ICONS OF LATINO AMERICA

Recent Titles in
Greenwood Icons

Icons of Horror and the Supernatural: An Encyclopedia of
Our Worst Nightmares
Edited by S.T. Joshi

Icons of Business: An Encyclopedia of Mavericks, Movers, and Shakers
Kateri Drexler

Icons of Hip Hop: An Encyclopedia of the Movement, Music, and Culture
Edited by Mickey Hess

Icons of Evolution: An Encyclopedia of People, Evidence, and Controversies
Edited by Brian Regal

Icons of Rock: An Encyclopedia of the Legends Who Changed Music Forever
Scott Schinder and Andy Schwartz

Icons of R&B and Soul: An Encyclopedia of the Artists Who Revolutionized Rhythm
Bob Gulla

African American Icons of Sport: Triumph, Courage, and Excellence
Matthew C. Whitaker

Icons of the American West: From Cowgirls to Silicon Valley
Edited by Gordon Morris Bakken

ICONS OF LATINO AMERICA

Latino Contributions to American Culture

VOLUME 2

Roger Bruns

Foreword by Ilan Stavans

Greenwood Icons

GREENWOOD PRESS
Westport, Connecticut · London

Library of Congress Cataloging-in-Publication Data

Bruns, Roger
  Icons of Latino America : Latino contributions to American culture/Roger Bruns.
    p. cm. — (Greenwood icons)
  Includes bibliographical references and indexes.
  ISBN 978-0-313-34086-4 (set : alk. paper) — ISBN 978-0-313-34087-1 (v. 1 : alk.
paper) — ISBN 978-0-313-34088-8 (v. 2 : alk. paper)
  1. Hispanic Americans—Biography. 2. Hispanic American celebrities—Biography.
3. United States—Civilization—Hispanic influences. I. Title.
  E184.S75B78 2008
  920′.009468073—dc22   2008013646

British Library Cataloguing in Publication Data is available.

Library of Congress Catalog Card Number: 2008013646
ISBN: 978-0-313-34086-4 (set)
      978-0-313-34087-1 (vol. 1)
      978-0-313-34088-8 (vol. 2)

First published in 2008

Greenwood Press, 88 Post Road West, Westport, CT 06881
An imprint of Greenwood Publishing Group, Inc.
www.greenwood.com

Printed in the United States of America

The paper used in this book complies with the
Permanent Paper Standard issued by the National
Information Standards Organization (Z39.48–1984).

10 9 8 7 6 5 4 3 2 1

Contents

Volume 2

Photos

Desi Arnaz, 1958 (page 1). Courtesy of Library of Congress.

Ruben Blades (left) and Mickey Rourke in *Once Upon a Time in Mexico*, 2003 (page 25). Courtesy of Columbia Pictures Corporation/Photofest. © Columbia Pictures Corporation.

Fabiola Cabeza de Baca Gilbert in front of rural New Mexico schoolhouse (page 49). Fabiola Cabeza de Baca Gilbert Pictorial Collection, Center for Southwest Research, University Libraries, The University of New Mexico.

Cesar Chavez, 1966 (page 71). Courtesy of Library of Congress.

Woman removing chile peppers from stove, Taos, New Mexico, 1939 (page 101). Courtesy of Library of Congress.

Sandra Cisneros, 1991 (page 121). AP Photo/Dana Tynan.

Baseball player Roberto Clemente (page 145) of the Pittsburgh Pirates vs. the Mets at Shea Stadium, 1966. Courtesy of Photofest.

Celia Cruz, 1962 (page 167). Courtesy of Library of Congress.

Placido Domingo, 1970 (page 189). Courtesy of Photofest.

Jaime Escalante (page 213) teaching math at Garfield High School, in California, 1988. AP Photo.

Thirteen-frame comic strip by Gus Arriola (page 237). Gordo and his young nephew Pepito wish to return home to their friends and relatives after assisting some Mayan archaeologists. Having killed Japanese troops who were trying to sabotage their excavations by posing as Mayan ghosts, the archaeologists arrange for Gordo and Pepito to go home. August 13, 1945. Courtesy of Library of Congress.

Series Foreword

Worshipped and cursed. Loved and loathed. Obsessed about the world over. What does it take to become an icon? Regardless of subject, culture, or era, the requisite qualifications are the same: (1) challenge the status quo, (2) influence millions, and (3) impact history.

Using these criteria, Greenwood Press introduces a new reference format and approach to popular culture. Spanning a wide range of subjects, volumes in the *Greenwood Icons* series provide students and general readers a port of entry into the most fascinating and influential topics of the day. Every title offers an in-depth look at approximately 24 iconic figures, each of which captures the essence of a broad subject. These icons typically embody a group of values, elicit strong reactions, reflect the essence of a particular time and place, and link different traditions and periods. Among those featured are artists and activists, superheroes and spies, inventors and athletes—the legends and mythmakers of entire generations. Yet icons can also come from unexpected places: as the heroine who transcends the pages of a novel or as the revolutionary idea that shatters our previously held beliefs. Whether people, places, or things, such icons serve as a bridge between the past and the present, the canonical and the contemporary. By focusing on icons central to popular culture, this series encourages students to appreciate cultural diversity and critically analyze issues of enduring significance.

Most importantly, these books are as entertaining as they are provocative. Is Disneyland a more influential icon of the American West than Las Vegas? How do ghosts and ghouls reflect our collective psyche? Is Barry Bonds an inspiring or deplorable icon of baseball? Designed to foster debate, the series serves as a unique resource that is ideal for paper writing or report purposes. Insightful, in-depth entries provide far more information than conventional reference articles but are less intimidating and more accessible than a book-length biography. The most revered and reviled icons of American and world history are brought to life with related sidebars, timelines, fact boxes, and quotations. Authoritative entries are accompanied by bibliographies, making these titles an ideal starting point for further research. Spanning a wide range of popular topics, including business, literature, civil rights, politics, music, and more, books in the *Greenwood Icons* series provide fresh insights for the student and popular reader into the power and influence of icons, a topic of as vital interest today as in any previous era.

Foreword

Ours is a society defined by the cult of personality. The famous make a constant demand on our attention. They want to be admired, imitated, and eulogized. Their life serves as a collective mirror. Through them, we measure our own qualities. Do we have the same stamina? Are we also capable of battling adversity like they do? What makes their place in the world unique?

Of the almost 50 million Latinos in the United States, less than two dozen are profiled in the following pages. The ratio is crunched: exactly one icon is selected for every two million people. Still, the percentage is standard. By definition, the number of celebrities at any given period in history is small. Our interest evaporates easily. We get tired rather quickly of the same old faces.

Are the stars in this set the best endowed? The answer, of course, is relative. Every society has the luminaries it deserves.

What makes them representative? Through a Darwinian law of evolution, they have been embraced by the environment as the most salient—and the most symbolic. Cesar Chavez overcame poverty to become a fundamental Civil Rights leader. Celia Cruz sang her way—¡azúcar!—from the Havana slums to Madison Square Garden. Roberto Clemente was a slugger with a philanthropic heart. And Ruben Salazar used the pen and the microphone to remind others of the unfinished quest for Chicano self-realization.

These chosen ones are role models. Yet they are unlikely to stand the passing of time in equal measure. In a decade or so, the list of role models will be different. With other needs to satisfy, some figures now eclipsed will be revamped while others currently basking in the sunlight will be forgotten. This is as it should be. Every community has the icons it deserves.

Roger Bruns' selection is a thermometer of our health. It includes one teacher, one playwright, two journalists, two writers, and two labor activists. Aside from mice and myths like Speedy Gonzalez and Zorro, the rest are actors, musicians, and athletes. No Nobel Prize-winning physicists, chemists, economists, and medical researchers. No philosophers. No inventors. And no U.S. presidents.

This is not necessarily bad news. It ought to serve as a reminder for Latinos of where improvement is needed.

Ilan Stavans

Preface

Icons of Latino America focuses on men and women with Latin American or Hispanic cultural roots who have made important contributions to American society and who are either U.S. citizens or who have spent much of their lives in the United States. This two-volume set includes essays on some of the most significant exemplars of the Latino experience, whose lives and careers have pushed cultural boundaries, effected social change, and expanded artistic expression in the larger U.S. culture. It also includes, in a few cases, inanimate Latino icons that have also had a strong cultural impact.

When we think of the word "icon," we think of individuals whose names can be identified in the public mind by a single thought or one name. When we think of farm workers, we think of Cesar Chavez. When we think of Tejano music, we think of Selena. We think of people whose names can be seen on T-shirts in barrios; whose images appear on walls in simple home shrines; whose lives have been celebrated in corridos, poetry, folk songs, and murals; whose identity sparks emulation and loyalty; and whose work inspires followers. The figures selected in this work are mostly individuals not only of achievement but of inspiration, of legendary proportion. Some of the individuals gained this status through long, productive careers; others gained it in the space of a few years cut short by premature death. In many cases, their iconic status resulted not only from their own personal activities and accomplishments but also from circumstance. Icons from a wide range of fields are included: sports, entertainment, journalism, music, education, labor, and literature. Most figures made their mark in the latter part of the twentieth century, and many continue to add to their iconic stature through new work. Family background, schooling, career trajectory, and further contributions to society are discussed. The few non-human Latino icons profiled include fictional and cartoon or comic characters and representative Latino food.

A Latino here is defined as a person in the United States with heritage going back to any of the Spanish-speaking cultures of the Western Hemisphere. The terms Latino and Latina include many aspects of cultural and linguistic identity. A Latino may be an immigrant or someone born in the United States; may be fair-skinned or dark-skinned; and may speak Spanish only, English only, or both.

Readers will find that a number of the icons profiled were influenced by or may have an important connection to other profiled icons. For example, Tito Puente and Celia Cruz performed together for many years. Actress Jennifer Lopez portrayed the singer Selena in a biographical film. Edward James Olmos portrayed teacher Jaime Escalante in the film *Stand and Deliver*. Cesar Chavez and Dolores Huerta together made the United Farm Workers union a reality. Furthermore, in telling the story of an icon, each essay relates many of the historical and social issues of the times. Thus, reading these essays gives students and other readers a good sense of recent Latino and Latin American history and progress.

The biographical profiles are presented in alphabetical order. Each essay concludes with suggested reading, including websites, and a list of relevant movies, recordings, or books. All profiles are accompanied by a sidebar that further illuminates the icon. A timeline of events provides a framework for the lives, contributions, and places of the icons in history.

Timeline

Icons profiled in volumes 1 and 2 are indicated with bold text.

7500 B.C.	Chile peppers are likely used in the diets of native Americans.
1941	Hundreds of thousands of Latino Americans serve in armed forces during World War II.
	Cartoonist Gus Arriola introduces the character **Gordo** in his nationally syndicated cartoon strip.
1943	The U.S. government forges an agreement with the Mexican government to supply temporary workers, known as *braceros*, for American agricultural work.
	The so-called Zoot Suit riots take place in southern California. Bands of sailors, marines, and other soldiers in southern California range the Hispanic neighborhoods, assaulting Latino youth who were wearing a teenage fashion called a zoot suit. The incident would later be made the subject of a play and film by the writer **Luis Valdez.**
1944	The Puerto Rican government begins Operation Bootstrap, a program to help meet U.S. labor demands caused by World War II. The program begins a wave of worker migration to the United States.
1951	In October, the "I Love Lucy" show begins an unprecedented run on national television. Starring Lucille Ball and Cuban bandleader **Desi Arnaz**, the situational comedy is the most-watched television show in four of its six seasons. Arnaz not only stars in the series but establishes one of the most successful entertainment production companies, Desi-Lu Productions.
1954	In the landmark case of *Hernandez v. Texas*, the U.S. Supreme Court recognizes Hispanic Americans as a separate class of people suffering profound discrimination, paving the way for

	Hispanic Americans to use legal means to battle all types of discrimination throughout the United States. It is also the first U.S. Supreme Court case to be argued and briefed by Mexican-American attorneys.
1954–1958	Operation Wetback, a government effort to locate and deport undocumented workers, results in the deportation of 3.8 million persons. Few are allowed deportation hearings. Thousands of U.S. citizens of Mexican descent are also arrested and detained.
	In the early 1950s, Latinos buy time on local television stations for Spanish-language programs in such cities as New York, San Antonio, Corpus Christi, and Harlingen, Texas. The first Spanish-language television station in the United States is San Antonio's KCOR-TV in San Antonio.
1956	Social worker and teacher **Fabiola Cabeza de Baca** publishes *Historic Cookery*. Formerly published in 1939 in pamphlet form by the New Mexico State University Extension Service, the work, which is the story of the cultural evolution of cuisine in the southwest, is as much about cultural icons such as chili as it is a cookbook. Many credit *Historic Cookery* as being the first critical influence in introducing Latino food preparation to a wider Anglo audience. In 1983, *Historic Cookery* appears in a hardcover edition from the Museum of New Mexico Press.
1959	Fidel Castro's Cuban Revolution overthrows the repressive regime of Fulgencio Batista. As Castro moves the country toward a communist state, Cuban immigration to the United States increases sharply. A number of entertainers are among those who choose to live in the United States, including famed salsa singer **Celia Cruz** and talk show personality **Cristina Saralegui**.
	Young Latino rock and roll singer **Ritchie Valens**, along with Buddy Holly and the Big Bopper, is killed in a winter plane crash in Iowa during a music tour. Because of the circumstances of his death, Valens, considered to be the first Latino rock and roll star, would become an almost mythic figure.
1960s	Young Mexican Americans throughout the United States become caught up in the struggle for civil rights and seek to create a new identity for themselves. These efforts become known as the Chicano Movement. The movement sparks a renaissance in the arts among Mexican Americans.
1961	In April, anti-Communist Cuban exiles, trained and armed by the United States, attempt a foray into Cuba that is doomed from the beginning. The so-called Bay of Pigs fiasco embitters thousands of exiled Cubans while strengthening Fidel Castro's position at home.

The movie *West Side Story*, loosely based on Shakespeare's play "Romeo and Juliet," opens to rave reviews. The story of street gangs—one made up of Puerto Rican youths and the other of European immigrants—at war in New York showcases the tensions of modern life in the big cities. Although the film was notable for the performance of **Rita Moreno**, a Puerto Rican actress playing a Puerto Rican character, the leading stars were Anglos playing Puerto Ricans. The film featured music by Leonard Bernstein and choreography by Jerome Robbins.

1964   The Civil Rights Act of 1964 establishes affirmative action programs. Title VII of the Act prohibits discrimination on the basis of gender, creed, race, or ethnic background, "to achieve equality of employment opportunities and remove barriers that have operated in the past." Discrimination is prohibited in advertising, recruitment, hiring, job classification, promotion, discharge, wages and salaries, and other terms and conditions of employment.

The *bracero* program ends. After a brief decline in immigration, numbers of workers from Mexico increase, either under the auspices of the Immigration and Nationality Act of 1952 and for family unification purposes, or as undocumented workers.

In October, the United States blocks a Soviet plan to establish missile bases in Cuba. Soviet Premier Khrushchev agrees to withdraw the missiles with the proviso that the United States declare publicly that it will not invade Cuba.

1965   The end of the *bracero* program in 1964 had forced many Mexicans to return to Mexico. To provide jobs for them, the Mexican and U.S. governments begin border industrialization programs, allowing foreign corporations to build and operate assembly plants on the border. These plants are known as *maquiladoras*.

A farmworkers union organized by **Cesar Chavez** engages in the successful Delano, California, grape strike and first national boycott. It becomes part of the American Federation of Labor and Congress of Industrial Organizations (AFL-CIO) in 1966 and later changes its name to the United Farmworkers of America.

For the first time, the United States enacts a law placing a cap on immigration from the Western Hemisphere, becoming effective in 1968.

Fidel Castro announces that Cubans can leave the island nation if they have relatives in the United States. He stipulates, however, that Cubans already in Florida have to come and get their relatives. Nautical crafts of all types systematically leave Miami, returning laden with anxious Cubans eager to rejoin their families on the mainland.

1966   A program is started to airlift Cubans to the United States. More than 250,000 Cubans are airlifted to the United States before the program is halted by Castro in 1973. About 10 percent of the island's population emigrates to the United States between 1966 and 1973.

1968   Chicano student organizations spring up throughout the nation, as do barrio groups such as the Brown Berets. Thousands of young Chicanos pledge their loyalty and time to such groups as the United Farmworkers Organizing Committee, which, under Cesar Chavez and **Dolores Huerta**, has been a great inspiration for Chicanos throughout the nation. An offshoot of both the farm worker and the student movements is the La Raza Unida party in Texas, an organization formed in 1968 to obtain control of community governments where Chicanos are the majority.

A Chicano Moratorium organizes in Los Angeles to protest the Vietnam War. More than 20,000 Chicanos and supporters draw attention to the disproportionately high number of Chicano casualties in the war. Conflicts erupt between police and demonstrators; journalist **Ruben Salazar** is killed by police.

In June, at the Oak Hill Golf Club in Rochester, New York, a short, stocky, jovial Mexican American accepts the trophy for one of the most prestigious tournaments in golf: **Lee Trevino** wins the United States Open.

1969   In August, an estimated 400,000 young people turn up for a three-day event to hear big-name bands play in an open-air venue near the town of Woodstock, New York. The name "Woodstock" would become emblematic of the anti-Vietnam war movement and the youthful, hippie drug culture of the 1960s. **Carlos Santana**, a young Latino guitarist destined for a long and celebrated career, makes his national debut.

1970s–   The rise in politically motivated violence in Central America
early 1980s spurs a massive increase in undocumented immigration to the United States.

1972   On December 31, New Year's Eve, famed baseball player **Roberto Clemente**, along with four other men, takes off from his native Puerto Rico on a mission to deliver supplies to hurricane-racked victims in Nicaragua. He, along with the others, is lost in the storm and never found. Clemente becomes the first Latino player ever inducted into baseball's Hall of Fame.

1973	The right of the Puerto Rican people to decide their own future as a nation is approved by the United Nations.
1974	Congress passes the Equal Educational Opportunity Act. One aspect of the law makes bilingual education available to Hispanic youth. According to the framers of the act, equal education means more than equal facilities and equal access to teachers; students who have trouble with the English language must be provided with access to programs to help them learn English.
1975	The Voting Rights Act Amendments extend the provisions of the original Voting Rights Act of 1965 and make permanent the national ban on literacy tests. Critical for Latinos, the amendments make bilingual ballots a requirement in certain areas.
1978	The United Nations recognizes Puerto Rico as a colony of the United States.
1979	Political upheaval and civil wars in Nicaragua, El Salvador, and Guatemala contribute to large immigrations of refugees to the United States.
1980s	The rates of immigration to the United States approach the levels of the early 1900s. During the first decade of the century the number of immigrants was approximately 8.8 million; during the 1980s, 6.3 million immigrants are granted permanent residence.
1980	Fidel Castro, reacting to negative worldwide press, announces that anyone who wants to leave Cuba should go to the Peruvian embassy. Ten thousand Cubans descend upon the embassy grounds and receive exit visas. Cuban Americans in Florida organize a fleet of boats to pick up the Cuban exiles at Mariel Harbor. The Mariel Boatlift continues from April through September. By the end of the year, more than 125,000 "Marielitos" arrive in the United States.
1982	A class of students at Garfield High School in a barrio of Los Angeles passes an Advanced Placement calculus examination under the tutelage of Bolivian-born teacher **Jaime Escalante**. So incredulous are testing officials that this group of students from a low socioeconomic background had passed the exam that the students are forced to take the exam again. They again pass. Their experience leads to a 1988 movie called *Stand and Deliver*. The part of Escalante is played by veteran actor and political activist **Edward James Olmos**.
1983	**Sandra Cisneros'** novel *The House on Mango Street* bursts on the international literary scene.

1986	After more than a decade of debate, Congress enacts the Immigration Reform and Control Act (IRCA), creating a process through which illegal aliens could become legal immigrants by giving legal status to applicants who had been in the United States illegally since January 1, 1982.
1989	Immigration to the United States from Central and South America increases from 44.3 percent in 1964 to 61.4 percent. Of the major countries of immigrant origin, Mexico accounts for 37.1 percent of total documented immigration to the United States; the next highest proportion of immigrants comes from El Salvador, 5.3 percent.
1991	Musician and actor **Ruben Blades**, a native of Panama, returns to Panama for a time to found the *Movemiento Papa Egoró*, which translates roughly into Mother Earth Party or Motherland Party in the language of the local Choco Indians. The party promises to fight drugs, hunger, and unemployment and expresses concern for ecology and the environment. Blades would return to Panama in 1994 to run for the presidency of Panama, an unprecedented move by a U.S. Latino; Blades garners 18 percent of the popular vote in 1994 but fails in his bid for the Panamanian presidency.
1994	The North American Free Trade Agreement (NAFTA) takes effect, eliminating tariffs between trading partners Canada, Mexico, and the United States within fifteen years from the date.
	In November, Californians pass Proposition 187 with 59 percent of the vote. The initiative bans undocumented immigrants from receiving public education and public benefits such as welfare and subsidized health care, except in emergency circumstances; makes it a felony to manufacture, distribute, sell, or use false citizenship or residence documents; and requires teachers, physicians, and other city, county, and state officials to report suspected and apparent illegal aliens to the California attorney general and the Immigration and Naturalization Service (INS). California Federal District Court Judge William Matthew Byrne, Jr., temporarily blocks the enforcement of Proposition 187, stating that it raises serious constitutional questions. Judge Byrne exempts the provisions that increase penalties for manufacturing or using false immigration documents.
1995	A nationwide boycott of ABC-TV by Hispanic Americans is held in Los Angeles, New York, Chicago, Houston, San Francisco, and Fresno, in protest of the network's failure to provide Latino-themed programming in its 1994 line-up.

Selena, age 23, a young Tejana music star murdered by her fan club president and boutique manager, is laid to rest on April 3. Six hundred people attend her private funeral. Before the funeral, thousands view her casket at the Bayfront Plaza Convention Center in Corpus Christi. In Los Angeles, four thousand people gather at the Sports Arena Memorial to honor the slain singer. Mourners also gather in San Antonio. The gravesite services were broadcast live by San Antonio and Corpus Christi radio stations. Her death by gunshot at the hands of her boutique manager makes her a Latino heroine.

1996   Proposition 209, introduced as a ballot initiative, is passed by California voters. The initiative bars preferential treatment on the basis of race or gender, virtually eliminating affirmative action in state hiring, public contracts, and education. Although challenged in court, the U.S. Supreme Court refused to hear the appeal, and Proposition 209 eventually takes effect in California.

Placido Domingo is named artistic director of the Washington Opera.

1997   Bandleader and musician **Tito Puente,** called "King of the Mambo" or usually "El Rey," receives a National Medal of Arts from President Bill Clinton. At the ceremony the President says, "Just hearing Tito Puente's name makes you want to get up and dance. With his finger on the pulse of the Latin American musical tradition and his hands on the timbales, he has probably gotten more people out of their seats and onto the dance floor than any other living artist."

1998   California voters pass Proposition 227, which bans bilingual classroom education and English as a second language programs, replacing them with a one-year intensive English immersion program.

Four years after Proposition 187, the growing Latino electorate helps make Lieutenant Governor Cruz M. Bustamante the first Hispanic statewide official in California in more than a century.

In *The Mark of Zorro*, Antonio Banderas becomes the first Latino actor to star in a major film based on the famed Latino character.

2001   Antonio Villaraigosa, former speaker of the California State Assembly, wins a commanding first-place primary finish in the race to succeed Republican Richard J. Riordan as mayor of the country's second largest city, Los Angeles.

2003   Hispanics are pronounced the nation's largest minority group—surpassing African Americans—after new U.S. Census figures are released that show the U.S. Hispanic population at 37.1 million as of July 2001.

2006   Thousands of people join rallies in cities across the country to protest proposed immigration reform. The protests, organized by labor, civil rights, community, and religious interests, culminate on April 10 in a "National Day of Action."

2007   Univision, the most-watched Spanish language broadcast television network in the country, is sold for a reported $13.7 billion.

In 2007, film and recording star **Jennifer Lopez**, known popularly as J-Lo, stars in a film called *El Cantante* about salsa legend Hector Lavoe.

2008   Cartoon series such as **"Baldo"** and **"La Cucaracha"** continue to inform and entertain American audiences.

Latino population in the United States surpasses 40 million individuals.

Jennifer Lopez

In the 1990s, millions of people around the world came to know singer, dancer, and actress Jennifer Lopez simply as J. Lo. Lopez was a dancing "Fly Girl" on the 1990s television show *In Living Color*, and she got her acting break in the lead role of *Selena*, a 1997 film about the murdered Tejano pop star. She became the first Latina actress to have a lead role in a major Hollywood film since Rita Hayworth, and she has become the highest-paid Latina actress ever. Her early films included *Anaconda*, *U Turn*, *Jack*, and *Out of Sight*.

In 2007, Lopez starred in the biopic *El Cantante*, which told the story of salsa legend Hector Lavoe. In the same year, a *Chicago Tribune* survey reported that a majority of middle-school students, when asked to choose from a list of famous people with whom they would like to dine for one evening, selected Jennifer Lopez as their first choice.[1] *New York Times* columnist Lynette Holloway wrote in December 2002:

> Forgive yourself if you are seeing Jennifer Lopez in your sleep. She is everywhere else these days too. You can hardly pass a billboard in New York City without seeing her face plastered on advertisements ... she could be seen on 'The Today Show,' bellowing out three singles from her new album.... Ms. Lopez's singing and acting talents have received mixed reviews, but that has not stopped her from becoming a cultural icon."[2]

GIRL FROM THE BRONX

Lopez was born on July 24, 1970, in Castle Hill, a section of the Bronx, New York, and she grew up on Blacklock Avenue. Her father, David Lopez, worked nights as a computer technician and, later, as an agent for the Guardian Insurance Company. Her mother, Guadelupe, taught kindergarten in Westchester County.

Her parents both grew up in Ponce, the second largest city in Puerto Rico, and both moved to the United States in their early childhood; eventually they met in New York. Like their parents and grandparents before them, both David and Guadelupe strove to fit into mainstream America. They rarely spoke Spanish in the home.

Jennifer was the middle of three girls. All of them, from their earliest years, displayed a great deal of musical ability. Jennifer's oldest sister, Leslie, sang opera for a time; her younger sister, Lynda, became a disc jockey on a New York radio station and an entertainment correspondent for a morning television show.

Music was always present in the house as the girls were growing up. David said later, "We played all kinds of music ... musicals, salsa, merengue, rock & roll, doo-wop, you name it. Music permeated the house. The girls would put on shows in the living room, acting out scenes from *West Side Story*—Jennifer was always Anita, the fiery one."[3]

The Lopez family lived in a small apartment that was always cold in the winter and hot in the summer, but they were a close-knit family. Although the neighborhood was one of the more crime-ridden areas in the Bronx, the sisters seldom felt threatened or intimidated by the surroundings. Jennifer later said that it was only after her teenage years that she understood the reputation of the neighborhood as a dangerous place.

> I only found out when I was in my 20s and dated a cop who worked in my neighborhood. I told him I grew up on Castle Hill, and he said, 'That's the worst crime area.' I knew nothing of it. My parents had three girls and raised us to do the right things—go to school, get good grades, try to get into college. It was about trying to have a better life. We weren't allowed to hang out on the streets. Parties—God forbid. I'd beg for weeks to go, then have to be home by 11 P.M., when everybody else was just getting there.[4]

Although David and Guadelupe were strict and careful about the activities and hours of the girls, they were always supportive and close by. "Our parents had a strong work ethic—there wasn't really any other way," said Lynda. "They led by example. They would tell us we could never miss a day of work—and they didn't. They told us we had to go to church every week, which they did. They never had any down time. I didn't realize people were any different until I was a teenager."[5]

All three children fondly remembered their mother organizing singing and dancing performances in the living room and remembered watching the movie *West Side Story* numerous times, with its Latin theme and rocking music and the fabulous performance of the Puerto Rican actress Rita Moreno, who had become a much idolized figure in the Latino community. Later, Jennifer told a reporter that she had seen the film more than a hundred times. Although she admired Moreno at the time, she said, she had always wanted to be Maria, the star of the story, played by Natalie Wood.

David and Guadelupe Lopez found enough extra cash from their jobs to pay for singing and dancing lessons for Jennifer. At the age of seven, the precocious youngster performed with one of her dance classes at various locations in New York, in particular the Kips Bay Boys and Girls Club in the Bronx.

At the Catholic Holy Family High School in the Bronx and later at the all-girl Preston High School, Lopez continued the singing and dancing lessons. She also showed off her athletic skills, playing softball, tennis, and, especially, gymnastics. The gymnastics routines naturally fed into her conditioning for rigorous dance maneuevers that she would master as she grew older.

Lynda Lopez later said that Jennifer's ultimate success did not surprise anyone. She was one of those people, she joked, that you tend to hate because she was so proficient and skilled and beautiful, and when she tried seriously to do anything, she could be successful. Nevertheless, Jennifer's looks, athleticism, competitiveness, and vivacious personality did not translate into excellent academic achievement—her grades were average. "I wasn't the most popular girl in class," she remembered later. "I had my friends, but I was comfortable with myself. There's always those most popular girls and I wasn't one of those. My parents wanted me to be a lawyer. But I don't think I would have been very happy. I'd be in front of the jury singing."[6]

While in high school, Lopez performed in a few musicals and on chorus lines. The strikingly attractive teenager also appeared in local productions of such classics as *Oklahoma* and *Jesus Christ Superstar*. Looking back on these early years, Lopez later saw in her young life the characteristics that would emerge strongly as she grew older and more mature. She was always a romantic, she said, emotionally drawn to loving relationships, always seeking companionship and close friends. She said, "Like, I remember a teacher saying to me when I was eleven years old—I was crying at the graduation so much that it was unnatural—and she was like, 'You feel things so deeply, on a different level.' I didn't understand—I was just a little girl crying over the fact that my friends were going away and that I wasn't going to see these people anymore. It destroyed me inside, I felt it so much. And I had to let it out, and I express myself that way—that's how I was born."[7]

At age sixteen, her boyfriend years began. Her first boyfriend was David Cruz. Although her family worried about the budding romance, Cruz would remain a long-time friend. The relationship had its ups and downs, Lopez joked, referring to the numerous times she was climbing out windows, jumping off roofs, and stealthily sneaking away to meet with him. She later looked back on those days as her own crazy but innocent version of *West Side Story*.

Also at age sixteen, Lopez, thanks to contacts made in dance classes around New York, was asked to appear in a bit part in a major motion picture. Directed by David Saperstein, *My Little Girl* involved a young teenager's social and emotional growth as she worked at a halfway house for troubled and homeless kids. Played by Mary Stuart Masterson, the lead character Franny leaves behind a pampered life of yachting parties to take up a summer job in Philadelphia that opens her eyes to a world she never knew existed. She decides to organize a talent show in which the young orphans will understand that they can achieve something worthwhile. Playing Myra, one of the youngsters at the halfway house, Lopez had the extraordinary opportunity at such a young age to work alongside actors like Masterson, James Earl Jones, and Anne Meara. Although the role was a mere bit part, the experience for the aspiring performer was invaluable.

After graduating from high school, Lopez enrolled at Baruch College in Manhattan. She also followed her most intense passion—dancing. Still living at home, she and her parents, especially her mother, were increasingly at odds. Guadalupe Lopez did not believe that professional dancing in night-clubs was an appropriate career direction for her eighteen-year-old daughter. Even though Lopez never drank alcohol, her parents felt strongly that work-ing in clubs would put her too close to potentially dangerous people and sit-uations. With the family conflict growing more intense, Jennifer decided to move out of the family house and to find a place on her own. She began liv-ing in an apartment that also housed one of the dance studios at which she took lessons.

Her college life at Baruch lasted for only one semester. To pay for the apartment and to keep taking the dance lessons, she worked part-time at a law office. Later, she also began to perform at clubs on gigs that her dance instructor set up, most of them earning $150 or less. For a year and a half, Lopez struggled. Numerous auditions led to polite turndowns but no work. One of the auditions was to be a "Fly Girl," one of the dancers who appeared between skits in the Fox television series *In Living Color*. She was especially disappointed when she did not land the job after giving what she thought was a strong audition.

The rejections were not only dispiriting but humbling. As her disillusion-ment turned toward depression, Lopez finally received an offer to join a group called the Golden Musicals of Broadway Revue. The dance job sent the aspiring performer on a brief tour in Japan, a special opportunity not only to display her talent but to travel to an exotic location. Perhaps the youngster from the Bronx could make it as a performer after all. She returned to New York from Japan to exciting news. The producers of *In Living Color* had reconsidered. They offered her a contract to be a "Fly Girl." Excited but also apprehensive, Lopez boarded a plane for Los Angeles. A job in Hollywood awaited.

IN LIVING COLOR

She was now a small part of a huge hit television show. She was performing alongside exceptional talents such as Keenan Ivory Wayans, Jim Carrey, Jamie Foxx, Chris Rock, and others. She came under the tutelage of the highly-respected actress Rosie Perez, and the two became friends. Neverthe-less, the first few months were excruciating. Los Angeles seemed almost like another planet; it was so different in pace and appearance from New York and so foreign to her background and tastes. She felt uprooted. It was not until her friend David Cruz decided to move to Hollywood to be at her side for a time that she began to feel somewhat at ease.

"*In Living Color* was nice because it was my first steady paycheck," she said, "but I was miserable living in L.A. I'm a total New York/Bronx girl, with the accent and the whole nine. I was hating it. It's a really lonely city when you're an East Coast person. But now I love L.A." During her first year on the show, she spent most of her money flying home every weekend. "It didn't get better until the second year," she says. "David and I got back together, and he moved to L.A., and that made it more bearable. He wound up staying out there for four years with me. I was stable at home, so I was able to excel and work. He was my stability."[8]

In 1993, Lopez grabbed a part in the made-for-TV movie *Nurses on the Line: The Crash of Flight 7* starring Lindsay Wagner and Robert Loggia. The plot: Three planes on their way to a remote medical outpost crash in the Mexican jungle. Immediately the search is on to locate and rescue any survivors. Jennifer plays a heroic nurse named Rosie Romero.

In 1995, she won a spot dancing for Janet Jackson in the video production of "That's the Way Love Goes." When Jackson's producers offered Lopez a gig dancing on the upcoming world tour, the increasingly confident young performer declined, deciding instead to concentrate on other film opportunities in Hollywood.

With her successful work on *In Living Color*, other opportunities did open up. Lopez appeared in the television film *Second Chances*, created by husband and wife Lynn Marie Latham and Bernard Lechowick. Three women, each finding her life in chaos, draw together as they find new opportunities. The planned production turned disastrous when most of the sets were destroyed in one of Los Angeles' frequent but minor earthquakes. Although the show ended in disarray and lost revenue, the producers had been so impressed with Lopez's performance that they took a nearly unprecendented move to write her character into a new series called *Hotel Malibu*. Joanna Cassidy played a tough-minded owner of a family hotel wrapped up in difficult circumstances involving corrupt government officials. Lopez's character Melina Lopez, was now an assistant in the hotel's bar. The spin-off was short-lived, and Lopez appeared in only one epoisode.

Lopez then moved on to a television film called *South Central*, an inner-city drama of the streets and a mother who tries to keep her children shielded from the culture of guns, drugs, gangs, and illegal money. Lopez appeared as a cashier in a local business.

She was on the move now. Talented, athletic, so stunning and curvaceous that many thought she should be on a short list of the most glamorous young women in Hollywood, she grew more confident with each new challenge, constantly setting her sights higher. Dance and television had gained her recognition and respect in the entertainment field, but her friends and associates saw in this talented young woman the makings of a superstar.

TOWARD A BIG SCREEN CAREER

In 1995, nine years after her small role in the film *My Little Girl*, Lopez returned to the big screen, an ambition she had harbored for several years.

Behind her now were several years of dancing experience, roles in a number of television productions, and the realization that she was on track to fulfill her dreams of an entertainment career.

The movie was called *Money Train*. Starring big-name actors Woody Harrelson and Wesley Snipes, the story revolves around two New York City transit cops who decide to rob a subway train carrying the subway system's weekly earnings. The schemes of the two are compromised by the character Grace Santiago, played by Lopez, who becomes the love interest for both lead characters. The film was mediocre, and Lopez's part lacked depth, but the film became controversial. As a result of a few incidents of arson on the transit system after the opening of the film—incidents blamed by many in the media and by some government leaders on copycat crooks who got their inspiration from scenes in the movie—a brief campaign to ban the film took root. Although the suggested boycott never materialized, a number of well-known public figures, including Senator Robert Dole, were among those who denounced the film.

In the same year, Lopez secured a role much better suited to her interests and inclinations, and one that promised an opportunity for serious film work. *My Family/Mi Familia* was directed by Gregory Nava and Anna Thomas, the husband and wife team who earlier created *El Norte*, a movie about Guatemalan refugees. The film was a major effort to portray the challenges facing several generations of a Mexican-American family living in Los Angeles.

For many Latinos, this was a film that spoke much about their lives. They could see in the various characters images from their own past and reminders of friends and relatives that they encountered in their own struggles. For Lopez, as for other Latino actors and actresses who appeared in the film, *My Family/Mi Familia* seemed to carry with its roles an obligation to tell the story correctly. Here was a film that sought to break through the stereotypes that had plagued Hollywood films for so long, the portrayals of dirty, stupid, or malevolent Latino types from banditos to the Cuban mafia.

Featuring such film stars as Jimmy Smits, Jenny Gago, Esai Morales, and Edward James Olmos in powerful performances, the story began in the 1920s, when one of the family members attempted to walk from his Mexican village to Los Angeles. Woven through the individual family stories are major conflicts and issues such as immigration, the illegal deportation of United States citizens of Mexican descent during the Depression, the growth of Latino gangs, the woes of political impotence, and the traditions and cultural practices from birth to death. It showed religious practices, family customs, and family solidarity. It was a unique look at a part of American life and a growing portion of American society so overlooked up to that point in Hollywood films.

Director Gregory Nava, looking back on Lopez's role as a young peasant woman in the film, said, "The first time we see Jennifer in *Mi Familia* it's

Did You Know That These Celebrities Were Latino?

The astounding career of Jennifer Lopez is notable for her success in a variety of areas, from acting to music. It is also notable that she represents a refreshing trend in American entertainment—that Latinos can make a powerful mark in industries in which a half century ago they were nearly invisible.

When the actor Victor Argo began his career in the 1950s, he found that he had to drop Jiménez, his real surname, if he wanted to win a part. Speaking of the producers and directors of the time, he said, "They couldn't conceive that someone with an obvious Latino name could play anything. The only actor working was José Ferrer, and I don't think people knew he was Puerto Rican."[1]

You may be surprised that the following celebrities had Latino roots:

Raquel Welch

One of the most popular Hollywood actresses of the 1960s and 1970s, Raquel Welch was born Raquel Tejada on September 5, 1940. At home near San Diego, California, her Bolivian-born father, Armando, an engineer, preferred to distance the family from its Latino roots. The family members did not speak Spanish in the home.

While still a teenager, Raquel married her high school sweetheart, James Welch. When she launched what would become a forty-year career as a movie star and Broadway performer, it was with the name Raquel Welch. Long after she was a Hollywood star, Welch decided to get more in touch with her heritage, to connect more closely to her roots. She traveled to Bolivia where she was greeted warmly.

Martin Sheen

Ramón Gerardo Antonio Estévez, known later as Martin Sheen, was born on August 3, 1940, in Dayton, Ohio, to Spanish-born Francisco Estévez and Irish-born Mary Anne Phelan. After his graduation from Chaminade High School, Ramón headed to New York to pursue his dream of becoming an actor.

He decided to change his name, taking the last name of the popular Catholic archbishop and theologian, Fulton J. Sheen, whose weekly television show was popular among millions of viewers. Martin Sheen's major role in the television production of *The Execution of Private Slovik* led director Francis Ford Coppola to choose him for a starring role in the 1979 film *Apocalypse Now*, which gained Sheen wide recognition. He later starred as the President of the United States on a popular television series called *The West Wing* from 1999 to 2006.

---

[1]Mireya Navarro, "Actors in all-Latino cast savor a 'historic moment,'" *New York Times*, December 2, 2003, http://query.nytimes.com/gst/fullpage.html?res=9505E6DC113AF931A 35751C1A9659C8B63&sec=&spon=&pagewanted=print.

Sheen is father to two actors who made different decisions about their stage names. Charlie Sheen kept his father's stage name; Charlie's older brother Emilio Estevez decided to use his father's real surname.

Rita Hayworth

Considered Hollywood's first Latina superstar, Rita Hayworth was born Margarita Cansino in Brooklyn, New York, on October 17, 1918. Her father, a professional dancer, was born in Spain; her mother was Irish-American. When Margarita was eight years old, the family moved to California where her father opened a dancing school on Sunset and Vine Streets. As the business declined during the years of the Great Depression, Margarita's father asked her to join him as a dance partner as he resumed his stage career. As a member of "The Dancing Cansinos," she was now in show business.

Her stage career eventually led to a career in movies with such actors as Cary Grant and Fred Astaire. Early in her career, she changed her stage name to Rita Hayworth. In 1941, she played in the film *Blood and Sand* opposite Tyrone Power. For the part, director Darryl Zanuck asked that she dye her jet-black hair red. For the rest of her career, her Latino name and features were forever lost on screen.

Lynda Carter

Born in Arizona on July 24, 1951, to a Mexican-American mother and an Anglo father, Linda Jean Córdova Carter grew up to become one of America's most iconic fantasy figures: Wonder Woman. Because her last name was Carter from birth, she never really thought of herself as truly Hispanic. Although her father did not speak Spanish, she heard it often from other relatives and later remembered sitting at her childhood home in Globe, Arizona, eating big stacks of tortillas and menudo, a spicy soup.

In 1972, after entering a local beauty contest in Arizona, Carter won the Miss World USA competition and reached the semi-finals of the Miss World pageant. The publicity launched a career that reached its height with the wildly popular fantasy-adventure television show, *Wonder Woman*, which aired from 1975 to 1979. Later in her career, as her ethnicity became more widely known, she embraced her Latino roots and spoke of them proudly.

Ted Williams

Teddy Samuel Williams was born in San Diego, California, on August 30, 1918. Williams' mother, May Venzor, was born in El Paso, Texas, and married Samuel Williams in 1915. Williams' father, a soldier and photographer, admired President Teddy Roosevelt. Samuel and May, a Salvation Army worker who had come to the United States from Ciudad Juarez, Mexico, decided to give their son the informal name, Teddy. May's parents, Williams' maternal grandparents, were Natalia Hernandez and Pablo Venzor, and her family originated from the state of Chihuahua, Mexico.

From his early days in the North Park neighborhood of San Diego, Teddy Williams seemed destined for a career in baseball. His uncle, Saul Venzor, played semi-pro baseball and, while living near his nephew, spent many days teaching him how to hit. Many family members credit Venzor with being an exceptional influence on the young man's early career. From his first days with the major-league Boston Red Sox in 1939, Williams made a tremendous impact. In 1941, he ended the season with a batting average of .406. No player since Williams has finished a season with a batting average higher than .400. He is considered by many to have been the greatest hitter in baseball history.

David Blaine

Although the details of magician David Blaine's early life are sketchy, they do reveal that his father was of Puerto Rican and Italian stock; his mother was a Russian Jew. Tumultuous childhood years spent in Brooklyn and then in Little Falls, New Jersey, gave to his life a sense of danger and dread, especially after his father left home when he was four years old. David's mother took an assortment of jobs to keep the family from breaking apart. She reportedly had gypsy ancestors and knew much about magic and the occult. When his mother remarried a man named John Bukalo, Blaine's legal name became David Blaine Bukalo. David dropped the name Bukalo for his career in show business.

While waiting tables to pay living expenses, David studied acting and performed magic at private parties, often for celebrities. After striking up friendships with such show business stars as Christopher Walken, Robert De Niro, and Leonardo DiCaprio, his career took off. In 1997, his first television show, called "David Blaine: Street Magic," was presented by DiCaprio and launched a spectacular career.

through the eyes of the gardener she will marry. Then it cuts to her first close-up on film. And for it, I used a silent-film technique: I put an iris around her, you know, where there's a circle around her face and everything else is blacked out? In that one shot, everyone knew she was a movie star."[9] Gregory Nava would be a critical influence in Jennifer's career. After Lopez's successful experience in *Mi Familia*, Nava would, in less than two years, select her for the lead role in a film that would, indeed, make her a star.

In 1996 Lopez appeared in a film directed by another Hollywood celebrity, Francis Ford Coppola. The film was called *Jack* and starred Robin Williams playing a ten-year-old boy who, because of an aging disorder, looks like a forty-year-old man. Jack's fifth-grade teacher is Miss Marquez, played by Lopez. When Jack gets a severe crush on Miss Marquez, he invites her to the school dance and woos her with Gummi Bears. Also in 1996, Lopez appeared in another film featuring other big-name Hollywood actors. In *Blood and Wine*, Jack Nicholson plays Alex Gates, a wine dealer turned thief, who steals a diamond necklance from a wealthy couple and falls for their curvacous Cuban nanny, Gabriella (Gabby), played by Lopez. The affair is further complicated by the stepson of the thief who also falls for the nanny. It was during the shoot for *Blood and Wine* that Lopez had met Ojani Noa, a Cuban immigrant and aspiring model and actor who was waiting tables at Gloria Estefan's Larios on The Beach restaurant in Miami. The two began a relationship and married a year later.

The marriage only lasted a year. "It was nice," Lopez said later of the relationship. "A love-at-first-sight situation," she said. "We got married. He was young, twenty-one, and I was twenty-five. It was premature, I guess. I don't think we had a fair shot as far as where we both were in life. It wasn't for a lack of love—that was genuine. Sometimes things just don't work out. But it did make me realize that love isn't the only thing that makes a marriage work—it's also about compromise, sacrifice, and understanding."[10]

PLAYING SELENA

Selena Quintanilla Perez, a Mexican-American singer from Texas, was a top performer of Tejano music. The music mixed rock and roll, rhythm and blues, Latin cumbia rhythms, and even the polka music so popular along the Texas-Mexico border. Tejano originated from Hispanic immigrant descendants in south and central Texas. Selena was one of the first popular crossover artists melding Latin and American pop music. Vivacious, with a powerful voice and alarmingly sensual stage presence, she became extraordinarily popular, first among Texas Hispanics, then in Mexico, even though Spanish was not her native tongue.

In March 1995, Selena was murdered at the age of twenty-three by the president of her own fan club. Her growing fame and then shocking death at such an early age resonated with an almost religious-like intensity in Latino communities. A mere month before her tragic and unfathomable murder, she had packed the vast Houston Astrodome with 61,000 excited fans. So powerful were the cultural forces surrounding her death that Governor George W. Bush of Texas saw fit to proclaim April 16 "El Dia de Selena."

Film director Gregory Nava, who had given Lopez an extrordinary opportunity to display her acting skills in a serious role in *My Family/Mi Familia*, decided to do a biographical film about Selena shortly after her death. As Nava began to interview possible actresses to play the part of Selena, Lopez became an obvious candidate. It was not a sure thing that she would be a candidate or picked for such a role. Selena's father, Abraham Quintanilla, Jr., who acted as executive producer for the film, decided to cast a wide net to look for the right actress. When word of the planned Selena film project reached the public, the producers were swamped with requests from more than ten thousand invidivuals asking to audition.

After Lopez made the first cut, she auditioned in Los Angeles with Selena's real-life father present in the theater. His presence in the room, she said later, gave her a special feeling, and she won over his pivotal support. She also won the part, her first starring role in a major motion picture.

Once she landed the role, Lopez did everything she could to get inside the character. She moved in with Selena's sister in Corpus Christi, Texas, and even took a scolding from the singer's mother for not eating enough. "She told me I was just like Selena, who became so worried about eating too much and getting fat that she almost passed out." When the filming started, Lopez spent more than two hours a day in the makeup chair to get the Selena look down pat. "But I didn't want to merely impersonate or caricature her," she recalled. "I wanted to capture her personality, down to the tiniest details—even the way she rubbed her nose."[11]

With his commitment to films that stressed family values and the struggle of Latinos to find a place for themselves in American culture, Nava gave to *Selena* the kind of understanding and depth that inspired the actors, especially Lopez. On playing the character of Selena, Lopez said, "It was a big moment in my life for many reasons. First of all, it was a great role for me, and it was my first big starring role. Gregory Nava, the director, has become a big part of my career. I don't know how much things would have been different. It is hard to say what makes your career."[12] The 1997 film also benefited from the solid performance of the famed Latino actor, Edward James Olmos, who played Selena's father. Olmos said to Lopez during the filming, "You'll never have another part like this again, where you're perfectly suited, in the right time in your life, where you understand."[13]

Lopez was later asked if the experience of playing Selena was difficult and challenging, given her almost saintly status in the Latino community. "There was a lot of pressure," Lopez said. "All the other roles I've gotten were like, you audition, you get the part, and that's it. This one was publicity-ridden from the first day. Suddenly my name was in the papers, and some people were happy and some weren't. I don't think it was personal toward me—at least I hope it wasn't." On her portrayal, Lopez said, "I do not naturally look like her, though we have similar bodies.... Being Latino in this country, we're all looked at the same. They don't look at us and go, 'She's Salvadoran,' or, 'She's Puerto Rican.' I grew up in the Bronx, she grew up in a working-class neighborhood in Texas, but where she was at when she passed away ... I know that we were going through a lot of the same things.[14]

Her performance of the legendary Tejano singer was inspired, leaving an impression of both wholesomeness and sensuality. Highly respected film critic Roger Ebert wrote of the film, "Selena's original recordings are used, with Lopez lip-synching and doing a convincing job of being Selena onstage; she has the star presence to look convincing in front of 100,000 fans in Monterrey, Mexico. *Selena* succeeds, through Lopez's performance, in evoking the magic of a sweet and talented young woman. And, like Nava's *My Family*, it's insightful in portraying Mexican-American culture as a rich resource with its own flavor and character."[15] Ebert's praise was echoed by many other film critics, and the film was a great box office success. Lopez earned a Golden Globe nomination for her performance and had reached such heights that she soon became the highest-paid Latina actress in U.S. history.

After the critical success of *Selena*, Lopez was no longer searching for roles. Producers and directors lit up the phones with various proposals for roles in big production films.

She played a documentary film director in the horror film *Anaconda*, about the world's largest and deadliest snake. She took on a steamy role in director Oliver Stone's film *U Turn*, in which Lopez played a young woman who seduces a drifter, played by Sean Penn, and then hires him to murder her husband, played by Nick Nolte.

In 1998, Lopez starred with George Clooney in *Out of Sight*, a film directed by Seven Soderburgh and based on an Elmore Leonard crime novel. Witty and imaginative, the film received plaudits from a variety of reviewers, some of whom considered it one of the best of the year. Clooney's character, Jack, opens the action by walking out of a Florida bank with an envelope full of cash only to find that his getaway car will not start. Whisked off to jail, he soon escapes to a waiting car on the other side of a fence driven by his friend Buddy, played by Ving Rhames. Federal Marshal Karen Sisco, played by Lopez, is nearby when the escape occurs and confronts the two, only to be overpowered and thrown inside the trunk of their car. And thus the action heads into overdrive, with Clooney and Lopez trading barbs along with flirtations. The superb cast also included Albert Brooks and Steve Zahn.

According to film reviewer Mike McGranaghan, it was Lopez who stole the show. "I think the performer who really walks away with the film is Jennifer Lopez. Her role must have been difficult to cast; Karen is supposed to be as tough as she is sexy. It's obvious that Lopez has the sexy part down, but she nails the toughness surprisingly well. Late in the picture, she sits in a car, chewing gum and silently observing the break-in at Ripley's house." With a simple expression, McGranaghan said, Lopez shows toughness along with confusion. "Busting Jack will mean busting a guy she really desires, but then again, you gotta do what you gotta do. Contrast this scene to the seduction that takes place in a hotel room and you see an actress who has a lot of dimensions to her talent. This is one of the best female roles of the year...."[16]

In 2000, Lopez starred alongside Vince Vaughn in the science fiction-thriller *The Cell*, in which she played a child psychologist helping track a serial killer. Film critic James Berardinelli wrote of Lopez's performance, "In *The Cell*, she does not smolder the way she did in *Out of Sight* but she gets an opportunity to display a broad range—from a hard-working therapist to a regal fantasy figure in white to a drugged-out succubus to a leather-clad martial arts babe. Lopez rolls from personality to personality without missing a beat. She's the glue that holds the film together."[17] Lopez had in the course of only a couple of years performed alongside some of Hollywood's most popular leading men.

Lopez's work had vaulted her career to new heights. From Hollywood papers to tabloids to the mainstream news media, the number of articles on the curvaceous entertainer exploded. She now appeared in various magazine lists as one of the world's sexiest women and most beautiful women. *People* magazine, one of the country's favorite supermarket publications, ran numerous articles on Lopez's early life, her ambitions, and her romances. She even appeared in the British *Celebrity Bodies* magazine, once taking top honors as the woman with the best female body.

Early in her career, Lopez had some difficult moments with the press. Word circulated in Hollywood that she was difficult to manage, and one public-relations firm even declined to represent the blossoming star. In some interviews she seemed irritated. In others, she took shots at other actors including Gwyneth Paltrow and Wesley Snipes. As her career progressed, Lopez gradually relaxed with the media, consciously steering clear of controversy, especially love interests. "In this business," she said in *Rolling Stone*, "your soul is so public and open and out there for everybody. There is no privacy. At the end of the day, you really have to fight to keep certain things sacred so that they survive."[18]

Nevertheless, she was not one to run away from her growing celebrity. She began to appear more frequently at Hollywood gatherings and awards ceremonies sporting extraordinarily flashy and often revealing fashions. This was now the world of J. Lo, much of it a kind of fantasyland of rumors and gossip, most of it contrived and inaccurate. Throughout the early ride on the celebrity trail, Lopez mostly took it in stride.

J. LO THE SINGER

One of the thrills Lopez enjoyed in her performance in *Selena* had been the extensive number of stage routines for which she had to prepare. Although the director decided to use Selena's recorded voice in the film, Lopez relished the part. It took her back to the days in the Bronx and the early times of her career showing off her best moves on stage. Those big stages were in her blood, and now, even though she had already established herself as a serious actress both in television and in motion pictures, she wanted more. She wanted some of what Selena herself had experienced—singing before live audiences.

Because of some of her early performances in a number of musical productions over the years, some record companies had shown some mild interest in pushing her career in a new direction. Now, with all of the glamour and publicity surrounding her growing star quality, the record executives began to line up, especially when Lopez herself announced an interest in recording. Indeed, she sparked a bidding war. The winner was Work Records, a label run by Sony Music.

Lopez was aware that many talented, well-known actors and actresses who had leaped from an acting career to music had suffered embarrassing setbacks. She was determined not to endure the same fate. In 1999, surrounding herself with top-flight writers and producers, she worked doggedly in the studio honing her debut album, "On the Six." The album featured such talented musical artists as Puff Daddy, Emilio Estevan, Rodney Perkins, and Marc Anthony, along with rap artists Fat Joe and Big Punisher. The result was a brilliant mix of hip-hop, Latin, and pop sounds. The first single, "If You Had My Love," raced to number one on the Billboard charts. "On The Six" sold more than eight million copies.

Rolling Stone magazine noted the extraordinary difficulty for a film star of Lopez's calibre to muscle her way successfully into the music field. The happy surprise of this first album, the review went on, is that Lopez knew what she was doing. "Instead of strained vocal pyrotechnics, Lopez sticks to the understated R&B murmur of a round-the-way superstar who doesn't need to belt because she knows you're already paying attention. When she gets the right support from a top-shelf song daddy like Rodney Jerkins, she's all brassy, breathy confidence, evoking her great precursor Ann-Margret's 1964 classic with Al Hirt, *Beauty and the Beard*. Behold jiggy Jennifer Lopez, song-and-dance woman: She makes a little va-va and a whole lot of voom go a long way."[19]

With "On The Six" and her subsequent releases, Lopez soon reached a high mark in the recording industry. Along with Ricky Martin, Marc Anthony, and others, she was an influential force in driving a growing Latin cultural influence in popular music.

MEDIA SENSATION

Lopez's media profile was now soaring. Sony began a major push to feature Lopez with other big-name entertainers. On one of those video productions, she appeared in "Around the World," created by Puff Daddy. Puff Daddy (Sean "Puffy" Combs) was born in Harlem, New York, in 1970. His father was a street hustler who was killed when Combs was three years old. His mother later moved the family to the suburbs, where Combs went to a private school. It was as a member of the school's football team that he got the famous nickname "Puffy" because he would puff out his chest to make his slender body seem bigger. After attending Howard University, the young man began his career in the music industry as an intern at Uptown Records, a position from which he quickly rose to vice-president. He later established a company called Bad Boy Entertainment. His spiraling success as a record producer, rap singer, and performer made him one of the richest men in the music industry. For a time, his major love interest was Jennifer Lopez.

After her divorce from Ojani Noa in January 1998, the tabloids began reporting that Lopez was involved romantically with Puff Daddy. For a time she characterized the relationship as "just friends," but by 1999 she went public with the romance. Throughout her entire life and career, Lopez had worked hard to show everyone, from her mother and father to friends and fans, that she was not the usual celebrity type, breezing through affairs and living on the edge. In December 1999, that image took a hit.

At a New York City nightclub, she was detained by the police along with Combs after a shooting that injured three people. Chased by police through numerous red lights, Puffy, with Lopez at his side, was finally pulled over and detained for more than fourteen hours. An unregistered pistol was found in Puffy's SUV, and the rap singer and promoter was indicted on a weapons charge. Lopez was released without being charged. For more than a year, the fiasco wound to a slow but agonizing conclusion. Rumors abounded that Puffy had bribed his driver into taking responsibility for the gun possession. Finally, Puffy was acquitted. One of his young rapper proteges was indicted and sentenced to ten years in jail. Lopez stuck by Puffy until the acquittal; shortly thereafter, the two split.

Lopez was soon seen in public on the arm of Cris Judd, a dancer she'd met while filming a video called "Love Don't Cost a Thing." Lopez and Judd married in September 2001. Pressed to comment on the several men in her life, Lopez said, "I don't look at people and see color and race. I see inside.... When you look at the people I've been with, there's no type. Ojani was from Cuba—different from me, a Latina born here. Puffy and I grew up in the same kind of background, but he's African-American. You have Cris, who was Asian, Filipino."[20] Like her first marriage to Ojani, the union with Cris Judd did not survive a year—they separated just nine months later.

Lopez fought off the image that her love life as in shambles. "It might look to the outside world that I've made mistakes, but I don't regret anything," Lopez said. "I've always followed my heart and it's never steered me wrong."[21] If her personal life seemed at least shaken, her career success rolled on. In 2001, her album *J. Lo* debuted at No. 1 on the pop charts. Meanwhile, she starred in a romantic comedy with Matthew McConaughey called *The Wedding Planner*. Like the *J. Lo* album, the film, although generally panned by critics, shot to the top of box office lists in its first week of release.

Lopez scored another successful double in 2002 with the release of the album *This Is Me ... Then* and a starring role in the comedy *Maid in Manhattan*. Playing opposite Ralph Fiennes, Lopez stars as a kind of Cinderella whose beauty and charm overwhelm a rich, political figure. *New York Post* critic Lou Lumenick wrote, "This is not the movie for hard-hearted realists bothered by the idea that an assemblyman's dates would be front-page news in the tabloids, even on a slow news day—or that a Senate candidate like Christopher would seem so utterly disinterested in politics. It is, however, just the ticket for anyone who delights in the idea of a spunky, single Latina mom from the Bronx who works her way into management and snags a millionaire...."[22]

In 2002, Lopez co-starred with Ben Affleck in a box-office disaster called *Gigli*. Although far from Lopez's proudest accomplishments, the film led to a relationship with Affleck. Here was a match that tabloid reporters and gossip columns fell all over themselves to track, a romance of two of Hollywood's brightest and most attractive stars. Media intensity reached such levels that any piece of news, however slight, false, misleading, or made up, could be lumped into one large category many began to dub "Bennifer." In November 2002, Affleck and Lopez announced their engagement, even before Lopez's divorce from Cris Judd was final. To one reporter, Lopez said, "I'm a creature of love—I was raised with a lot of it. It's funny: When you have somebody there, you don't think about it or worry because they're there for you.... I'm the type that needs family and love. I need love. I'm addicted to love, just like the song!"[23] Nevertheless, the relentless media hoopla and the nearly delirious, fast-paced schedules of the two celebrities wore down the relationship. Affleck and Lopez called off their 2003 wedding only four days before the event and ended the relationship a few months later.

After the affair ended, Lopez decided that her personal life was now off-limits in any of her interviews. Following the lead of countless celebrities who have vowed to keep their intimate lives to themselves, almost always a futile effort, Lopez lashed out at the media. "When everything was happening with Ben," she said, "I realized talking about that stuff just feeds the machine. It threatens what I love most: my work. And it's also very, very dangerous for my personal life. I was very open, and it didn't work for me. Because as much as you try to keep that stuff away, it seeps in under the doors and in through the cracks of the windows."[24]

Shortly after Lopez and Affleck ended their relationship, she became involved with Latino singer Marc Anthony. Like Lopez, Anthony grew up in East Harlem, and, also like her, he was the child of parents who moved to New York from Puerto Rico. Anthony and Lopez were born just two months apart in 1969. They met in 1998 during the production of Lopez's first album. A Grammy-winning star very popular in Latin America, Anthony successfully crossed over into mainstream American pop music. Lopez said, "I think there are a lot of people with fantastic voices, which he obviously has, but the thing that makes him special is that he can make you want to cry when you listen to him sing. I think he is a very one-of-a-kind artist of our time. I was always a fan of his. Ever since we worked together, even before then. My family was, too."[25] In June 2004, Lopez married Anthony at a private ceremony at her Los Angeles mansion.

LOPEZ FASHIONS AND SCENTS

By 2005, Lopez was one of the highest-paid performers in Hollywood, with a long list of television and motion picture credits. She had produced several highly-successful albums and record videos. She had danced, acted, and sung her way to the top. She had also become an entrepreneur.

In 2001, Lopez began to fulfill one of her fondest dreams; she launched a signature collection of clothing. Joining forces with clothing designer Andy Hilfiger, she formed the J. Lo brand company called Sweetface Fashion. "I've always had great respect for fashion icons and their impact on society," Lopez said, "I'm working to fulfill my vision of creating a brand that incorporates every aspect of my life. I am in the fashion business to create a brand that will have an effect on the women's marketplace."[26] From dresses to an assortment of swimwear, hats, gloves, footwear, handbags, and outerwear, Sweetface Fashion is not only sold in the United States but internationally, first in Canada, Central America, and Russia, and later in other countries.

Lopez also made a big mark in the perfume business. From the early days of Hollywood, a number of leading actresses have made contract arrangements with perfume companies lending their name to a product. In the 1930s Schiaparelli designed a bottle of perfume to look like Mae West's figure. In the 1950s, Givenchy created a perfume with the name of Audrey Hepburn. Over the years other stars were linked with scents, but it was not until 1987 that Elizabeth Taylor put her name on a perfume called Passion. The product became a sales phenomenon.

In 2002, Coty approached Jennifer Lopez shortly after she had appeared at a Grammys ceremony wearing a startling green dress that was the fashion talk of the evening. "She had just become the first person to ever have a No. 1 movie and album at the same time," said Coty representative Walsh. "That green dress made her a fashion icon—a triple threat."[27] Working with Lopez, Coty introduced a fragrance called "Glow." It proved to be one of the most successful launches ever in the perfume industry. Subsequently, Lopez put her name to other Coty perfumes called "Miami Glow," "Still," and "Live." All were successful.

Asked about her daring line of clothing, Lopez said, "I just don't have fashion fear. I've always been able to see how many different styles can work. I find beauty in so many things. Being an actress is about being fearless, vulnerable, not afraid to make a fool of yourself. I guess that's why I've been able to take so much criticism and not jump off the roof. I've gone through crazy times, doubtful times. But being able to be creative always helps me through. Even when it feels like the world's against you, you have your creativity."[28]

She did admit to one instance of fashion fear. In February 2005, backstage at her debut on a New York runway show for Sweetface Fashion, she panicked. "It was the most nerve-racking thing I've ever done.... I'm a performer. I can sing in front of huge crowds. But I was so nervous about my own fashion show." Nevertheless, as with most of her efforts across a variety of undertakings, she triumphed.[29]

LATINA SUPERSTAR

By 2005, Lopez had become an international movie star, singer, and fashion entrepreneur. Now thirty-five years old, her nickname was recognized by millions of people around the world. But Lopez's identity was not necessarily that of a young Latino woman of Puerto Rican descent who had marched down a truly remarkable career path from the Bronx to Hollywood. It was not as if Lopez purposefully tried to escape from her roots in her professional career. Nevertheless, she had not explored them beyond her film roles in *Selena* and *My Family/Mi Familia*.

When Lopez starred in *The Wedding Planner*, she took on the role of an Italian-American. Some Latino writers and observers were perplexed. Why was this character not a Latino? With so few movies portraying Latino characters as anything above gang members, comic caricatures, or menial laborers, here was an opportunity for a Latino star to portray a Latino professional woman. Did Lopez make an effort to persuade the producers and writers to fit the role to the actor? When she played a maid in the 2002 romantic comedy *Maid in Manhattan*, did she think about the fact that a Latino would be characterized, yet again, as an individual filling one of these stereotypical roles?

Latino writer Celia San Miguel, who, like Lopez, was of Puerto Rican background, wrote, "I couldn't believe someone of her stature would be complicit in perpetuating such stereotypes. Yes, there are Latina maids out there, but we also have saleswomen, teachers, doctors, lawyers, and artists, so why is it we always have to be either packin' heat or pushing brooms onscreen?"[30]

San Miguel wrote of such Hollywood celebrities as Rita Hayworth, Lynda Carter, and Raquel Welch, all of whom changed their names and disguised their ethnic backgrounds to get ahead in the film industry. San Miguel wrote, "When so many older Latino actors had to battle with being subjected to these roles (Lupe Ontiveros, for one, has played a maid more than twenty times in TV shows such as *Who's The Boss?* and *Charlie's Angels* and films such as *As Good as It Gets*), why would someone who has choices take on such a role?"[31]

Yet, Lopez would soon begin to make Celia San Miguel change her mind and in a convincing fashion. Aided by new spouse, Marc Anthony, she began to explore in unique ways her cultural underpinnings. She began working on her first Spanish-language studio album. *Como Ama Una Mujer* (How a Woman Loves) was released in March 2007. One of the songs, "Baila Lola," is a tribute to Lola Flores, a legendary flamenco dancer from Spain. She described the project as "... the biggest passion project I've ever done." *Como Ama Una Mujer* quickly moved to No. 1 on Billboard's Latin Album Chart and No. 10 on Billboard's Top 200 chart.[32]

Lopez considered the album some of her best work. "I think one of the things about people who want to do a lot of things—and I think it is often true of artists—is that there's this unquenchable thirst. Like you said, if you don't have the hurdles, then there's nothing to reach for or to stretch to, and you have to keep stretching. You have to. You have to keep growing in all directions." Anthony said, "She's not faking it.... Not too many people understand; the powerful, independent Latina woman is not the easiest thing to get."[33]

By this time, Lopez had formed her own company, Nuyorican Productions. She had the money, influence, and skilled collaborators to begin to produce films that aroused her interest and passion. Working with Simon Fields, her partner at Nuyorican, she began to emphasize to reporters and friends that the film industry must deal with topics that would not only entertain but would also educate, especially films that could make a difference in the lives of children. "She has a vision, she sticks to that vision," said Fields, "and even though she is realistic about some of the production changes that need to be effected, somehow she preserves the original vision."[34]

In 2007, Lopez received the Artists for Amnesty International Award, recognizing her work as producer and star of *Bordertown*. Directed by Gregory Nava, the film explored the rapes and murders of close to 400 women since 1993 in Juarez, a Mexican town near El Paso, Texas. Lopez teamed with actor Antonio Banderas, who played a former boyfriend who runs the local newspaper. Nobel Peace Prize winner Jose Ramos Horta presented the award to Lopez at the Berlin International Film Festival. Lopez was also honored by the organization Nuestras Hijas de Regreso a Casa (Bring Our Daughters Home), an organization of mothers and families of the murdered women in Juarez, for her work in *Bordertown*. "Since first hearing of these atrocities in 1998, when Gregory Nava came to me with this project, I desperately wanted to tell this story. I began working to ensure we made this film in order to bring the attention of the world to this tragedy and to pressure the Mexican government to bring to justice those responsible for these horrible crimes." said Lopez.[35]

Larry Cox, executive director of Amnesty International USA said, "It sends a strong message to the public when someone like Jennifer Lopez demonstrates her personal commitment to a cause. We are thrilled that her support will help us reach entirely new audiences who can invigorate an international movement to save women's lives."[36]

In the summer of 2007, Nuyorican Productions released the film *El Cantante*, the story of Hector Lavoe, a music pioneer who helped introduce salsa music to U.S. audiences. The film traces the genius of his work but also the tragic descent of his life into drugs and his death caused by AIDS. Lopez plays his wife Nilda Rosado, known as Puchi, a tough, resilient partner who channeled all energies in trying to help her husband conquer his demons. The part of Lavoe was played by Marc Anthony.

Although the film received mixed reviews, famed movie critic Rex Reed wrote of Lopez's performance, "J-Lo really delivers the goods. I haven't always been a fan, but she makes this movie a must-see. Shaking her booty in backless gowns with balls of brass, a hornet's nest of hair by Westinghouse, oversize sunglasses and cherry red lipstick on fire, she is shockingly good. The music is unforgettable, but she brings a pulsating rhythm to *El Cantante* that is uniquely her own."[37]

In 2007, Univision and Nuyorican productions announced the creation of Lopez's first Spanish-language television project. Called *Como Ama Una Mujer*, the same title of her first Spanish-language album, the five-episode series premiered in October 2007. The series was scheduled for release on a two-disc DVD set in December 2008. The series featured some of the biggest names in Spanish-television and film such as Chilean actor Leonor Varela, Columbian singer and songwriter Karoll Marquez, and Mexican stars Raul Mendez, Gabriela de la Garza, Rebecca Jones, Rocio Verdego, and Martin Altomare.

In the fall of 2007, about the same time as *Brave*, her sixth studio album, was released, Lopez and Anthony began a tour to a number of cities. They played a mix of Spanish and English music. A dollar from every ticket sold was donated to "Run for Something Better," a children's fitness and healthy lifestyle program. United States childhood obesity rates have tripled within the last thirty years, and the effect has been especially prevalent in the Latino community. Lopez's participation and commitment was yet another indication of just how far she had come in her career.

Still well under forty years old, Lopez has become one of the most influential and recognized figures in the entertainment industry and beyond.

Singer, dancer, actor, producer, business leader—she persists, seemingly inde-fatigable. There is so much music and film and business enterprise ahead, and Jennifer Lopez keeps up the pace.

SELECTED RECORDED MUSIC

Lopez, Jennifer. *On the 6*. Sony, 1999. CD.
Lopez, Jennifer. *J to the L-O! The Remixes*. Sony, 2002. CD.
Lopez, Jennifer. *This Is Me … Then*. Sony, 2002. CD.
Lopez, Jennifer. *Rebirth*. Sony, 2005. CD.
Lopez, Jennifer. *Brave*. Epic, 2007. CD.
Lopez, Jennifer. *Como Ama Una Mujer*. Epic/Sony BMG Latin, 2007. CD.

SELECTED MOVIES AND TELEVISION

Second Chances (series). Directed by Gene Reynolds. Lorimar Productions, 1993–1994. Television.
My Family. Directed by Gregory Nava. American Playhouse, 1995. Film.
Blood and Wine. Directed by Bob Rafelson. Fox Searchlight Productions, 1996. Film.
Jack. Directed by Francis Ford Coppola. American Zoetrope, 1996. Film.
Anaconda. Directed by Luis Llosa. Cinema Line, 1997. Film.
Selena. Directed by Gregory Nava. Esparza/Katz Productions, 1997. Film.
Out of Sight. Directed by Steven Soderbergh. Jersey Films, 1998. Film.
The Cell. Directed by Tarsem Singh. Avery Pix, 2000. Film.
Feelin' So Good. Directed by Gary Shimokawa, 2000. DVD.
The Wedding Planner. Directed by Adam Shankman. Columbia Pictures, 2001. Film.
Maid in Manhattan. Directed by Wayne Wang. Revolution Studios, 2002. Film.
Gigli. Directed by Martin Brest. Revolution Studios, 2003. Film.
Jersey Girl. Directed by Kevin Smith. Miramax, 2004. Film.
Monster-in-Law. Directed by Robert Luketic. Bender Spink, 2005. Film.
An Unfinished Life. Directed by Lasse Hallstrom. Initial Entertainment Group, 2005. Film.
Bordertown. Directed by Gregory Nava. Mobius Entertainment, 2006. Film.
El Cantante. Directed by Leon Ichaso. Nuyorican Productions, 2006. Film.
Jennifer Lopez Presents: Como Ama una Mujer. Directed by Antonio Serrano. Epic, 2007. DVD.

NOTES

1. Eric Zorn, "Change of Subject," *Chicago Tribune*, August 24, 2007, http://blogs.chicagotribune.com/news_columnists_ezorn/2007/07/index.html.
2. Lynette Holloway, "Keeping J. Lo in Spotlight Has Risks for Her Career As Well as Rich Rewards," *The New York Times*, December 9, 2002, http://query.

nytimes.com/gst/fullpage.html?res=9F0CE0DF1F3BF93AA35751C1A9649C8B63&
sec=&spon=&pagewanted=print.

3. Anthony Bozza, "Jennifer the Conqueror," *Rolling Stone*, February 15, 2001, 44, http://web.ebscohost.com/ehost/detail?vid=3&hid=9&sid=e9ddbd7f-afc3-4aa8-8afb-381130d417dd%40sessionmgr8.

4. Sara Davidson, "Jennifer Lopez Interview: The Little Latina Girl from the Bronx Is All Grown Up," *Reader's Digest*, August 2003.

5. Bozza.

6. "Jennifer Lopez: Into the Limelight," http://www.superiorpics.com/jennifer_lopez.

7. Susan Dominus, "Jennifer Lopez," *Vanity Fair*, Fall 2007, 114.

8. Bozza.

9. "Jennifer Lopez: Profile," *Premiere*, August 2000, http://www.eonline.com/celebrities/profile/index.jsp?uuid=a3197077-232b-4a31-957d-0017cadf0ac7.

10. Bozza.

11. Jeffrey Ressner, "Born to Play the Tejano Queen," *Time Canada*, March 24, 2007, http://web.ebscohost.com/ehost/detail?vid=44&hid=6&sid=3ebaf63d-944a-47f5-9f0e-b18b1434c9c1%40sessionmgr7.

12. "10 Questions," *Time*, October 29, 2007, 6.

13. Davidson.

14. Barney Hoskyns, "Selena: Interview with Actress Jennifer Lopez," *Interview*, April 1997, http://findarticles.com/p/articles/mi_m1285/is_n4_v27/ai_19382610.

15. Roger Ebert, "Selena," *Chicago Sun-Times*, March 21, 1997, http://rogerebert.suntimes.com/apps/pbcs.dll/article?AID=/19970321/REVIEWS/703210306/1023.

16. Mike McGranaghan, "The Aisle Seat: 'Out of Sight,'" http://www.rottentomatoes.com/m/out_of_sight.

17. "The Cell," http://www.reelviews.net/movies/c/cell.html.

18. Bozza.

19. "Jennifer Lopez: On the Six," http://www.rollingstone.com/artists/jenniferlopez/albums/album/174131/review/6067496/on_the_6.

20. Davidson.

21. "Jennifer Lopez," *Contemporary Hispanic Biography*, Vol. 1, Gale Group, 2002, reproduced in *Biography Resource Center*, Farmington Hills, MI: Thomson Gale, 2007, http://galenet.galegroup.com/servlet/BioRC.

22. "J. Lo's Got It 'Maid,'" *New York Post*, December 13, 2002, http://allstarz.hollywood.com/~jlo/maidreview.htm#NYPost.

23. Bozza.

24. Jonathan Van Meter, "The Girl Can't Help It: Jennifer Lopez Has a New Husband, a New Album, and a New Lease on Life," *Vogue*, January 2005, 110.

25. Van Meter.

26. "JLO Company History," http://www.shopjlo.com/aboutus.

27. Julia Boorstin, "The Scent of Celebrity," *Fortune*, November 14, 2005, http://web.ebscohost.com/ehost/detail?vid=12&hid=117&sid=7a78317e-024f-4e25-99ea-51f97a88defd%40sessionmgr102.

28. Merle Ginsburg, "Couture: Jennifer Lopez Style," *Harper's Bazaar*, May 2006, http://web.ebscohost.com/ehost/detail?vid=5&hid=117&sid=7a78317e-024f-4e25-99ea-51f97a88defd%40sessionmgr102.

29. Ginsburg.

30. Celia San Miguel, "Jennifer Lopez: The Brave One," *Giant*, October 8, 2007, http://www.giantmag.com/2007/10/movies/jenniferlopez1007/2.

31. San Miguel.

32. Van Meter.

33. Van Meter.

34. Dominus.

35. "Jennifer Lopez Working Alongside Amnesty International," http://www.amnestyusa.org/Bordertown/Jennifer_Lopez_Working_Alongside_Amnesty_International/page.do?id=1101537&n1=2&n2=22&n3=795.

36. "Jennifer Lopez Working ..."

37. Rex Reed, "J-Lo Glows," *The New York Observer*, July 31, 2007, http://www.observer.com/2007/j-lo-glows.

FURTHER READING

Bozza, Anthony. "Jennifer the Conqueror," *Rolling Stone*, February 15, 2001, 44, http://web.ebscohost.com/ehost/detail?vid=3&hid=9&sid=e9ddbd7f-afc3-4aa8-8afb-381130d417dd%40sessionmgr8.

Ginsburg, Merle. "Couture: Jennifer Lopez Style," *Harper's Bazaar*, May 2006, http://web.ebscohost.com/ehost/detail?vid=5&hid=117&sid=7a78317e-024f-4e25-99ea-51f97a88defd%40sessionmgr102.

Hoskyns, Barney. "Selena: Interview with Actress Jennifer Lopez," *Interview*, April 1997, http://findarticles.com/p/articles/mi_m1285/is]_n4_v27/ai_19382610.

San Miguel, Celia. "Jennifer Lopez: The Brave One," *Giant*. October 8, 2007, http://www.giantmag.com/2007/10/movies/jenniferlopez1007/2/.

Van Meter, Jonathan. "The Girl Can't Help It: Jennifer Lopez Has a New Husband, a New Album, and a New Lease on Life," *Vogue*, January 2005, 110.

Rita Moreno

One of the great all-time Latino entertainers, Rita Moreno (born 1931), a skillful actress who could also sing and dance, proved that Latino performers were not limited to "ethnic" roles, and in the process became one of few artists ever to win the four major entertainment awards: the Oscar, the Tony, the Grammy, and the Emmy.

FROM PUERTO RICO TO WASHINGTON HEIGHTS

Moreno was born Rosa (Rosita) Dolores Alverio on December 11, 1931, in the small town of Humacao, Puerto Rico, close to one of Latin America's great rainforests, El Yunque, located in the rugged Sierra De Luquillo mountains southeast of San Juan. Her parents, Paco and Rosa Alverio, were *jibaros*, independent farmers who tried to be self-sufficient by growing crops on small parcels of land away from the large cities.

As young children, Rosita and her younger brother Fernando enjoyed the lush surroundings close to the rainforest. Her mother was fond of showing various plants to the children, and, by the time she was three, Rosita often surprised friends and neighbors with her ability to name many of the plants in the area.

Although the family was poor, living in a very small white stucco house with no indoor plumbing, Rosita never felt deprived. All of her young friends and their families and relatives, including grandparents, lived nearby in the same conditions.

Nevertheless, in the 1930s, the pressures of the Great Depression were just as severe for residents of Puerto Rico as they were for those in the United States. Family life for the Alverios suffered as the fear of losing even the small tract of farmland and the house became more intense. Under the strain, Rosita's parents grew more hostile and distant from each other and finally divorced when Rosita was only four years old.

Rosa Alverio, still a very young woman with ambitions and a sense of independence, decided to take a step on her own that relatively few single women with children in Puerto Rico would undertake at the time—she decided to seek employment in the United States. Leaving Rosita and Fernando with their father and his new girlfriend, Rosa packed up a few belongings, boarded a boat for New York, and moved in with an aunt named Tomasita Lopez. Rosa found a job as a seamstress in a garment factory and began to save a little money.

Within a year, she was back on another boat headed to Puerto Rico, armed with a few presents for the children. She had saved enough money to bring one of the children with her to New York, she said, and planned to return a year later to do the same for the second child. Although Rosita seemed to look forward to the boat ride and the move, her brother, who had grown quite attached to his father, defiantly said that he would not go to New York. Soon, Rosa and Rosita, along with a host of other *jibaros*, also looking for something better, were headed toward New York. As the boat headed out of San Juan Harbor, Rosita and her mother looked forward to a new life.

The small tenement room that Rosita shared with her mother in Washington Heights seemed a drastic change for the young girl who was used to romping outside in the lush greenery of rural Puerto Rico. But this was the chance, Rosa Alverio knew, for both of them to rise above the life of poverty on the small farm. Soon after their arrival in New York, Rosa married once again, this time to a Cuban watchmaker named Enrique Cossio. They moved into a larger apartment.

Rosa's work in the garment factory was the kind of arduous, low-paying job that most newly arrived Puerto Ricans found. Others worked on the waterfront, as maids, or as janitors. Rosa worked for ten hours a day and, because she was paid according to the number of garments she sewed, she rarely took breaks, sometimes not even to eat. Without a union in the establishment, she had no benefits, little job security, and very little chance of advancing beyond her piecework job.

Minerva Torres Ríos, another young woman who came to El Barrio from Puerto Rico in the early 1930s and took a job in a factory, recalled her own experience, similar to that of Rosa and thousands of other women: "On Mondays and Tuesdays we worked until 8 P.M. On holidays we had to work half-days. The summer was when I really suffered, between the work and the heat. When the temperature outside was 90 degrees, it was more than 100 inside the laundry. I sweated miserably between those two ironing machines, but what could I do? Nothing but keep on working in order to keep my job. The Depression was gripping the country and there were no jobs; anyone lucky enough to have one wanted to keep it, no matter how small the salary."[1]

Outside the tenement, the streets were filled with a rush of people heading every direction. Life was tense, fast-paced, and far different from the pastoral life of a remote Puerto Rican village. As other ethnic groups wedged into the various neighborhoods of New York, families groped for acceptance, trying to learn as much of the English language as possible and, on most occasions, staying close to others of their own culture and class. They formed associations to help each other cope in the new surroundings. Teenagers often formed gangs, many establishing rites and rituals that would last for generations. Violence, poverty, crowded conditions, unsanitary living—all of it weighed heavily on the families trying to make a life in New York City, but most, like Rosa, persevered, hoping that better days were ahead.

With two salaries helping to stabilize their financial situation, the couple was able not only to make ends meet but to have a little money available to spend beyond necessities. They decided to send Rosita to dance classes. Even in these early years, the precocious child showed marvelous agility and grace, and she seemed to love being the center of attention. Rosita had a sparkling beauty and an engaging personality.

New York Public School 132 was a challenge at first. When Rosita came to the United States she knew little English. Even though she was very bright, she rarely spoke up in class, embarrassed by the language barrier. Although she worked hard to learn English, she never shone in her early classroom work as she did on a stage.

Years later, when Rita looked back over her life and especially her days in Washington Heights, she said that from her earliest years she knew that she wanted to be an entertainer. It was, she said, something deep within, and she always remained surprised when one of her friends or an acquaintance remarked that they never had any idea in their youth what they wanted to be in life. She had always known from the beginning.

Rosita's dance teacher, Paco Cansino, was a member of the professional Dancing Cansinos. Recognizing her as an exciting child talent, he took special interest in Rosita's training, at one point even taking her to a Greenwich Village nightclub where, at age seven, she joined him in dancing the *sevillanas*, a popular flamenco-style dance from Seville. Soon, she was performing in the children's theater at Macy's and dancing at bar mitzvahs and weddings. The avocation would quickly lead to a career. Rita later saw those early days performing as both a joy and an opportunity. She said, "It was accepted at the time that as Puerto Rican boys could achieve success by excelling in boxing or baseball, girls could achieve success by becoming exceptional dancers."[2]

Rosita's mother, who saw her daughter's future career as a ticket out of the tenements, soon broadened Rosita's dance training, enrolling her in schools that taught tap dancing and ballet. Her mother also began taking her to radio auditions and talent agencies, usually dropping off a picture and resume at each location. At age eleven, Rosita began a series of jobs in which she would dub voices in English-speaking motion pictures to be exported to Latin America. As a young teenager she became the Spanish talking voice of such Hollywood stars as Elizabeth Taylor and Judy Garland. In 1945, while perusing the trade magazine *Cue* for lists of auditions, her mother saw a listing for a young actress for a Broadway play written by Harry Kleiner called *Skydrift*. Rosita would be at the audition.

ON STAGE AND SCREEN: THE LATIN FIRECRACKER

Accompanied by her mother, thirteen-year-old Rosita walked into a Broadway production company to audition for a play. Although the producers were looking for an "Italian-looking" youngster to play an eleven-year-old character, Rosita, with her young, attractive features and stunning smile and presence, won the job. She had never acted before. Her mother had assumed all along that the big break for her daughter would be as a dancer. Nevertheless, she joined a cast that included Lily Valente as the lead actress and actor Eli Wallach, also playing in his first Broadway show.

A World War II drama about the spirits of young soldiers who had died in combat returning home one last time to say good-bye, *Skydrift* was an emotional and sentimental play, not one destined for a long run on Broadway. Playing the daughter of an Italian soldier, Rosita managed to memorize the few lines for the short part and deliver them without a hint of stage fright. On opening night, her mother sat in the audience transfixed. It was the first time she had ever seen a Broadway play—her young daughter was in it. *Skydrift* closed after only seven performances. Nevertheless, Rosita was now in show business at a level that only months before would have seemed impossible.

At the same time, Rosita's home life was again rocked. Her mother met a Mexican radio entertainer named Edward Moreno. Soon, she left Enrique and moved with Rosita to live with Moreno in a small house in Valley Stream, Long Island. Upset by the sudden dislocation in the family and attached to Enrique, Rosita displayed outbursts of defiance and anger she had rarely shown before. Eventually, Rosa married Edward Moreno. They soon bore a son they named Dennis. It was this family name—Moreno—that the young child entertainer would soon take for the rest of her life.

After her appearance in the Broadway play, word spread through the New York talent agencies about the thirteen-year-old girl with the dazzling looks and natural stage presence. At one of her dance recitals, a talent scout for Metro-Goldwyn-Mayer Studios (MGM) watched intently as she breezed through her performance. The scout handed his card to Rosita's mother. He would return a number of times, he said, to watch her progress. Hollywood now seemed much closer.

For a time, Rosita attended the Professional Children's School in Manhattan, a private institution combining the usual school curriculum with other classes geared for the entertainment niche to which each of the students aspired. Founded in 1914, the school's graduates over the years have included some of the most accomplished names in the entertainment world: Milton Berle, Elliot Gould, Sidney Lumet, Donald O'Connor, Christopher Walken, and many others. Most of the students were primarily actors. Even though Rosita had an appearance on Broadway listed on her infant resume, she still felt she was primarily a dancer. She felt uneasy and out of place with the other students and soon transferred to a less pressure-filled private school.

Through the swirl of auditions and tryouts and dance lessons, Rosita's adolescence seemed nearly consumed by the time commitments required by such activities. One of the few respites for the teenager was a weekly Saturday trip to the movies, where her mind raced through the possibilities that might be ahead. She admired such glamorous stars as Lana Turner and, later, Elizabeth Taylor. But on that silver screen were no Latina actresses with major roles.

Rosita did not have a real date until she was seventeen years old, and that experience was with a young man in his twenties who worked for a talent agency. The experience left her uneasy and unsure. Later, she lamented the fact that in her young years she never dated boys her own age.

Rosita began to perform regularly with variety acts in nightclubs, even though at her young age she could not have walked through the front doors as a patron. She performed locally in Spanish Harlem and Greenwich Village, and she traveled to gigs as far away as Canada. A typical show would include a comedian, an accordion player, a band, and Rita, the Spanish dancer. Even for a teenager, working the nightclubs was a rigorous test of endurance. At five feet two inches and weighing little more than 100 pounds, she chased around the New York area on buses and subways carrying two large suitcases filled with clothes.

As she continued the nightclub circuit, she learned that the image that was expected of her was that of the Latin spitfire. One of the clubs in which she performed in New Jersey was decorated like a jungle and the management of the club asked her to go by the name of "Rosita the Cheetah." She reluctantly agreed. She became keenly aware of the stereotypes to which she was asked to conform. As her career progressed, she would increasingly reject those kinds of roles. But it would take some time. For now, she would go along.

In 1949, Rosita met Louis B. Mayer, head of MGM. His talent scout had kept him informed about Rosita's fledgling career, and now he considered taking the next step. As she prepared to meet the Hollywood giant in person, she did not dress as a Latina spitfire or Rosita the Cheetah but, instead, did her best physical impression of Elizabeth Taylor. Reportedly, when Mayer first met the young performer, he did remark that she reminded him of a Latin version of the famous star.

The day after Christmas in 1949, Rosita Moreno signed a contract with MGM. The management asked her to change her first name to Tina; she compromised with the name Rita. And so began the movie career of Rita Moreno. She was eighteen years old. Before leaving for Los Angeles, however, Moreno completed what would be her first part in a motion picture, a movie released by United Artists called *So Young, So Bad*. An agent had helped Moreno get the part before she signed the contract with MGM. The film was the kind of cheap, black-and-white, B-movie, juvenile delinquent production that became popular with teenage audiences in the 1950s. On the film's billing as Rosita Moreno, she played the part of a young Latina picked up for vagrancy and sent to a girls reform school only to be mistreated and eventually commit suicide. Although the part carried a modicum of sympathy for the plight of a Latina trapped in a foreign culture, it also generally reinforced prevailing attitudes that such ethnicity meant dysfunctional behavior. Despite the relative obscurity of the film, Moreno received a few positive reviews by critics after the film's release in 1950. After completing the film, she prepared to move to Hollywood.

Later, Moreno recalled a wonderful teenage letter she wrote to a friend, handwritten on lined paper and about twelve pages long. She told her friend that her life was about to begin, that she was thrilled, and that it was as if she was in a fantasy with all its glory. In late 1949, Moreno traveled to Los Angeles with her mother and half-brother, Dennis, at her side. Her stepfather soon joined them in a cottage in Culver City, California, near the MGM studios. He later joined the U.S. Army, and Rosa again divorced.

For a time, the family waited for the MGM contract to pay dividends, waited for the first opportunities for Rita to launch a serious movie career. But MGM was the largest of the film corporations with over eighty stars under contract including Gene Kelly, Lana Turner, June Allyson, and Esther Williams. For Moreno, the parts would come but they would be specialized, tailored to fit roles the company representatives believed were appropriate for a young Latina.

In 1950, Moreno was asked by MGM to appear in two films, *The Toast of New Orleans* and *Pagan Love Song*. In the first film, she played a tempestuous Cajun woman in love with a local fisherman played by Mario Lanza. In the second, she was cast as a very young Tahitian girl employed by an Anglo character played by Howard Keel. In neither role did Moreno's character have the kind of intelligence, maturity, or serious thoughts that the Anglo characters had.

This was the case in all Hollywood productions. No director or producer would think of casting a Latino actor or actress in a role with depth. Latino roles in films were those of fantasy objects or exotic dancing partners, or native indigenous people in bare feet, more background than substance. Hollywood studios, in fact, did not quite know what to do with talented, promising entertainers such as Moreno. In her case, MGM, after only these two films, decided to do nothing more and they did not renew her contract.

Confused and devastated, Moreno did not give up. Although only in her early twenties, she had already been a professional entertainer for nearly a decade. Even though she now realized, as she not had before, the hurdles and challenges dictated by her ethnicity, she also believed in her own talent. She was now used to the cheers and adulation from audiences. She had read the favorable reviews in newspapers. She was stung mightily by this rejection, but she stayed in Hollywood. She would, as she had done before, work without a contract. She would show up at the auditions and make the rounds of the studios and other players in the filmmaking community.

But the bitterness about the stereotyping never abated. Moreno said, "I think my ethnic background has affected my career enormously. I have a feeling that had I not had the name Rita Moreno even, for starters... because of my particular looks... I know that my career would have been a very different one, a more active one and less of a struggle."[3]

In the early 1950s, Moreno appeared in several movies including *The Fabulous Senorita, Latin Lovers,* and *Javaro*. Most of the time she wore what she called her "Rita Moreno costume"—a dangling, off-the-shoulder peasant blouse, long earrings, and sandals. It was her job to look seductive and voluptuous, a task not particularly difficult for the stunning Moreno. Sometimes, she took on other ethnic roles. She was an Arab in the war drama *El Alaméin*, and she portrayed Native American characters in both *Fort Vengeance* and *The Yellow Tomahawk*. In many of her Indian maiden roles she walked around barefoot.

The B-pictures passed through Moreno's life like normal days at the office. Indeed, she often referred to them as "jobs" rather than roles. She also took most opportunities to appear in minor television series, anything to keep the career going and the hopes for something better alive.

But she began to feel trapped in an isolated corner of Hollywood and the entertainment world, her talents buried in bit parts and spitfire characters. "The more I played those dusky innocents, the worse I felt inside," Moreno said later. "I was a kid who wanted to do Chekhov, and there I was in movies ... dancing barefoot and looking terrifically sulky and sultry."[4]

The closest she got to what she saw as a truly legitimate part in these years was in the film *The Ring*, produced by the King Brothers and distributed by United Artists in 1952. Playing a romantic lead opposite Mexican-American actor Lalo Rios, Moreno was Lucy, the girlfriend of a boxer. Unlike most characterizations of Mexican Americans coming out of Hollywood in these years, these figures were sympathetic, experiencing the trials of loss and separation and the redemption of love. Her character had integrity and enduring attachment to her lover.

Looking back to those years in a cultural wasteland, Moreno later saw *The Ring* as almost unique for the time. "All the family in it are good people," she recalled. "He is not a gangster, he is not a bad boy, she is anything but a bad girl, she is a good girl. She has very traditional Mexican values."[5]

Even with favorable reviews of a film she regarded with some pride and satisfaction, Moreno still faced the usual newspaper and tabloid take on her career. One Los Angeles critic said in 1952, "It's rather surprising to hear this pretty, black-haired Latin beauty rattle off the dialogue like some doll who had been raised in Manhattan all her life... Rita, whose black eyes constantly remind you of her colorful and robust ancestry, would rather be an ordinary American on the screen than anything else.... Now don't forget that free rumba lesson, kiddo."[6]

In trying to come to grips with the perception that Hollywood producers, directors, and critics had of her persona and seeking ways to break through the barrier, she saw a number of psychiatrists over the years. "It took six years of therapy," she said, "trying to get my 'ethnic' problems untangled.... I'd get to the point where I'd feel great, really sure of myself, and then audition for an important part only to have the producer say, 'Terrific. But really, honey, for this part we need a Mitzi Gaynor—we need an American.'"[7]

Shortly after her arrival in Hollywood, Moreno moved into her own apartment and began a social life that would rank in tabloid interest with many other well-known starlets. Even though the sex kitten roles had come easily to Moreno on her career path to Hollywood, her personal life had been sheltered. In certain ways of the world she was, indeed, a relative innocent. Her first dating partner in Hollywood was Hugh O'Brien, a young, aspiring action hero who would soon make a name for himself on the long-running television series *The Life and Legend of Wyatt Earp.* Her subsequent dates and relationships in these years were mostly with actors several years older than she. At one point in her early twenties, she went through an abortion procedure and suffered complications that nearly cost her life.

She began a relationship with the brooding and rebellious star Marlon Brando. Seven years older than Moreno, Brando was already a star, having astonished the acting world with his performance as Stanley Kowalski in Tennessee Williams' play *A Streetcar Named Desire.* So creative and inspiring were Brando's stage and film abilities that he was able to follow the Stanley Kowalski role a few years later with a stirring screen performance of Mark Antony in Shakespeare's *Julius Ceasar.* After completing the film, veteran film director Joseph Mankiewicz recalled Brando's performance as "the greatest moment I have ever felt as a director…. It's what made [my] whole career worthwhile."[8]

The relationship between Moreno and Brando lasted several years and was filled with great affection and, sometimes, tumultuous jealousy. They were both outspoken, highly intelligent, and passionate, not only about each other but also about those things they regarded as unfair or unjust. Both would become ardent activists in a number of reform areas, especially the civil rights movement. They had endured stormy childhoods; they compensated with wit and sharp humor. They loved engaging in the unconventional, sometimes merely for its shock value.

With his uncontrolled womanizing, Brando often strained the relationship to the breaking point. They quarreled and came back together in regular cycles. Neither one spoke extensively about the other either during or after their close personal relationship that lasted for nearly a decade. Moreno once told a reporter in Hollywood that she had too much admiration and respect for her friend Marlon than to talk about him, especially when she knew that he did not like her to do that.

During one of the times that her relationship with Brando cooled, Moreno began to date George (Georgie) Hormel, heir to the fabulous Hormel meat-packing fortune. Dark and attractive, Hormel was in the middle of divorce proceedings with dancer Leslie Caron when he met Moreno.

The short affair with Hormel did not end without controversy and embarrassment. While Moreno slept on Hormel's couch one evening in 1954, Los Angeles police raided the premises after learning of a possible stash of marijuana. Moreno awoke to see two undercover policemen flanking Hormel, one of them rummaging through her purse. Instinctively, she fought back, kicking the startled detective in the leg and belting him in the stomach. Although both Hormel and Moreno were escorted to jail, all charges were dismissed at trial. Not surprisingly, the tabloid papers had much sport with the case. Moreno had reached celebrity status with all its attention, much of it definitely unwanted.

In the same year, however, Moreno got a totally unexpected, career-jolting boost. When *Life* magazine sent reporters to Hollywood to cover a story on a number of new television series, Moreno had landed a small gig as Ray Bolger's dancing partner in a pilot for "The Ray Bolger Show." Reporters interviewed many performers, producers, and writers for the story and took a large number of photographs.

Back in New York, *Life's* editors, while reviewing the photographs for the story, saw several shots of Moreno dancing with Bolger. Although most of the editors did not know her name, *Life* sent reporters and a photographer back to the west coast for a follow-up. Much to her amazement, one of those shots of Moreno appeared as the cover of *Life* on the March 1, 1954, edition.

Millions of people around the world saw the picture, no one more important for Moreno than Darryl Zanuck, the head of Twentieth Century-Fox. Intrigued by the sensuous-looking portrait, Zanuck ordered his staff to find out more about the young woman, especially whether she could speak English. Soon, Moreno and Twentieth Century-Fox agreed to a seven-year contract. She was only twenty-three years old.

ESCAPING THE WASTELAND

Moreno was again under contract. At least for a time, she would be on much firmer ground financially, unburdened from the constant search for bit parts that could keep her afloat. Still, the roles for the Latina actress amounted to no more than the sultry, Latina vamp wasteland. In the film *Seven Cities of Gold*, she played an Indian savage who, before a suicidal leap from a cliff, asks a U.S. soldier, "Why joo no luv Oola no more?"

In 1953, Moreno suffered one of the great humiliations of her career, one that over the years kept reminding her of the racial taunts of her childhood and the inflexibility of the entertainment industry to change with the times. Pigeonholed in what she called "Conchita-Lolita" roles, Moreno had, nevertheless, been signed up to play in a stage production of *Camino Real*. During rehearsals, she was kicked off the production by the playwright himself, Tennessee Williams, who reportedly said to one of the producers, "She can't read my goddamn poetry. Get rid of her." Moreno later recalled the experience: "I'll never forget the phone call. 'Don't come into work today.' That was it. Theater people can be very cruel. That was my introduction to a kind of terror I've never gotten over."[9]

In 1956, Moreno appeared in the most substantive role of her film career up to that point, appearing as the Asian princess Tuptim in *The King and I*. The casting was something of an accident of fate. Two different actresses slated to play the role of the Asian character dropped out. For the first time on film, Moreno was able to show off her range of talents. She sang "We Kiss in a Shadow" and "I Have Dreamed" with Carlos Rivas, and she did the narration for the ballet within the film, "The Small House of Uncle Thomas." The ballet sequence was choreographed by the highly respected Jerome Robbins. For once, she was able to wear an array of costumes rather than going the entire movie dressed in tattered rags and buckskin.

But even this role, with resplendent clothes and an opportunity to contribute something substantial to the production, left Moreno unsatisfied and increasingly defiant. At a later point in her career she would look back at *The King and I* as yet another insipid role that marked her early years in Hollywood. She initially blamed her intimidation by the system and her own youth and lack of confidence, but in taking a closer look Moreno realized how passive she had been. She had taken the roles as written, had tried to do a workmanlike job, and had fulfilled all her obligations. Yet, in retrospect, she realized that she had not put the full force of her creative energies into the parts, had not given all of herself to the parts.

In *The Vagabond King*, an operetta set in court of French King Louis, Moreno played Huguette, a sassy tavern wench. She falls in love with the dashing bandit hero of the film but loses both her lover and her life. The hero once again finds happiness in the arms of an Anglo-Saxon. Moreno's role not only added the usual titillation to the production but also some ill-used, Latin-type musical pieces including one called "Viva La US!"

Unlike MGM, Twentieth Century-Fox at least worked on publicity packages for Moreno and attempted to come to grips with the possible ways they could use the actress beyond the usual "Viva La US!" She interviewed with a number of entertainment writers and appeared in the gossip columns of newspaper and fan magazines. The usual words were "fiery," "sultry," and "firecracker." One local newspaper even ran the results of an informal poll of Los Angeles policemen who, when asked which star would be the most fun to ticket, placed Rita Moreno at the top of the list.

As her career progressed, Moreno, realizing her own potential as a Latina actress to make a difference, began to turn down film parts. When television producers asked her to consider the role of a young Eurasian woman who could speak only a few words of pidgin English, Moreno read the script and said that the role was not for an actress but a limp, formaldehyde-filled body.

Moreno appeared in few films during the later years of the 1950s. Like MGM had done before, Twentieth Century-Fox also declined to renew its contract with Moreno. In 1957, she appeared as Hetty Hutter in the Twentieth Century-Fox adaptation of James Fennimore Cooper's novel *The Deerslayer*. Filmed in the High Sierras, the story follows a young white man reared by an Indian father named Chingachgook who rescues a hunter and his two daughters from the Hurons. For the good deed, the Deerslayer is rewarded with the hand of one of the daughters, Judith. The other, Hetty, returns to her tribe. Once again, Rita Moreno lost the leading man to another. At least this time, she wore shoes.

Frustrated with her screen roles, Moreno turned in the late 1950s to the theater, performing in a summer tour of Arthur Miller's play A *View from the Bridge*. She did a number of gigs in summer stock and regional theater, hitting the road to venues from Seattle to New York. She played Lola in *Damn Yankees* and Adelaide in *Guys and Dolls*. The summer stock and small theater appearances did little to break the movie role barriers for Moreno. She still hoped for the break that could lead her out of the wasteland.

WEST SIDE STORY

In September 1957, the Broadway play *West Side Story* opened at the Winter Garden Theatre in New York City. Created by an extraordinary group of writers, directors, and musicians, the tale of Romeo and Juliet was set against the modern backdrop of the 1950s and New York's Puerto Rican tenements. The production ran for more than 700 nights, toured, and then returned again for over 250 more performances.

In 1960, director Robert Wise searched for actors for the screen version of *West Side Story*. With the collaboration of a team of storied creators—Jerome Robbins, director-choreographer; Robert Wise, director; Leonard Bernstein and Stephen Sondheim, songs and lyrics; Arthur Laurents and Ernest Lehman, writers—the musical's plot revolved around the hostility and confrontation of two rival gangs—the Sharks, a group of Puerto Rican youth, and the Jets, children of white European immigrants. The story is not only about the clash of races and cultures but also about a struggle for territory within a tight urban setting. As in the case of *Romeo and Juliet*, this modern fable has no consoling conclusion; it ends in tragedy and grief that holds little promise for relief.

Three of the central characters in the film are Puerto Rican. In casting those characters, however, the directors employed only one performer of Latino descent. Choreographer Jerome Robbins, who worked on the stage version and continued in that role for the film, had not forgotten the work of a young actress with whom he had worked on *The King and I* four years earlier. Rita Moreno, he suggested, would be perfect for the role of Anita. Not only was the ethnic fit right, he told his colleagues, she also had considerable acting skills and musical talent. For the part of Anita, the girlfriend of the leader of the Sharks, they selected Moreno. Although only twenty-six years old, the striking actress with a spitfire reputation was a veteran of stage and screen and had grown up in New York's Upper West Side, Washington Heights area where thousands of Puerto Ricans lived. She had seen the world of street gangs, had played hopscotch and jump rope on the sidewalks of "El Barrio," and had experienced firsthand the racism and cultural stereotypes that went with the territory. She had endured the taunts that Anita endures in the play. At one point, when Anita enters a candy store, one of the Jets whistles "La Cucaracha." Stopping her, one of the Jets says, "She's too dark to pass."[10]

When Moreno first auditioned for the part in *West Side Story*, the racial epithets and insulting language directed at Puerto Ricans in the play and the memories of her own childhood drove Moreno momentarily to tears. But this was a part, she believed, that she was born to play. For Moreno, the role was a godsend. Even though it was a supporting role, here was a character with depth and humanity. Here was a role that called for character development and understanding. Also, it was a role that would showcase Moreno's considerable musical talents.

The film was a major cultural breakthrough. For the first time, a Hollywood film confronted the issues of assimilation, ethnic identity, and the tensions not only among Anglos and Latinos but between Latinos themselves. Puerto Rican characters in the film are torn between the conflict of identifying with their native homeland and making their mark in a new society.

Although the story retained a dark and ominous side of Puerto Rican life, with its backdrop of gang violence, poverty, and an air of hopeless/perpetual gloom, its message was against intolerance. And even though the lead actors portraying Puerto Rican characters were not of Latino descent, there was Moreno, bringing wit and pathos to the role of Anita. And there was her rousing rooftop musical triumph with the song "America." Moreno once said of her singing, "I have a messianic side that comes out when I perform, when I sing. I feel I have something very special and unique to impart to people, as a performer who's also a human being." In this case, the musical number in *West Side Story* became one of the most remembered and celebrated in the history of American film.[11]

Puerto Ricans, whatever their overall feelings about the portrayal of Puerto Rican life in America, have felt a special relationship to the film. Jennifer Lopez, the highest-paid Latina actress in Hollywood today, recalls that her favorite movie as a child was *West Side Story*. "I saw it over and over," she said.[12]

If the filming of *West Side Story* was a career breakthrough for Moreno, the circumstances of her personal life, at the same time, were shattering. Her affair with Marlon Brando, passionate but rocky, exploded into the news in 1961. While testifying in court in a custody trial with his former wife, Brando made the astonishing admission that he had secretly married one of his girlfriends, a Mexican film actress named Movita. He also claimed that they had an eleven-year-old son.

Nine days after newspapers reported the testimony from the trial, Moreno drove to Brando's house, and, in the living room, swallowed many sleeping pills. At the time, Brando's secretary happened to be the home, discovered Moreno, and called a hospital in Santa Monica. When she arrived at the hospital, doctors found no immediate reflexes. Nevertheless, with quick medical action, she survived. Looking back over her emotional crisis, Moreno later said, "It's unfortunate that I once described my suicide attempt as therapeutic because suicide is not therapeutic. It was a turning point in my life, though. Life is really very precious, and I was reminded of that."[13]

In the fall of 1961, *West Side Story* opened to mostly glowing reviews. Bosley Crowther of the *New York Times* wrote: "What they have done with *West Side Story* in knocking it down and moving it from stage to screen is to reconstruct its fine material into nothing short of a cinema masterpiece."[14] Even a review that was less than sparkling pointed to the unique effort of the film to come to grips with racial divides. *Time* magazine said, "Sociologically, the film bids to be taken seriously: At a hundred points it sinks a *daga* of ridicule into the affluent society that has carelessly betrayed the people this movie portrays. A number called "America!" lets the hot air out of the *norteamericano* ideal of freedom. You are free to do anything you choose, the song says, and that amounts to waiting on tables and shining shoes.[15]

Early in 1962, the film was nominated for many Academy Awards. Among the nominations was Rita Moreno for Best Supporting Actress. In the jungles of the Philippines filming a movie she hated, *To Be a Man*, Moreno decided to take a break to travel to Los Angeles for the award. She asked a Filipino seamstress to sew a gown for the occasion, bought a ticket, invited her mother, and flew to the ceremony, never expecting to win the award—Judy Garland was the favorite to win.

With her mother sitting beside her, Moreno was astonished to hear her name called as a winner. Even though she had not expected to make the walk to the stage, she had thought about what she would do. "I remember thinking," she recalled. "Whatever you do, don't run to the stage. So I didn't run, but when I got there I said something absolutely stupid like, 'I don't believe it!' I couldn't believe that this little girl from the ghettos of Puerto Rico was wearing this gown and clutching an Oscar. Later I realized I was the first Latin actress to win an Oscar."[16]

Especially for Puerto Ricans on the West Side of New York, Oscar night, April 9, 1962, was a little like Harlem had been on fight nights when Joe Louis had taken the ring in the 1940s. On the doorsteps, in the bars, and in groups on the streets, people waited expectantly. Puerto Rican singer Liz Torres remembered the night: "You know, when Rita won her Oscar for *West Side Story*, I lived in the Hispanic ghetto in New York, and that's a

The Winner Is: Rita Moreno

Rita Moreno is one of only a handful of entertainers who have won all four of the major entertainment awards: an Oscar (motion pictures), an Emmy (television), a Tony (stage), and a Grammy (music). The following is a list of those awards:

1962: the Oscar for Best Supporting Actress as Anita in *West Side Story.*

1972: a Grammy, along with others in the cast, for a soundtrack recording of the popular children's television program "The Electric Company."

1975: a Tony for her performance as Googie Gomez in *The Ritz.*

1977: an Emmy as a guest artist on an episode of "The Muppets."

1978: an Emmy for her portrayal of a prostitute on "The Rockford Files."

pretty noisy place, but I have to tell you that when they started to name the names of the nominees, that neighborhood got absolutely silent. And when Rita's name was called, it went up in flames."[17]

Winning the Oscar would not materially change the kind of roles that Hollywood producers and directors would offer Moreno. But it did change the view within the Latino community itself about the actress. Moreno said:

> I cannot tell you how many Hispanic stars have since then either said in print or told me personally that my appearance in that movie and then getting the Oscar meant all the difference to them to the extent that they then felt that they could be in show business and that somehow they could make it happen for them. Edward James Olmos, Jimmy Smits, and John Leguizamo told me that. Rosie Perez told me that. And Jennifer Lopez has said it in print tons of times.[18]

Through the success and tumult of her life in the early 1960s, Moreno seemed to gather a growing self-confidence. She seemed more willing to take personal stands, to speak out against injustices not only in her own profession but also in the larger issues of the time. On a Saturday afternoon in November 1961, she led a group of protestors on a march along Sunset Boulevard on behalf of the campaign for HELP (Help Establish Lasting Peace). Along with fellow entertainers such as Brando, Shelley Winters, Kim Novak, and Rita Hayworth, the marchers carried signs such as "Ban All Atomic Weapons" and "The Only Defense Is Peace." She told a *New York Times* reporter, "We have one objective: total world cessation of nuclear bomb tests." For the rest of her career, Moreno would be an outspoken activist for a variety of causes.[19]

And now, for the first time, she told the press and the world what she thought of the way in which Hollywood treated Latino and other minority actors and actresses. In 1962, when veteran actress Betty Davis criticized efforts by activists to increase minority representation in the film industry, Moreno fired back with a letter in the press. Betty Davis did not speak for everyone in Hollywood on this issue, Moreno said. "So long as any American citizen or group of citizens is deprived of dignity and freedom, then my own freedom and sense of personal dignity are also inevitably threatened."[20] Moreno had called to account one of the towering legends in Hollywood. If Rita Moreno had been typecast as a firebrand in early years as an actress, this was a new kind of firebrand. She now carried a large protest banner for large numbers of minority actors and actresses who had been marginalized in the Hollywood system.

TO LONDON AND BACK

Although her celebrity had grown immensely after *West Side Story*, and even though she had publicly made very clear her position on the need to broaden Hollywood's portrayal of minority subjects, the choice roles still failed to come her way. Frustrated, she decided to change course; she traveled to London, hoping to land thoughtful and challenging roles on the London stage.

When she arrived, a part quickly opened at the Lyric Theatre in London's West End. Well-known director Hal Prince, who was directing an American musical called *She Loves Me*, was looking for a replacement for the part of Ilona Ritter, an important character in the play, because the actress scheduled for the part had become ill. He soon approached Moreno, who eagerly accepted. But Moreno faced a new problem in London—the actor's union, whose rules required that certain British productions use only British actors. Although the union protested Moreno's participation in the play, it went on as scheduled. She received rave reviews from British stage critics. However, the union problem was not one she had anticipated. Hal Prince offered her a quick way out of the dilemma. A new part was available back in New York at the Longacre Theatre. The play was Lorraine Hansberry's *The Sign in Sidney Brustein's Window*; Moreno's character was Iris Parodus Brustein.

For Moreno, this was an especially rich play. Hansberry, a black playwright, had written a tense drama surrounding Sidney Brustein, a disillusioned white intellectual, his wife, Iris, an aspiring actress who leaves him to act in television commercials, and his friend Alton Scales, a black activist who loves Sidney's sister-in-law, Gloria, who turns out to be a prostitute and not a model as she had claimed and who eventually commits suicide. The play opened in October 1964 and ran for approximately one hundred performances.

During the Broadway run of the play, Moreno met a New York cardiologist and internist at Mount Sinai Hospital named Leonard Gordon. He was twelve years older than Moreno. Short and bespectacled, he was very different from the usual run of actors that Moreno had dated over the past decade. The two loved each other's company. He was supportive and deeply interested in her work. On June 18, 1965, they walked up the steep steps at New York's City Hall for a simple wedding ceremony in the chambers of New York State Supreme Court Justice Samuel Gold. Moreno was thirty-three years old. In 1967, the two had a daughter they named Fernanda Luisa, who would follow in the footsteps of her mother, becoming both an actress and dancer. Leonard continued his practice until 1970, when a congenital heart problem from which he suffered became more serious. He gave up his career in medicine and, after a time learning about the entertainment business, became his wife's manager.

Moreno appeared in a number of plays in the late 1960s. None of the performances were as memorable or satisfying as Anita in the film version of *West Side Story*. Nevertheless, enough of them were of such quality as to fortify her reputation as a greatly respected actress. In November 1968, Moreno played in the starring role as Serafina in a revival of Tennessee Williams' *The Rose Tattoo*. Directed by George Keathley at the Ivanhoe Theatre in Chicago, the play earned Moreno the Joseph Jefferson Award given by the Chicago Theatre critics. Moreno took special delight in the standing ovations night after night during the performance run and her later award for excelling in a play written by the man who had once personally fired her from a cast.

Moreno remained friends with Marlon Brando, and over the years he took a strong interest in her career and offered a great deal of professional encouragement. At his suggestion, Moreno decided in 1968 to appear again in Hollywood productions. She traveled to France to play with Brando in the film *The Night of the Following Day*. An elaborate plot involving a gang planning to kidnap an heiress, Moreno played one of the schemers, a woman on drugs. Although the film did poorly at the box office, Moreno herself garnered a number of favorable reviews. She followed up the Brando film with a performance in *Marlowe*, a detective film starring James Garner, and then she portrayed Alan Arkin's Puerto Rican girlfriend in the United Artists comedy *Popi*, set in East Harlem.

After performing in two more plays on Broadway, Moreno played a prostitute in the dark drama/comedy *Carnal Knowledge* (1971), which was directed by Mike Nichols and starred Jack Nicholson, Candace Bergen, Art Garfunkel, and Ann-Margret. Influential film critic Robert Ebert of the *Chicago Sun-Times* raved about the film, remarking that the acting and direction were superbly understated.

In the early 1970s Moreno, now the mother of a three-year-old daughter, set her sights on helping to improve children's television. In 1971, the Children's Television Workshop, produced by the creators of Sesame Street, created a program called *The Electric Company* designed to improve the reading skills of children between the ages of seven and ten. A multiracial group of actors, including such stars as Bill Cosby and Morgan Freeman, played numerous characters on the rapid-paced series broadcast on the Public Broadcasting Service. Over the course of six seasons and nearly eight hundred episodes, the show used various musical and comedic sketches. In the second season, Moreno began to open the show by screaming "Hey, you guyyyyys!!" One of her characters, Pandora, was a curly-headed blond who tried to outwit the adults in her life. In 1972 Moreno received a Grammy award for her contribution to *The Electric Company* soundtrack album. Moreno hoped that her involvement with *The Electric Company* would help inspire Latino children to improve their reading skills. She said, "I am Latin and know what it is to feel alone and ignored because you are different... my presence can tell a lot of children and some adults, 'Yes, we do exist, we have value.'"[21]

PLAYING "GOOGIE"

When Moreno was filming *West Side Story* in the early 1960s, she often entertained cast and crew members with an outrageous parody of a star-struck Latino bathhouse entertainer with an exaggerated Spanish accent singing such songs "Everything's Coming Up Roses." The name of the character was Googie Gomez. In many ways Googie was the sum of Moreno's frustrations with the kinds of roles typically directed her way, the stereotypical, zany Latina making merry and making a fool out of herself. Her characterization of Googie was a slap at the writers, producers, and directors who refused to take Latino roles or Latino performers seriously.

Sometimes, Moreno would be asked to do an impromptu rendition of Googie at parties. She would break up the house, even if many of those at the parties were the writers, producers, and directors at whom the character's pitiful but hilarious antics were directed. At one such party in 1973, a birthday celebration for actor James Coco, she was asked to do Googie. Among the guests that night was a talented young writer named Terrance McNally, who had already written one very successful play. Like many others over the years, McNally rolled with laughter at Moreno's character who, on this particular night, recited a passage from Shakespeare's *Hamlet*. Unlike the others, however, McNally immediately saw an opportunity. He approached Moreno and told her he was going to write a play for Googie.

Moreno thought little of the encounter. But in 1974, her husband Leonard happened to see James Coco while walking along Broadway in New York. The writer asked Leonard if he had seen the script. At that point neither knew what Coco was talking about. A few days later, the mystery was unveiled: In a package mailed by McNally, Moreno first saw a play called *The Tubs*, a gay farce set in a bathhouse and featuring Googie Gomez.

In 1975, Moreno took Googie to Broadway. The play, renamed *The Ritz*, opened at the Longacre Theatre. It was a smash hit. Moreno told reporters that she was thumbing her nose at all the writers who had written such lines as "Yankee peeg, you rape my sister, I keel you" for so long. For Terrance McNally, she said, those kinds of lines were farce and he understood that.

When asked later what she remembered most about performing the role of Googie, Moreno said, "I'd never laughed so hard in all my life. And the cast was like that, too. The hardest thing we had to do on that show was to keep a straight face. I broke myself up all the time. I just thought Googie was so hilarious. It was like I was schizophrenic, like I was two people. I was always Rita listening to this other character and the character would make Rita laugh. I can still break myself up by thinking of things to do with her attitude and her accent and, well, I would fall on the floor myself."[22] For her tour de force performances as Googie Gomez, Moreno won a Tony Award.

FROM THE MUPPETS TO OZ

In 1977, Moreno continued her work on children's television. Jim Henson, creator of "The Muppets," asked her to be a guest star for a special to be filmed in London. In one skit, she played the part of a French apache dancer. Normally, the man tosses his dancing partner up and about while swirling around. In this case, Moreno took the opposite path. While dancing with a life-sized Muppet, Moreno becomes enraged when her partner begins flirting with a Muppet pig. Responding to the insult, Moreno tosses her partner around the stage. In another skit, Moreno engages in a hair-pulling standoff with Miss Piggy. For her work on the episode, Moreno won yet another award, the Emmy for Best Performing Artist in a Variety Show.

Throughout the last part of the twentieth century and into the new millenium, Moreno continued to perform in film, television, and theater as if she were at the beginning of her career. Her energy and stamina have been remarkable.

Moreno won another Emmy for Outstanding Lead Actress for a Single Appearance in a Drama or Comedy Series for her performance in an episode of *The Rockford Files*. She created a one-woman nightclub act that she performed over the years in various cities. In 1982, she starred on an ABC situation comedy called *Nine to Five*. She performed numerous times with her daughter Fernanda in productions of *Steel Magnolias* and *The Taming of the Shrew*.

Her later film roles included *Wharf Rat* in 1995 with Lou Diamond Phillips and the 1995 feature film *Angus* with George C. Scott. She appeared in the 1999 feature *Carlo's Wake*, and she starred opposite Ben Gazzara in the

2000 film *Blue Moon*. In 2000, she appeared in the highly acclaimed movie *Pinero* starring Benjamin Bratt, and in 2002 she appeared in the John Sayles film, *Casa de los Babys*.

Moreno's later stage roles included such diverse characters as Lola in *Damn Yankees*, Annie Sullivan in *The Miracle Worker*, Doris in *The Owl and the Pussycat*, Amanda Wingfield in *The Glass Menagerie*, and Mama Rose in *Gypsy*.

In 1977, Moreno began working on a hard-edged, critically acclaimed series on HBO called *Oz*. The series portrayed the daily tensions and challenges of inmates and guards at a maximum-security prison. Moreno was Sister Peter Marie, one of a team of psychologists treating prisoners. The part was the antithesis of the sexy spitfires that Moreno had played in her early years. No one who had seen Moreno perform during those years would have recognized her as a nun in *Oz*. "I didn't look good," she said. "It gained me a new kind of respect in the business. It made a big difference. Allowing myself to look unfrivolous, unsexy."[23]

Throughout her career, Moreno continued to give a great deal of time and energy to a number of causes. She lobbied on Capitol Hill for a program to keep disadvantaged Latino children in elementary school. She campaigned for bilingual education. She was a determined supporter of a woman's right to reproductive privacy and freedom. She supported AIDS charities and was one of the first major stars to promote awareness. "A lot of us saw it early on as a plague and a scourge and that it needed immediate attention because our government was turning the other way," recalled Moreno. "Back then, there was so little known about the disease. Now we have treatments that prolong life and we continue to hope for a vaccine or cure."[24]

In 2004 Moreno received rave reviews for her portrayal of Maria Callas in another Terrance McNally play, *Master Class*. In 2006 she received similar praise for her portrayal of Amanda Wingfield in The Berkeley Repertory production of *The Glass Menagerie*. And in 2007 Moreno appeared in a cameo role on the hit television series *Ugly Betty*.

Looking back over her long distinguished, and varied entertainment career, Moreno has said, "I'm a dinosaur, a dying breed ... I sing, dance, act. Now performers are so specialized."[25]

Moreno's enormous contribution in so many entertainment fields, however, is not just in the diverse talent she brought to stage, screen, and television, but in her ability and willingness to rise above the proscribed roles that had been in place for Latino characters and Latino performers. Moreno's career says to all in the field of entertainment that richness and depth and understanding in all those mediums come not from cultural isolation but from inclusion. Comedian Paul Rodriguez said, "I just want you to know that when I was a kid living in East L.A., none of us in that neighborhood had a clue who our congressman was, who our councilman was, who our senator was, but we knew who Rita Moreno was."[26]

SELECTED MOVIES AND TELEVISION

Pagan Love Song. Directed by Robert Alton. Metro-Goldwyn-Mayer, 1950. Film.

So Young, So Bad. Directed by Bernard Vorhaus. Danziger Productions, 1950. Film.

Cattle Town. Directed by Noel M. Smith. Warner Bros. Pictures, 1952. Film.

The Fabulous Senorita. Directed by R. G. Springsteen. Republic Pictures, 1952. Film.

Singin' in the Rain. Directed by Stanley Donen and Gene Kelly. Metro-Goldwyn-Mayer, 1952. Film.

El Alaméin. Directed by Fred F. Sears. Columbia Pictures, 1953. Film.

Fort Vengeance. Directed by Lesley Selander. Allied Artists Pictures, 1953. Film.

Latin Lovers. Directed by Mervyn LeRoy. Metro-Goldwyn-Mayer, 1953. Film.

Garden of Evil. Directed by Henry Hathaway. Twentieth Century-Fox Film, 1954. Film.

The Yellow Tomahawk. Directed by Lesley Selander. Bel-Air Productions, 1954. Film.

Seven Cities of Gold. Directed by Robert D. Webb. Twentieth Century-Fox Film, 1955. Film.

Untamed. Directed by Henry King. Twentieth Century-Fox Film, 1955. Film.

The Lieutenant Wore Skirts. Directed by Frank Tashlin. Twentieth Century-Fox Film, 1956. Film.

The Vagabond King. Directed by Michael Curtiz. Paramount Pictures, 1956. Film.

Summer and Smoke. Directed by Peter Glenville. Hal Wallis Productions, 1961. Film.

West Side Story. Directed by Jerome Robbins and Robert Wise. The Mirisch Corporation, 1961. Film.

Cry of Battle. Directed by Irving Lerner. Petramonte Productions, 1963. Film.

A World of Stars. Directed by Buddy Bregman. 1963. TV Special.

The Night of the Following Day. Directed by Hubert Cornfield. Gina Production, 1968. Film.

Marlowe. Directed by Paul Bogart. Cherokee Productions, 1969. Film.

Popi. Directed by Arthur Hiller. Herbert B. Leonard Productions, 1969. Film.

The Electric Company. Children's Television Workshop, 1971–1977. TV.

The Ritz. Directed by Richard Lester. Courtyard Films, 1976. Film.

Italian Movie. Directed by Roberto Monticello. 1993. Film.

Where on Earth is Carmen Sandiego? Directed by Stan Phillips. DiC Enterprises, 1994. TV.

Angus. Directed by Patrick Read Johnson. Atlas Entertainment, 1995. Film.

The Wharf Rat. Directed by Jimmy Huston. All Media, Inc., 1995. TV.

Oz. Levinson/Fontana Company, 1997–2003. TV.

Slums of Beverly Hills. Directed by Tamara Jenkins. Twentieth Century-Fox Film, 1998. Film.

Blue Moon. Directed by John A. Gallagher. Blue Moon Pictures, 2000. Film.

Piñero. Directed by Leon Ichaso. GreeneStreet Films, 2001. Film.

Casa de los Babys. Directed by John Sayles. IFC Films, 2003. Film.

Copshop. Directed by Anita W. Addison and Joe Cacaci. David Black Production, 2004. TV.

Play It by Ear. Directed by Lauren Flick. USA, 2006. Film.
Cane. ABC Studios, 2007. TV.

NOTES

1. "Old Voices, New Voices: Mainland Puerto Rican Perspectives and Experiences," *OAH Magazine of History*, Winter, 1996, http://www.oah.org/pubs/magazine/latinos/old%20voices.html.

2. Mary Caudle Beltran, *Bronze Seduction: The Shaping of Latina Stardom in Hollywood Film and Star Publicity*, dissertation for the degree of doctor of philosophy, The University of Texas at Austin, August 2002, 147, http://dspace.lib.utexas.edu/handle/2152/1154.

3. Beltran, 156.

4. "Puerto Rico Profile: Rita Moreno," August 10, 2000, http://www.puertorico-herald.org/issues/vol4n32/ProfileMoreno-en.html.

5. Beltran, 158.

6. Beltran, 160.

7. Beltran, 160.

8. Maggie Van Ostrand, "Brando," *TesasEscapes*, April 3, 2007, http://www.texasescapes.com/MaggieVanOstrand/Marlon-Brando.htm.

9. Glenn Lovell, "Digging Deep: Moreno's Emotional Scars Mark Menagerie Effort," *The Mercury News*, May 8, 2006, http://findarticles.com/p/search?tb=art&qt=%22Glenn+Lovell%22&sn=50.

10. Alberto Sandoval Sanchez, "*West Side Story*: A Puerto Rican reading of 'America,'" *Jump Cut*, June 1994, 59–66, http://www.ejumpcut.org/archive/onlinessays/JC39folder/westSideStory.html.

11. Elisabeth Laurence, "Lives of Style: Rita Moreno and Fernanda Fisher," http://www.clipclip.org/clips/detail/24371/lives-of-style-rita-moreno-and-fernanda-fisher-examiner-com.

12. Frances Negron-Muntaner. *Feeling Pretty: West Side Story and Puerto Rican Identity Discourses*. Social Text–63 (Vol. 18, No. 2), Summer 2000, 83–106, http://muse.jhu.edu/login?uri=/journals/social_text/v018/18.2negron-muntaner.html.

13. Ron Arias and Michael Lipton, "Entertaining Rita," *People Weekly*, September 21, 1998, 167.

14. Bosley Crowther, "Screen: 'West Side Story' Arrives," *New York Times*, October 19, 1961, 39.

15. "Sweetness and Blight: West Side Story," *Time*, October 20, 1961, 94.

16. David Hutchings and Mark Morrison, Is There an Oscar in the House? *InStyle*, March 2006, http://web.ebscohost.com/ehost/detail?vid=15&hid=102&sid=c97c5e06-d172-4129-8662-32afe7501673%40sessionmgr102.

17. Blasé DiStefano, "Rita Reigns," http://www.outsmartmagazine.com/issue/i02-01/rita.html.

18. DiStefano.

19. *New York Times*, November 11, 1961, 54.

20. Beltran, 175.

21. "Puerto Rico Profile."

22. DiStefano.

23. Laurence.

24. "Moreno and Tilly Team Up against AIDs," USA Today, May 25, 2003, http://www.usatoday.com/news/health/spotlighthealth/2008-05-28-aids_x.htm.

25. Arias and Lipton.

26. DiStefano.

FURTHER READING

Arias, Ron, and Michael Lipton. "Entertaining Rita." *People Weekly*, September 21, 1998, 167.

Beltran, Mary Caudle. *Bronze Seduction: The Shaping of Latina Stardom in Hollywood Film and Star Publicity*. Dissertation for the degree of doctor of philosophy. The University of Texas at Austin, August 2002, http://dspace.lib.utexas.edu/handle/2152/1154.

DiStefano, Blasé. "Rita Reigns." http://www.outsmartmagazine.com/issue/i02-01/rita.html.

"Puerto Rico Profile: Rita Moreno," August 10, 2000, http://www.puertorico-herald.org/issues/vol4n32/ProfileMoreno-en.html.

Sanchez, Alberto Sandoval. "*West Side Story*: A Puerto Rican reading of 'America.'" *Jump Cut*, June 1994, 59–66, http://www.ejumpcut.org/archive/onlinessays/JC39folder/westSideStory.html.

Edward James Olmos

"I come from a dysfunctional family," actor Edward James Olmos once said. "I'm a minority, I have no natural talent, but I did it. If I can do it, anybody can do it. I take away all the excuses."[1]

Olmos is one of the most influential voices of the Latino community in the United States. As an actor, he has produced a commendable body of work that has earned him numerous awards and accolades. But Olmos' life is more than a story of a poor kid from the barrio who made it big in Hollywood. He is not only an actor but also an activist with a deep commitment to his community. His greatest joy comes from influencing young people to do something good with their lives.

Journalist Ralph Cruz wrote of Olmos: "As an actor who created the standard for portraying modern-day urban Latinos in movies, and a human being who has spent twenty-five years campaigning against violence, Olmos has become a cultural icon: a no-backing-down preacher of peace."[2]

BARRIO-BORN

Born on February 24, 1947, Olmos was the second of three children of Pedro and Eleanor Olmos. Pedro was an immigrant who had left Mexico City with only a few dollars in his pocket and a sixth-grade education. The former Eleanor Huizar was a Mexican-American who had completed the eighth grade. Her grandparents had been journalists in Mexico City during the Mexican Revolution in the early part of the twentieth century. Eleanor Huizar met Pedro Olmos while visiting Mexico City. Their first child was a boy they named Peter; Edward, the second child, was followed by Esperanza, six years younger than her oldest brother.

Olmos' childhood years were spent in a small house on Cheesbrough's Lane in the Boyle Heights section of Los Angeles. Situated on the east bank of the Los Angeles River, Boyle Heights was named for the bluffs overlooking the muddy flats below. The area was bordered by the river on the west, Mission Road on the north, and Los Angeles city limits on the east and south.

Throughout Olmos' childhood and teenage years, East L.A. was in the process of becoming an area populated largely by Mexican immigrants. At the time he was born, however, Boyle Heights was a racially mixed neighborhood where Latinos, Koreans, Chinese, Russians, and other ethnic groups intermixed. Olmos later remembered it as a place where immigrants of all nationalities were merged together to become Americans. On his particular street, Olmos recalled, there was a Hispanic family with thirteen children, a Native American family, and an assortment of Korean, Chinese, and Russian families.

To Olmos, it was fascinating: "I was raised in what I consider to be not a melting pot," he said, "but a salad bowl. The onion stayed the onion, the tomato stayed the tomato, the lettuce stayed the lettuce, with maybe a little

Olmos and the Mayans of Chiapas

In the Chiapas Mountains of southern Mexico, there are people whose ancestors can be traced directly to the native Mayan tribes that inhabited the area hundreds of years earlier, long before Spanish adventurers arrived. One can still see the rich past in thousand-year-old ruins in places with such names as Palenque and Yaxchilan.

Chiapas did not become a Mexican state until 1824, and it remained a remote frontier until the Pan American Highway opened in the 1950s. The tangles of mountain ranges, rivers, and jungle discouraged the invasion of modern civilization. Throughout the centuries, the region attracted explorers and conquerors. From the invasions of the Spanish hundreds of years ago through the battles over land that continue today, the area has been the scene of rebellions, ruthless rule, and suppression. At the same time, much of the native culture that existed before the Spanish conquerors lived on in language, customs, and religion.

The Chiapas Maya kept their history alive in folk tales, in memories handed down through generations, and in colorful rituals. Edward James Olmos' own family was in part descended from those early Mayan natives. His commitment to those people and their culture is powerful and deeply personal.

Russian or Italian dressing. And it tasted real good. No one lost their identity, and I thought that was what life was like."[3]

Inside this world, Olmos said, everyone had similar struggles. They were all poor. They all faced the daunting challenge of keeping up their spirits, of trying to make each day better than the one before. Olmos believed from early on that the cultural diversity of that Boyles Heights neighborhood contained within it the kind of camaraderie that society lacks when it separates into more self-contained, private worlds determined by wealth and ethnicity.

Over the years, the area east of downtown Los Angeles began to shed much of that diversity as it became home almost entirely to thousands of Mexican immigrants. Most of the people were laborers and working poor. The community began to reflect much of the character and many of the traditions of the Latino people—a strong sense of family, strongly Catholic, and a rousing love of fraternity and social and cultural celebration. Along Whittier Boulevard and other main streets in East L.A., churches, schools, social clubs, newspapers, and storefronts gradually took on the look of cities in Latin America.

Nevertheless, as many other developing immigrant populations had experienced throughout U.S history, the community in East L.A. found itself lagging in educational opportunity, employment, and political clout. It also experienced from the greater Los Angeles population a dispiriting racism and discrimination. Many young Latino boys took refuge from the poverty and bigotry in a growing number of street gangs. Here, they looked for the power and respect that eluded them in the larger society. Instead, they often found juvenile delinquency, jail, drug and alcohol abuse, and, sometimes, death.

It was in this atmosphere that Olmos' earliest memories of the poor and struggling were formed. Both of his parents taught the boy acceptance and respect for the underclasses. His father, who had earned only a sixth grade education in Mexico City, worked many jobs, as a postal worker, a slaughter-house laborer, and as a welder, and he eventually gained a high school diploma from the Los Angeles school district. His mother, who worked most of her life as a nurse, also completed her education late in life. They never gave up or gave in to their challenging circumstances, and they always were there to lend a hand. Pedro Olmos took time off to coordinate little league baseball youth programs; Eleanor Olmos later cared for AIDS patients.

Olmos was asked many times where he got his passion for helping others. He especially thought of his mother. "My mother is the reason I know God is a woman," he said. "She's worked for twenty years—from age fifty-four to seventy-four—at County General Hospital in Los Angeles. She has worked from eleven o'clock at night to seven in the morning in the AIDS ward, where she's held the hands of many, many people as they died. It's a gift."[4]

His parents divorced in 1955, shortly before his eighth birthday. Along with his brother and sister, Olmos lived with his mother but was able to see his father often during his teenage years. The lures of gang life and other troubles that captured the minds and hearts of many adolescents in East L.A. did not capture Olmos.

From his earliest boyhood days, he was fascinated by baseball. Days and evenings, weekdays and weekends, one would find him on the ball fields, rousing his friends to start another game, to shag some flies, to keep improving the hitting swing. Dreaming about playing major league baseball occupied his thoughts so much that hanging around seemed useless, a waste of time. He became a star player in Little League, his hitting exploits gaining the attention of folks outside of East L.A. At every game, his admiring father was among the families and friends of the youngsters, cheering on his boy, whom, he was convinced, was headed for a baseball career.

Encouraged by his father, Olmos took whatever opportunity he had to listen to games on the radio or, on occasion, attend one in person. The Brooklyn Dodgers moved to Los Angeles in 1958 and became the Los Angeles Dodgers. Olmos was eleven years old and thrilled. Baseball, he said later, kept him out of gangs. It "taught me self-discipline, determination, perseverance, and patience—all of which have been key ingredients to what I have done since."[5]

Olmos later moved with his family to a more suburban area of East L.A. known as Montebello. He joined the 1964 class at Montebello High School. Although the facilities at the school were somewhat better than many of the other high schools in the area, the school administrators and faculty struggled with low budgets and declining resources.

The two largest high schools in the district, Garfield and Roosevelt, were built in the 1920s to house about one thousand students each. By the mid-1960s they housed several thousand. Most schools had too many unqualified teachers, too few textbooks, and not enough guidance counselors. Their facilities were outdated. Few students leaving the school system attended college; many were not able even to get skilled work. Many of the boys were part of a growing gang population.

More than half of the children under the age of eighteen lived in poverty in East Los Angeles; more than 50 percent of the adults over twenty-five years old did not have a high school diploma. Some of the families had recently arrived from Mexico; many of the families were large with several children, and a large percentage spoke only Spanish in their homes.

In addition to the usual challenges facing a high school student in what many began to call "the barrio" because of its Latino imprint, Olmos suffered from a reading disability that forced him to work especially hard in his academic subjects. Nevertheless, the youngster gamely carried on with a determination and fire that were commendable.

As Olmos reached his later teenage years, his interest in baseball waned, replaced by a sudden desire to be a singer. Although he had never displayed much natural ability to sing, he moved ahead with his newest goal, set on making a name for himself. He began to teach himself to play the piano. With his close friend Rusty Johnson and others, he formed a rock-and-roll group they called Eddie and the Pacific Ocean. With long hair streaming down to the middle of his back, Olmos was lead vocalist and keyboarder. He later admitted to being a terrible singer but was able, on the other hand, to scream and dance with the best of them. The group became proficient enough to land some gigs at local venues in Los Angeles, especially along Sunset Strip, and Eddie and the Pacific Ocean earned some extra money. The entertainment career of Edward James Olmos was launched.

BUDDING ENTERTAINER

The band was good but not great, certainly not destined to make it to the heights of the Billboard listing. Although the group had gotten exposure in downtown Los Angeles at some ritzy bars, especially at a nightclub called Gazzari's, no record company executive or agent was anxious to take them on.

At one of the Pacific Ocean's gigs, Olmos met Kaija Keel, the daughter of actor Howard Keel. She had recently broken off a relationship with actor Jeff Bridges. She and Olmos hit it off immediately. As the two became seriously involved, the Keels became concerned that their daughter was dating a Latino rock and roll singer. "I was *Guess Who's Coming to Dinner* before the movie appeared," recalled Olmos. "It was quite a dinner. They served artichokes, and I'd never eaten one." In 1971, Olmos and Kaija Keel decided to marry. Kaija said later of her parents, "I was very mad at them for a while, but now that I'm a parent, I can understand. They were worried about me going off so young with a crazy person with no money."[6]

By the age of twenty-five, Olmos was a husband and father of two boys, Mico and Bodie. Mico's name came from the Spanish *mi hijo* (my son), and Bodie was named after a ghost town in eastern California. The family stayed together for more than twenty years, the couple divorcing after the children were adults.

After high school Olmos enrolled in East Los Angeles City College, where he earned an Associate of Arts degree in sociology. He also studied at the California State University at Los Angeles. At first he took some psychology and criminology courses and then signed up for a drama course that, he hoped, would improve his presence on stage with the Pacific Ocean group. It was in the course of his work in the drama class that Olmos became convinced that rock music was not a career path leading to the promised land of entertainment success; he now found that he enjoyed acting. He told friends that he was surprised that it was easier to talk an emotion on stage than to sing it. As with other of his preoccupations and infatuations in his young life, Olmos turned to acting with much enthusiasm, determined to give it maximum effort.

With Rusty Johnson's agreement and support, Olmos broke up the band. To make enough money to provide for his family, Olmos bought the band's large van and began a business delivering antique furniture. He also began to find work with experimental theater groups and, for a time, took small roles on television. He won parts on such shows as *Kojak* and *Hawaii Five-O*, invariably playing a "bad guy" role. Olmos once joked that in one of the *Hawaii Five-O* episodes, his character was so bad that he was the only person that Jack Lord, the hero of the series, ever shot in the back.

In 1975, Olmos played a bit part in a film called *Aloha, Bobby and Rose*. Directed by Floyd Mutrux and starring Paul Le Mat as Bobby, the film was essentially a teenage car-chase road film. An auto mechanic and his girlfriend, responsible for an accidental homicide, take to the open road and flee from the law. Although the film was little noticed, along with his own part in it, Olmos' career on the silver screen had begun.

Two years later, Olmos played a drunk in the film *Alambrista*. Written and directed by Robert Young, the film follows Roberto, a young Mexican man who slips across the border into the United States after the birth of his first child. Seeking work to support his family back home, he finds hardship and exploitation. Young later became a long-time Olmos friend and co-owner of his production company.

For Eddie Olmos, the world of acting opened up in 1978—and it opened on stage. He played the part of "El Pachuco" in the celebrated play *Zoot*

Suit. Written by the esteemed playwright Luis Valdez, who had for a time worked with Cesar Chavez in organizing the farm workers' union, the musical drama evoked strong memories shared by Latinos in Los Angeles about racial prejudice and perverted justice. The play evoked the drama played out in Los Angeles over the so-called Sleepy Lagoon Murder and the Zoot-Suit Riots.

As early as the 1940s, young Mexican Americans, especially members of various gangs, began calling themselves *pachucos* and wearing so-called zoot suits as a cultural symbol. With its oversize coat, gaucho pants, and broad-brimmed hat, the zoot suit fashion gave a youngster a defiant identity. With their long, swept-back "ducktail" hair and their key chains dangling to the ground, the pachucos seemed a dangerous force to the larger Los Angeles community, a symbol of violence and upheaval.

Tension between the pachuco gangs and the Los Angeles police department escalated, especially after the roundup of a group of zoot-suiters thought to have killed a young Mexican national near a reservoir named Sleepy Lagoon. With a media onslaught directed at the pachuco gangs, the police swept up more than six hundred Latinos in August 1942. Twenty-four members of a gang were falsely charged with the murder. From those early days of the pachuco phenomenon, distrust and anger swelled over the years between East L.A. and the rest of the greater Los Angeles area. On January 12, 1943, three of the twenty-four defendants were convicted of first-degree murder and sentenced to life in prison; nine were convicted of second-degree murder and sentenced to five years to life, and five were convicted of assault and released for time served.

On the night of June 3, 1943, eleven sailors on leave in Los Angeles precipitated another incident that made a fiery situation even more combustible. After the eleven claimed to have been attacked by a group of pachucos, a group of more than two hundred uniformed sailors chartered twenty cabs and charged into the heart of the Mexican-American community in East L.A. Marching in orderly lines, they broke into stores, bars, and theaters, assaulted any individual wearing a zoot suit or anything close to it, and beat up numerous citizens.

The impact of the Sleepy Hollow Lagoon murder case and the subsequent Zoot-Suit Riots was a glaring testament to the climate of racial tension pervading Los Angeles. Luis Valdez's play struck at the heart of the sense of alienation and ostracism felt by Latinos in East L.A. For Valdez, the pachuco figure represented a symbol of mythic power and ancestry that gave a disenfranchised people a sense of their roots. The main character of *Zoot Suit* is El Pachuco, a dashing figure in a zoot suit, swishing a switchblade knife and snapping his fingers while he narrates the events played out in those critical days of the early 1940s. He is a super-macho, street-smart, smirking emblem and voice of conscience as he struts about the stage commenting on the action. To Valdez, the figure of El Pachuco represented the Chicano spirit of pride and individualism, and the play, featuring exact courtroom testimonies and press quotes, was a searing indictment of misunderstanding, racial prejudice, and violence.

In early 1978, Olmos and some three hundred other aspiring actors showed up to try out for the part of El Pachuco. At the audition, Olmos later remembered, he marshaled all the street lingo and mannerisms he could bring. He spoke in *calo*, a street jive lingo that mixed Spanish, English, and Gypsy. When they asked him to dance, he hit a perfect set of splits, smiled menacingly, and turned up the brim of his hat. He was, almost everyone there agreed, perfect for the part. "He's a samurai, a warrior, very principled and loyal," Olmos said of the character El Pachuco. "But there's also the dark side—the ninja—in him. He knows he can use his powers in negative ways. His voice is very Zen."[7]

Opening at the Mark Taper Forum in Los Angeles, *Zoot Suit* was scheduled to run for ten weeks. Garnering favorable reviews and sold-out performances, the production returned for eight additional weeks and then moved on to Hollywood's Aquarius Theater for a full nine months. His performance won a number of awards, including a Los Angeles Drama Critics Circle Award and a Theater World Award.

The rave reviews and publicity for *Zoot Suit* landed the production a run in a major Broadway theater, the Winter Garden. From insignificant roles as bad guys who get shot in the back, Olmos was now on the Broadway stage. *Zoot Suit* raised its first curtain in New York in March 1979. Although the New York audiences did not flock to see the production as they did in Los Angeles, Olmos nevertheless was nominated for a Tony Award for Best Performance by a Featured Actor in a Play. Olmos later portrayed El Pachuco in a 1981 screen version of *Zoot Suit*. Also directed by Luis Valdez and distributed by Universal Pictures, the film was nominated for the 1982 Golden Globe Award for Best Picture—Musical or Comedy.

No longer did Olmos have to scrape for bit parts in Hollywood. Soon he landed a part as a Native American steelworker in *Wolfen*, a detective story that explored the lack of environmental concerns by big business interests. Olmos accepted the role only after he was assured that the producers of the film considered any Native American actors who might have been interested in the role.

Olmos played in the 1982 futuristic, science fiction thriller *Blade Runner*, directed by Ridley Scott and starring Harrison Ford. Although the film did not fare well in reviews or at the box office when it was released, it became in later years something of a cult classic, appreciated by science fiction fans worldwide.

Olmos was now in a position to be selective in the kinds of roles he accepted. Increasingly sensitive to the ways in which Latinos were portrayed on stage, screen, and television, he made it clear to his agents and to prospective producers and directors that his feelings about his cultural roots and the ways in which he portrayed Latino figures was more important than financial gain. Also, he made it clear that he did not want to be cast in a part if he did not feel an emotional connection to the character.

In 1983, he was approached to appear in Brian de Palma's film *Scarface*, a story about a Cuban immigrant who turns to the illegal world of drug dealing, a kind of Latino Godfather figure. Olmos turned down the opportunity to appear in the film. "I just couldn't find myself inside that movie," he said later.[8] In the early 1980s, he also refused parts in *Red Dawn*, a film that envisioned America under siege from invading Russian and Cuban armies; *Firestarter*, a film based on the Stephen King novel about a young girl who possessed the power of pyrokinesis, the paranormal ability to ignite and control fire using only the mind; and *Streets of Fire*, a film about the abduction of a young woman at the hands of a biker gang.

PLAYING A MEXICAN FOLK HERO

One character portrayal that Olmos enthusiastically took on was in the 1982 Public Broadcasting Company (PBS) *American Playhouse* production of *The Ballad of Gregorio Cortez*, in which Olmos was offered the title role. Based on the true story of a Mexican folk hero who was traditionally known as a fierce outlaw, the film explores the facts behind the myth surrounding a stolen horse, mistaken identity, murder, and a manhunt.

Gregorio Cortez, a poor rancher in Gonzales, Texas, was wrongly accused of murder in 1901 and chased by an enormous posse across the state. The local Anglo population in Texas was so convinced of Cortez's guilt and angered by the difficulty in capturing him that a number of violent incidents occurred against Mexican Americans during the manhunt. He was finally apprehended and sentenced to fifty years in prison; Cortez served twelve years of the sentence before being pardoned by the Texas governor, who, by his action, finally admitted that Cortez was innocent. However, through misunderstanding and false interpretation, the legend of Cortez had turned the real life Cortez into a bandit. At the time of the real-life events, the story of Cortez was carried in newspapers across the country and popularized by a number of ballads including *El Corrido de Gregorio Cortez*. Folklorist Américo Paredes published the story in a 1958 book called *With His Pistol in His Hand*.

With his characteristic zeal for the parts that he took, Olmos personally researched historical archives on the chase, studying old photographs and newspaper clippings. He considered the role of special cultural significance, noting that the figure of Cortez was one of the first legendary Latino heroes ever shown on screen. He was determined to show that figure in as clear a historical light as possible. He even was able to convince the PBS producers and director Robert Young that his character of Cortez should speak only Spanish in the film and that there should be no sub-titles. In this way, he believed, the audience would be given a legitimate feeling about the ways that language barriers can cause deep division. He wanted the audience to feel the lonely burden of miscommunication and misunderstanding.

After the film aired on public television, Olmos tried to persuade major studios to release it commercially. None of them decided to take the risk, mainly because of the language element. Olmos took the rebuff as a personal challenge. Determined that the largest number of people possible would see the film, he began a five-year crusade to show the film himself. He rented a Hollywood theater and showed the film every Saturday morning for free. At considerable personal cost both in time and money, he distributed it to schools, boys and girls clubs, and libraries. He traveled across the country showing the film and lecturing about the importance of cultural awareness and understanding. Highly acclaimed director John Sayles wrote of the film, "The oppressor's need to demonize the oppressed has seldom been better realized."[9]

MIAMI VICE

In 1984, NBC launched a television series that helped change many American ideas about police. It was called *Miami Vice*, and it centered on two detectives, Sonny Crockett, played by Don Johnson, and Ricardo Tubbs, played by Philip Michael Thomas, who worked undercover to infiltrate the South Florida drug scene.

The show had a particularly distinctive look—the colorful hues of white and light blue; the sporty fashion with designer Gianni Versace dressing the actors; the luxurious sports cars, especially Ferraris, whizzing around the streets of Miami; the hip music featuring top vocalists of the day such as Phil Collins and Glenn Frey as well as the memorable theme song.

The series changed the life of Don Johnson, launching him into a film career. It changed the career of executive producer Michael Mann who went on to produce many feature films. It also changed the career of Edward James Olmos.

Olmos played Lieutenant Martin Castillo, the dark, brooding, complex commanding officer of the two colorful undercover cops. No one quite knew what his background involved, although some tidbits of information linked him to former espionage activities. He was a Latino in a position of authority, a fact that Olmos appreciated as he made decisions on which roles he felt were appropriate in his career. He also found in the character qualities of discipline, determination, and patience, a complex figure unlike so many of the stereotypical Latino characters routinely portrayed in Hollywood pictures and on television.

When he was first approached by Mann to appear in the series, Olmos balked. He was already getting a reputation for inflexibility, an actor who demanded more than the usual control over a part. Telly Savalas, the notable star of the television series *Kojak*, had become particularly irritated with Olmos during a screening of one of the few episodes in which Olmos appeared. He was a prima donna, Savalas told friends. Olmos demanded changes in lines that he felt detracted from the creative avenues in which he felt a particular character should travel.

And now, when Mann looked to Olmos to play Martin Castillo on *Miami Vice*, Olmos first backed away, saying he did not have enough time, that he did not want to tie himself down to a grinding life in a television series, and that the part was not quite right. Mann did not give up, calling back time and again. Finally, with an offer that promised Olmos more money in one year than he had made in his entire life, he accepted. Still, he wanted a creative role in fashioning the character—Mann agreed.

Castillo came to represent a kind of moral center of the show. A number of critics said that the character was by far the most complex and compelling in the series. Olmos said, "He's mysterious because you don't know very much about his life. Actually, he's a fairly normal guy who has been beaten back by life. In one early episode, it was revealed that he had lost his family and all his friends, he was betrayed by his own country, by the CIA. So what he learned about life made him very bitter." Mann said to Olmos in the beginning that he could see the character as something like a stern Jesuit priest. Olmos agreed. "You know, Jesuits are very strict with themselves, very disciplined, and so is Castillo. I would like to think of myself and my own values that way."[10] It was not until about the thirteenth episode that the character caught on with the large national viewing public. People began to understand that this was a man who had suffered, Olmos explained, a man overcoming wounds and a painful past, a man of depth.

The portrayal rejuvenated Olmos' life. Financially, he could breathe a little easier and keep alive his determination to make a difference in the way in which Latinos were shown on the screen. The critics also noticed: In 1985 Olmos won an Emmy award for Best Supporting Actor in a drama series, and in 1986 he won a Golden Globe award.

STAND AND DELIVER

If *Miami Vice* delivered Olmos to millions of television viewers, his breakthrough movie performance came in 1988. He played the educator Jaime Escalante in the film *Stand and Deliver*. In 1974, about the same time that Olmos had begun to appear in small roles on television, a middle-aged computer scientist and math teacher who had first learned to teach in his native Bolivia joined the faculty at Garfield High School in the East Los

Angeles barrio. A man of very modest means but with a burning desire to teach math to students that many educators claimed could not learn the subject, Escalante went about the task with highly unconventional but effective strategies. He challenged the students, convinced them that they could do the work, and treated the group like a team preparing for serious competition.

Within eight years, Escalante had prepared a group of students to take the very difficult national Educational Testing Service (ETS) mathematics test for high school students, an examination usually attempted only by select students in predominantly suburban, well-equipped schools. As he pushed and prodded his students to do their best, Escalante's favorite word was *ganas* (desire). They needed to have *ganas*. For many Latinos, *Stand and Deliver*, above all else, proclaimed this message. They could lift themselves out of challenging circumstances, rise above their previous expectations, and become much more than they ever imagined.

The result was shocking. Eighteen students from this unknown inner city school passed the national advanced calculus examination. Educators across the country could not believe the story. Neither could the Educational Testing Service. After conducting an investigation, the ETS informed Escalante and Garfield High School officials that they suspected that cheating had been involved. They asked that the students take the examination a second time.

Insulted, disappointed that the students at Garfield would be subjected to this kind of inquiry, Escalante agonized over whether to ask the boys and girls to repeat the test. In the end, fifteen of the eighteen students decided on their own to sit for the test a second time. Each of them again passed the test. It was a stirring vindication of Escalante's teaching methods and of the perseverance and drive of the students themselves.

Soon after the story ran in the newspapers, film producer Tom Musca and director Ramón Menéndez collaborated on a project to bring the inspirational story of the triumph of Latino children to the screen. They turned to Olmos to play the part of Escalante.

With the support of Garfield's principal Henry Gradillas, Escalante agreed to allow Olmos to accompany him eighteen hours a day for one month to prepare for the role. Olmos also gained forty pounds in an attempt to capture the physical appearance of Escalante and spent hours studying tapes of Escalante to perfect his speech patterns and mannerisms, especially the way the teacher interacted with the Latino students using banter and slang. Olmos even asked whether it would be possible for him to move in with Escalante for a time. Escalante's wife said no.

Nevertheless, Olmos transferred to the screen Escalante's features and persona with uncanny accuracy. Written and directed by Ramón Menéndez, and featuring Lou Diamond Phillips as student Angel Guzman and Andy

Garcia as a representative of the ETS, the film was released by Warner Brothers Pictures in 1988. It was a box office success and won several awards. For Olmos the portrayal of Jaime Escalante was particularly satisfying. He said, "The film is really about the triumph of the human spirit.... It's about something we've lost—the joy of learning, the joy of making our brains develop."[11]

Moctesuma Esparza, a film producer whose credits included *The Milagro Beanfield War* and *The Ballad of Gregorio Cortez,* raved about Olmos' performance as Escalante. Olmos, he said, was "very inspirational, a real hero to the Hispanic community... he not only has star quality but belief and drive." The film grossed more than nine times its modest production costs. For his superlative performance, Olmos received an Academy Award nomination.[12]

Much as he had done after the completion of *The Ballad of Gregorio Cortez,* Olmos engaged in an intense effort to make the film available to the widest possible audience. He secured the financial backing of several corporations to place copies in schools, libraries, prisons, hospitals, youth organizations, and other locations across the country. He regarded the story of Escalante's determined work as an inspiration not only to other educators but also to young people in school who overcame the kinds of seemingly insurmountable odds as those students at Garfield High. As he traveled to Indian reservations, youth detention centers, and veterans' hospitals speaking about the film, Olmos burned with passion. "It's addictive," he said of his travels. "A few hours of energy come back in waves for years. It's a wonderful feeling to make people forget about themselves. It's real soul food for me."[13]

In 1989, Olmos appeared in a supporting role in the film *Triumph of the Spirit.* The film chronicles the story of Salamo Arouch, a Jewish middleweight boxing champion in the Balkans who was captured by the Nazis during World War II and sent to the concentration camp at Auschwitz. The fighter was forced to fight for his life more than two hundred times at the camp. Olmos played a fellow prisoner named Gypsy, an entertainer who was forced to carry on his vaudeville act to amuse Nazi guards.

Now more than forty years old, Olmos had forged a solid acting career and gained national recognition as a performer. He had also gained a nearly heroic image among many in the Latino community who recognized his passion for improving the lives and cultural image of his forebearers.

He now spent more time with his wife Kaija and the two boys, who were twelve and fifteen years old. The family lived most of the year in Encino, California, but also had an island house off the coast of Florida. Although Olmos tried to keep the family out of tabloid range, he did ask the boys to appear in small roles in some of his movies. Also, he loved going on long bicycle rides with his sons, sometimes as many as three times a week. Like their father, both excelled athletically.

Kaija helped Olmos screen some the scripts that came from agents and producers, answered much of the fan mail, and helped on many of the charity drives that her husband constantly formed or joined. As did most families in show business, she and the boys endured long separations from their celebrity husband and father.

Latino artist Joe Gonzalez, who had painted a number of murals on the sides of buildings in East L.A., was asked to create a mural of Olmos. He selected a spot on Cheesbrough's Lane, a gray concrete block wall off a parking lot of El Mercado, a Latino center that featured food and shopping stalls and mariachi bands. Gonzalez and fellow artists Tony Ramirez and Xavier Quijas teamed up to complete the mural. It was a short distance from the house in which Olmos grew up.

Olmos' national recognition was graphically illustrated in July 1988. He graced the cover of *Time* magazine. It was a special issue on Hispanic culture, and one of the longer articles focused on Olmos. On the *Time* magazine cover was the photograph of the mural. *Time* staff writer Guy D. Garcia, author of a novel called *Skin Deep*, wrote the story on Olmos for the magazine edition. He said, "Olmos is a symbol of Hispanic Americans' newfound self-assurance.... Because the muralists are part of the Hispanic cultural movement, the medium really is part of the message."[14]

Gonzalez said of his work on Olmos, "We wanted to help instill pride. Eddie Olmos is the perfect example. He grew up in the barrio and became somebody. That gives inspiration to kids who might otherwise give up."[15]

EXPLORING THE NATURE OF GANGS

In 1992 Olmos completed a film project that was as much a lesson on social behavior as any on which he had ever worked. The project dealt with the pathology and extreme personal destruction caused by gangs. The film was called *American Me*. Created by screenwriter Floyd Matrux, co-produced and directed by Olmos, the story, which spans three decades, involves a gang member who grows up in East Los Angeles, spends time in juvenile jail, and is finally incarcerated in Folsom State Prison near Sacramento, California. The character's name is Santana and he is played by Olmos. Although behind bars, Santana continues to run his gang on the outside, a collection of thieves and drug dealers who peddle everything from prostitution to gambling.

So persuasive was Olmos in explaining his purpose in creating the movie that prison authorities allowed some of the filming of savage scenes to be done inside the prison walls. In the course of the filming, many of the 3,400 inmates were used as extras. Graphic, violent, and disturbing, the film showed the deterioration of personal ethics and morality into a kind of brutal, animalistic battle for survival.

Newsweek movie reviewer Jack Knoll wrote that *American Me* was "a fiercely impressive film; it butts its way inside you and stays there long after you've seen it. The mostly Latino cast pops through the screen with passion, gravity, and humor. Olmos himself is a splendidly smoldering presence; he's like a Latin Bogart with his oblong head, sidelong gaze, cigarette squint, and panther slouch."[16]

"This film is not for one race, one subculture, or age range," Olmos said. "Gangs teach a distorted discipline, a distorted familial bonding, a distorted sense of pride and power. I made this movie to allow all society to take a journey into an uncharted land that they would never have the opportunity to go into."[17]

As he had done with other films, Olmos attended special screenings around the country for teenagers and community leaders. He talked to gatherings of gang members. He also took part in the production of a follow-up documentary film called *Lives in the Hazard*. Released in 1994, the documentary explored the lives of some of the real-life gang members who served as extras in *American Me*.

Olmos was treading into dangerous territory. Federal and state authorities learned that members of the Mexican gang underworld were furious at the film depiction of their world and that Olmos had become a target. One gang member in the United States even attempted to sue Olmos claiming that the character of Santana was based on him. Another gang member admitted a few years later that Olmos was lucky to get away with his life.

Nevertheless, Olmos continued his personal appearances. As he walked down the aisle at a prison in California toward the stage, many of the inmates began to applaud. He stopped along the way to shake a few hands. Others wanted nothing to do with him. Dressed in a black leather jacket, he climbed the stairs to the stage and looked out at the mostly brown and black faces, many in their teens and early twenties. "How many of you guys think I'm smarter than you?" he asked. Half the inmates raised their hands. "I ain't smarter than anyone here, man," Olmos retorted. "I may have developed my brain a little more in high school, but I think we're pretty equal. I grew up in East L.A., just a few miles from here. You might say I was lucky. And I was. But I made a choice."[18]

In 1992, when race riots broke out on the streets of Los Angeles after the police beating of an African American named Rodney King, Olmos became something of an unofficial leader of the city's clean-up committee. The morning after the riot he took a broom to the streets and began to sweep. With a number of friends he began to sweep outside a church. Soon, others joined—there were a hundred people, then five hundred people, and the next day there were thousands.

Olmos later became executive director of the Lives in Hazard Educational Project, a national gang prevention program funded by the United States Department of Justice. He continued to speak out against gang violence at schools, reformatories, and jails. He worked with organizations to discourage youth gangs and gave motivational speeches to students, migrant workers, prisoners, and juvenile delinquents.

MISSION FOR THE MAYANS

Olmos' personal life overturned in the early 1990s. He and his wife Kaija, who had been married since 1971, divorced. In early January 1994, he married actress Lorraine Bracco, whom he had met on the set of a film. They would also later divorce.

In the same month that Olmos married for the second time, violence erupted in the Chiapas Mountains in southern Mexico. The indigenous people of the Chiapas region, whose ancestors were of the Mayan culture, were mostly poor farmers. They were forced to pay absentee landlords for use of the land despite the fact that the Mexican constitution of 1917 had guaranteed that the land would be made available to all. The Chiapas people had long but unsuccessfully sought to have those constitutional guarantees upheld. But, in 1994, their efforts were dealt a stunning blow. The Mexican government repealed that part of the constitution that called for the land to be used by the people. The struggling, poverty-ridden farmers were in an even more precarious position.

The unfair treatment of the Chiapas people by the Mexican government led to the formation in early 1994 of the so-called Zapatista Army of National Liberation, a band of armed resisters determined to foment rebellion against the government. The leaders gathered whatever arms they could and organized themselves in the Chiapas Mountains.

The organization was led by a man who called himself "Subcomandante Marcos." The group was named after the revolutionary leader Emiliano Zapata who, during the Mexican war in 1910, had fought on behalf of poor agricultural people. The band soon issued a proclamation:

> We have nothing to lose, absolutely nothing, no decent roof over our heads, no land, no work, poor health, no food, no education, no right to freely and democratically choose our leaders, no independence from foreign interests, and no justice for ourselves or our children. But today we say enough is enough! We are the descendants of those who truly built this nation, we are the millions of dispossessed, and we call upon our brothers to join our crusade, the only option to avoid dying of starvation."[19]

In this land of the ancient Mayan civilization, there was now a small army of masked men carrying AK-47 rifles. After a series of skirmishes with elements of the federal army and with mercenaries hired by the local landlords, the Zapatistas were largely bottled up in their rural strongholds. In addition, a series of raids on communities suspected of supporting the Zapatistas led to massacres of women and children.

Olmos, whose great-grandmother was Mayan, had great personal concern for the plight of the Chiapas people. Soon after the first military clashes had taken lives, Olmos visited southern Mexico in 1994, learning as much as he could about the struggle. He organized a relief effort to raise money for beans, corn, salt, cornmeal, and other food to help stave off the certain starvation of many of the people as they became more and more isolated during the conflict. "I don't care about the politics and the war," he told a reporter. "These people cannot starve to death. Not my people. I won't allow it."[20]

By 1996, hundreds of Chiapans had been killed as a result of the fighting and many thousands fled their homes. The others who saw nowhere to run continued to live in the middle of the crisis while in constant fear. In April 1996, Olmos, through contacts he made earlier in his stay in southern Mexico, was able to meet the leader of the Zapatista Army, the elusive "Subcomandante Marcos," one of the men most wanted in Mexico. The two met in a wooden shack in the mountains; when Olmos arrived, Marcos stepped up and greeted him in Chicano slang. "*Orale vate!*" (Hey, man!), he shouted to Olmos. The line was more than just slang; it was a line said often by Olmos in playing the teacher Jaime Escalante in the movie *Stand and Deliver*. The leader of this small rebel force in the southern mountains of Mexico was familiar with the film.

They talked about the uprising and the needs of the people. When he returned to the United States, Olmos made it clear that he was not a Zapatista. He also made it clear that he was not a supporter of the Mexican government. In his visit, he saw the devastation of military raids on the villages and crops throughout the region. He saw many villagers with cases of dysentery. "Did we make a dent?" Olmos asked rhetorically after the large food drive. "No. But did we save lives? Yes." Norberto Tapia, media-relations coordinator for the government's delegation to the Chiapas, agreed. "What he's doing," said Tapia, "is a true social labor."[21]

The revolt continued into the new century. By 2003 the Zapatistas claimed control over a portion of the area and declared the territory independent of the government of Mexico. The rebels even sought outside help to begin to improve medical conditions and educational facilities for the people. The uneasy, complex circumstances remained, and Olmos continued to help.

LATINO CULTURE, LATINO PRIDE

Much of Olmos' work was shaped by the social and cultural circumstances of his own life and the struggles of those around him to make a place in American society. From those early days on Cheesbrough's Lane in East Los Angeles, he had experienced the strong sense of family, the disappointments of being poor, and the stings of insensitivity and prejudice directed at his fellow Latinos. He had come through his adolescence in far better shape than most of his friends and companions from those early years. But he never lost his sense of place. Indeed, with each new career success he seemed more determined than ever to reach out and give back in ways that could make a difference for other youngsters growing up in similar circumstances.

In September 1994, Olmos appeared in an HBO made-for-television film on the life of Chico Mendes, the Brazilian labor leader who fought against the destructive practices of large corporations that were destroying much of the Amazon jungle. Mendes' non-violent fight for a return to sustainable agricultural systems led to his assassination. Called *The Burning Season*, the production was directed by John Frankenheimer and starred Raul Julia as Mendes and Olmos as labor leader Wilson Pinheiro, another environmental labor leader who was also killed. The subject of the film, the preservation of the rainforest, was of particular importance to Olmos. For his work in the award-winning production, Olmos was presented a Golden Globe award for best supporting actor in a television movie, and he was also nominated for an Emmy award.

A year after his performance in *The Burning Season*, Olmos played in another production that was close to his heart, the film *My Family/Mi Familia*. It was directed by Gregory Nava and Anna Thomas, the husband and wife team who earlier created *El Norte*, a movie about Guatemalan refugees. *My Family/Mi Familia* traced the lives of generations of a Mexican-American family in Los Angeles. Produced by Francis Ford Coppola, the film was a major breakthrough in portraying the Latino experience in America. Members of the Sanchez family included an uncle called "El Californio," who was born in Los Angeles when it was still Mexico; Maria, a Mexican-American mother who was deported during anti-immigrant hysteria in the 1930s, and Isabel, a Salvadoran political refugee who married into the family. Olmos' character, a writer, was the film's narrator. Syndicated columnists Patrisia Gonzales and Roberto Rodriguez, whose joint works on the Latino experience earned them both a number of writing awards, said of the film:

> Anyone from an immigrant family, or even a large family, should see a part of their own lives in this film. We did. *My Family* is part of a larger effort by Latinos to recover that dignity through film, documentaries and the written word. Latinos everywhere are recording a different memory of how we see ourselves, how we narrate ourselves and our place in America.[22]

In April 1999, Olmos followed up his work on *My Family/Mi Familia* with a multimedia project called *Americanos: Latino Life in the United States*. Through film, music, a book, and photography, the project, co-sponsored by Time Warner, Inc., celebrated Latino culture and involved a traveling photography exhibition organized by the Smithsonian Institution that toured the country for five years, a music album featuring Latino artists, a documentary on HBO, and a book of essays and photos co-edited by Olmos.

Three years after the start of the *Americanos* project, Olmos joined the cast of a television series produced by PBS. Entitled *American Family*, the series portrayed the lives of members of a Latino family, much like *My Family/Mi Familia* had done on film. Olmos played Jess Gonzales, a conservative, old-fashioned father, much like the character of Archie Bunker in the long-running television show *All in the Family*. The show was the first on television ever to feature a Latino family.

Olmos felt the show was a positive reinforcement of family values from the perspective of a Latino family. "It's wonderful," he said. "It's very simple, but very direct. The Gonzalezes are wholesome people. I don't think there's a malicious moment in any of the scripts. There's no car crashes. There's no drugs. There's no violence per se. It's drama, human values in drama, comedy. It makes for fun, thought-provoking moments. I like it, personally."[23]

ACTOR AND HUMANITARIAN

As on a train, Olmos' career rolled along on two rails. His acting made possible his numerous humanitarian enterprises. His acting also reflected the concerns and social awareness expressed in those activist efforts. Olmos continued to produce, direct, and act in films that carried a message that he was convinced could make a difference. His time and efforts, he knew, were limited. Whatever projects he took on, he promised himself and his legions of fans, would be ones that had the best chance to help produce change and to make people think, projects that meant more than mindless entertainment.

In 2002, Olmos became the U.S. Goodwill Ambassador for UNICEF. The world's leading charitable organization for children, UNICEF had created projects in more than 160 developing nations to feed, educate, and inoculate children against diseases like polio, to rescue them from crushing poverty. In his work to raise money for UNICEF, Olmos took donors into devastated areas in which their contribution could make a difference. "When I take them to places where they can see what their support has done," he said, "they break down and cry. It's a gorgeous experience when you watch a person turn on a faucet and clean water comes out in a town that has never had clean water or electricity. Or when you see the eradication of infant mortality from diarrhea, just by giving seven cents for rehydration materials."[24] Olmos did his best to raise awareness and money and considered the experience one of the most rewarding experiences of his life. Olmos has also been a spokesman for the Diabetes Research

Institute Foundation, Mothers Against Drunk Driving (MADD), Students Against Destructive Decisions (SADD), and for foundations to fight Parkinson's and Alzheimer's diseases.

In 2003, Olmos joined a television series that on the surface seemed an unlikely choice for him. *Battlestar Galactica* was a science-fiction thriller based on an original television series that aired from 1978 to 1980. It involved a fleet of human survivors from the destroyed colonies of a planet called Kobol in search of a planet called Earth. The dwindling band was led by Admiral William Adama, played by Olmos, and President Laura Roslin, played by Mary McDonnell. *Battlestar Galactica* immediately won a legion of admiring fans and rave reviews from major magazines such as *Time*, the *New Yorker*, and *Rolling Stone*. It also won a prestigious Peabody Award in 2006 for its creativity.

When he was first approached about the series, Olmos was, as always, careful about what he was getting into. When he saw the first scripts and talked with the producers he was intrigued. This was not a series about outer space creatures or alien attacks on earth; this was about human emotions, survival, and comradeship. When he agreed to take the part, he told executive producer David Eick that if he ever saw a four-eyed monster introduced in the series he would immediately leave.

Olmos saw the series in the context of the tragedy of the terrorist attacks of September 11, 2001. "You had a whole different perspective on the end of the world," he said, "that whole philosophy ... the script was very powerful. It was completely different." As the series headed into its final episodes in 2007, Olmos remained deeply committed, calling it the best television in which he had ever been involved.[25]

In 2005, the people of the Chiapas Mountain area of Mexico were again in the news when the area was hit by a devastating hurricane. It seemed incomprehensible to Olmos that once again the poor inhabitants of that area would be struck with yet another tragedy. He quickly went to work. Through the establishment of a community action center called Sexto Sol, Olmos labored tirelessly to find funds to provide relief. He especially appealed for funds to repair damaged schools for the indigenous children.

In 2006, the seemingly tireless Olmos directed a powerful HBO film that depicted events of 1968 in East Los Angeles, when Olmos himself was twenty-one years old. The film was called *Walkout* and covered the activities of a group of high school students who mobilized a non-violent protest against the Los Angeles school system. They rebelled because of the dire conditions of schools in the barrio and the complete disregard of their cultural backgrounds in the curriculums. At the height of the student protest, more than 22,000 children walked out of their classes in the Los Angeles area, not only students in East Los Angeles but also from schools in various other parts of the county who joined them in solidarity. It became the largest single student walkout movement in the history of the United States.

A number of students were beaten by police. One of the student leaders, Moctesuma Esparza, who had become a distinguished film producer, worked on the project for five years and persuaded Olmos to direct the film. Olmos said,

> I think the idea of bringing about social change by way of non-violent behavior is the strongest single method that we have, of making ourselves understood and understanding ourselves better. Non-violent social change is to me the best kind of change for the communities at large. Because it really speaks from the core of our humanity rather than a political or a religious belief; it really comes from the core of the human being and it encompasses all religions, all cultures, and all political types. And I think that we've had some wonderful examples of that in our lifetime. With Cesar Chavez, Ghandi, and Martin Luther King.

Olmos hoped the film would be not only entertaining to younger viewers but also inspirational. For his work on *Walkout*, Olmos received a nomination by the Directors Guild of America for Best Director of a television movie.[26]

And so, his work as actor and activist continued. In both of those roles Olmos brought extraordinary determination and passion. "I would hate to look back on my life," he said, "and only see myself as a person who made lots of money." Instead, he would hope that his great-great-grandchildren could look back on his accomplishments and say, "Well, grandpa really did some extraordinarily different kinds of work."[27]

MOVIES AND TELEVISION

Actor

Aloha, Bobby and Rose. Directed by Floyd Mutrux. Cine Artists International, 1975. Film.

Wolfen. Directed by Michael Wadleigh. Film Capital Associates, 1981. Film.

Zoot Suit. Directed by Luis Valdez. Universal Pictures, 1981. Film.

The Ballad of Gregorio Cortez. Directed by Robert M. Young. Embassy Film Associates, 1982. TV.

Miami Vice. Michael Mann Productions, 1984–1989. TV.

Saving Grace. Directed by Robert M. Young. Embassy Film Associates, 1985. Film.

Stand and Deliver. Directed by Ramon Menendez. American Playhouse, 1988. Film.

American Me. Directed by Edward James Olmos. Universal Pictures, 1992. Film.

The Burning Season. Directed by John Frankenheimer. HBO, 1994. TV.

My Family/Mi Familia. Directed by Gergory Nava. American Playhouse, 1995. Film.

Caught. Directed by Robert M. Young. Cinehaus, 1996. Film.

Disturbing the Peace. Directed by Thomas Patrick Smith. Lightview Entertainment, 1996. Film.

The Disappearance of Garcia Lorca. Directed by Marcos Zurinaga. Antena 3 Television, 1997. Film.

Selena. Directed by Gregory Nava. Esparza/Katz Productions, 1997. Film.

Bonanno: A Godfather's Story. Directed by Michel Poulette. Armeda Limited, 1999. TV.

In the Time of the Butterflies. Directed by Mariano Barroso. Metro-Goldwyn-Mayer, 2001. TV.

American Family. Directed by Gregory Nava. Twentieth Century-Fox Television, 2002. TV.

Jack and Marilyn. Directed by Edward James Olmos. FOCUS Institute of Film, 2002. Film.

Battlestar Galactica. British Sky Broadcasting, 2004–2008. TV.

Splinter. Directed by Michael D. Olmos. Splinter Film LLC, 2006. I. Film.

Walkout. Directed by Edward James Olmos. Esparza/Katz Productions, 2006. TV.

Director

American Me. Universal Pictures, 1992. Film.

Jack and Marilyn. FOCUS Institute of Film, 2002. Film.

Walkout. Esparza/Katz Productions, 2006. TV.

NOTES

1. Gabriela Velazquez, "Edward James Olmos: Fighting for Justice and Defying Gangsters," *Latino Leaders*, December 2003, 46.

2. Ralph Cruz, "Olmos Asks Questions We Need to Address," *Knight Ridder/Tribune News Service*, January 21, 1996, 121, http://www.latinohistory.com/people.php?id=64.

3. Terrie Rooney, ed., *Contemporary Heroes and Heroines, Book III*, New York: Gale, 1998, 452.

4. Kathryn Hart, "Edward James Olmos Stands and Delivers: As an Ambassador for UNICEF, Olmos Follows in Audrey Hepburn's Formidable Footsteps to Protect the World's Children from Poverty and Disease," *In Style*, February 1, 2002, 156; General Reference Center Gold, Gale, http://find.galegroup.com/itx/start.do?prodId=GRGM.

5. Rooney.

6. Guy Garcia, "Burning with Passion: Despite a Low-Key Exterior, Edward James Olmos Ignites the Screen," *Time*, July 11, 1988, 54.

7. Garcia.

8. Rooney.

9. "Filmmaker John Sayles Gives Us His Take on the 20 Best Political Films of the Past Two Decades," *Mother Jones*, May/June 1966, http://www.motherjones.com/arts/film/1996/05/sayles.jump.html.

10. Louise Mooney, ed., *Newsmakers*, Detroit: Gale Research, 1990, http://find.galegroup.com/srcx/infomark.do?&contentSet=GBRC&type=retrieve&tabID=T001&prodId=SRC-1&docId=EK1618000670&source=gale&srcprod=SRCG&userGroupName=chan86036&version=1.0.

11. Hispanic Heritage Biographies, Gale Resources: Edward James Olmos, http://www.gale.com/free_resources/chh/bio/olmos_e.htm.

12. Garcia.

13. Garcia.

14. Robert L. Miller, "Artist Joe Gonzalez Painted Edward Olmos for *Time* Magazine Special Hispanic American Issue Cover." *Time*, July 11, 1988, 4.

15. Miller.

16. Jack Kroll, "Eddie Olmos' East L.A. Story," *Newsweek*, March 30, 1992, 67.

17. Kroll.

18. Garcia.

19. The Zapatista National Liberation Army, http://www.mtholyoke.edu/~lkchandr/zapatista.html.

20. Peter Carlin and Betty Cortina, "Stand and Deliver," *People*, September 9, 1996, http://web.ebscohost.com/ehost/detail?vid=5&hid=5&sid=7541e540-8265-4d63-92e4-55db38b93a01%40sessionmgr7.

21. Carlin and Cortina.

22. Patrisia Gonzales and Roberto Rodriguez, "My Family/Mi Familia: A Milpa Grows in East L. A.," *Chronicle Features*, May 8, 1995, http://www.killermovies.com/m/myfamilymifamilia/reviews/22o.html.

23. "American Family: Journey of Dreams: An Interview with Edward James Olmos," 2004, http://www.pbs.org/americanfamily/behind6.html.

24. Hart.

25. Sarah Kuhn, "Event Horizon: Edward James Olmos and Mary McDonnell Explore the Line between Sci-Fi Settings and Real-Life Pathos on 'Battlestar Galactica.'" *Back Stage East*, December 14, 2006, http://find.galegroup.com/itx/start.do?prodId=GRGM.

26. "*Walkout*: Interview with Edward James Olmos," HBO Films, http://www.hbo.com/films/walkout/interviews.

27. *Contemporary Hispanic Biography*. Vol. 1. Gale, 2002. Reproduced in *Biography Resource Center*, Farmington Hills, MI: Gale, 2007, http://gale.cengage.com/free_resources/chh/bio/olmos_e.htm.

FURTHER READING

Carlin, Peter, and Betty Cortina. "Stand and Deliver." *People*, September 9, 1996, http://web.ebscohost.com/ehost/detail?vid=5&hid=5&sid=7541e540-8265-4d63-92e4-55db38b93a01%40sessionmgr7.

Contemporary Hispanic Biography. Vol. 1. Gale, 2002. Reproduced in *Biography Resource Center*. Farmington Hills, MI: Gale, 2007, http://gale.cengage.com/free_resources/chh/bio/olmos_e.htm.

Garcia, Guy. "Burning with passion: Despite a low-key exterior, Edward James Olmos ignites the screen." *Time*, July 11, 1988, 54.

Olmos, Edward James, Lea Ybarra, and Manuel Monterrey. *Americanos: Latino life in the United States*. Boston: Little, Brown, and Company, 1999.

Rooney, Terrie, ed. *Contemporary Heroes and Heroines, Book III*. New York: Gale, 1998.

Velazquez, Gabriela. "Edward James Olmos: Fighting for justice and defying gangsters: On charity boards, UNICEF goodwill ambassador, Oscar nominee." *Latino Leaders*, December 2003, 46.

Tito Puente

NIGHTS AT THE PALLADIUM

In 1949 a nightclub called the Palladium opened in New York City at 53rd Street and Broadway. The second-floor ballroom soon became an entertainment magnet, drawing large crowds of Latin music aficionados and dancers. The dance hall sizzled with the rhythms and beats of Latin music. This was the height of the mambo craze, and the Palladium was a house of the mambo. Its dance floor could hold a thousand couples at the same time while the orchestra played non-stop.

One of the Palladium's legendary performers was percussionist and bandleader Tito Puente. Forming the nine-piece Piccadilly Boys in 1947 and then expanding it to a full orchestra two years later, Puente recorded for Seeco, Tico, and eventually RCA, helping fuel the mambo craze that gave him the unofficial—and ultimately lifelong—title "King of the Mambo," or just "El Rey." Puente also helped popularize the cha-cha during the 1950s, and he was the only non-Cuban who was invited to the government-sponsored "50 Years of Cuban Music" celebration in Cuba in 1952. He became a towering, iconic Latino figure, hailed in the United States and abroad.

Puente later said of those days at the Palladium: "The Palladium was a phenomenon ... the place was a big melting pot ... Jews, Italians, Irish, Blacks, Puerto Ricans, Cubans—you name it. Everyone was equal under the roof of the Palladium, because everyone was there to dig the music and to dance."[1] These were the memories of Tito Puente. He was "El Rey," the King of Latin Music, and the Palladium was his playground.

SPANISH HARLEM

On April 20, 1923, at Harlem Hospital in New York, Ercilia Puente gave birth to a son that she and her husband, Ernest, named Ernesto Anthony Puente, Jr. His mother began to call her son "Ernestito" (Little Ernest), and eventually shortened the name to Tito. Ernest Puente worked as a foreman at the Gem Razor Blade Company in Brooklyn. The Puente family soon grew to five, as Ercilia gave birth to a daughter named Anna in 1928 and a son named Robert Anthony a year later. The family scraped by and suffered through a grievous loss when Tito's younger brother, Robert, died from a fall from a fire escape when he was only four years old.

Ercilia and Ernest had migrated to New York from Puerto Rico shortly before Tito was born, Ernest from Guanadillas and Ercilia from Coamo. Their house at 1850 Madison Avenue was in the heart of East Harlem, an area that became known as Spanish Harlem and "El Barrio." Squeezed in a strip between 3rd and 5th Avenues, stretching from 125th Street south to 96th Street, Spanish Harlem was alive with rich Latino traditions. From the hot sounds of Latin music to the aromas of tamales and fried plantains and the bright reds and yellows of the bodegas and eateries along Broadway and Amsterdam Avenues, El Barrio was the home of thousands of people who had traveled north from Latin America, especially Puerto Rico.

Puerto Ricans had been arriving in the United States since the middle of the nineteenth century. After the Spanish-American War in 1898, Puerto Rico began the twentieth century as a United States possession under military rule, with governing officials appointed by the President of the United States. By 1917, Puerto Ricans were granted U.S. citizenship, a status they have continued to hold. After the grant of citizenship to residents of Puerto Rico, the numbers of immigrants to the United States increased dramatically. Many established communities in Chicago and Philadelphia as well as in mid-Atlantic villages and the mill towns of New England. The largest migration of Puerto Ricans, however, was to New York City. Many, like the Puente family, moved into Spanish Harlem.

Although many of the new arrivals had been farm workers in Puerto Rico, they now began to work in a wide variety of city jobs in hospitals, hotels, garment factories, and the fire and police departments. Many Puerto Rican migrants struggled with poverty, unemployment, and racial discrimination. The language barrier often made it difficult to find well-paying work or to deal with government agencies or other English-speaking organizations and institutions.

Tito's mother first noticed her eldest son's musical interests when he was seven years old, and the family managed to enroll him in 25-cent piano lessons. Neighbors often directed yells at the Puente house when young Tito furiously banged on pots and pans. Little did they know where that banging would lead.

Tito kept his ears pinned to the radio and on occasion managed to get into the theaters. "I would listen to the great dance bands of the day on the radio," he said. "Benny Goodman, Artie Shaw, Duke Ellington, Chris Webb, and I'd go to theaters like the Paramount and the Strand to see them perform."[2]

Throughout his early years, Tito's precocious musical talents became increasingly known around the neighborhood and school. While attending Public School 184, he spent Saturdays learning to play the piano at a branch of the New York School of Music at 125th Street and Lenox Avenue. He continued piano lessons for seven years, eventually being tutored by pianist Victoria Hernandez, sister of Puerto Rico's most renowned composer, Rafael Hernandez, and Luis Varona, an early pianist in the Machito Orchestra. These were serious musicians who saw in the young boy unmistakable talent and energy. From them, Tito received an invaluable introduction into the Latin music of his heritage.

After his lessons Tito would entertain his parents, playing everything from semi-classical pieces to the current pop tunes of the day. One of his most vivid memories, he said later, was playing the Puerto Rican danza, "Mis Amores," for his mother.

Recognizing the immense natural talent of Tito, Ercilia found a drum teacher who could teach the boy another instrument along with the piano. "He knew absolutely nothing about Latin music," remembered Tito, "but I wasn't going to him for that. He gave me a good foundation: snare drum technique, how to interpret figures in charts and accompany shows.... I even won a drum contest playing his solo on "Sing, Sing, Sing," note for note."[3]

Encouraged by his mother, Tito and his sister Anna, who was called Annie, joined a musical group called "Stars of the Future." It was sponsored by a local Catholic church, La Milagrosa, at 115th Street and Lenox Avenue, where Tito made his first communion and confirmation. Each year the church sponsored a coronation of the king and queen of music. Anna was crowned Queen of the Stars of the Future in 1935; her brother carried away the King's crown four times, largely because of his dancing skills.

As his dancing talent made clear to everyone, Puente was athletic and highly coordinated. He also loved baseball.

By the age of fifteen, Puente had been studying music for seven years. He was already skilled at the piano and drums. While Tito attended Cooper Junior High School and then Galvanni Junior High School, he was already playing weekend gigs with small music groups near his home. He listened intently to the radio, soaking up as much of the new music, especially from Cuba, as he could hear. He joined a vocal quartet, and he also began sitting in with a band called Los Happy Boys who performed at the Park Place Hotel at 110th and 5th Avenues, playing an assortment of music, from pop and Latin to swing and jazz.

In addition to the piano and drums, Tito was also introduced to the xylophone, saxophone, guitar, and the timbales, which are twin hollow steel or brass percussion drums, usually with two bells that spark most Latin rhythm sections. Jose Montesino, an accomplished timbalero, helped Puente develop the rhythms and techniques that would one day mark his own spectacular career.

In 1937, Tito enrolled at Central Commercial High School. His thoughts, nevertheless, were always on music. At lunch breaks, on school stairways, on street corners after school, Tito drew crowds at improvised performances with a variety of instruments. Often he would head to the auditorium to use the piano while crowds gathered around to hear boogie-woogie beats. He put together trios of performers who played and sang. Songs by the Ink Spots were favorites.

He also studied dance with his sister, Annie. They watched films of Fred Astaire and Ginger Rogers. They tried tap and various acrobatic moves and became a child song-and-dance team. He later said that he prided himself on being one of the few bandleaders who really knew how to dance.

While still enrolled at Central Commercial High School, Tito began a heavy schedule of weekend gigs with Cuban musicians. "I would do jobs four to six hours long," he said. "The pay was two to three dollars and

I would be falling asleep by midnight. The musicians would sometimes tie my feet to the bass drum and hi-hat pedal so that when I woke up I would trip all over myself."[4]

A TEENAGE PRO

In 1939, Tito's father agreed to allow the young and gifted musical talent to drop out of Central Commercial High School to become a full-time musician. In the same year, Tito met another sixteen-year-old music phenomenon named Pablo Rodriguez, a singer and bongo player, who had left Puerto Rico to pursue a career in music. They met at a teenage hangout in the neighborhood, became members of the same club, and began working a few gigs together. Rodriquez would later change his first name to Tito. Like Puente, he also would form his own orchestra.

In December 1939, Puente worked with another young musician who was also generating much notice in the music community, pianist Jose Curbelo, newly arrived from Cuba. When Curbelo heard Puente perform, he asked the young percussionist if he would join him for a few months on the road. The two roomed together in Miami and became close friends. Curbelo said that he thought he had seen the best Puerto Rican drummer alive when he saw Puente.

The partnership was invaluable to Puente, offering not only additional exposure, but also a lasting collaboration. Curbelo later formed his own band and Puente joined him. Puente and Curbelo melded Cuban and Puerto Rican sounds, and their work together led to much innovative work by each of them. Later, when Curbelo disbanded his group in 1957, he set up the Alpha Booking Agency and became Puente's agent. When a hot gig had to be filled, Curbelo always looked first to Tito.

By the late 1930s a number of elegant nightspots had opened in the midtown district of Manhattan that attempted to capitalize on the growing craze for the rumba and other Cuban dance forms. Such hot dance spots as the Havana-Madrid, Club Yumuri, La Conga, and Casa Cubana were filled night after night and even some hotels moved to set up ballrooms especially for Latin orchestras and dances. Cuban-style bands often alternated sets with the regular swing bands on long-term engagements at the major hotels.

Although only in his early teens, Tito's extraordinary talent, broad smile, and an intensity that seemed to radiate with each movement on stage landed him short gigs with some of the most prominent Latin bands of the day. He played at the Stork Club in New York, traveled to Chicago to join a group at the Colony Club, and also joined a band headed by legendary pianist Noro Morales. The Morales gig landed Puente in Hollywood for a time to perform with the band in a number of films. Whatever the challenge, it seemed, Puente was there to take it on with exuberance and a confidence that defied his years.

When the regular drummer for the great Machito Orchestra was drafted into the army, Tito became a regular member of one of the premier Latin bands in the world. Machito, whose birth name was Frank Grillo, had moved to New York from Cuba to join the popular Xavier Cugat orchestra. A first-class vocalist, Machito assembled several respected musicians and became one of the pioneers of so-called Latin jazz or "Cubop." It was under Machito that Puente began to experiment with fusing the rhythms and beats of various Latin sounds. Even at this early stage of his career, Puente was an electrifying performer.

As his young career moved forward, it was clear that Puente's specialty was playing the timbales. When he first played the timbales, they were usually physically located at the back of an orchestra as a minor instrument with the musician seated. Under Puente's hands, they soon became a lead sound, with Tito on his feet, moving and pounding, and not only playing the music with power and precision but also playing to the audience. Orchestras now moved Puente and his timbales front and center.

Slightly built, with dark eyes and good looks and a shock of black hair that over the years would turn white, Puente definitely belonged out front. With his effervescent smile and revved-up energy, he became, in many instances, the pace setter, the spot on the floor where the audiences' eyes naturally moved. He was a born showman, unable for a moment to contain his boundless enthusiasm and infectious sense of rhythm and beat. With the Machito Orchestra Tito was featured as a soloist.

In 1942, at age nineteen, soon after the Japanese attack on Pearl Harbor and the United States entry into World War II, Puente was drafted into the U.S. Navy. He completed boot camp on Long Island in New York and served as Seaman First Class in the U.S. Navy. Serving on the *USS Santee*, a converted U.S. Navy aircraft carrier that was used to escort supply and passenger ships, he loaded ammunition into the ship's guns and survived a number of naval encounters, bombing raids, and torpedoes.

Along with his responsibilities to load ammunition and other military duties, he played conga and alto saxophone to entertain the troops with the ship's band, playing such favorites as "Sweet Georgia Brown," "How High the Moon," and "One O'Clock Jump." He was also the ship's bugler. "I would play reveille to wake up the crew. One morning I was on the bridge and I started to warm-up by playing general quarters, the signal to man battle stations.... Man, the whole ship went crazy; everyone thought we were being attacked. I had to hide for a week; everyone wanted a piece of me."[5]

While in the South Pacific, Puente befriended a young Navy aircraft pilot who had played tenor sax and had done arrangements for a major band. During breaks in the work and action, Puente learned the basic techniques of arranging from the veteran musician and began his first attempts at writing music.

It was while at sea that Puente learned of the death of his beloved sister Annie after a long fight against spinal meningitis. On an emergency furlough, a grieving Puente returned home for the funeral. At a memorial service at a Puerto Rican social club called La Perla del Sur, he sat at the piano and played "Mis Amores" in honor of his mother and Debussy's "Clair de Lune" in honor of Annie.

By the time of his discharge from the Navy in 1945, Puente had seen action in nine battles. He returned home with a Presidential Commendation, some new musical knowledge and skills, and an intense anticipation to get back to what he was meant to do—perform.

Puente soon hooked up with his old friend Jose Curbelo in New York, who had formed his own band and played for Frank Marti's Copacabana orchestra while Charlie Palmieri was the pianist. He also worked as drummer and arranger for a time with a band formed by Cuban Pupi Campo, at one time sharing the billing at the Havana Madrid with comedians Dean Martin and Jerry Lewis.

At such Manhattan locations as the Copacabana and the Conga, Puente performed an ever-widening array of music. "You had to be a good musician because we played the show too, not just dance music or barrio music like in Spanish Harlem," recalled Puente. "You had to play waltzes, tangos, sambas, boleros. That's how I developed my experience in reading and playing all types of music." It was also a time when he knew he had to become more of a student of music. "Most of the Latin percussionists didn't read much music," he said. "Really, you just have to learn your profession, your instrument. This is it. You have to study."[6]

And he did study. Tito used money from the G.I. Bill to take classes in conducting, orchestration, and theory at the prestigious Juilliard School of Music from 1945 to 1947. Although sometimes chafing from the school's emphasis on classical music, Puente gained substantial perspective and insight into the larger musical world.

He had now played with some of the top Latin bands and bandleaders; he had done arrangements and begun composing. He even had learned how to play the vibraphone, adding a new sound to his growing repertoire. So enamored did Puente become with the vibes that he would increasingly use it in new compositions. Some of the musicians who had little experience with the vibes even joked with Puente that they looked like Venetian blinds. But Puente was now ready to launch a big-time career. He had the formal training, a wide range of experience for a man at such a young age, and numerous friends and contacts in the world of Latin music. The break came in 1947 and he seized it.

THE PALLADIUM YEARS

At the Alma Dance Studios on 53rd Street and Broadway, dance promoter Federico Pagani began lining up major Latin orchestras. For the first time, the migration of those dancers and music lovers who wanted to lose themselves in the Latin beat would now be to midtown, amidst the playhouses, recording studios, and movie theaters north of Times Square. To hear some of the great Latin sounds of the time, Latinos and blacks would travel from El Barrio to the heart of Manhattan.

To attract the interest of blacks and Latinos to travel to the new venue to hear Latin music, Pagani gave away discount cards at subway stations and bus stops in Harlem. As the first performance neared and several Latin band groups waited in the ballroom, long lines began to form on the streets outside. Even Pagani could not have known the enormous success that awaited his new dance emporium.

Pagani had recently heard Puente rehearsing a piece of music that he had not yet given a name. So arousing was the rhythm and beat, Pagani said, that it made his blood turn cold. When Pagani asked Puente about the music, Tito said that it was a "picadillo," a mish-mash of ideas, including a touch of Chinese. Pagani asked Puente to put together a band of his own that would be part of the Sunday matinees at the dance studio. Pagani suggested that Puente bring together a few musicians and that he should call the group The Picadilly Boys. From such a quiet conversation and meeting did the career of Puente leap forward. This was the beginning of two eras: the Alma Dance Studios would now become known as the Palladium, and Tito Puente would begin his career as a bandleader.

At the Palladium, which soon became known as "Home of the Mambo," cultures and music blended. Jazz musicians became interested in the mambo. Latino and black dancers and musicians learned from each other. "Tito was incredibly good," recalled Pagani, "He had a fresh sound with a jazz influence. For weeks thereafter his name kept popping up ... dancers wanted to hear more of his music."[7]

The Palladium began to attract the elite of New York's art and literary community along with Hollywood movie actors. Sammy Davis, Jr., Jackson Pollock, and Marlon Brando were frequent visitors. An excellent dancer and aspiring percussionist and conga player, Brando befriended Puente, who gave him some instruction. Brando frequently went to Latin Nights at the Palladium. Even after theater performances, the young actor rushed over to 53rd Street and Broadway after the show. "No one who went to the Palladium could think about anything but dancing," said Brando. "The atmosphere was fabulous. It gave you the idea that all the Puerto Ricans in New York were on the dance floor and they got rid of the frustrations they had worked up during the week, while working as waiters or pushing carts in the part of the city where they sold women's garments. People moved their bodies in incredible ways to the rhythm of the mambo—the most beautiful dance I had ever seen."[8]

Tito recalled those early nights at the venue in mid-Manhattan: "It was the explosion of dance. Remember, the Palladium was a big dance hall. I've always maintained that without a dance the music cannot be popular... and so here was a place, the Palladium, where everybody could come to dance or learn the mambo." It was at the Palladium where Puente would fuse various forms of Latin jazz and the emerging mambo style that would set him apart from other creative musical leaders.[9]

Along with other Latino bandleaders such as Perez Prado and Tito Rodriguez, Puente popularized the mambo, a fast-paced, staccato form from Cuba. Emphasizing Afro-Cuban instruments such as the conga and timbales, mixing with African-American jazz and big band swing, the mambo gradually became associated in the public mind with other Latin dances such as the cha-cha, samba, cumbia, and merengue. The mambo was a variation on the rumba, and the cha-cha was a further development of the mambo. The merengue was actually a dance that hailed from Venezuela, Haiti, and the Dominican Republic with influences from Afro-Cuban dance styles. But now, in its variations, it all became a version of "salsa."

Puente often joked that salsa was a sauce and not a dance. Nevertheless, he went along with the commercialization of the art form and became one of its leading practitioners. From his earliest days as a bandleader, Puente was an innovator, experimenting with combinations of musical forms, marrying various styles and cultures. His experimentation and inclusion drew many non-Latinos to his dances, not only in Manhattan but also in Brooklyn and Long Island.

Down the street from the Palladium on Broadway was Birdland, a club named after the heralded saxophonist and composer Charlie Bird Parker. Here, just around the corner from the Palladium, was the center of the American jazz scene, a place where, for seventy-five cents, a visitor could see such greats as Parker, Dizzy Gillespie, and Thelonious Monk. When the Palladium opened its doors to its Latin music, there quickly emerged a beaten path between the two musical emporiums.

The Latin musicians flocked to see the jazz players; the jazz players returned the compliment. The friendships and interaction affected all of them. The Palladium and the mambo rave it produced influenced the work of many emerging musicians. Max Roach, Monk, and others began to incorporate the new mambo forms in their own work. The emerging mixture of jazz and Latin sounds profoundly changed the American music scene.

Puente played Birdland and other jazz clubs like The Royal Roost. He struck up close working arrangements with such jazz greats as trumpet player Doc Severinsen. Drawing on his early musical experience and his training at Juilliard, Tito put together a band so versatile that it could play a wide range of music from jazz to pop to varieties of Latin. The band's range enabled it to play to a wider audience and at a larger number of venues. He was trying, he said, "to find a marriage between Latin music and jazz.... I was trying to play jazz but not lose the Latin-American authenticity."[10]

Larry Harlow, "El Judio Maravilloso" as he was known in music circles, one of the great innovators in salsa music, recalled seeing Puente at the Palladium when Harlow was first studying music at the age of fifteen. Although he was underage, he managed to convince some at the Palladium that he was serious about music and that they should let him watch. "I would stand in front of the bandstand and watch and listen and learn," he said. Every time Tito would break a timbale stick I would run and fight for it with the many young fans and budding drummers. I collected his broken sticks and finally bought a pair of ZimGar Mexican-made cheapy timbales. I would come home from school and practice with Tito's recordings. I was a terrible timbale player, but by playing along I developed a feel for Latin music."[11]

In the late 1940s, Jackie Robinson, Larry Doby, and other black professional ballplayers were breaking the color barriers in baseball. During the same period, Puente and other Latino bandleaders, with their new fusion of musical forms, were drawing interracial crowds to dance floors. People of all races and backgrounds came together at the Palladium. The music and the dance broke down cultural barriers, at least for the moments inside those walls.

A MAN OF MUSICAL INNOVATION

In late 1948, at WOR studios on 48th Street and 7th Avenue, Puente and his band recorded their first hit record, *Abaniquito*. The recording featured the orchestra's fabulous Cuban singer Vicentico Valdes. In Spanish the title word of the album means "little fan." The arrangement of *Abaniquito* included a mambo riff but also incorporated Cuban dance music and bop.

Tico Records, a company that featured a number of Latin artists, produced *Abaniquito*. Over the next few years Puente recorded numerous singles for Tico, including a remarkable thirty-seven titles in 1952. His first album, *Tito Puente and Friends*, appeared on the Tropical label in 1951.

During most of the time that he and his fellow band members were not in a recording studio, they were playing in various clubs in New York or on the road in such venues as Los Angeles, Miami, Philadelphia, the beach clubs on Long Island, and the resorts in the Catskills.

New York Times music critic Peter Watrous wrote of Puente's jovial presence, his arms and elbows flailing away, a musician who, by all usual standards of appearance would be "a mess." Yet, it was all deceptive, Watrous said. He talked about Puente's "eruptions of sounds that accentuate and power his roaring bands... as graceful as percussion gets. A virtuoso whose playing drives people onto the dance floor, Mr. Puente's improvisations also offer rhythmic variations that allow listeners to revel in his ingenuity." Most of all, Watrous said, Puente had the ability "to make people feel better."[12]

In 1955, the band recorded *Puente in Percussion*. Using no pianos or horns, the recording featured only percussionists along with a bass. Although executives at Tico were worried that the effort went too far, that the public and reviewers would find an album strictly made up of percussion too limited and esoteric, Puente continued to press the idea, emphasizing the importance of beats and rhythms and syncopation that could be highlighted in such a recording. Puente later said, "I explained... the significance of the drum in Africa, its use in religious dance rituals and communication, and how the tradition was handed down to us in Latin America." Puente's instincts and spirit of innovation won out. The company agreed to produce the recording. It was a masterpiece of quality drumming and musical experimentation that garnered favorable publicity and sales.[13]

In 1955, Puente signed an exclusive contract with RCA Victor, a major company but not one that traditionally recorded Latin music. Nevertheless, RCA quickly released *Mambo on Broadway*, a compilation of Tito's previously recorded albums. A year later he recorded *Cuban Carnival* and *Puente Goes Jazz*. Both albums were major commercial successes. Music critic Fernando Gonzalez said of *Cuban Carnival*: "With an orchestra powered by a rhythm section that included bona fide stars such as Mongo Santamaria, Carlos "Patato" Valdez, and Candido Camero on percussion, *Cuban Carnival* shows Puente at the top of his game, pushing the standards of the music but never forgetting the dancers on the dance floor. The excitement of "Pa'Los Rumberos" (later revisited by Santana), the elegance and muscle of the cha cha "Que Sera," or the rootsy flavor of "Elegua Chango" and "Oye Mi Guaguanco" come through clearly ... this is Puente at his best."[14]

The experimentation continued and so did the album sales. In 1956, Tito expanded his percussion concept that had been so successful on *Puente in Percussion* to include voices along with the instruments. *Top Percussion* was a successful experiment that included a range of Afro-Cuban drumming along with a chorus performing the cants and songs of Lucimi, a West African religion that had taken root in Cuba and throughout Latin America. Through much research, imagination, and daring, Puente was exposing the public to the connections between African religion and music and Latin forms.

So influential did Puente's music become in Cuba that in 1957 the Cuban government honored Puente in a ceremony recognizing the greatest Cuban musicians of the past fifty years. Puente thus earned the distinction of being the only non-Cuban ever so honored. In the same year, Puente and his orchestra recorded an album that, in its commercial appeal and artistic expression, was the most successful effort in his young career. It was called *Dance Mania* and it featured the vocal stylings of Santos Colon, who had left Jose Curbelo's orchestra to join Puente. The album included a variety of Cuban dance rhythms, including mambo, cha-cha, and bolero. With such notable tracts as "Cayuco," "3-0 Mambo," and "Hong Kong Mambo," the album not only continued to sell decades after it was recorded but also became a favorite tool of dance instructors across the country and world.

Max Salazar, influential Latin music journalist, disc jockey, and friend of Puente, said that *Dance Mania* revolutionized dance music. The pulsating rhythms, the hard-hitting horns, and jazz harmonies were a dancer's dream. "There was no question about what Tito had done to the music," Salazar said, "He took it light-years ahead. When *Dance Mania* came out, that's all you heard for three years."[15]

INTERNATIONAL ARTIST

In 1960, Puente collaborated with trombonist Buddy "Night Train" Morrow. Like Puente, Morrow had paid his dues appearing with a number of big bands including Paul Whiteman, Artie Shaw, and Tommy Dorsey. Like Puente, he had briefly studied at Julliard and was interested in music experimentation and the fusion of sounds. After organizing his own band, Morrow and Puente conceived an idea of creating an album in which each orchestra would in turn play various songs in their own style. The album would showcase ways in which big band jazz sounds and Latin rhythm could treat the same basic material. "Revolving Bandstand" was unlike any album ever produced.

In the 1960s rock music swept the United States and many other countries like a cultural hurricane. Influential artists and bands flooded the airwaves with new sounds and beats. For many Latin artists, these were tough times. The Latin dance crazes and its music that had proven so popular and profitable were now being moved aside in the venues and the record stores for the rock music. In the 1950s, names such as Elvis Presley, Fats Domino, and Chuck Berry were now the rage, and, later, musicians and bands such as The Beatles and The Rolling Stones and myriad others began to dominate.

For Puente, the new times and the popular music mattered little. He was now a star of international acclaim. As always, he kept experimenting with new sounds and arrangements and kept adapting. In the 1960s he began what would be a lifelong series of appearances abroad. In Japan, for example, he made the first of a number of visits, popularizing Latin music, along with other such artists as Perez Prado. He also began to take his music and his own persona to different mediums. In the late 1960s he hosted his own television program, *El Mundo de Tito Puente*, on a Spanish-language network.

Puente worked with two extraordinary female vocalists. The first was La Lupe. Born in a small rural town in Cuba, she had launched her singing career in concerts and on the radio in Havana. A bombshell singer on stage—emotional, unpredictable, and rebellious—she left Cuba with the onset of the revolution, arriving in New York in 1962. After working for a time with percussionist Mongo Santamaria, she started appearing with Puente.

Although she was never officially part of the Puente orchestra, she worked with Tito frequently in the 1960s, appearing on stage and recording five albums.

In 1964, Puente and La Lupe recorded what became a classic hit: "Que Te Pedi" (What Did I Ask of You)." La Lupe accompanied Puente on tours through Mexico, Puerto Rico, Panama, and Spain. The two appeared together on several television shows in the United States, including those hosted by Dick Cavett and Johnny Carson. Puente appreciated her enormous talent and energy, and allowed her room to express both. He became something of a mentor, helping her develop her singing style. Nevertheless, the two had frequent volcanic disagreements. Her stormy personality was finally too much for Puente, and the two went their separate ways.

The second female vocalist of international acclaim who worked with Puente was Celia Cruz. In 1950, she became the lead singer of one of the most important Cuban orchestras, La Sonora Matancera. Cruz sang at the Tropicana Casino in Havana throughout the 1950s, and she toured with La Sonora Matancera throughout South America and Mexico. When she left Cuba in 1960, she exploded onto the New York scene, recording classic albums with the biggest names in the field, such as Willie Colon and Johnny Pacheco. Puente and Cruz recorded six albums together.

A *New York Times* reporter covered a concert at the Village Gate in which Cruz and Puente performed together:

> Miss Cruz is the kind of singer who electrifies not just audiences, but musicians. With her rough-and-ready contralto voice, she rips into the rhythmic exhortations of salsa tunes far more boisterously than most male salsa singers. She rolls her r's with a percussive vengeance, and sometimes lets loose a raspy holler.... Mr. Puente's band responded with its usual drive and then some. Mr. Puente answered Miss Cruz with intricate salvos of timbales and cowbell, twirling his drumsticks with elaborate flourishes, and his horn section shouted out its parts.[16]

As Puente collaborated widely with other jazz and Latin musicians in New York and across the country such as Woody Herman and George Shearing, he constantly sought new sounds and mixes. If some in the music business began to refer to him as a "crossover" artist, he shrugged off the description. He had always crossed over into all kinds of music, he said. That was the essence of his work.

In 1967, Puente presented a concert at New York's Metropolitan Opera. From small clubs in El Barrio to the great hall of the Met, he had made enormous strides in taking Latin music to new levels.

Puente's career was a multicultural experience as well as a cross-generational one. Fusing the sounds of Latin countries, African tribes, Cuban music, jazz, and, later, rock and roll, he became something of an ambassador for collaboration. He worked with musicians of many races and generations. His music, ever innovative, has appealed to listeners for more than half a century.

In his increasing travels abroad in the 1960s, he always carefully pointed out that first and foremost he was a Puerto Rican and a Latino. But he vigorously sought the broadest possible audiences, appealing to the mass market, attempting to break into places where Latin music was only a recent phenomenon.

The big thing, he said, was to make certain that Latin American music struck through the cultural barriers. "That's what my object is," he said, "to get recognition for our Latin American music throughout the world, where throughout, when people talk about one kind of music in Europe, they can compare it with Latin music." His own career, he hoped, would spark other young artists to take the music to new levels and to new places.[17]

THE SEVENTIES AND SALSA

As Puente experimented with combinations of blues, rock, soul, jazz, and Latin influences, he remained ebullient and enthusiastic about the music, a storm of energy on stage, and a professional bandleader increasingly respected and guided by his peers.

In 1971, the cross fertilization of music for which Puente had worked so energetically was rewarded through a surprising entertainer. In the streets of the San Francisco Mission District, a teenage guitarist from Autlán del Alto in Jalisco, Mexico, heard Tito Puente's band and Celia Cruz's voice blaring from AM car radios and sidewalk markets and record stores. It influenced his own work. The son of a great mariachi violinist, Carlos Santana took violin lessons at the age of five. When his family moved to Tijuana, he learned to play the guitar, and in 1961 he moved to San Francisco and formed the Santana Blues Band. Surrounded by innovative rock groups such as the Grateful Dead, Santana added his own unique dimension to the rock scene with music full of soul and rhythm. By the time of his appearance at the Woodstock Festival in 1969, his guitar talent and exuberance had taken him to new dimensions—a unique combination of rock and blues with an Afro-Cuban blend.

In 1970, Santana recorded Tito Puente's "Oye Como Va," recorded originally by Puente in 1962. It was a hit that rose to the higher echelons of the rock charts. Santana said later

> We did it differently than el maestro Tito Puente, and that's why they recognized it [around] the whole globe. We took something wonderful to begin with and we injected something different. It's called multidimensional consciousness. The way Tito did it was more Cuban and Puerto Rican. But we put a multidimensional clave in it, multidimensional feel and color. Therefore, not only Cubans and Puerto Ricans liked it. The whole world liked it.[18]

What Santana had done and expressed so well is what Puente had encouraged—constant fusion, development, and mixing. When asked about Santana's recording of his music and its innovative sound, Puente had nothing but praise. After all, he said, this was yet another step in the drive to create and blend Latin sounds with various musical roots. And, besides, he said, he got some nice royalty checks from Santana's recording that kept giving and giving.

In 1965, *Santana III* included another Puente classic, "Para Los Rumberos." Both "Oye Como Va" and "Para Los Rumberos" became something of cult hits receiving consistent airplay internationally over the years, and both Puente and Santana repeatedly played them to audiences in their respective concerts.

Seven years later the two teamed up for a memorable Manhattan concert at the Roseland Ballroom. As Pablo Guzman described in *Village Voice*, "Puente conducted his fifteen-piece orchestra with snaps of his head and sweeps of his hands while playing timbales; at one point, when he signaled with his trademark stick over the head gesture, the entire brass section, spread in a row along his left, rose as one and played counter to itself. Folks went wild."[19]

To Santana and other rock groups, then, Puente's music transcended boundaries of style, time, and method. Grateful Dead drummer Mickey Hart said that his first memory of live music occurred when his mother took him to see Puente when he was a child. Later, after he began playing the drums, he had the good fortune to work in the right place. "I started playing timbales and shakers and guiro, and I worked in a restaurant at Atlantic Beach [in the suburbs of Manhattan, in Nassau County], where Tito Puente was playing upstairs in the ballroom. At night, Tito used to let me come backstage and play guiro and shakers, behind the bandstand. I was too young to be on the bandstand—I was a kid, thirteen or fourteen years old."[20]

Over the years, Puente worked with a wide variety of pop artists ranging from Sugar Hill Gang to Tower of Power. Puente toured extensively in Europe in 1979 to large and enthusiastic audiences. He also visited Japan. So receptive to the Latin sound were Japanese listeners that a group of Japanese musicians formed a group called Orquesta de la Luz. Not only did the group make an impact on Japanese concertgoers and record buyers, but it became a favorite group of many music fans in the United States and other countries. Inspired by Puente, Celia Cruz, and others, Orquesta de la Luz later shared the stage with them. Puente's international influence had extended to audiences and musicians alike in ways that surprised even "El Rey."

Puente also won his first Grammy award in 1979 for an album called *Homenaje a Beny.* It was a tribute to the memory of Cuban legend Beny More—singer, composer, and guitarist. At a celebration of Puente's award sponsored by *Latin New York* magazine, the hosts and guests established The Tito Puente Scholarship Fund to help support the education for musically gifted children. Touched and truly appreciative of the actions of his friends to set up the scholarship fund, Puente over the years appeared in annual fundraising events to help extend the scholarships' reach. Originally associated with the Julliard School of Music, the fund later became affiliated with the Spanish Harlem's Boys Harbor Conservatory for the Performing Arts.

Not only did the scholarship fund fulfill its original intention of providing support to aspiring young artists, its annual event was often a major musical attraction. At a concert in 1994 at the Apollo Theater in Harlem, for example, artists such as Dizzy Gillespie and Muchito performed along with Puente. "The scholarship fund," said Tito, "was a dream of mine for a long time. In the Latin community we have a lot of gifted youngsters who don't get an opportunity to develop their talent because of lack of money. Long after I'm gone the fund will be helping kids."[21]

OVER SIXTY AND STILL ROLLING

As Puente continued experimenting with new musical forms, he added a new small horn section to his band and named it the Latin Percussion Jazz Ensemble. He signed with Concord Records, a company that was increasingly active in recording Latin jazz. In 1983, Puente recorded *On Broadway*, and with it earned another Grammy award. He also won a Grammy for *Mambo Doable*.

Puente was over sixty years old now but was as vibrant a force in the field of music as ever. Constantly recording and playing gigs, he seemed to have inexhaustible drive and energy. His looks were only marginally different: the full head of jet-black hair was turning to white hair, and the trim physique had a slightly softer look. But behind the timbales, night after night, he could raise the roof with the youngest of his musical colleagues.

A seemingly endless number of major entertainers such as Frank Sinatra and Rosemary Clooney approached him to record or share stages. His music began to show up more frequently in Hollywood productions. Nevertheless, despite the acclaim, he regularly returned to the old haunts, performing in clubs around New York, from El Barrio to Brooklyn. His music, he said, had always been for dancers. They had supported him throughout his career and he would never stray far from the ballrooms.

He had always kept his personal and family life as far from scrutiny as possible. While on leave during the war, he had married his girlfriend, Mirta Sanchez, and they had a son they named Ronald in 1947. The marriage ended in divorce. In the 1950s his relationship with dancer Ida Carlini led to another son, Richard.[22]

Puente then had a long relationship with singer Margaret Ascencio, who sang backup with the band on several of Puente's albums. Margie gave birth to a daughter, Audrey Puente, who later became a well-known news

Tito Puente and The Simpsons

In 1995, Tito Puente played the most unusual venue in his career. He became a character in a two-part episode of the hit television cartoon series *The Simpsons*. His cartoon caricature was one of the suspects in the mystery of "Who Shot Mr. Burns?"

At the beginning of the episode, oil is discovered at Springfield High School. Many suggestions come forth as to what to do with the money. One of the suggestions comes from Lisa Simpson, the school's smartest student, who suggests that they hire Tito Puente to teach Latin jazz at the school. The school agrees and Puente accepts the offer. However, his hiring and other plans for the money suddenly evaporate when the town's wealthy ogre, Mr. Montgomery Burns, sets up a diagonal drilling operation from his own property that drains away all the oil at the school.

If that were not enough, Burns reveals his next scheme to add to his fortune. He plans to construct a giant, movable disc that would permanently block out the sun in the town so that the residents would have to use additional electricity from his nuclear power plant and thus earn for him even more profits.

Naturally, many residents want to remove Mr. Burns permanently from the scene. Sure enough, someone shoots him. He survives, but the hunt is on for the shooter. The list of suspects seems endless, including Tito Puente, who lost a chance to teach at Springfield's school as a result of Mr. Burns's schemes.

When the police visit Puente to interrogate him, he and his band are playing in a nightclub that looks like the Tropicana from the series *I Love Lucy*. The club is called 'Chez Guevara,' a pun referring to the Cuban revolutionary Che Guevara. Puente and his orchestra are playing a song called "Señor Burns." The lyrics deride the old, evil Burns—Puente will "settle the score," the song goes, "on the salsa floor." The police decide that Puente is not their man.

The investigation finally reveals who actually shot Mr. Burns. It was Maggie, the infant daughter of Homer and Marge Simpson. Mr. Burns had seen Maggie in her car seat with a lollipop, looking happy and content. He asked her what she was so happy about. As he talked to Maggie, he accidently dropped his gun, which he naturally carried for protection. As she dropped her lollipop and he reached for his dropped gun, the scuffle resulted in the gun being discharged.

With the investigation concluded, Mr. Burns demands that Maggie be arrested for attempted murder. A law enforcement official tells Burns that no jury in the world would convict a baby—except maybe in Texas.

reporter in New York, and a son, Tito Puente, Jr. "It's funny" Margie said later, "I met Tito at the Palladium in the 1960s but at the time I was a big fan of Tito Rodriguez. Ain't that a kick?"[23]

All of Puente's sons played music for a time. Tito Puente, Jr., followed closely in his father's footsteps, putting together a percussionist band. Tito Jr. once said of his father's relationship with Margie: "My mom is the epicenter of the Puente *familia*. Nothing can be done without her approval. She is the CFO-executive producer of the Puente family. I don't think my dad would exist without her. Thirty-three years, they've been together, and he still doesn't know what a beeper is! He's old-fashioned. He's still looking for the rotary phone. What? E-mail? No, put it in the mail with a stamp on it."[24]

Through all of his work on stage and in the recording studio, Puente continued to branch out in all sorts of artistic endeavors. In 1986, Puente collaborated with well-known playwright Maria Irene Fornes on her play *Lovers and Keepers*. Puente composed the score for the work, which was presented at the INTAR Hispanic America Theater in New York. Puente also worked with legendary bandleader Xavier Cugat to conduct the Cugat Orchestra for a television special produced in Barcelona Hall and devoted in part to Cugat's music.

In 1986 Puente appeared in a film called *Armed and Extremely Dangerous*, starring John Candy. A year later, he was in director Woody Allen's film *Radio Days*. He also appeared on *The Cosby Show* and performed in a commercial for Coca-Cola with Cosby. The two became good friends. Over the years, Puente appeared with numerous television personalities including Arsenio Hall, Jay Leno, David Letterman, and on shows such as *The Simpsons*.

THE MAMBO KING AND 100 RECORDS

In early 1992 Universal Pictures released the film *The Mambo Kings*. Based on Oscar Hijuelos' Pulitzer-Prize winning novel, *The Mambo Kings Play Songs of Love*, the film follows the lives of two Cuban brothers, Cesar and Nestor Castillo, both musicians, who leave their native Cuba for the United States in the 1950s hoping to make it in the Latin music scene. Older brother Cesar, played by Armand Assante, is the business manager and aggressive ladies' man. Nestor, played by Antonio Banderas, is a brooding songwriter, still longing for a woman in Cuba who had broken off their relationship.

Working as musical coordinator, recording sound tracks, and acting in the film as a bandleader at the Palladium, Puente was a central creator of the production. Celia Cruz also appeared in the film, cast as Evalina Montoya, a popular club singer. The film was a remarkable recreation of the spirit of the Latin music scene, from the mesmerizing atmosphere of the Palladium to the rich sounds of Puente's music. Film critic Roger Ebert described *The Mambo Kings* as "so filled with energy, passion, and heedless vitality that it seems new, anyway." He pointed to its evocative opening sequence "of dancers swooning as the camera flies above them" and "a wonderful scene where Assante climbs up on the stage with the legendary Tito Puente and insinuates himself into a performance with sheer gall."[25] The film achieved such widespread box office success and critical praise that the resulting publicity reached audiences that had never before been exposed to Puente. His work with the film coincided with another milestone in his already illustrious career.

At the same time that Puente was working with Universal on *The Mambo Kings*, he saw a tremendous opportunity to make the film coincide with yet another of his many accomplishments—the recording of his 100th album. Remarkably, the figure of one hundred did not include any reissues of albums or compilations of previously recorded music. Puente gloried in the accomplishment. "A lot of people say they've done 100 albums," Puente chuckled, "but we checked and didn't find anybody else with that many."[26]

For the special album called *Tito Puente: The Mambo King*, Puente made special arrangements. He decided to record the 100th album through a new record company that had been launched by his long-time agent, Ralph Mercado. The new label was RMM Records. For the recording, Puente assembled a host of top-flight singers and musicians with whom he had been associated over decades of performing. It would be new musical material with a dance orchestra style that he helped develop from his earliest years as a bandleader. The group included Celia Cruz, bandleader Tito Nieves, Puerto Rican salsa singer Santitos Colón, and composer and singer Ismael Miranda (also known as the Pretty Boy of Salsa).

Time magazine reported that "Tito Puente hasn't had this much fun since the '50s. The once and future mambo king is celebrating his 100th LP... with a world tour on both coasts and will head for Spain and Latin America this summer. But this is no finale. At 68, the salsa-hot percussionist still plays some 300 gigs a year—and modestly plans another 100 records."[27]

Puente remarked about his 100th album: "I did this album live.... I had everybody come in and play at the same time—not the trumpet on Monday and the sax on Thursday [because] I'm a dancer. I must dance in the studio while the whole band is playing to see if it really works.... When you hear this album... you'll feel the beat, you'll feel the vibrations—because this type of music was played and recorded like I did in the old days."[28]

On February 15, at Madison Square Garden, Puente celebrated the 100th album with his friends and admirers. A huge cast of entertainers paid tribute, opening with a young musician, Marc Anthony, who had recently released an album featuring a guest appearance by Puente. Celia Cruz was on stage that night along with bandleaders Oscar D'Leon, Tito Nieves, Ismael Miranda, and Jose (El Canario) Alberta.

THE LEGEND AND THE LEADER

As Puente reached his 70th birthday, the world was almost literally his stage. In the early 1990s, he took his band every year to more than twenty jazz festivals in countries around the world. The staggering list of countries included England, Germany, France, Italy, Holland, Finland, Sweden, Russia, Japan, Australia, Argentina, Canada, Mexico, and the country of his parents, Puerto Rico. Throughout the early 1990s he also played clubs from the Bronx to Hollywood.

In 1996 Puente had the great personal joy of performing on his son's first album. Tito Puente, Jr.'s premiere work, recorded on the EMI-Latin label, was called *Guarachando* and it launched him into a successful music career. The album included the hit made famous by his father and Santana, "Oye Como Va."

"In the early 80s while I was in high school, I had a rock band," Tito Puente, Jr., recalled, "I rarely traveled with Dad, so I didn't understand his role in the Latin music scene. It wasn't until after high school that I traveled some with my Dad and I started understanding that he was this icon. I got to meet people like Celia Cruz, etc., and they really had a profound effect on me." Shortly after the tragedy of the World Trade Center on September 11, 2001, Tito Puente, Jr., recorded a CD single called "Here's to You," dedicated to his father. He donated part of the proceeds to the American Red Cross.[29]

In August 1996, at the closing ceremony of the 1996 Olympic games in Atlanta, Georgia, Puente joined B.B. King, Wynton Marsalis, Stevie Wonder, and Gloria Estefan in an extraordinary production. At the end of the individual acts, the group formed a conga line that continued to grow and grow with the music whipping up a feverish beat. The Olympics had been marred early on by a deadly bomb that had been set off by a political fanatic. The celebration at the closing ceremony marked a special moment in the life of Latin music, bringing a sense of community and a spirit of inclusion. Puente's musical career had been devoted to fusing musical elements from various cultural backgrounds. At the Olympics, especially at these Games, it seemed particularly suited.

During his career Puente performed at the White House for three presidents—Jimmy Carter, George H.W. Bush, and Bill Clinton. "When I was there with Carter, they didn't know what title to use to introduce me to the President," he chuckles today. "They couldn't call me 'The King of the Timbales,' because what the hell does he know about timbales? So, they came up with a new one, 'The Goodwill Ambassador of Latin American Music!'"[30]

In 1997 he received a National Medal of Arts from President Clinton. At the ceremony Clinton said, "Just hearing Tito Puente's name makes you want to get up and dance. With his finger on the pulse of the Latin American musical tradition and his hands on the timbales, he has probably gotten more people out of their seats and onto the dance floor than any other living artist. For fifty years now, the irrepressible joy of his irreplaceable music has won him four Grammy awards, countless honors and a wide world of fans."[31]

In February 2000, Puente won another Grammy award for best traditional tropical Latin performance for *Mambo Birdland*. The album was a live recording from the Birdland, where Tito played some sets that took the listeners and dancers from the days of the 1940s and 1950s to the end of the century, from the days of the Palladium and the Afro-Cuban rhythms to the Latin Jazz and other musical composition that had been his life's work. When the night was over, Tito called out to the crowd, "Did you feel it?" They responded with a roar of joy.[32]

In late May 2000, Puente was in San Juan, Puerto Rico, to perform with the Puerto Rican Symphony Orchestra, where he fell ill and returned to New York. On Wednesday, May 31, at New York University's Medical Center, he died from complications after heart surgery. He was seventy-seven years old.

The tributes and remembrances were many and heartfelt. They not only spoke to Puente's artistry and musical genius but also his graciousness of spirit and the profound ways in which he promoted his culture and its music. On June 1, the day after his death, the Puerto Rican government declared three days of official mourning. "He put Puerto Rico's name in lights," said the island's U.S. Congressional delegate, Carlos A. Romero-Barcelo. "He incorporated our music in the international vocabulary," said artist Nestor Otero.[33]

The esteemed Latino music historian and critic Max Salazar said that Puente was not only a truly innovative musician and bandleader but "also a world VIP, not just a Latin bandleader or a Puerto Rican. He was special, he was our ambassador, our Bach and Brahms and Beethoven, and he was all those things... King Kong rolled into one."[34]

"Tito Puente was a great musician with great musical styling," said Michael Greene, President/CEO of the National Academy of Recording Arts and Sciences. "As an ambassador he provided the world with a window of access to Latin culture and put a face on Latin music.... He actively participated in the Grammy Foundation's programs for children and was one of the founders of the Latin Academy of Recording Arts and Sciences." Greene added. "Tito lived a life full of music and mischief and meaning right up to the end. He will be missed."[35]

"So many young musicians talked about the kind of mentor he was to them," said Little Judy, executive producer of the New York–based LaMusica. com, one of the largest and oldest Latino Web sites. "What struck me was that they all said that Tito would speak well of them to other people, and what he said always boosted their careers. That told me two things," she added. "How much influence he had, but also how much he cared about all those younger musicians."[36]

Many famed musical artists paid tribute. One of Puente's close friends, the pianist and bandleader Eddie Palmieri, recalled how Latin bands competed for dancers' hearts and feet in the heyday of the mambo. On many occasions, the bands would hold what amounted to competitions in the same venue, trying to wring every last feverish beat out of the music. "Tito was the greatest dance-band warrior there ever was," said Palmieri, "He was a natural genius who took dance music to its highest level."[37]

"This is such a great loss," said Bill Marin, former vice president of Puente's record label, RMM. "He was truly the ambassador of Latin music for the world."

Upon learning of Puente's death, Carlos Santana released a statement saying he felt honored to have known him, crediting Puente with "opening doors for him and other artists."[38] The Spanish word *puente* means bridge. From great dance halls such as the Palladium to recording studios to small, intimate clubs he had brought together the rhythms and beats of myriad musical cultures. "Did you feel it?" he asked. The tapping shoes and the exuberant dancers made the answer obvious.

SELECTED RECORDED MUSIC

Puente, Tito. *El Rey.* Concord Records, 1990. CD.
Puente, Tito. *Dance Mania.* Sony International, 1991. CD.
Puente, Tito. *Top Percussion.* Sony International, 1992. CD.
Puente, Tito. *The Best of Tito Puente: El Rey del Timbal!* Rhino/Wea, 1997. CD.
Puente, Tito. *50 Years of Swing: 50 Great Years & Tracks.* RMM Records, 1997. CD.
Puente, Tito. *Oye Como Va: The Dance Collection.* Concord Records, 1997. CD.
Puente, Tito. *Mambo Birdland.* RMM Records, 1999. CD.
Puente, Tito. *Party with Puente!* Concord Records, 2000. CD.
Puente, Tito. *King of Kings: The Very Best of Tito Puente.* RCA, 2002. CD.
Puente, Tito. *Dance Mania, Volume 2.* Sony International, 2003. CD.
Puente, Tito. *Live in Montreal (Montreal Jazz Festival).* Image Entertainment, 2003. DVD.
Puente, Tito. *The Essential Tito Puente.* RCA, 2005. CD.

NOTES

1. Steven Joseph Loza, *Tito Puente and the Making of Latin Music,* Urbana, IL: University of Illinois Press, 1999, 8.
2. Jim Payne, *Tito Puente: King of Latin Music,* Briarcliff, NY: Hudson Music, 2006, 12–13.

3. Bobby Sanabria, "Tito Puente: Long Live the King: Early Years," http://www.lpmusic.com/Pros_That_Play_LP/players_spotlight/tito_early_years.htm.

4. Sanabria, "Tito Puente, Early Years."

5. Sanabria, "Tito Puente, Percussionist."

6. Payne, 19.

7. Loza, 7.

8. "Marlon Brando: The Conga Man," http://www.cubanow.net/global/loader.php?secc=6&cont=people/num21/hipercongaman.htm.

9. Sanabria, "Tito Puente, Early Years."

10. "Hispanic Heritage: Tito Puente," http://www.gale.com/free_resources/chh/bio/puente_t.htm.

11. Larry Harlow, "A Salute to Tito Puente," http://www.larryharlow.com/new content/tito_puente.htm.

12. Peter Watrous, "Tito Puente Celebrates 100 Albums," *New York Times*, February 4, 1992, C3.

13. Loza, 12.

14. "Cuban carnival," http://www.amazon.com/Cuban-Carnival-Tito-Puente/dp/B000005LCY.

15. Payne, 32.

16. Jon Pareles, "Salsa: Celia Cruz and Tito Puente," http://query.nytimes.com/gst/fullpage.html?res=9B04E6DB1739F930A35752C1A965948260.

17. Loza, 226.

18. Leila Cobo, "Santana: Lara's Person of the Year," *Billboard*, August 14, 2004, 21.

19. Hispanic Heritage.

20. Wes Orshoski, "Grateful Dead Drummer Thinks Globally," December 6, 2006, http://www.relix.com/content/view/2003/117.

21. Loza, 18.

22. Barry Willis, "Latin Jazz King Tito Puente Dies at 77," *Stereophile*, June 4, 2000, http://www.stereophile.com/news/10765.

23. Sanabria.

24. Luther Orrick-Guzman, "On Top of the World! Tito Puente, Jr. reveals the details of his life as the son of a living legend," http://www.qumagazine.com/qu12/tito.html.

25. Roger Ebert, "The Mambo Kings," *Chicago Sun-Times*, March 13, 1992, http://rogerebert.suntimes.com/apps/pbcs.dll/article?AID=/19920313/REVIEWS/203130304/1023.

26. Payne, 41.

27. "Giving the World an Earful," *Time*, April 20, 1992, 85.

28. Hispanic Heritage.

29. "Exclusive Interview with Tito Puente Jr.!," http://www.salsapower.com/interviews/titojr.htm.

30. Mark Holston, "The One-Man Band of Latin Jazz," *Americas*, Nov–Dec 1990, 56.

31. "Remarks by the President at Arts and Humanities Ceremony," The White House: Office of the Press Secretary, September 29, 1997, http://clinton2.nara.gov/Initiatives/Millennium/19970929-2360.html.

32. "Latin Jazz Club: Tito Puente, Mambo Birdland," http://www.latinjazzclub. com/TP_MamboBirdland.html.

33. Willis.

34. Joe Hernández, "Max Salazar on Tito Puente," *Latin Beat Magazine*, April 1, 2002, http://www.encyclopedia.com/doc/1G1-86040805.html.

35. Ramiro Burr, "Puente's Life, Artistry Praised by Admirers," *Billboard*, June 17, 2000, 5.

36. Burr.

37. Larry Blumenfeld, "Farewell to 'The King': In his 50-year reign, mambo master Tito Puente put the Latin in America," *Entertainment Weekly*, June 16, 2000, 89.

38. Blumenfeld.

FURTHER READING

Harlow, Larry. "A Salute to Tito Puente." http://www.larryharlow.com/newcontent/ tito_puente.htm.

Hispanic Heritage: Tito Puente, http://www.gale.com/free_resources/chh/bio/puente_ t.htm.

Loza, Steven Joseph. *Tito Puente and the Making of Latin Music.* Urbana: University of Illinois Press, 1999.

Payne, Jim. *Tito Puente: King of Latin Music.* Briarcliff, New York: Hudson Music, 2006.

Salazar, Max. "Max Salazar on Tito Puente." *Latin Beat Magazine*, April 1, 2002, http://www.encyclopedia.com/doc/1G1-86040805.html.

Sanabria, Bobby. "Tito Puente: Long Live the King." http://www.lpmusic.com/Pros_ That_Play_LP/Players_Roster/sanabria.html.

Ruben Salazar

CORRIDO FOR A MARTYR

On August 29, 1970, Los Angeles news reporter Ruben Salazar became a martyr, a symbol of the unjust treatment of Latino minorities by the police. Salazar, a news director and reporter for the Spanish-language television station KMEX in Los Angeles, was covering the National Chicano Moratorium March, organized to protest the disproportionate number of Hispanic Americans killed in the Vietnam War. The peaceful march ended with a rally that was broken up by the Los Angeles police with such force that a riot ensured, during which Salazar, seated in a bar at the time, was shot in the head at short range with a tear gas projectile. A coroner's inquest ruled the shooting a homicide, but the police officer involved was never prosecuted. At the time many believed the homicide was a premeditated assassination of a very vocal member of the Los Angeles Hispanic community.

Salazar's death has been commemorated in many ways, especially in murals and *corridos* (songs). *Corridos* are stories set to music in poetic form and sung much like English ballads. They developed as a musical form in Mexico during the nineteenth century. Although sung throughout Mexico, corridos became especially connected with the border; sometimes they have been called *musica de la fronterea* (border music). Traditionally sung in Spanish, corridos often are a mix of Spanish and English. Most contain thirty-six lines, seven to ten syllables per line, with a varied rhyme scheme. The traditional corrido tells of actual events, especially involving heroic exploits or tragic death. The subjects of corridos are often icons of the people.

"El 29," a corrido written by the legendary Chicano singer and songwriter Lalo Guerrero, tells the story of the Chicano Moratorium March of 1970. The song tells of the people's wrath spilling out after years of unjust treatment, not only in the war but in the barrios. The song then tells of the martyrdom of "a great man and human being"—Ruben Salazar. He died on "El 29," the 29th of August.

A JUARITO IN EL PASO

Ruben Salazar was born in Ciudad Juarez in Chihuahua, Mexico, across the Rio Grande River from El Paso, Texas, on March 3, 1928. Mexican Americans in the United States referred to children across the border as *juaritos*. On February 15, 1929, Ruben's parents immigrated to the United States. For the Salazars, the move was, at least physically, a mere crossing of a river because they settled in El Paso.

Like most border towns, El Paso struggled mightily with its racial policies. Mexican-American children, for example, were not allowed to swim in the same public swimming pools as Anglo children. But El Paso was far from the most segregated border town. The cultural divides, although serious and always stacked against Mexicans and Mexican Americans, gradually eased in El Paso. By the end of World War II, a Mexican American was mayor of the town.

The family remained in El Paso throughout Ruben's childhood. His father, Salvador Salazar, worked as a watch repairman and later as head of the silver department in a downtown jewelry store. The job paid well, and the Salazars lived relatively modest but comfortable middle class lives while Ruben, who became a naturalized citizen, attended both primary and secondary schools, graduating from El Paso High School.

After high school, Salazar entered the United States Army, serving a two-year stint in Germany. After leaving the service, he returned to El Paso. His parents encouraged him to consider a college education, a move that few young Mexican Americans attempted in the early 1950s. Intelligent and energetic, Salazar decided to take on the challenge. He enrolled in Texas Western College (later the University of Texas at El Paso). In the mid-1950s, Texas Western College gained national attention by becoming the first college in a Southern state to integrate its intercollegiate athletic teams.

Salazar developed an interest in newspaper work while in college. He wanted to be where the action was, to find out what was going on underneath the appearances and facades. Majoring in journalism, he began to write articles for the school newspaper, *El Burro*. In 1954, Salazar earned a Bachelor of Arts degree. Few Latinos in the United States had earned journalism degrees by that time, and he was determined to make a life as a reporter.

Salazar took a job as a cub reporter at the *El Paso Herald Post*, an established newspaper that had been in operation since the 1920s. While at the *Herald Post*, he wrote a number of articles about the brutal treatment of Mexican and Mexican-American prisoners in Texas and also about police brutality. In May 1955, he persuaded his editors to do a piece on the conditions in the El Paso city jail. He dressed appropriately for the part, got himself arrested on a drunk and disorderly charge, and joined other prisoners in "Tank 6." The young reporter planned on staying a couple of nights. After a single day and night, twenty-five hours to be exact, he managed to call the paper and get released.

The article that appeared in the *Herald Post* explained why. "I spent a night in a Chamber of Horrors," he wrote. An encounter with a fellow prisoner named Red came early in the evening. "He was sitting on a high bunk surrounded by his henchmen. Red took me by the collar and his vile breath hit me in the face. He said, 'First timer, ain't you?' I said 'Yes.' He let go of my collar and showed me his yellow shaking hands. 'See these hands?' he asked. 'They can beat you up or kill you and no one here will say anything about it.'" Through a night of fights, drug dealing, and other assorted fearful activities, young Salazar had seen enough. "I had intended to stay longer," he said. "I couldn't."[1]

Such investigative reporting had been almost unheard of in El Paso. And it was being done by a Latino fresh out of college. Ken Flynn, another young reporter for the *Herald Post*, was astonished at Salazar's aggressiveness and ingenuity and the way he leaped into action. "I tried to emulate him," Flynn said. First of all, Flynn went on, Salazar was a good journalist. In addition, "He was a daring kind of reporter ... always for the underdog, and he had a tremendous winning personality." Flynn later remembered the city jail investigation as an amazing journalistic feat, especially for someone so new to the game. "The authorities didn't realize it was him," Flynn said. "He wrote a blistering account."[2]

For another story, Salazar posed as a drug user. After befriending an addict, the two visited the home of one of El Paso's drug dealers in the barrio. He described the woman pusher, the house, the children, and the deal the two made to purchase heroin. He watched in a hotel room as the addict shot up. This was not cheap fiction from bad magazines but life for many in the dives and underclass areas of the border town. His stories neither preached nor condemned. They were graphic, shocking revelations about a world within El Paso about which most citizens were unfamiliar.

Again going undercover, Salazar found his way to the home of one of the major El Paso speakeasy operators, a woman famous for her ten-cent shots of liquor. Its fame was not just the price but the potentially lethal combination of ingredients that gave the brew its wallop. The determined reporter drank the smoky-looking liquid from a pint bottle. "It rasped my throat like sandpaper. A few minutes later I felt the results. I didn't get drunk—I was dazed."[3]

This was a kind of muckraking journalism that Salazar had read about in classes at Texas Western—but this was the real thing. Dangers of all kinds lurked around the shadowy places that the young reporter traveled, seemingly without fear. For many in El Paso, the Latino kid reporter quickly gained a following. Some of his colleagues later said that he was the best reporter that the city of El Paso ever had.

As his later career matured, he returned to these themes of police abuse, especially of Mexican Americans, and the horrors of the prison system. Such articles did not approach the entire body of his work, but they marked his special place in American journalism and in the evolving history of Latinos in the United States.

With a growing reputation, new opportunities arose. The goal of most reporters in the Southwest was eventually to migrate to California. It was there, in San Francisco or Los Angeles, that the bigger jobs and the bigger stories awaited. Salazar took one of those offers and left El Paso and the Southwest where he had spent all of his youth. He took a job with a small newspaper called the *Press Democrat* in Santa Rosa, California, a small town near San Francisco in the heart of wine country. After short stints with the *Press Democrat*, the *San Francisco News*, and the *Los Angeles Herald-Express*, Salazar landed the position he had sought all along—the *Los Angeles Times*. It was here that he would truly make his mark.

WORKING FOR THE *TIMES* IN LOS ANGELES

By the time Salazar arrived at the *Los Angeles Times*, the paper had begun to shed its provincial, small-town character. Under the ownership of Otis Chandler, Jr., and the guidance of managing editor Nick Williams, the *Times* sought to expand its horizons from beyond the city of Los Angeles to become a source of regional and national news. It bolstered its staff and began, as never before, to encourage vigorous investigative reporting. The vision of Williams was that the *Times* would no longer merely record the events of the growing metropolitan area but would branch out. Soon, he hoped, newspapers in the Midwest and the East would be reprinting stories that originated with the *Times*.

Chandler and Williams especially wanted the *Times* to be the paper of record on news affecting the border between the United States and Mexico. To achieve this transformation, Chandler, using some of his publishing family's fortune, dramatically increased its budget. It was in this new era of the newspaper's history and the beginning of its rise to a newspaper of national prominence that Salazar joined the staff. When Salazar arrived at the *Times*, he was reluctant to be cast only as a reporter of Mexican-American issues. Nevertheless, because of his background, he took on the assignment of covering border issues with much zeal and commitment. Above all, he wanted, through both his willingness and talent, to demonstrate the best in professional journalism.

For the Mexican-American community in Los Angeles, the appearance of Salazar as a reporter of consequence, one who was attuned to their cultural and social problems and challenges, was a vital signal that the *Times* was committed to fair news coverage.

East Los Angeles was the largest barrio in the United States, with more than 500,000 inhabitants. Unemployment rates for the local male labor force hovered between 15 and 20 percent. The average Latino in Los Angeles had completed less than nine years of schooling, four years fewer than anglos and two years fewer than blacks. Latinos had no political muscle in the city or the state—no Mexican-American city council member, no supervisors. And this phenomenon was in a city founded at the time of the American Revolution by Mexicans.

Early on, Salazar intensely took on the challenge of reporting these conditions to the greater Los Angeles area. He charged around the city getting to know the Latino community as no other reporter had ever done. He began to demonstrate through his own personal contacts and in his writing that he and the *Times* would treat the issues that involved the Mexican-American community with the understanding and seriousness they deserved.

In 1959, Salazar met a former *Times* employee named Sally Robare through a mutual acquaintance. She had lived in Alhambra, a small city in the western San Gabriel Valley near Los Angeles, and also in Whittier, a small city east of Los Angeles. She had worked in the classified section of the paper but had taken a job as a department store clerk by the time she met Salazar. After a brief courtship the two were married in 1960. They had three children together: Lisa Marie, Stephanie Ann, and John Kenneth.

During the first six years of his career at the *Times*, Salazar concentrated on the growing sense of frustration among Mexican-American leaders in gaining traction in local politics, in improving conditions for the growing immigrant population, and in developing strategies that promised a real chance for social and political change. Extremely bright but easygoing, his language often breaking into barrio slang, a man who on occasion drank too much and enjoyed a good time, Salazar was not a political activist. With an Anglo wife and a middle-class home in the Orange County suburbs, he was apart from the everyday conflicts and tensions of the inner city. Nevertheless, his journalistic instincts were acute. He hungered for the secrets behind the scenes, the stories of those who lived on the edges, who faced the uncertainties and trials that he had managed personally to escape. As he dug deeper, his passions and outrage grew along with the first-hand evidence he gathered day after day.

In the 1960 presidential election, a large proportion of the Latino leaders worked on John F. Kennedy's campaign for the presidency through "Viva Kennedy" clubs and other outreach efforts. Nevertheless, with the advent of the Kennedy presidency, the patronage and programs they had hoped would flow to the Mexican-American community because of their support did not significantly materialize. Few Mexican Americans garnered appointments, and the administration promoted very little legislation to improve the lives of the growing immigrant population in the city on such issues as discrimination, schools, poverty, and jobs.

Especially critical to the Latino community were the problems brought on by the *bracero* program. Since World War II, the program had brought thousands of Mexican contract laborers to work the fruit and vegetable fields of the American Southwest, especially California. Paid very low wages and housed in miserable conditions, the exploited Mexican workers came to America during the picking seasons and were then sent back across the border after the seasons ended.

Not only did the *bracero* program exploit poor Mexican laborers, it had deleterious effects on those Mexican-American workers who could have worked in those jobs. It also hampered early efforts of Mexican-American workers to organize in unions to fight for decent working conditions and fair pay. With the *bracero* program supplying much of the labor necessary for American businesses, Mexican-American workers had little power or bargaining influence. It was this program, along with the many other towering obstacles of discrimination and powerlessness, that Mexican-American leaders would combat in their fight to organize migrant field workers.

Salazar interviewed farmers, growers, government officials, lawyers, and townspeople throughout much of the rich farming areas of southern California. In Brawley, he met a physician who had lived for a long time in the area and had seen firsthand the exploitation meted out to poor Mexican laborers. His name was Ben Yellen, and he was angry. He told Salazar that the farmers claimed they did not have enough U.S. workers because the domestic work force would not take on the menial jobs in the fields, such as stoop labor. It was basically a lie, he said.

"In the old days," he said, "there were labor contractors who would bring crews of domestic farm workers to different farms. These domestic farm workers had their permanent homes in the Valley. In the summer they left to work in northern California." But the farmers naturally wanted laborers who would work for the lowest wages. Also, they did not want to deal with an increasingly agitated U.S. work force that was beginning to demand greater wages and better working conditions. "If the lettuce growers need farm workers," said Yellen, "let them pay decent wages and they will get farm workers. But they do not want to pay American wages. They want the cheap labor from Mexico."[4]

In his journalistic forays into the tangled issues of workers' rights, immigration, undocumented workers, racial discrimination, cultural barriers, and the needs of agricultural businesses, Salazar saw clearly that the issues were long-lasting, deep, and nearly intractable. There were no easy solutions, he realized—no quick fixes.

Salazar focused on the social plight of Mexican-American families attempting to make a life in southern California. He wrote about the extremely low median income of average Mexican-American households; he reported on the lack of jobs, the problems of discriminatory practices in housing, the derision with which many Mexican Americans were treated in the United States, and the language challenges facing new immigrants.

He especially concentrated on the school system. He talked with teachers, school administrators, parents, and students. He visited schools. He bristled at the suggestions he heard from those in power that dealing with Mexican-American children in the California school system was nearly impossible, that much of the teaching was wasted on those whose cultural and language facility was so much inferior to that of Anglo children. He began to doubt the commitment of the educators and their administrators and began to believe that a certain laziness and weariness was draining the energy of many, even those whose motives were sound.

Salazar began to report on the growing movement among Mexican-American leaders to push for reforms within the school system that would place greater emphasis and awareness on the cultural and language differences facing minority students. Only through a system that took account of bilingual and bicultural factors could Mexican-American youngsters receive fair treatment and a decent chance to succeed.

Salazar pointed to the experiences of a boy named Pablo Mendez. Seventeen years old, born in the United States to Mexican-American parents, Pablo dropped out of high school to keep a summer job. Pablo's father, Benito, believed that the boy should not have gone to high school in the first place and that he was destined, because of his class and background, to work with his hands. College was out of the question.

The boy spoke a Mexican-American slang that sounded neither Anglo nor Spanish. "Though he looks like a Mexican," Salazar wrote, "Pablo is not. He's an American, but doesn't think of himself as one, and in many respects is not looked upon as one by non-Mexican Americans." His speech patterns, Salazar said, would sound ridiculous among a group of high school students in Tijuana. But among his "gringo" acquaintances, his English is labored, peppered with phrases and idioms that, to them, also make little sense. Naturally, a boy in this kind of situation struggles with his identity, pulled by two cultures and identities that "can leave you with only the hyphen."[5]

The expectations for the boy's future, Salazar lamented, were limited and grim. He might seek training for relatively unskilled work. He might compete in a growing army of unskilled workers. He also might drift, a path that could lead to crime, drugs, and other delinquencies. Salazar's tragic portrait of Pablo was a call for action, a plea for the thousands of youngsters trapped in poverty, alienation, and a culture of low expectations.

Salazar's reporting laid out the developing agenda for Mexican-American leaders as they attempted to wrestle with the problems of the educational system. They began to call for the teaching of Spanish, the introduction of Mexican and Latino literature into the curriculum, and the hiring of bilingual teachers who could help guide students with special needs toward graduation.

When the Los Angeles school system and other schools in the Southwest where large numbers of Latinos mixed with Anglos did not respond favorably to these suggestions, the two sides on the education debate became increasingly polarized. The arguments became expressions more of fury and anger than of constructive reform. The bitterness and hostility over the school system would grow even more intense through the 1960s and lead to mass protests and confrontation.

In 1963, Salazar focused his reporting in a six-part series called "Spanish-speaking Angelenos." He related the unique culture and identity of Mexican Americans, who, like Salazar himself, had been born in the border areas. These people were not like any other immigrant group that had made their way into the mainstream of American culture, he said. Most of the individuals claim a heritage within the United States itself; their culture is indigenous to southern California and the Southwest. Their ancestry can be traced to a time when Anglos were a minority in the region, before the Mexican War had changed the face of the Southwest. American society, Salazar wrote, needed to appreciate this cultural past, to celebrate its traditions, to honor its history.

Salazar's six-part series fueled much passion in the *Times* readership. Some recoiled at the barroom slang of the pieces and the notion that somehow the Mexican-American community in Los Angeles was being wronged. Some Hispanics resented the pieces. Richard Valdez of Los Angeles wrote that "We, of Mexican ancestry, born in the United States, are Americans. 'Mexican Americans' implies dual citizenship, and nothing could be further from the truth. We in East Los Angeles resent our area being referred to as 'Little Mexico.' This is an American community, lived in by Americans." But despite some criticism and misunderstanding, the series had, as no other California newspaper had ever done, unflinchingly explored these critical social and political issues. "This is the first letter I've written to a newspaper," wrote Julia Cereceda of Montebello, California, "but I feel I have to thank Ruben Salazar for the articles he has written. I am glad he works for a newspaper such as the *Times* that allows him to write blunt truth."[6]

SALAZAR ABROAD

In 1965, the *Times* had a new assignment for one of its star reporters. The paper had made remarkable progress in establishing itself as a national newspaper of influence. In the space of a few years, it had assembled an impressive group of correspondents, had undertaken aggressive investigative reporting, and had gained a tremendous increase in readership as well as the respect of the journalistic community across the country. It was now ready, its owners and editors believed, to make an increasing impact in the largest arena as a top-flight news organization reporting firsthand outside of the United States.

The *Times* began to assemble a team of foreign correspondents to cover hot international stories. In addition to securing a number of veteran reporters who had previous experience outside the country, foreign editor Bob Gibson turned to Salazar. His first assignment was the Dominican Republic.

In the fall of 1963, the elected President of the Dominican Republic, Juan Bosch, was overthrown by a military coup. Bosch's government had begun to institute various left-wing policies, including land redistribution. The coup that drove him from power was led by a right-wing faction of the Dominican military led by General Elías Wessin. Wessin and his cohorts were determined to keep the country out of the hands of socialist or communist control, despite the election results earlier in the year. Wessin and his allies hunkered down, formed a governing junta, abolished the constitution, built up the military, and prepared to fight off any counterinsurgency that might follow.

In April 1965, a group of young officers who remained sympathetic to Bosch mounted a rebellion. Calling themselves "Constitutionalists" for their determination to restore the constitutionally elected presidents, they gathered supporters, took to the streets, and managed to seize the national palace and the government radio and television stations in Santo Domingo, the capital city. Both sides of the civil uprising were heavily armed, and the prospect of a deadly standoff, with many civilians caught in the crossfire, loomed. The United States began preparations to evacuate its citizens in the Dominican Republic.

U.S. President Lyndon B. Johnson and his advisors became convinced that the supporters of Bosch, although fighting for a democratically elected regime, were a communist force. These were the days of the Cold War, and Johnson was determined that the Dominican Republic would not become another Cuba in the Western Hemisphere, another Communist nation at the doorstep of the United States. On April 28, 1965, U.S. military forces landed in the Dominican Republic. A fleet of forty-one vessels blockaded the island, and eventually more than 40,000 American Marines and Army troops began to attempt to restore order. In addition, the Organization of American States and the United States formed an inter-American force to assist in the intervention in the Dominican Republic. Troops from Brazil, Honduras, Paraguay, Nicaragua, and other countries joined the U.S. troops.

Salazar arrived in May 1965. He did not wait around with other reporters in American-owned hotels for official briefings by the U.S. military. As he had done in those early days in El Paso, when he got himself arrested to spend time in the local jail to get a story, Salazar went into the streets, a rather dangerous proposition with so much unrest and violence occuring daily. Not only did he make contacts with the government in power, he also managed to find enough underground information to arrange a meeting with insurgent forces, those fighters whom many journalists were simply referring to as Communists.

In a story filed in mid-May of 1965, Salazar interviewed one of the men considered a dangerous Communist by the U.S. Embassy. His name was Hector Olivarez, a twenty-two-year-old college student. Olivarez admitted

---

The Freedom Forum's Memorial for Journalists and Photographers Killed on the Job

The Freedom Forum in Washington, D.C., maintains an online memorial for journalists and photographers killed on the job through nearly two centuries. The list starts with James Lingan, who was stomped to death in Baltimore in 1812 by an angry mob upset by his reporting about local politicians. As of 2006, the names of 1,665 journalists from around the world are etched on the memorial's glass panels. The memorial is rededicated each year to include the names of journalists who died on the job the previous year. A total of 299 names are journalists from the United States. A handful of these journalists have Latino surnames—one of those names is Ruben Salazar.

his socialist leanings to Salazar but denied he was a Communist or that Communists were heavily involved in the rebel effort to oust the military junta. Impressed by his intellect and zeal for a democratic government, Salazar began to sense that perhaps the United States, through its intervention, should not be supporting the current brutal regime.

In late May, Salazar found himself not only in the middle of reporting the chaos, but also in the middle of the action. At a rally of approximately one thousand demonstrators in the town of San Francisco de Macoris, Salazar was ordered out of the plaza by junta police. His car with its press sign, the police claimed, was helping to incite disorder. When Salazar left the plaza, many of the demonstrators charged after him, shouting "Constitucion! Constitucion!" Many yelled at him to tell the world their story. When Salazar got out of his car, police unloaded several bursts of rifle fire at his feet. Finally, the rally dissolved.

The fighting continued in the Dominican Republic until late August 1965. When a truce was finally declared, most American troops left shortly afterwards. Policing and peacekeeping operations were turned over to Brazilian troops. Former President Joaquin Balaguer, backed by U.S. interests, was elected over Bosch, who would never regain power. Balaguer would go on to dominate Dominican politics for over twenty years.

After his coverage of events in Santo Domingo, Salazar left for a brief stint in Vietnam. When he arrived in the fall of 1965, the U.S. military commitment to South Vietnam had intensified. Salazar spent nearly a year covering various aspects of the conflict. Many of his stories involved the personal tragedies and occasional triumphs of average soldiers. From the town of Bien Hoa, South Vietnam, for example, Salazar wrote of Private First Class Jimmy Williams, a black soldier from Wetumpka, Alabama, who had been killed by Viet Cong mortar fire in the jungle southeast of Saigon. The story was not about Williams' bravery or courage, or of the admiration and respect he had earned from his fellow soldiers of the 173rd Airborne Brigade, but of his pending burial. Salazar and Williams' buddies had learned that, because he was black, the town of Wetumpka had refused to allow Williams to be buried in its main cemetery, close to where the Williams family lived. Instead, Williams had to be buried in the Andersonville National Cemetery.

For Williams' friends and for Salazar, this kind of unbelievable racial discrimination, this blind injustice and hidebound adherence to prevailing social norms, was a startling reminder of how far America still had to go in the area of race relations. "He deserved to be buried any place—even in the White House grounds," one of Williams' friends told Salazar. "That he was not permitted to be buried where his parents wanted him to be is going to bother me for a long time." It also deeply bothered Salazar who wrote, "Jimmy Williams' platoon has suffered heavy casualties. All of Williams' buddies killed with him were resting this Memorial Day where their survivors wanted them to be. All but Williams."[7]

In the fall of 1966, Salazar was called away from Vietnam by the *Times* to take over the job of bureau chief in Mexico City. He became the first Mexican American to hold such a position at a major newspaper. This time, Salazar did not travel alone. The entire Salazar family relocated with him to Mexico City. The assignment put Salazar back in a familiar environment, where he covered events not only in Mexico but also in Central America and the Caribbean. Here, the language and culture were assets for Salazar as a foreign correspondent.

Salazar wrote on the extreme poverty of Honduras. He wrote about the political discontent and lack of democracy in Nicaragua. He wrote on the marginalization and poor living conditions of the various native Indian groups in Mexico. He wrote a first-hand account of the Mexican government's brutal reaction to students demonstrating against the administration of Gustavo Diaz Ordaz and in favor of a democratic movement that would sweep away entrenched power and control in Mexico. The Mexican student movement was an outgrowth of student movements across the world in the late 1960s, most notably in France. Students from such institutions in Mexico as the Polytechnic Institute, the national Agricultural School, several prep schools, and high schools rallied in events leading up to a climactic clash.

It came to be known as the massacre at Tlatelolco. On the evening of October 2, 1968, troops opened fire on some 5,000 people gathered in Tlatelolco Square, or the Square of the Three Cultures, in the center of Mexico City. The tragedy occurred ten days before the inauguration of the nineteenth Olympic Games in Mexico's capital. The student-government unrest had lasted for nine weeks. During the afternoon of October 2, an estimated 15,000 students marched through the streets carrying red carnations. By evening, the number of protestors, some with spouses and children, had remained after the march for a planned concluding rally.

At sunset, violence erupted. Police and military forces, including armored cars and tanks, charged into the square and indiscriminately began firing live rounds into the crowd. The shrieks and screams of scattering demonstrators mixed with the incessant ringing of bullets and small explosions. Later, the police would blame agitators for instigating the riot and starting the battle. Thousands of people who were caught in the melee, at least those who survived, would all dispute that account.

Throughout the night, sporadic gunfire could be heard in the capital city. Soldiers scoured the area for snipers and any demonstrators still willing to try to retaliate. They broke down doors and searched from house to house. Witnesses later claimed that bodies were removed from the scene in garbage trucks. Some 2,000 students were dragged into police and military jails and stripped and beaten.

No one knows precisely how many people died that infamous night. Even the lowest estimate exceeded fifty people. Hundreds were seriously injured.

For Salazar, the night of October 2, 1968, was a prelude. He would be in the midst of such violence again.

RETURN TO LOS ANGELES

While Salazar was covering events in Mexico, the scene in Los Angeles was growing more tense and confrontational. The Chicano movement was proving to be the most heated social protest among Mexican Americans in the history of the American Southwest. Amidst escalating tensions in the city, the *Times* decided it needed to recall its most respected and knowledgeable correspondent on the growing unrest of Mexican-American communities. After Salazar had left the country in 1965 to be a foreign correspondent, the *Times* had hired no other Mexican-American reporters. There was no one better than Salazar to cover these developments, and the leadership of the *Times* knew it. The newspaper asked Salazar to return with his family from Mexico City and take over the reporting of this dynamic time of Chicano protest.

Although Salazar had mixed feelings about returning to Los Angeles to take over essentially the same position he had left, he recognized the dimensions of the Chicano story to Los Angeles and the Southwest. He already had numerous contacts in the Mexican-American community. He realized that his stature within that community would pay huge dividends as he explored various angles in the Chicano movement. In late 1968, he accepted the offer and returned to Los Angeles.

There were fighting words now on the lips of young Mexican Americans. Much like the student protests Salazar had covered in Mexico City, youngsters in East Los Angeles now talked about justice and liberation. The slogans were "Chicano Power," "Viva La Raza," and "Brown is Beautiful." The movement signified a culture of opposition.

It was no more dramatically expressed than in a so-called "Plan de Aztlan," written at a 1969 Chicano Youth Liberation Conference in Denver, Colorado. The plan set out the vision of the recovery of Aztlan, the mythical original homeland of the Aztecs, which the movement equated with the American Southwest—those areas taken by the United States from Mexico in the nineteenth century. If the dream was fanciful, the growing spirit of unity and protest among Chicanos was not.

Much like the students in Mexico City, several thousand youngsters in a number of schools in East Los Angeles such as Robinson, Wilson, Lincoln, and Garfield had, just a few months before Salazar's return, staged their own student strike. Supported by Chicano college student groups as well as community organizations, they began a campaign to protest the poor quality of education, overcrowded conditions, and racist curriculum. They pushed for bilingual classes and for the teaching of Latino cultural and historical themes. They walked out of their classes. They called the protests "blowouts." In the end, city education officials offered a few token responses to the protests. They developed courses in Chicano studies, for example, but overall the city did little to change conditions.

As Salazar soon realized upon his return, the Mexican-American community in Los Angeles was, as never before, galvanizing various elements into an increasingly unified protest force, from high school and college students to countercultural youth organizers and civil rights organizations. The issues had remained mostly the same: racism, poverty, educational discrimination, and police oppression. But the difference was in the confrontational spirit to fight against the status of inferiority that had been forced on them.

"Most Mexican Americans have experienced the wary question from an Anglo: 'You're Spanish, aren't you?' or 'Are you Latin?'" Salazar wrote. "Rarely will the Anglo venture: 'You're Mexican, aren't you?' The reason is that the word Mexican has been dragged through the mud of racism since the Anglos arrived in the Southwest. History tells us that when King Fisher, the famous Texas gunman, was asked how many notches he had on his gun, he answered: 'Thirty-seven—not counting Mexicans.'"[8]

Salazar had been away from the United States during the momentous events surrounding Cesar Chavez's United Farm Workers first strikes and boycotts in 1966 and 1967. The success of Chavez in mobilizing groups of farm workers to a cause and in persevering through the creation of an actual union of farm workers was, to Salazar, one of the most impressive accomplishments imaginable. It was an inspiration to all Latinos, Salazar believed, including those outside the farm worker community, those Latinos in East Los Angeles, and in other urban areas.

"You know, Cesar is our only real leader," Salazar told a friend. "Chavez organized a broad-based appeal and non-violently resisted every effort to make him compromise. The growers seemed so strong—too strong—yet Chavez demonstrated that the best approach is still 'Power through Unity.'" This was the example—non-violent grass-roots organizing and growing political force in numbers—that inner-city Latinos must follow to succeed.[9]

Salazar began to report on a variety of Chicano movement issues. He gathered information and personal testimony on the substandard educational facilities in the city. He carefully laid out the position of Chicano activists that the Spanish language should be promoted and not punished in the public schools as a way to break through some of the culture barriers separating Anglos and Mexican Americans. He wrote on the work of various organizations attempting to make it possible for Chicanos to gain greater control over the institutions that affected their lives. He wrote about individuals such as Joe Ortiz, a former drug addict who beat his addiction, joined the League of United Citizens to Help Addicts, and worked to encourage other junkies to find help.

Salazar also wrote about the origins, views, and work of the Brown Berets, a pseudo-military organization patterned in some ways after the

Black Panthers, the militant black power group. To most of the Anglo community and especially to Los Angeles law enforcement officials, the Brown Berets represented a serious threat to law and order. Salazar gave the readers of the *Times* a totally different image, portraying the Brown Berets as young, aggressive advocates for change. He pointed out that the Brown Berets had chapters in twenty-seven other U.S. cities and that their message was not of revolution or violence but of community service and cultural awareness. He also pointed out that with help from the Ford Foundation the Brown Berets opened the East Los Angeles Free Clinic and offered free medical, social, and psychological services to Mexican Americans. In answer to the charge that many of the members of the Brown Berets were former barrio gang toughs, Salazar said simply that the group was trying to change rebels without a cause into rebels with an important cause.

In April 1970, Salazar made a critical career decision. He accepted an offer from KMEX, the Spanish-language television station in Los Angeles, to become news director. The position had been held by Danny Villanueva, a former National Football League player. Villanueva was moving up to be the station manager. In his own tenure as news director Villanueva had pushed for vigorous, investigative reporting in the Mexican-American community. He and the station owners saw Salazar, with his reporting skills, his knowledge of the issues, and the trust he inspired among the Latino population, as the perfect choice for news director.

Although surprised by the offer, Salazar immediately saw the potential to reach new audiences with his work through Spanish-language media. He realized that much of the Spanish-speaking community did not receive their news through the print media but through radio and television. The KMEX job, he realized, would give him fresh opportunities to communicate directly, in their own language, to many of the people he had written about in his newspaper work.

At KMEX, with a staff of three reporters and one cameraman, Salazar sent his news team into the barrios to cover stories that the English-language media ignored. His crew covered the protest demonstrations held by Chicano activists. It was Salazar's news team that covered the fatal shooting of two unarmed Mexican cousins, Guillermo and Gildardo Sanchez, by the Los Angeles police in July 1970 in a tragic case of mistaken identity. The two were gunned down in their apartment when officers broke through the door looking for a criminal suspect. Seven police department members were indicted on federal charges of violating the victims' civil rights; all were acquitted. The case caused a major outcry in the Latino community. The Los Angeles Police Department blamed much of the criticism on KMEX's intense, day-to-day coverage.

With his move to KMEX, Salazar did not sever his ties with the *Times*. The paper asked him to write a weekly column on Chicano issues; he would be paid for the columns but would no longer be an official *Times* staffer.

Salazar welcomed the chance to take on both opportunities to explain and interpret Chicano life and culture to the greater Los Angeles community.

Salazar's *Times* column became nationally recognized for its tough approach to questions of poverty, discrimination, and racism. Salazar told a reporter that his bosses at the newspaper wanted him to explain the Chicano to the white community. The best way to do that, Salazar believed, was not through columns about how Mexican Americans make the best enchiladas but to give them the hard-hitting stuff, the conflicts and underlying hopes and aspirations.

In one column, Salazar suggested that everyone associated with the Mexican-American community begin to use the term "Chicano." The term, he said, had become a badge of honor and defiance, a term through which the community could come together for change. "A Chicano is a Mexican American with a non-Anglo image of himself," he said. "He resents being told Columbus 'discovered' America… that Chicanos are "culturally deprived," or that the fact that they speak Spanish is a "problem."[10]

In other columns, Salazar attacked racism, talked about poverty, and lamented the miserable living conditions in much of the Chicano community. He also talked about unequal justice under the law. Salazar quoted a Los Angeles Brown Beret leader, David Sanchez, who said, "To Anglos justice means 'just us.'" Salazar continued: "*La Ley* or the Law, as Mexican Americans call the administration of justice, takes forms that Anglos—and even Negroes—never have to experience. A Mexican American, though a third-generation American, for instance, may have to prove with documents that he is an American citizen at border crossings, while a blue-eyed blond German immigrant, for example, can cross by merely saying "American."[11]

Salazar talked about the pull of two cultures and identities within the Mexican-American community. The hyphen, he said, was symbolic of the forces tugging at Chicanos, torn between the culture of their forebearers and that of the Anglos. The Chicano movement itself provided a foundation for a new identity, one that not only counteracted the racist attacks on Chicanos but also led to feelings of self-worth.

In his dual journalistic role in both television and print media, Salazar was gaining increasing notoriety in the city. He insisted on a number of occasions that he never thought of himself as a Chicano reporter and that he resented that characterization of his work by others. He was a reporter, he said, who happened to be Chicano.

As the strains and tensions in Los Angeles between Chicano activists and the police intensified, Salazar found himself the target of investigations. The Federal Bureau of Investigation looked into his background, trying to determine whether Salazar's connections to Chicano radicals were more than journalistic, whether he had ties to Communist organizations or militant activist groups.

Salazar told friends that he suspected that he was being followed by the police. "I definitely felt the word was out among the cops to get Ruben one way or another," said Charlie Ericksen, publisher of Hispanic Link news service in Washington. Ericksen was a friend of Salazar at the time and set up a meeting in which the newsman told friends that police were after him.[12]

In fact, Police Chief Ed Davis, annoyed with the content, tone, and hostility of the columns and KMEX's coverage, claimed that Salazar's reporting was inciting the Chicano population. The police pressured both the *Times* and KMEX to fire him. Police even visited Salazar at his office. Earl Shorris, an old friend and colleague of Salazar during his early years at *Herald Post* in El Paso, recalled Salazar telling him that the sheriff had threatened him directly, saying, "You had better stop stirring up the Mexicans." Shorris also remembered that the threats bothered Salazar but did not stop him.

"What are you going to do?" Shorris asked Salazar.

"Keep writing," Salazar responded.[13]

NATIONAL CHICANO MORATORIUM AGAINST THE WAR IN VIETNAM

In the fall of 1969, massive demonstrations against the war in Vietnam rocked cities across the country. In California, several hundred thousand participated in rallies from Berkeley to Los Angeles. In this swirl of protest and activism, Chicano leaders decided to mount their own protest marches. They formed the National Chicano Moratorium against the War in Vietnam. By the spring of 1970, more than a dozen local Chicano moratoriums across the country were making plans. Like the other anti-war marches, these Chicano protests would also lash out against the death, destruction, and folly of the war. But the genius of the plan put forth by Chicano leaders was that the moratoriums would use the anti-war theme for a broader cause.

Yes, Latinos were dying at a greater rate in Vietnam than other segments of the United States. Yes, the war itself was illegal, unjust, and causing America great harm both at home and in the eyes of the world. But beyond the evils of the war were the social and cultural deprivations being suffered in the Mexican-American communities. Through the moratorium, leaders sought to mobilize the Mexican-American population, not just against the war but also against domestic problems confronting Chicanos. David Sanchez, founder of the Brown Berets and one of the original members of the Chicano Moratorium committee, said that anti-war protest was "a trend, a national trend, and we just made it into a Chicano trend."[14]

The leaders scheduled the Los Angeles march for August 29, 1970. It was the largest anti-war demonstration ever organized in the United States by people of Mexican descent. Demonstrators would come not only from California but also from other southwestern states.

A few weeks before the moratorium, Salazar openly expressed fear that the police were out to crush the movement. He wrote on June 19, 1970, that the "mood is not being helped by our political and law-and-order leaders who are trying to discredit militants in the barrios as subversive or criminal."[15]

On Friday afternoon, before the weekend's events, he made careful preparations with the various staffers at KMEX who were to cover the activities. Salazar mobilized all the station's news resources to cover what he expected to be a big event, even though he appeared to have forebodings of the tragedy that loomed.

Years later, Sally Salazar remembered her husband's unusual behavior in the days before the moratorium. Whenever he left the house, he made a point to tell her exactly where he was going, something he had never done regularly from their earliest days together. He also began to return straight home after work. At the office at KMEX, Salazar took pictures off the walls and packed some of his belongings. His desk, always a state of seeming chaos, was now clean and tidy, as if he were preparing for a long vacation.

The day before the Chicano Anti-War demonstration, Salazar wrote his final column. It was on the need to take drastic measures to improve the school system. When his friend Danny Villanueva said goodnight, Salazar told him that he would see him if he survived.

August 29, 1970, was warm and pleasant in Los Angeles. By the thousands the demonstrators arrived, greeted with Mexican music and a festive atmosphere. They sat on the grass to listen to the entertainment and speakers and prepared to begin a march that would follow a six-mile trek from Belvedere Park to Laguna Park in East Los Angeles.

The 30,000 marchers were there not only to protest the Vietnam War, a conflict that was taking the lives of a disproportionate number of Latinos; they were also there to give witness to a Mexican-American community that they felt was under siege in their own land. They protested against police discrimination and brutality, in favor of better schools, for better cultural awareness and appreciation, for greater acceptance of the use of the Spanish language in the United States, for increased political activism among Chicanos, and for a rousing pride in their heritage and people. They sang, waved flags, and enjoyed the camaraderie of the moment.

But once the marchers began the walk toward Laguna Park, a sense of ominous apprehension began to grip the scene. First, there were intermittent blasts of police sirens; then rumors began circulating that police were beginning to rough up and arrest some of the marchers in the front.

By 3:00 P.M., when most of the marchers had reached Laguna Park, a S.W.A.T. team of more than five hundred policemen began to sweep through the park. When police fired volleys of tear gas and stormed the crowd with nightsticks, the crowd stampeded. Some began to loot and trash property. Deputies later said that they were responding to a reported burglary at a liquor store and had been the targets of bottle and rock throwing. Panic and chaos soon engulfed the area. Tears from the gas mingled with blood and streamed down the faces of the demonstrators. Moratorium leaflets were dropped and scattered on the streets. It seemed like a scene from early Civil Rights marches in the South.

Cesar Chavez, the head of the United Farm Workers, was scheduled to speak that afternoon to the marchers. As the police sweep took effect, Chavez never reached the podium. One of the protesters who participated in the march said later:

> Once the riot broke out, all I remember is the chaos and fear. People screaming and scattering. Clusters of cops and civilians flailing at one another. Looters smashing shop windows. We had driven from Berkeley to Los Angeles to participate in the National Chicano Moratorium, a protest against the disproportionate number of Latinos dying in the Vietnam War. Suddenly, we found ourselves in the middle of a war right here at home.[16]

Bob Navarro, one of Salazar's colleagues, was with Salazar at the Moratorium. As the melee intensified, the two separated. Later, Navarro remembered Salazar calling out to him, "'Be careful, Bob,' he said. 'You be careful,' I replied, 'I'm leaving.'"[17]

To avoid the violence, Salazar ducked into a crowded local bar called the Silver Dollar shortly before 8:00 P.M. Police later claimed that they had information that suspected militants responsible for the riot were inside the Silver Dollar and were armed. A squad from the Special Enforcement Bureau surrounded the bar and demanded that those inside come out and surrender.

In the tense atmosphere, with people in the bar now becoming more fearful of their predicament, one of the policemen got ready to fire a tear gas canister through the window. As most of the patrons rushed out the back door, Salazar was still sitting at the bar. One of his friends yelled out to him to leave, that the police were going to shoot.

In the next instant, a quick volley of three, 10-inch tear gas projectiles ripped through one of the windows; one of them ripped through Salazar's head.

Octavio Gomez, a KMEX cameraman, was with Salazar in the Silver Dollar. When the lights in the bar went dark and the police began yelling, Gomez, along with other patrons, rushed to the back and then outside. Moments later, after the tear gas explosions, he became very concerned about Salazar and tried to get back inside. The police stopped him. He rushed back to KMEX and talked with Roberto Cruz, head anchorman of the station. "When Octavio came back to the station," Cruz remembered, "I asked, 'How about Ruben?' He said, 'I think he was hurt. Maybe he's in the hospital.' We didn't know he was already dead."[18]

The investigation into Salazar's death became a major media event in Los Angeles. For sixteen days, live television broadcasts riveted the attention of the city as the police defended their actions at the march while Chicanos blamed Salazar's death on police brutality and overreaction. Some Chicanos suggested that the police had purposely targeted Salazar and that his death was not an accident but an assassination.

A well-known Chicano attorney and writer, Oscar Zeta Acosta—also known as the Brown Buffalo—accused authorities of criminal conspiracy. The shooter was identified as Deputy Thomas Wilson. When asked where he was aiming when he fired the projectiles, he said he was aiming at the ceiling of the bar. Speaking of the police shooter, Acosta railed at the inquest, "He was aiming at Ruben Salazar, that's what he was aiming at! This is an obscenity.... We are sick of it. This room is polluted with perjury and you know it!" Acosta then led a group of about twenty-five Chicano militants out of the court and announced that the group would boycott the rest of the hearings.[19]

Aside from Acosta, Cora Barba was perhaps the most compelling witness. One of the marchers, who had been a tear-gas victim, she told the inquest gathering that the violence had not been perpetrated by the marchers but by a zealous police force: "I don't want people to be blaming my people. Everybody blames all Chicanos. And I'm proud to be a Chicana. I will always be a Chicana and if I have to die being a Chicana, I'm going to die being a Chicana. And I don't want them talking about my people that way."[20]

District Attorney Evelle Younger concluded that the facts from the inquest did not justify criminal charges against Deputy Wilson or the sheriff's department. The U.S. Department of Justice also refused to get involved in the matter of Salazar's death, even after twenty-two California state legislators asked for an investigation. Although authorities ruled Salazar's death accidental, Los Angeles County paid $700,000 to his widow and three children.

Shortly after Salazar was killed, the famed journalist Hunter Thompson, who had himself been assaulted during the protests at the 1968 Democratic National Convention in Chicago, came to Los Angeles to investigate the story. In the April 29, 1971, issue of *Rolling Stone*, Thompson wrote "Strange Rumblings in Aztlan." Thompson's masterful piece about the rise of the Chicano movement, the oppression of Latinos, and the tragedy in the Silver Dollar made the life and death of Ruben Salazar a national and international story. Thompson wrote:

> Middle-aged housewives who had never thought of themselves as anything but lame-status 'Mexican Americans' just trying to get by in a mean Gringo world they never made suddenly found themselves shouting 'Viva La Raza' *in public*. And their husbands—quiet Safeway clerks and lawn-care salesmen, the lowest and most expendable cadres in the Great Gabacho economic machine—were volunteering to testify; yes, to stand up in court, or wherever, and calling themselves Chicanos.[21]

LATINO HERO

In the life of Ruben Salazar, Chicano pride found a unifying symbol. From California to Texas, parks, libraries, university buildings, scholarships, and housing projects were named after him. Salazar's life inspired murals and other pieces of artwork. He appeared as a fierce symbol of resistance in a number of books including Lucha Corpi's 1992 thriller *Eulogy for a Brown Angel* and in Oscar Acosta's *The Revolt of the Cockroach People*.

In 1971, Salazar was posthumously awarded the Robert F. Kennedy Journalism Award. Known as the "Poor People's Pulitzer," the award honors outstanding reporting of the lives and strife of disadvantaged people throughout the world.

In 1999, the California Chicano News Media Association established the annual Ruben Salazar Journalism Awards. The awards recognize work published or broadcast in California that exemplifies journalistic excellence while contributing to a better understanding of Latinos.

The National Association of Hispanic Journalists established the Ruben Salazar Scholarship Fund to encourage Hispanic students to pursue careers in the field of print, photo, broadcast, or online journalism.

At the time of Salazar's death, his children were quite young: Lisa, the eldest, was nine years old, Stephanie was seven, and John was five. Twenty years after her father's death, Lisa said, "Because I was so young at the time of his death, I fantasized that it was all a mistake and that one day he would be back. In the very short time that I did have my Dad, I remember a happy, funny man who always told us he loved us and had special nicknames for us. He took good care of us, and we shared special times together as a family. It hurts, but I often like to look back at family photos because there on his face it is very clear to see the love he had for us."[22]

Even to his wife Sally, the honors and awards seemed to obscure the man behind the myth. On the tenth anniversary of his death, Sally Salazar wrote, "My memories are confused by the murals and memorials and a creation built in the public mind—someone other people call Ruben Salazar, but someone to this day I don't fully recognize… someone he himself may have just been in the process of discovering."[23]

"Salazar's death was a devastating loss to a community that was just starting to find its voice," wrote Frank del Olmo, a *Times* editor who knew Salazar personally. "For he seemed to be taking not just his own journalism but that of the *Times* to a new level that matched the passion being expressed on the city's streets."[24]

He tackled issues still being hotly debated today: immigration, race, affirmative action. Journalist Juan Gonzalez, a prominent member of the National Association of Hispanic Journalists, said, "The death of Ruben Salazar really sparked the organization of Latino journalists around the country, and there are many organizations, including our own, who have scholarship funds in his name. He was well loved throughout the Latino community of Los Angeles, but has become sort of a martyr figure among Latino journalists in terms of his work, his dedication to the Latino community, and his journalism."[25]

Nevertheless, the road to respect and recognition for the Latino community has been slow. In May 1995, at the opening of the new headquarters of the Mexican American Opportunity Foundation, a number of speakers praised Salazar as an icon. Unveiling a hall of fame of heroes of Mexican descent, the members of the Foundation made Salazar the first member and, in addition, called it the "Ruben Salazar Mexican Hall of Fame." Many of the speakers said that Salazar would be horrified at the anti-immigrant sentiment sweeping southern California. One of the speakers, Antonio Barrajas, said, "Can you imagine that after all Chicanos, and other Latinos for that matter, have done for this country, people still want to kick us out?"[26]

Salazar had written shortly before his death:

> There is much bitterness in our Mexican-American community, an ever-increasing bitterness against school systems that psychologically mutilate the Chicano child, against certain police who habitually harass our brown brothers, against local and federal governments that apparently respond only to violence.[27]

Salazar was the first Latino journalist to cross into big-time English-language journalism. He was also the first Mexican-American journalist to become an important foreign correspondent. He was a bridge builder, trying to bring reluctant people together and to bring greater understanding of the lives of Latinos.

Shortly before his death, Salazar was interviewed on a Los Angeles television station. The interviewer asked Salazar if he was an advocacy journalist. Salazar said that if the question was whether he advocated for his people, a people who have been silenced in the rest of the media, then he pleaded guilty.

NOTES

1. Mario Garcia, ed., *Border Correspondent: Selected Writings, 1955–1970: Ruben Salazar*, Berkeley: University of California Press, 1998, 41–42.

2. Michael Quintanilla, "The Trailblazer," *Los Angeles Times*, August 21, 1995, 1.

3. Garcia, 47.

4. Garcia, 78.

5. Garcia, 70.

6. Garcia, 109.

7. Garcia, 171.

8. "Ruben Salazar: Honoring an Icon in L.S.'s Latino Community," *Los Angeles Times*, October 13, 2006, B2.

9. David Gomez, "The Killing of Ruben Salazar: 'Nothing Has Been Changed in the Barrio.'" *The Christian Century*, January 13, 1971, 50.

10. Quintanilla.

11. "The National Chicano Moratorium: Ruben Salazar, Digital History," http://www.digitalhistory.uh.edu/mexican_voices/voices_display.cfm?id=117.

12. Robert J. Lopez, "FBI Files Shed Little Light on Ruben Salazar's Death," *Los Angeles Times*, November 18, 1999, 1.

13. Earl Shorris, *Latinos: A Biography of the People*. New York: Norton, 8.

14. Lorena Oropeza, "Making History: The Chicano Movement, Occasional Paper No. 17, The Making of the Moratorium and the History of the Movement," Julian Samora Research Institute, http://www.jsri.msu.edu/RandS/research/ops/oc17.html.

15. Garcia, 261.

16. Agustin Gurza, "A Reporter's Contribution to the Latino Movement," *Los Angeles Times*, December 5, 1999, 6.

17. Bob Navarro, "Commentary: The Day the Latino Beacon Died," *Los Angeles Times*, August 30, 1990, 1.

18. Valerie Nelson, "Octavio Gomez, 71; Cameraman Helped Cover Latino Civil Rights Movement," *Los Angeles Times*, January 27, 2006, B10.

19. Gomez.

20. Gomez.

21. Hunter S. Thompson, *Fear and Loathing in Las Vegas and Other American Stories*, New York: The Modern Library, 1996, 220–221.

22. Garcia, 36.

23. Garcia.

24. Gurza.

25. Amy Goodman and Juan Gonzalez, "Remembering Latino Journalist Ruben Salazar Who Was Gunned Down in 1970 by the LAPD," February 24th, 2005, http://www.democracynow.org/article.pl?sid=05/02/24/155226.

26. George Ramos, "Angry Words of Ruben Salazar Remain Potent," *Los Angeles Times*, May 15, 1995, 3.

27. David Gomez, *Somos Chicanos: Strangers in Our Own Land*, Boston: Beacon Press, 1973, 131–132.

FURTHER READING

Garcia, Mario. *Ruben Salazar: Border Correspondent*. Berkeley, University of California Press, 1998.

Gomez, David. *Somos Chicanos: Strangers in Our Own Land*. Boston: Beacon Press, 1973.

Salazar, Ruben. *Strangers in One's Land*. Publication No. 19. U.S. Commission on Civil Rights Clearinghouse, May 1970.

Shorris, Earl. *Latinos: A Biography of the People*. New York: W. W. Norton & Co., 1992.

Thompson, Hunter S. *Fear and Loathing in Las Vegas and other American Stories*. New York: The Modern Library, 1996.

Thompson, Hunter S. "Strange Rumblings in Aztlan." *Rolling Stone*, April 29, 1971.

Courtesy of Photofest

Carlos Santana

Music fans across the globe called it "The Santana Sound." It was hard to describe but unmistakable, a haunting mix of guitar, organ, percussion, and rocking bass, all with an Afro-Cuban flavor. Its creator was Carlos Santana. From dirt-poor beginnings in Mexico to San Francisco, Santana followed the footsteps of his musician father and then discovered his own signature blend of sounds. Always innovative, ever changing, and growing with the times, the renowned guitarist remained a musical force from the early 1970s through the beginning of the new century.

Santana created a highly successful blend of salsa, rock, blues, and jazz. He became an icon in both rock and Latin music, a guitarist who took the blues as preached by B. B. King and played them with the soul of a world-class Mexican mariachi musician.

A spiritual man with deep humanitarian instincts, he became not only a towering musical figure but also a philanthropist, an individual driven in his pursuit to give to as many people worldwide as he could a deeper appreciation and sense of discovery of music and other artistic expressions that enrich the soul.

FAMILY ROOTS

Carlos Santana was the middle of seven children of Jose and Josefina Santana, and he was born on July 20, 1947, in Autlan de Navarro, a small village in Mexico. A subtropical agricultural community in the Costa Sur region in the southwestern state of Jalisco, the town had few of the creature comforts found in larger cities and was home mostly to a peasant lifestyle. There were no paved roads, and only a scattering of buildings that had electricity. It seemed almost like a place out of another century.

Santana's father was a mariachi violinist, well known to locals, who played at many community events and gatherings. "My memories… were that everyone loved my Dad," Santana remembered. "He was the darling of the town. Everybody wanted my Dad to play for their weddings, baptisms, whatever. My father supported my mom, my four sisters, and two brothers in Mexico with his music."[1]

Both Jose Santana's father and grandfather had been musicians. Carlos also seemed drawn to music at an early age. His father tried to teach him the violin when he was five years old, but, looking back, Carlos joked that the violin seemed outside his inner being. No matter how hard he tried, he later remembered, the sounds seemed infantile and awkward. Nevertheless, under his father's patient tutelage, he became increasingly competent with the instrument.

Jose Santana's own musical ambitions were greater than weddings and baptisms. He had been schooled in classical music, played the music of Agustin Lara, the legendary Mexican composer, and was knowledgeable about folk music from around the world. In the Santana home, the sounds of Mozart and Beethoven often flowed from the radio or phonograph.

In the early 1950s, Jose Santana formed a band called Los Cardinales and took it to the bustling, small border city of Tijuana, a few miles from San Diego, California. Unlike the rural, agricultural area that he left behind, Tijuana offered Jose Santana the possibilities of gaining a name for himself and financial footing for his family.

Although the city itself was nearly barren of industry, it attracted many tourists from the United States looking for cheap nightlife. It boasted such establishments as "La Ballena" (The Whale), which claimed to have the longest bar in the world. In such establishments Jose Santana would try to turn his mariachi band into a successful venture.

With its proximity to the United States, Tijuana was also a major stopping point for Mexican citizens eager to become American citizens. In 1955, a year after Jose Santana took Los Cardinales to Tijuana, Josephina Santana sold nearly all of the family's personal possessions to get enough money to load her and the seven children into a taxicab for the thousand-mile trip to join her husband in Tijuana.

Tijuana was not a garden spot to raise a family. The town, with all of its trappings, was something of a way station for those looking for something better but now stuck in congestion and chaos. It teemed with hustlers and sellers, from cheap trinkets in the tourist shops to the sordid nightspots on the downtown strip.

Santana said of those first years in the city, "When we first landed in Tijuana from Autlan Jalisco in '55, we lived… in a house with no running water, no electricity, and so it smells the same thing in Tijuana or Hong Kong or India or Africa. Poverty," he said, "smells the same."[2]

For now, the Santana family would bide its time and seek to get ahead. Carlos joined his father's mariachi band, and later the family scraped together enough money to enroll the boy in a local music school. His father recognized the boy's musical ear and gifts, and they spent long hours together as Jose strove to give Carlos a grounding in the melodies of Mexican music, always emphasizing the importance of feeling and focusing on each note and gesture. The discipline and appreciation that the father instilled in these early years, as well as the lessons from music instructors, paved the way for the emergence of an extraordinary talent.

"My father turned me on to European music, very sophisticated music," Santana recalled. "Later on, when we came to Tijuana he taught me traditional Mexican songs. But what I received in my DNA from my father is charisma. My father has a lot of charisma. My mother has a lot of conviction. So between charisma and conviction, voila, you know, you have me."[3]

By the time he was ten years old, Santana could be seen on downtown Tijuana street corners with his father, his violin, and a hat on the ground. For fifty cents a song, tourists could hear a good rendition of "Mexicali Rose." On Sundays, young Santana often played music in the church orchestra.

On some nights, however, the scene was much different. Jose Santana would often take Carlos with him into some of the bars to play with the house bands. Here, the focus was never on the music but on hard-drinking, frequent brawls, and open sexual display—a scene in no way appropriate for a young teenager.

Later, Santana would say that the atmosphere in the bars, where no one was particularly interested or impressed with the music, was one of the reasons that he turned to other forms of musical expression. Mariachi music came to represent to him a form with little dignity. At one point, the young musician told his father that he no longer wanted to play mariachi. Nevertheless, with that outburst behind him, he would continue to help support the family and play the music for the dollars. He would never again, however, do it with much enthusiasm.

The young Santana was now in the grip of the new rock and roll sounds from the United States. At a downtown plaza, a rock and roll band played the latest hits from Chuck Berry, Little Richard, and B. B. King. Fascinated by the sounds of the electric guitar and the rich beats of rock and roll and rhythm and blues, he now sensed where his future in music might land.

After a few years in Tijuana, Jose Santana was prepared to begin the family's next journey. When his application for United States citizenship was granted, he moved to the barrio section of San Francisco, around Van Ness and Mission Streets. Just as he had done in Tijuana, he worked to establish a foothold and then asked that the family join him in the new home.

After a few months, he was able to put together a small band at a local Latino club and begin to earn some money. When he heard through family correspondence from Tijuana that his son had turned away from the violin and now wanted to become a guitar player, he did not hesitate to act. A few weeks later, in mail delivered from San Francisco, young Carlos Santana opened a package containing a hollow-bodied Gibson L5 electric guitar. The ecstatic youngster began the long process of mastering the new instrument. With his musical training and knowledge of other instruments he had gained from his father, the boy had a solid foundation upon which to build.

Young Santana was like a musical sponge. He soaked up sounds of rock and roll, Spanish ballads, everything he could find on the family's radio. He practiced endlessly the melodies and beats and experimented constantly, always keeping in mind the teachings of his father that each note deserved attention. The flourishes and lush sounds gradually evolved.

He especially liked the blues sounds of artists such as Chuck Berry, Bobby Bland, and John Lee Hooker. Sometimes, when he had studied his own father's playing, Santana had noticed that the sounds often resembled human voices, with all their passions and cries of both joy and despair. He heard those notes clearly in B. B. King's music and tried to match the intensity, all the while experimenting with various combinations of sounds.

He would take inspiration from many of the masters and work out his own sounds and interpretations. In these early months were planted the seeds that would become the Santana sound.

The youngster soon joined a local band called The Strangers. Playing dances and small gigs around Tijuana, he began to earn small amounts of money. Later, he quit the band and moved to a club called El Convoy, in the very heart of the Tijuana strip on Revolution Avenue. Beginning at 4:00 P.M. with shifts throughout the night until 4:00 A.M., the teenager took in all the sights and sounds of the strip shows, the drug dealing, the violent outbursts and rush of police, the prostitution, and the air of danger swirling around the mean streets.

All the while, the band at El Convoy was giving the young guitarist a fast introduction to playing before often indifferent crowds. The musicians, nevertheless, took their work seriously. Because the clientele of the club included blacks, Santana played with the band the latest blues and rhythm and blues hits, especially material from Ray Charles and Bobby Bland. From these early experiences with blacks in the club, Santana not only gained an appreciation of black music but also of black culture and both became musical inspirations throughout his life and career.

In the spring of 1962, Santana, not yet sixteen years old, received word, along with the rest of the family, that his father was ready for them to join him in San Francisco. He balked. He was happy with the way things were there on the strip. He was making money, hanging out with other musicians, enjoying the flirtations of many women, and generally feeling quite macho.

His mother finally persuaded the reluctant Santana to join the rest of the family as they stepped on the bus in Tijuana to head for San Francisco. For the duration of the journey and for the first three months in California, however, Santana complained about the disruption of his life. Although he gravitated toward a few musicians his own age in the city for a few weeks, he was not ready to let Tijuana go from his life. He decided to leave and return to Mexico.

Arriving back in Tijuana late one night with about twenty dollars in his pocket, the youngster managed to convince the owner of El Convoy to hire him once again. "First I stayed with the drummer at this funky hotel his aunt used to own," Carlos said later, "and then we both got thrown out and I started staying with one of my mom's friends back in the old neighborhood."[4]

Santana lived in Tijuana for a year making enough money to stay afloat while living with friends. But the family had not given up trying to convince the teenager to return to San Francisco. In the late summer of 1963, his mother and Tony, Carlos' older brother, traveled to Tijuana to try once again to convince the young guitarist that life held greater chances for success in northern California. There, far more than in Tijuana, a young, rock music scene was just beginning to develop. Carlos, they argued, could grow with it.

Finally, although angry and rebellious, he agreed to return. After arriving in San Francisco, he brooded, locking himself away in his room for hours on end. He threatened again to return to Mexico. After a few months, however, the anger subsided. He was ready to get on with his life in California.

A LIFE IN SAN FRANCISCO

In Tijuana, young Santana had gotten an adult slice of life. Now, in San Francisco, he again became a student, briefly at James Lick Junior High and then in Mission High School. He gradually improved his English and tried to fit in as best he could. When he looked back at those uneasy times, he said that it was enormously challenging to his psyche and ego to be dragged back into the role of an adolescent, a role that in his own mind he had long ago passed. After all, he had worked in nightclubs, watched strippers on stage, and hustled for quarters playing music on street corners. He was now a shaky high school student with a language problem and no study skills. It was all, he said, a drag.

He did encounter one art teacher at Mission High that challenged Santana to make the most of his talents. Whatever his immediate past, however little he had progressed as a student, Santana was made aware by that teacher that he had imagination and an eye for art, and that such gifts held great promise for him.

When the teacher took Carlos and other students to an art museum in San Francisco, Santana later remembered, "That's when he told me that in the real world, there was no room for fifty–fifty, meaning I had to give one hundred percent to become an artist or a musician, to follow my dreams. When he told me that, I started crying.... He had passion for me an as individual. He wasn't painting everyone with the same brush."[5]

Still, Santana's attention was less on school and almost totally on the musical talents of such legends as B. B. King and James Brown. His father was not enthusiastic about his son continuing his musical career. He had spent his whole life following that hard path, and it had led to infrequent work in Mexican restaurants and occasional small gigs that paid little. His wife was now working in a laundromat. He did not wish that fate upon his son.

But Carlos Santana was not deterred. "I had worked so hard to learn the guitar and worked strip clubs in Tijuana to buy my first guitar," he said. "I was so mad at him that I became more determined to play my music...."[6]

For a time, Santana lived with his family in San Francisco. Nevertheless, the tensions grew. He continued in high school but was often absent, cutting classes to hang out at music halls and bars. Not only did his father object to his ambitions to continue toward a career in music, but also relations between Carlos and his mother grew heated. That's when the youngster took another major step. Later he remembered, "Mom wanted us to live according to her rigid sense of right and wrong. I was a hippie, and we couldn't talk about anything, so I moved out, roaming San Francisco with my friends and playing my guitar to make money. We played at weddings and at the YMCA in the Mission."[7]

His break with his family did not shatter his emotional ties to them. His parents and brothers and sisters remained close to his heart and he would later share with them some of his triumphs. But he was now a teenager in the streets of the San Francisco Mission District, a young guitarist like others who had come to the city looking for their future.

Santana put together a small group to play parties, bar mitzvahs, and weddings. His music now had an authentic blues flavor that mixed with the Latin beats and melodies he had learned in his earliest years playing the violin. He also partnered with a vocalist named Joyce Dunn from nearby Daly City, a promising soul singer. In 1965, a local radio station sponsored a "battle of the bands" competition for local groups. Held in San Francisco's huge auditorium, the Cow Palace, Santana's group made a respectable showing.

Santana took a part-time job at a drive-in diner on Third Street named the Tic-Toc. Washing dishes, scrubbing floors, and peeling potatoes helped pay the bills along with his occasional music gigs. Never part of a growing number of teenage gangs in the lower-class neighborhoods of the city, Santana was, instead, focused almost entirely on music. One notable event in his life helped convince him that he would never turn back.

One day at Tic-Toc, he said later, things became clear in his mind. "Everything culminated to this time where the Grateful Dead pulled over in a couple of limousines to buy some hamburgers," he said. "They just did a gig and I was peeling potatoes, bleaching floors, busing dishes and washing dishes, and I saw them, you know. And something told me, if they can do this, I can do this…. That day was the beginning of the best part of my life because I discovered Carlos."[8]

In October 1966, life changed for Santana. He met music promoter Bill Graham. Born Wolfgang Grajonca in Berlin in 1931, Graham escaped Nazi persecution by walking hundreds of miles to safety. He made it to New York and was raised by foster parents. In the 1950s, he moved to San Francisco with dreams to be an actor. Instead, he connected with a number of performers as a business manager, including the San Francisco Mime Troupe.

When the troupe was arrested in 1965 on obscenity charges, Graham organized a benefit for their legal defense at a venue called The Fillmore, formerly a dance hall at Geary and Fillmore Steets on the outskirts of the city's black community. The event was a huge success and launched

Graham's career as a music promoter, using the Fillmore as his main concert site. One of the early concerts featured The Grateful Dead, and it began a close association between Graham and the increasingly influential group.

As the Vietnam War dragged on into the late 1960s, San Francisco and especially nearby Berkeley, California, home of the University of California, became a hotbed of left-wing, anti-war protest. The city had also witnessed the remarkable growth of a counter-culture movement, anti-establishment and communal, promoting a lifestyle of free love, peace, and the glories of psychedelic drugs. And music was its soul.

Bill Graham's shows became the center of the infant, vibrant San Francisco music scene, one that would become a mecca for counterculture ideas and music. Graham began slowly to create combinations of acts that fused jazz, blues, and folk artists, along with popular rock bands. One might walk into the Fillmore and find Miles Davis sharing a bill with the Staple Singers or Steppenwolf.

Another of Graham's early acts was the Butterfield Blues Band, featuring the hugely talented harp player, Paul Butterfield, and renowned guitarist Paul Bloomfield. On that October day in 1966, Santana was in the Fillmore watching Jerry Garcia of the Grateful Dead and others jamming on stage, preparing for the night's show. When one of the members of the Butterfield Blues Band did not show up, one of Santana's friends suggested to Graham that the kid from Mexico fill in at the night's concert. Graham agreed. What Graham saw that night was superstar quality and, with his sharp instincts for talent, he recognized it immediately. After the dazzling performance, Graham asked Santana if he had a band already in place or was looking to create one.

Throughout the Bay Area's music community, Santana's name was suddenly hot. At the performance at the Fillmore, a guitar player named Tom Frazier had been in the audience. Frazier was a friend of another musician named Gregg Rolie, a keyboard player from the San Francisco suburb of Palo Alto, home of Stanford University. When Frazier told Rolie what he had seen on stage that night, the two decided to locate Santana with the idea of forming a new group.

In 1966, Santana and Rolie formed the Santana Blues Band along with Tom Frazier on guitar, Gus Rodrigues on bass, Danny Haro on drums, and Michael Carabello on congas. They started rehearsing in a garage just outside the Mission District. Rolie, who owned his own car, would drive in from Palo Alto for the rehearsals. The others in the band, who had no cars, regarded him as wealthy. The group had little percussion equipment and nothing resembling sophisticated amplification. But they soon had a sound. It would take some time and some replacement parts, but the band was on its way.

In the hot music scene of San Francisco in the 1960s, new bands were appearing all the time. It was not easy to get noticed. But news of Santana and his group spread quickly. Blending an Afro-Cuban beat with a fast-tempo rock and blues base and low-key vocals, the band worked on a new fusion of blues, Latin, and rock. They experimented with blues versions of songs by Ray Charles, B. B. King, Little Milton, and others. This was a unique blend of jazz, salsa, and rock. It featured Carlos Santana's usual high-pitched guitar with such Latin instruments as timbales and congas.

"We were exclusively a blues band at first," Santana said. "People ask me how the change took place, and I think it was because we used to go to "hippie hill" at San Francisco's Aquatic Park, and there'd be people playing congas and drinking wine. That's where we got the congas in the band. And then I heard Gabor Szabo, and his *Spellbinder* album had congas on it. Somebody brought this conga player to jam with us, and he threw us into a whole different thing. Actually, we never play 'Latin music.' It's a crossover. I just play whatever I hear."[9]

At the beginning of 1967, the Santana Blues Band was mostly working just on weekends. Several months later, Bill Graham began to use the band at the Fillmore to stand in for acts that did not show up or as the opening act for such headliners as Sly Stone and Creedence Clearwater Revival.

By this time, Bill Graham and the Fillmore were attracting such talents as Jefferson Airplane, Led Zeppelin, The Doors, and Janis Joplin. He brought in not only famous rock groups but also singers such as Otis Redding and even poets.

It was in 1967 that Santana first saw B. B. King at the Fillmore. "That's when I knew I would be nothing else but that, no matter what. I'm very blessed," he said later. "I'm very fortunate, because what I know I've known all my life and that's all I want to know. I didn't want to know about algebra or George Washington's morals or wooden teeth or whatever. I could hardly wait to get out of school so I could go buy some John Lee Hooker records or Wes Montgomery records and tear 'em apart."[10]

In 1968, Bill Graham moved the Fillmore into another old dance hall, the Carousel Ballroom, and called it the Fillmore West. The Santana Blues Band made their first appearance at Fillmore West in the late summer. Graham also opened a club in New York called the Fillmore East.

By early 1969, the Santana Blues Band had made important changes. Carlos Santana and Gregg Rolie were now backed up by Michael Shrieve on drums, the returning Michael Carabello on congas, Jose Chepito Areas as percussionist, and David Brown on bass. The group was a veritable melting pot of nationalities—a Chicano, a Puerto Rican, a Nicaraguan, a black American, and two white suburbanites.

Realizing the enormous potential of the group, Bill Graham took over management of the band. In the spring of 1969, Graham scheduled a recording session at the Pacific Recording Studios in San Mateo to produce the band's first album. Graham even suggested that one of the tracks on the album be an urban-guitar mix of Latin and rhythm and blues called "Evil Ways." Graham knew he could get extensive radio play on this single.

Approximately a year after first playing at the Fillmore West, an accomplishment Carlos Santana would cherish for the rest of his life, thanks to the efforts of Bill Graham, the band had another date in the summer of 1969 that would live in Santana's memory forever. It was at a large field in upstate New York.

WOODSTOCK

In August 1969, an estimated 400,000 young people turned up for a three-day event to hear big-name bands play in an open-air venue near the town of Woodstock, New York. The name "Woodstock" would became emblematic of the anti–Vietnam War movement and the youthful, hippie, drug culture of the 1960s. It would also become emblematic of the growing popularity of young rock musicians and the vast potential that lay ahead for the music industry.

About 186,000 tickets had been sold in advance of the open-air concert, so promoters were expecting about 200,000 to show up. But on the first night, when the rickety fences failed to hold a growing swarm of humanity, organizers announced that the concert was free. Soon an ever-growing number of cars, trucks, motorcycles, and other vehicles began to clog traffic for some fifty miles leading to the town of Woodstock. Later estimates said that over 1,000,000 individuals made an effort to get to the site.

During those three days, there was a great deal of drinking, drug use, nudity, sex, rain, and mud, but little violence. Indeed, the festival's chief medical officer, William Abruzzi, said, "These people are really beautiful. There has been no violence whatsoever, which is really remarkable for a crowd of this size."[11]

Situated in the middle of the field, the stage was nearly surrounded by the crowd. The concertgoers reveled in the music of such artists as Janis Joplin, The Who, The Grateful Dead, Canned Heat, Crosby, Stills, Nash & Young, Joan Baez, Ravi Shankar, and Jimi Hendrix. "When I first heard Jimi Hendrix," Santana remembered, "I thought, 'My God, this guy has a different kind of brush. His was much thicker than everyone else's. They were using tiny little brushes and doing watercolors, while he was painting galactic scenes in CinemaScope.'"[12]

The concert also featured a young performer and his band that most had never seen or heard—Santana. Carlos was nervous and, like many of his fellow performers, somewhat high on drugs. Later, remembering the scene when he made his way up to the stage to face a seemingly endless landscape of faces, he said he kept asking God to help him stay in time and in tune.

The band played a piece specially written for the event called "Soul Sacrifice." Despite the array of talent that preceded and followed Santana on stage, his band and his own artistic wizardry were now imprinted on the

Memories of Santana at Woodstock

It was the largest rock concert ever—three days of music under the sun and stars. From all across the United States they came, hundreds of thousands drawn by the publicity, the lineup of rock sensations, and the promise to be part of the party to end all parties. Mostly they were young people—many were counterculture hippies, most were against the war in Vietnam.

For three days in August 1969, in a field in a small town of upstate New York, the legend of Woodstock began. From its opening act, when singer and guitarist Richie Havens took the stage at 5:07 P.M. on August 15, 1969, through Jimi Hendrix's "Star-Spangled Banner" to close the festival, the superstars of rock music performed, including Joan Baez; The Band; Blood, Sweat & Tears; Paul Butterfield; Canned Heat; Joe Cocker; Creedence Clearwater Revival; Crosby, Stills, Nash & Young; The Grateful Dead; Arlo Guthrie; Jimi Hendrix; The Jefferson Airplane; Janis Joplin; Country Joe McDonald; Melanie; Ravi Shankar; Sly and the Family Stone; The Who; and others. One of the performers was relatively unknown. Here are some reactions of those who saw Santana's unforgettable performance:

Kevin Galvin, nineteen-year old freshman at Lemoyne College, Syracuse, New York: "We eventually made our way toward the music and stage, hopping onto cars that were inching their way along. When we finally found a spot on the hill that formed a semicircle around the stage, we had to sit there for some very long periods. The soil was damp and giving off a strong smell of manure—it was farmland after all. But the people-watching was world class, as you can imagine. One of the highlights, musically, was that rockin' Spanish-looking band. Of course it was Santana, whom we had not heard of before that day."[1]

Richard "Cheech" Marin, twenty-two-year-old Californian who would soon form a comedy team with Tommy Chong: "When he stepped to the front of the stage and when he started playing there was, like, no separation between what he was thinking and what he was feeling and what was coming out of those speakers and those guitars."[2]

Mickey Hart, twenty-five-year-old drummer with The Grateful Dead: "It was all those guys coming out in the catharsis, this one great outpouring of magnificent energy and it just gave it up and people just sucked it in and they all came together in this one beautiful organism. And that's what did it."[3]

---

[1] "Woodstock memories abound 38 years later," *The Buffalo News*, August 15, 2007, http://www.buffalonews.com/opinion/myview/story/141353.html.

[2] "Carlos Santana: At Woodstock," http://www.biography.com/broadband/main.do?video= bio-top250-santana-woodstock.

[3] "Carlos Santana: At Woodstock."

minds of thousands. The power, the shuddering crescendos of sound, the energy—all of it was on full display. When a motion picture and other clips of the event were aired later, a much larger part of the music public knew what Bill Graham already knew—that this was a guitarist and a band destined for greatness.

The Woodstock event would also symbolize another aspect of Santana that Carlos and the other members of the band had never intended when they gradually came together as a unit. The band was racially integrated and, to many people, a symbol of third world achievement. After the release of the film, Carlos became an instant Latino celebrity, not only in the United States but also in other countries. Percussionist Chepito Areas was suddenly a hero in his native Nicaragua. The integration also took another form—that of the music. The roots were a fusion of Latin, Afro, blues, and other musical forms, a synthesis of sound that represented collaboration and respect.

For Carlos Santana, Woodstock seemed like something of a personal emotional watershed. He talked later of how it all symbolized the power of peace over violence. He talked about how those at the event and hundreds of thousands of others like them helped stop a wretched war. He talked about how the music raised the consciousness of a nation, about how the hippie generation demonstrated that thousands could gather to share and not to fight. "It was a celebration of people's principles and colors," he said, "a living, breathing ocean of flesh. The music made us feel that we were not alone, you know?"[13]

Max Yasgur, the forty-nine-year old dairy farmer who provided not only his land but also $50,000 for the concert, said it more simply: "You have proven something to the world... that half a million kids can get together for fun and music and have nothing but fun and music."[14]

CHANGING SOUNDS AND SPIRIT

With Santana's enormous success at Woodstock, doors began to open. The group appeared on one of the most influential and watched television programs in the history of the entertainment industry, the Ed Sullivan Show. They signed a contract with Columbia Records; their first album, recorded before the Woodstock appearance, rolled up the Billboard charts. Entitled *Santana*, the work eventually sold more than four million copies.

In 1970, riding a wave of success, Santana released its second album, *Abraxas*. This featured the classic rock staple "Oye Como Va," originally written and recorded in 1962 by the heralded Latino bandleader Tito Puente. It was a hit that rose to the higher echelons of the rock charts.

Santana said later, "We did it differently than el maestro Tito Puente, and that's why they recognized it [around] the whole globe. We took something wonderful to begin with and we injected something different. It's called multidimensional consciousness. The way Tito did it was more Cuban and Puerto Rican. But we put a multidimensional clave in it, multidimensional feel and color. Therefore, not only Cubans and Puerto Ricans liked it. The whole world liked it." What Santana had done and expressed so well, is what Puente had encouraged—constant fusion, development, and mixing.[15]

Asked later what was the one single moment that he felt was the defining moment of his career, Santana said, "When we played at the Fillmore West in 1970, and Tito Puente and Miles Davis were there three nights in a row in the balcony cheering for us. That's when I knew it wasn't a passing thing or something that was [just] OK. I knew we were bringing something to the table that was important. When I saw Mr. Tito Puente and Mr. Miles Davis cheering for us, that was confirmation that we were doing something right."[16]

In 1971 the group produced another highly successful album, *Santana III*. Meanwhile, Carlos became increasingly fond of jazz, and in 1972 he worked with Buddy Miles to record his first effort without the rest of the band.

As many music groups over the years had discovered, often the personal chemistry and individual idiosyncrasies of the members clashed. In many cases, the camaraderie of creating music could not overcome the personality differences. The Santana Blues Band experienced such a breakup in the early 1970s.

Members of the band began to shift, some moving on to other groups and others starting groups of their own. But the mainstay of the band had been Carlos Santana himself. A new generation of listeners had begun to hum and imitate such singles as "Evil Ways," "Jingo," and "Black Magic Woman," and fans were buying everything that he produced. He was now an established force in the music industry. He could go on with his musical career with new musicians at his side. His creative artistry and genius were free to range over new landscapes.

DEBORAH KING

Deborah King, Santana's future wife, was raised in San Francisco by her father, the respected black jazz guitarist Saunders King, "King of the Blues," who had worked with Billie Holliday, and her mother, Jo Frances Willis, a Texas woman of Irish-English ancestry.

When Deborah was in the third grade at San Miguel Elementary School, a group of older children confronted her. One girl snorted, "Your mama's as white as day, and your daddy's as black as night." As she later looked back on the incident, she realized that the moment was a turning point. Never again would she be able to see her family as colorless. But the moment was also a revelation. As she watched the events of the civil rights movement unfold over the years, she felt a growing appreciation of the struggles that had come before, the sacrifices and strength of those who had fought racism and bigotry. "I sought to make my biracial identity an asset to my philosophy of life," she wrote, "to rise above the perception that it was a negative."[17]

She was a cheerleader in high school and sang in the choir with her sister, Kitsaun. Intelligent and talented, she respected her parents and the strong family bond they fostered. Nevertheless, at age eighteen, she fell in love with rock star Sly Stone and followed him to Los Angeles and a world of hard drugs. After enduring an abusive relationship with the rock star, she finally broke away, returned to San Francisco, and in 1972 was accepted into the Creative Writing Program at San Francisco State.

In July 1972, at a concert at San Francisco's Marin Civic Center, she first saw Carlos Santana. "His handsome, mysterious face stayed in my mind," she wrote. "Without speaking a word, Carlos had imprinted a desire inside me to know him ... my mind lurched and my stomach rolled. *How can I be attracted to another famous musician?* Santana's songs "Black Magic Woman" and "Oye Como Va" were constantly on the radio."[18]

The two became inseparable. She began to see him as the opposite of Sly Stone. They both had spiritual inclinations that they freely shared. The two meditated together on their first date. Not long after the two began a relationship, they met a guru named Sri Chinmoy. Born in 1931 in what is now Bangladesh, he had spent years in an ashram in South India engaging in meditation and writing essays, poetry, and spiritual music. In 1964, he moved to New York City to begin to minister to seekers in the West. One of his converts was the musician John McLaughlin, a jazz-fusion guitar player from Yorkshire, England. When McLaughlin introduced Santana and King to the spiritual leader, they became as inspired by his teachings and words as McLaughlin had been.

Carlos cut his hair and began to wear white clothes. Deborah began wearing saris and started running marathons. The guru also suggested that they marry. Although the two shared a very special bond, marriage had not been on their immediate agendas. Nevertheless, as the guru asked, they soon arranged a marriage ceremony. On April 20, 1973, at the home of Deborah's aunt and uncle in Oakland, California, the two exchanged vows—he was twenty-five years old; she was twenty-two. A few months later, also at the suggestion of the guru, Deborah and her sister established a gourmet vegetarian restaurant in San Francisco called Dipti Nivas, "The Abode of Light," a cafeteria-style establishment. They sold bread they called "loaves of light" taken from a recipe in a Zen cookbook.

In the summer of 1974, Sri Chinmoy held a ceremony in which he gave Carlos and Deborah their spiritual names. Carlos was now to be called "Devadip," meaning "Lamp of God," and Deborah was now "Urmila," meaning "Light of the Supreme." The bestowal of such names was an affirmation by the guru that the two had made spiritual progress. Although

Santana's fans, friends, and, especially the press, had difficulty with the alteration of his name, within the year his tours carried the name of Deva-dip Carlos Santana. Deborah's parents never acquiesced in the change of her name and continued to call her by the name they had given her at birth.

When Carlos looked back at those times, he talked about the premature deaths of three towering figures in rock music—Jimi Hendrix and Janis Joplin in 1970 and Jim Morrison of the Doors in 1971. Like them, he had rocketed to fame in a short, breathtaking time and found himself indulging in the usual sports of a rock star, including casual sex and the use of drugs. But Santana was at heart a spiritual thinker. When Deborah came into his life, he began to take a close look at where his journey was headed. With her encouragement and the meeting with the guru, he moved radically in a different personal direction. "At that time, when I got into Sri Chinmoy," Santana said, "everyone was dying, OD-ing left and right. So it was either the stuff they put in your veins, or fold your hands and give yourself to the Lord. I never wanted to become a casualty. I was afraid that I wasn't strong enough to shake off the same road that everybody takes, which was booze and drugs ..."[19]

Santana's spiritual quest deeply influenced his music. For a time, he worked closely with the extraordinarily talented McLaughlin and members of his Mahavishnu Orchestra. They collaborated on an album that was, in part, a tribute to legendary jazz saxophonist John Coltrane. The album was called *Love Devotion Surrender*. On the album cover are photos of both Santana and McLaughlin, along with a smiling Sri Chinmoy.

Many of the contemporary reviews of the album praised the musical effort but puzzled over the photo of the guru and what it might represent. Thousands of Santana fans also undoubtedly squirmed. Where was their hero headed? Whatever the public thought of Santana's religious motivations, they turned out in massive numbers to hear him in person across the world. He made long, exhausting tours across the United States and to several countries from England and France to Japan and a number of Latin American countries.

Throughout the 1970s and into the 1980s, Santana released several other albums with spiritual themes, recording in collaboration with such jazz greats as Alice Coltrane and Herbie Hancock. His musical virtuosity with the guitar had become more complex with great technical proficiency.

But he still realized the limitations of technical genius and the importance of constantly reaching for the emotional high, the feeling, and the soul of the piece.

A lot of times you may hit some really ugly notes, but that's okay in the pursuit of that perfect thing. That's the whole romance of losing and finding yourself when you take a solo. You must lose yourself to find yourself. If you approach everything from an analytical point of view, the mind takes over. By the time you do your solo, it might sound great, but it's not going to penetrate. It will be like bullets that don't penetrate paper.[20]

In a fourteen-month period in 1972 and 1973, Santana recorded three albums that displayed the exciting experimentation that marked his career in these years. Fusing electric jazz with other musical elements that he had used in the past, the albums—*Caravanserai, Love Devotion Surrender,* and *Welcome*—showed his deep respect for the work of Miles Davis and John Coltrane. At the same time, Santana was edging more distinctly to works that tried to capture the spiritual side of his creativity. The works were contemplative and serious musical endeavors, if not commercially viable. The musical influences in his work now touched Afro-Cuban, classical, blues, jazz, soul, and others. The band clung precariously together as his music company, Columbia, encouraged albums that would appeal to a broader audience. But like his life, his music constantly sought new directions and meaning.

THE 1980S

For nearly a decade, Carlos and Deborah Santana had closely followed the teachings and spiritual direction of guru Sri Chinmoy. On his advice they had married. She had opened a restaurant at his suggestion. And now, in 1981, she aborted a pregnancy at his guidance. The guru's reasoning, Deborah told Carlos, was that having a family would lessen their dedication to the spiritual life. She had the abortion while Carlos was on the road and had not told him.

Revealing the abortion to Carlos upon his return was painful. But the guitarist vowed that they would again try to have a child. "Carlos whispered in my ear," Deborah recalled, "We are one with God and each other. No matter what happens, we are one. I love you."[21]

Shortly after the abortion, the two formally left behind the tutelage of Sri Chinmoy and his guidance center. The Santanas decided that the guru had gained far more control over their spiritual quest and everyday lives than they had wanted or anticipated. They told him, in no uncertain terms, that they were going their own way. Although an angered Sri Chinmoy insisted their path would lead to darkness, the couple moved on with their lives. In breaking their ties, the two even decided to sell the restaurant. Deborah chose to join Carlos on more of his tours.

In 1984, Deborah and Carlos welcomed into their life their first child, a boy they named Salvador. His skin was olive-colored like that of his father and his eyes were blue. At the early age of seven months, the boy accompanied his parents on a trip to Tokyo, Japan, and then to New York as Santana made stage appearances. His mother said he looked like a miniature sumo wrestler with a baseball cap and kimono. A year later, Deborah gave birth to a girl they named Stella. By the time she was three, Deborah said later, the young girl was twirling through the house in her ballet leotard and tutu. Her mother was convinced she was destined, like her famous father, for stardom. In 1987, the couple had a second daughter. They named her Angelica Faith. Deborah said that they chose her middle name for the quality she cherished most in the world—faith not only in God but also in humankind and in oneself.

During the 1980s, Santana and the band recorded less frequently, cutting only a few albums. But they were constantly on the road, selling out stadiums and auditoriums and appearing at high-profile occasions. In 1984, he joined Bob Dylan in a highly publicized European tour that filled large soccer stadiums in several countries. In 1985, he joined other top stars in a concert for Live Aid to assist famine victims in east Africa.

In 1987, Santana released an album called *Freedom*, a combination of works that reached all the way back to his early Tijuana days but included touches of gospel, blues, and soul. After the release of the recording, Santana was again on the road, including such stops as East Berlin and Tel Aviv, with an audience filled with both Jews and Arabs. Bill Graham later said, "Santana played the most inspirational show of his life at the foot of the great wall." For Santana, the point was that music could help bind the wounds of hate and mistrust. One of the songs they played that day was called "The Healer."[22]

On June 6, 1987, the city of San Francisco celebrated "Santana Day" in recognition not only of the guitarist's artistry but also of his public service. Against the backdrop of a huge mural between 22nd Street and Van Ness in the Mission District that featured the image of Carlos and two other Latino figures, the band played a free concert that drew an estimated 200,000 listeners. From atop buildings and lampposts, from the windows of nearby buildings, city residents strained to hear and get a glimpse of the figure that so many Latinos had embraced as a beloved figure.

In late 1987, the band, along with other performers, played in Moscow, Russia, as if on a peace mission. Boris Grebenshikoz, lead singer of an underground Russian rock group, said, "Basically, Santana commanded most of the admiration of the crowd. Santana is a name everyone knows in Russia from long years of listening to them. Santana, well, he's closer to the Russian consciousness because he presents the spiritual aspects. Carlos is something spiritual, he is so melodic and that is a sign of the spirit."[23]

For Santana himself, the Moscow experience left him emotionally moved like few other times in his life. "After the last note was played," he said, "and everybody was walking backstage, we started hearing all of a sudden 'Santana! Santana!' I broke down like a little kid and hid my head and face in my wife's chest."[24]

In 1988, Santana was again on the road, touring with saxophonist Wayne Shorter and also embarking on a tour with the original Santana band members Rolie, Areas, and Shrieve, who had not played together since the early 1970s. In addition, he released a thirty-song retrospective album featuring previous hits as well as unreleased studio tracks and live cuts. By 1998,

Santana's albums had sold more than thirty million copies and the band had performed for an estimated thirteen million people.

In 1992, Santana signed a deal with Polydor Records that included forming his own label, Guts & Grace. *Rolling Stone* magazine said that *Milagro*, the first album recorded under the new label, was one of Santana's finest efforts, establishing again his prominence as a standard-bearer for the fusion of music from various origins. Singer and songwriter Henry Garza said,

> Carlos Santana's music is a family thing for Chicanos. It's what you listen to when you're all hanging out: Drinking some beers, listening to "Oye Como Va," and cooking some barbecue is the best thing in the world. His music hits right to the pump—right to the heart. He's a pioneer of Latin rock & roll: His music was something new, but it was intertwined with everything else that was out there at the time—Sixties rock, Latin jazz, and more.... He incorporated his culture into the music, and he mixed English and Spanish in the lyrics.[25]

Garza also said that Santana was one of the greatest guitar players who ever lived. Sophisticated guitar players and the general listening audience alike immediately recognized his distinctive sound, like a fingerprint. His music spoke languages and culture to people across the world.

Shortly before the release of *Milagro* in June 1992, Santana made a stirring homecoming appearance in Tijuana. His appearance marked the first time the guitarist had played a note in the Mexican city since 1963. Many relatives and fellow musicians showed up at a seaside bullfighting ring that held over 17,000 people, including his father, Jose, who played with a local mariachi band, Tequila. The crowd treated Santana as a returning hero. When the band played "Oye Como Va," it was as if some kind of spiritual energy had been released in the crowd. As the set closed, fireworks lit up the skies around Tijuana, and Santana warmly embraced friend after friend.

Reflecting on the decades of his musical odyssey, Santana said after all those years that he rarely thought of the chords, notes, or techniques of playing. All of that, he said, should be instinctual for a professional musician. "When I'm playing a solo now, most of the time," he said, "I'm thinking of combing my daughter's hair before she goes to bed, and I have to do it a special way so I don't make her cry by pulling her hair. Believe me, that's what I'm thinking lately, man! I don't know if it's, like, domestic or mid-life or whatever, but I think of things about my family, because when I'm playing, it's automatic now."[26]

Although he continued to draw large crowds in the 1990s, Santana's national following was slipping. His fans were growing older now, and the usual string of hits reeled off by the band declined markedly. His 1987 solo effort, "Blues for Salvador," for example, had reached the Billboard Charts for only one week at number 195.

Never one to go quietly into obscurity, Carlos looked for a way to break out of the slide. He wanted to appeal to a younger group, wanted to make a difference in the lives of those now in their teenage years and early twenties just as he had always done. He turned to producer Clive Davis, who had first signed him to his contract at Columbia in the 1960s. Together they devised a plan to crack the airwaves with new music. They decided to fuse Santana's musical genius with that of younger musicians who had already begun to make their own influence felt. They would carefully mix sounds and coordinate styles and introduce a new Santana to the world.

SUPERNATURAL (1999)

In June 1999, Santana's *Supernatural* appeared, a diverse selection of Latin-rock riffs, Afro-Cuban rhythms, and mainstream pop singles. At a time when other groups of musicians who had come to prominence in the 1960s and 1970s had long since dispersed or were making retrospective appearances, Santana moved confidently into a new era. Carlos assembled some of the biggest names in the music industry for the new album, including Lauryn Hill, Wyclef Jean, Dave Matthews, and Rob Thomas of Matchbox 20.

With the release of the album, disc jockeys across the country began to air the single "Smooth," a salsa-laced, stylish production co-written and sung by Thomas. Soon, the song climbed the charts as no other Santana song had ever done, even outperforming "Black Magic Woman," which had reached the number four spot on the Top 40 list nearly thirty years earlier. Teenagers and people in their young twenties were now joining a generation of their fathers and mothers who followed the music of Santana, the vibrant and soulful sounds and that magical guitar that had evolved with the times. "Smooth" finally reached the number one spot and stayed there for twelve weeks. Santana was again riding high.

In addition, *Supernatural* also achieved a new first for Santana. It sold over one million CDs in the United States. Several months later, when the Grammy nominations were announced, the album garnered ten of those nominations. In February 2000, those nominations turned into awards. Santana won a startling eight Grammy Awards, including Record of the Year for "Smooth," and Album of the Year and Best Rock Album for *Supernatural*. He also won an American Music Award that year for Best Album.

Reflecting on his decision to bring together his own musical background and instincts with other, younger performers in a collaborative effort, Santana said, "My body's fifty-six; my soul is seventeen years old and very hungry to learn. It's not a gimmick, gizmo, gadget or formula. Basically, it's the principle to complement. Complement whatever they put in front of me. Even to the point of silence. If you don't hear anything, don't play anything. But if you're prepared to complement, you're going to be around for a while."[27]

Even with all the experimentation, Santana never discarded the things that worked best. He still had the old Paul Reed Smith guitars, made between 1979 and 1981, with their necks nearly as thick as baseball bats and so heavy that they nearly chewed the T-shirts off his left shoulder. He still had the heavy nylon picks that he said looked like tortillas.

Three years after *Supernatural*, Santana released *Shaman*, which took the same idea of assembling a stellar group of musicians to blend sounds. *Shaman* brought together musicians as varied in their musical backgrounds and talents as English soul singer Seal and operatic tenor Placido Domingo.

On producing *Shaman* and playing with Placido Domingo, Santana said,

> I wanted to transmute opera, symphony, Afro-Cuban beats, and blues into something new. I'm really grateful to Placido's spirit. Many opera singers don't want to sing in English—only Italian, Spanish, or German. When I asked him if he'd have a problem singing in English, he said, 'Of course not.' He's sixty years old, but when he hit that microphone from ten feet away, he sounded like two Marshall amplifiers. And hit those notes at 3:00 in the morning *after* doing two concerts with a sore throat.[28]

For Santana, *Shaman* represented something of his own worldview. With the war in Iraq and the general state of a world wracked with fear and anger, Santana, as he had done so many times in the past, called for healing. The tools were beauty, excellence, grace, and dignity, and they were badly needed, he said, to combat the old tools of guilt, contempt, and fear. To him, the new record resonated with the times. He was proud of it.

LEGENDARY JOURNEY

It had been quite an odyssey for the young Mexican, from the streets and bars of Tijuana to performing in venues around the world. "I started with a hat on the floor, a guitar, a harmonica player, and a conga," he said. "We say fifty cents a song, mister, fifty cents a song, mister. I'm the same person. The hat just got really, really, really big."[29]

In 1998, Deborah and Carlos established the Milagro Foundation. The word *milagro*, which he had used as the title of one of his albums, in Spanish means "miracle." Through this foundation the Santanas sought to strengthen arts and music education for children so that youngsters' lives could be enhanced in various ways, much like the arts had enhanced their own. The foundation supported band programs in schools, provided musical instruments to low-income families, and established various kinds of educational programs for low-income families and at-risk children.

In the summer of 2003, Santana went on the road for a summer tour, the proceeds of which were donated to Artists for a New South Africa (ANSA), an organization created to help fight the AIDS epidemic in Africa. The administrator of the fund, Nobel Prize winner Archbishop Desmond Tutu, said, "It's just a fantastic thing because it is going to save lives. It is, I hope, going to galvanize people.[30]

In 2004, the Latin Academy of Arts and Music honored Santana with its "Personality of the Year" award for his extraordinary impact on global music and culture. In April 2005, Broadcast Music, Inc. (BMI) honored Santana with its BMI Icon award. The designation is given to a creator who has been a "unique and indelible influence on generations of music makers." He joined a distinguished list of previous BMI Icons, including Brian Wilson, Chuck Berry, James Brown, Bo Diddley, and others.

For Santana, it has not been about the recognition so much as touching people with his art. "I want my music to clue my listeners into something beyond the song itself," he related to Dan Ouellette in *Down Beat*. "For example, this guy who had considered suicide wrote me a letter. He had seen the video of John Lee Hooker performing 'The Healer' and it inspired him to seek another way of dealing with his problems. Now that's more important to me than how many Grammys I get or how much money I could make selling Pepsi."[31]

Young Latino singer Henry Garza said, "People recognize that Santana has a really good message to send to the human spirit. He once said to us, 'You want to be like emissaries of light. When you're up on that stage or when you record, you want to be a tool that shines light through to everybody.' Santana has this awesome light that you're drawn to. You don't want to dwell in darkness. You want to go toward the light. And Santana is the light."[32]

For Santana, life has been a journey seeking harmony through music. His mysticism and spiritualism, and even his casual musings, have often seemed out of place and odd for a musician who has appealed to an enormous worldwide audience. But what has been most unusual has been his ever-evolving musical search for new sounds and innovative approaches, his enormous talent, and his appeal to the changing generations of people who love music. Santana said,

> What I'd like to do before I die is bring people closer to the same reality that John Coltrane and Bob Marley were trying to bring people to. "...no borders, one race, just one body, and we all take responsibility so nobody starves to death tomorrow morning.... Songs become like windows for people to look inside or look outside. That's why we love Jimi Hendrix. Because they're beautiful windows—when we look into them, we like what we see.[33]

Music, then, is a force that binds people together, that heals. The Mexican immigrant, the great guitarist who plays on to remove the borders for humanity, said,

> If I could establish one thing... it would be to plant the seeds of a vision that everyone all over the world would have water, electricity, food, and education

for free. In return, what we would like is to wake up and raise your consciousness to be a better person. That you have more passion for compassion, more gentle wisdom, more patience. So I do feel, in the words of Cesar Chavez, "Si se puede" (Yes, we can). That's the only agenda worth being passionate about.[34]

SELECTED MUSIC

Santana. *Havana Moon*. Sony, 1990. CD.

Santana, Carlos and Buddy Miles. *Live!* Sony, 1994. CD.

Santana. *Santana Jam*. Prime Cuts, 1994. CD.

Santana. *Abraxas*. Sony, 1998. CD.

Santana. *The Best of Santana*. Sony, 1998. CD.

Santana. *Supernatural*. BMG/Arista, 1999. CD.

Santana. *World of Carlos Santana*. ZYX Records, 2001. CD

Santana. *Shaman*. Arista, 2002. CD.

The Grateful Dead, Jefferson Airplane, Santana. *A Night at the Family Dog 1970*. Eagle Rock Entertainment, 2005. DVD.

Carlos Santana Presents: Blues at Montreux 2004. Eagle Rock Entertainment, 2006. DVD.

Santana. *Viva Santana!* Sony, 2006. DVD.

Santana. *Ultimate Santana*. Arista Records, 2007. CD.

Santana, Dave Matthews Band, Tony Lindsay. *Santana Live*. Hudson Street/New Media/Highline Play, 2007. DVD.

Santana, Carlos and Wayne Shorter. *Live at Montreux Jazz Festival*. Image Entertainment, 2007. CD.

NOTES

1. Simon Leng, *Soul Sacrifice: The Santana Story*, London: Fire Fly Publishing, 2000, 12.

2. "Profile of Carlos Santana, Alanis Morrisette, Part 1," *The America's Intelligence Wire*, August 23, 2003, http://www.accessmylibrary.com/coms2/summary_0286-24189695_ITM.

3. "Profile of Carlos Santana."

4. Leng, 23–24.

5. "Carlos Santana on recruiting minority teachers," *NEA Today*, May 2000, 21.

6. Deborah Santana, *Space Between the Stars: My Journey to an Open Heart*, New York: One World-Ballantine Books, 2006, 269–270.

7. Santana, 207.

8. "Profile of Carlos Santana."

9. Tom Wheeler, "Carlos Santana (Encore)," *Guitar Player*, July 2003, 25.

10. James Rotondi, "Healing Hands: Carlos Santana's Musical Mission," *Guitar Player*, January 1993, 58.

11. "1969: Woodstock music festival ends," http://news.bbc.co.uk/onthisday/hi/dates/stories/august/18/newsid_2760000/2760911.

12. Andy Ellis, "Music of the spheres: Santana conjures 6-strong magic with *Shaman*," *Guitar Player*, January 2003, 76.

13. Mark Marvel and Peter Galvin, "The Players," *Interview*, July 1994, 58.

14. "1969: Woodstock music festival ends."

15. Leila Cobo, "Santana: Lara's Person of the Year," *Billboard*, August 14, 2004, 21.

16. Cobo.

17. Santana, 14–17.

18. Santana, 119.

19. Rotondi.

20. Rotondi.

21. Santana, 261.

22. Leng, 142.

23. Leng, 143–144.

24. Leng, 144.

25. Henry Garza, "The Immortals 90: Carlos Santana," *Rolling Stone*, April 21, 2005, 98.

26. Rotondi.

27. "Profile of Carlos Santana."

28. Ellis.

29. "Profile of Carlos Santana."

30. "Profile ..."

31. Hispanic Heritage: Carlos Santana, Gale, Free Resources, http://www.gale.com/free_resources/chh/bio/santana_c.htm.

32. Garza.

33. Rotondi.

34. Cobo.

FURTHER READING

Hispanic Heritage: Carlos Santana, Gale, Free Resources, http://www.gale.com/free_resources/chh/bio/santana_c.htm.

Garza, Henry, "The Immortals 90: Carlos Santana," *Rolling Stone*, April 21, 2005, 98

Leng, Simon. *Soul Sacrifice: The Santana Story.* London: Fire Fly Publishing, 2000.

Rotondi, James. "Healing Hands: Carlos Santana's Musical Mission," *Guitar Player*, January 1993, 58.

Santana, Deborah. *Space Between the Stars: My Journey to an Open Heart.* New York: One World-Ballantine Books, 2006.

Santana official website, http://www.santana.com.

AP Photo/Tony Gutierrez

Cristina Saralegui

Many call television host Cristina Saralegui the Latina Oprah Winfrey. Cuban-born Saralegui hosts *El Show de Cristina*, a Miami-based Spanish-language television talk show on Univision with an audience of over one hundred million viewers throughout the United States and Latin America. She hosts a radio show, publishes a magazine, runs a production company with three soundstages from which she produces both the television and radio shows, heads companies that produce a clothing line and furniture, directs a bilingual website that averages over 50,000 hits a day, runs a foundation that educates Latinos and others about the dangers of AIDS, and engages in countless fundraising activities on behalf of programs to combat gang violence and racial intolerance.

"OPRAH WITH SALSA!"

That was the advertising line that Univision used in promoting Cristina Saralegui's Spanish-language talk show in 1989.

Years later, when Saralegui was also a star in her own right, she was in Chicago and dropped by Oprah Winfrey's studio to watch a taping of *The Oprah Winfrey Show*. The queen of daytime television suddenly told the audience that there was a woman in the studio who was known as Oprah with salsa. "But that's a lie," said Winfrey. "I am the black Cristina."

"I was so red," recalled Saralegui of the moment. "But I've been honored to be compared with Oprah."[1]

When *Television Week Magazine* interviewed Saralegui in 2006, she said that she used to be embarrassed by the comparison, worrying that Oprah may have thought that Saralegui made up the slogan for herself. But she finally realized, she said, "that when you have a new product, like in 1989 when we first started the show, nobody knew what to call me. So they started calling me Oprah with salsa. That was in the first Univision press release. And now eighteen years later, here I am."[2]

Saralegui, in many ways, does have career lines parallel to those of Oprah Winfrey. In 1986, Winfrey launched *The Oprah Winfrey Show*. It was the beginning of a remarkable career that catapulted her to a global media leader and one of the most admired public figures. In 1989 Univision launched *El Show de Cristina* (The Cristina Show). Modeled after shows such as Winfrey's and *The Phil Donahue Show*, it was the beginning of one of the most successful enterprises in the history of television.

---

[1]Ken Kerschbaumer, "Cristina Saralegui," *Broadcasting & Cable*, October 10, 2005, 30.

[2]"A Latina icon with multimedia presence: After 18 years on the air, talk show host Cristina Saralegui is a brand all her own," *TelevisionWeek*, October 16, 2006, 26, http://find.galegroup.com/itx/start.do?prodId=GRGM.

In 1988, Winfrey established Harpo Studios, a production facility in Chicago, making her the third woman in the American entertainment industry (after Mary Pickford and Lucille Ball) to own her own studio. In 2001 Saralegui became the fourth woman in the history of American entertainment to own her own studio with the creation of the Blue Dolphin Studios in Miami, a state-of-the-art television facility.

In 1991, Saralegui launched a monthly magazine called *Cristina La Revista* (Cristina the Magazine), which soon reached a circulation of more than 160,000 in the United States and Latin America. In 2000, Oprah and Hearst Magazines introduced *O, The Oprah Magazine*, a monthly magazine that has become one of today's leading women's lifestyle publications.

Through her private charity, The Oprah Winfrey Foundation, Oprah has awarded hundreds of grants to organizations that support the education and empowerment of women, children and families in the United States and around the world. In 1996, Saralegui and her husband founded an AIDS organization called "Arriba la Vida/Up with Life Foundation," which is dedicated to providing information, medicine, and support to Hispanic people afflicted with AIDS.

In October 1998, Saralegui started a bilingual website, Cristina Online (www.cristinaonline.com), providing access to all of the subsidiaries of her corporation, Cristina Saralegui Enterprises, Inc., and offering news, biographical information, photographs, and other aspects of her life and career. Oprah.com is a premiere women's lifestyle website, offering advice on everything from the mind, body and spirit to food, home and relationships.

In 2004, *O at Home*, a newsstand-only quarterly shelter magazine designed to help readers create a home that reflects their personal style, made its debut. By 2004, Saralegui's name was licensed to fifteen manufacturers of home-related products such as couches, mattresses, candles, bed linens, towels, dishes, glasses, and rugs. She started Casa Cristina, a furniture line manufactured by Pulaski, reflecting the culture in which Saralegui was raised.

Two remarkable women; two American icons.

In her role as a talk show host, Saralegui has addressed topics that many other shows could not take on with such a direct and frank approach. Homosexual marriage, menopause, AIDS prevention, plastic surgery—these and many other subjects have both educated and entertained millions. "I often make mistakes, and when I do, I tell my audience," she said. "They like my honesty." Her mission, she pledged, was to bring Latinos together. "In unity, there is strength."[1]

"She's a trailblazer in so many areas," says veteran Miami-based music and film producer Bruno del Granado. "Before Cristina, there were no strong Hispanic women on TV—it was always victim, victim, victim. She not only changed that, she did it her way, by her own rules."[2] Controversial and enormously energetic, she is an adored figure with legions of fans. They simply call her Cristina.

CUBAN CHILDHOOD

Cristina Maria Saralegui was born in Miramar, a wealthy suburb of Havana, Cuba, on January 29, 1948, to Francisco and Cristina Saralegui, both of whose families had come from the Basque region of Spain. The Saralegui family was one of distinction and wealth. Cristina's paternal grandfather, the elegant Francisco Saralegui y Arrizubieta, was known as the Paper Czar of Cuba after founding three leading Spanish-language magazines—*Bohemia*, *Carteles*, and *Vanidades*—and gaining a monopoly on paper distribution throughout much of Cuba.

Cristina's maternal grandfather, Jose Santamarina, was a pioneering advertising creator in Cuban television. One of his creations was a campaign for Cristal Beer in which a beer bottle wiggled and swayed like a girl dancing. The Santamarinas lived in the Cuban province of Pinar del Rio, in the eastern portion of the island where the best of the world-famous Cuban cigars are manufactured.

When Cristina's father, Francisco "Bebo" Saralegui, courted her mother, Cristy Santamarina, he wooed her with a series of love letters. Only later did she discover that the letters were not created in the head of her beloved but were copies of letters that the Emperor Napoleon of France had written to his lover Josephine more than a hundred years earlier.

Cristina was the oldest of five children in the family. She and her two brothers and two sisters grew up with personal nurses and servants. Surrounded by celebrities and political figures that her grandfather entertained at his seaside mansion, she later described herself at the time as spoiled and shy. She remembered Sunday mornings and the family gatherings at her grandfather's house. In the morning her grandfather would climb into his black Cadillac, driven by his chauffeur, pick up several of his grandchildren, and take them to mass at the Church of Santa Rita. After church, he would drive the children to a toy store where each could pick out one toy. "After that ritual," she said, "We had lunch at his house, each child with his or her nurse, dressed in starched white uniforms." The Spanish-style dining room with its large table seated eighteen guests. "Grandfather sat at the head of the table, and Grandmother at the other end. I remember that she insisted that we wear bibs she had made that said, 'Eat and keep silent.'"[3]

It was an idyllic, if controlled, life. Cristina took ballet and piano lessons and classes in Spanish folk dances. She attended a convent school in Miramar called Slaves of the Sacred Heart, where all of the students wore brown uniforms. The family spent three-month vacations at Varadero, the famous Cuban beach where the waters seem nearly transparent and where the children can catch starfish with their bare hands. In her early teens Cristina sometimes preferred to dress like character she saw on television called Zorro who wore black clothes, black cowboy boots, and a black mask.

She remembered going with her father and grandfather to see the printing press. "I grew up smelling ink," she said. "Being in print was all I ever wanted to do in my life. When I told my dad that I wanted to be a journalist, he said I was going to starve because they don't make any money. But it was a passion."[4]

Behind the privileged life of the upper classes that young Cristina experienced as a child was political turmoil that was leading to uprising and revolution. General Fulgencio Batista's military government that had seized power in 1952 and had ruled with ruthless authority faced a growing insurgency of rebels determined to overthrow it. The rebellion was led by a young lawyer named Fidel Castro.

Cristina's father, Bebo Saralegui, had known Castro as a schoolmate both at the Jesuits' school and at the University of Havana. He later remembered him as a serious student who spent many hours in the library studying anthropology. He also remembered him as a man on a mission. "It's not that Castro was so much a Communist as a young man as he was anti-American," Cristina Saralegui later wrote about her father's impressions. "From the time he was a boy," her father said, Castro "foamed at the mouth" when talking about Americans.[5]

A dynamic public speaker, Castro began to build a large following when he ran for Congress in 1952. When Batista took control of the country in that year, the young lawyer decided that revolution was the only way to drive Batista and his corrupt government from power. His first attempt to strike at the Batista regime was a pathetic assault on a Cuban army barracks in 1953. The ragtag group of 123 men and women were rounded up, and most were murdered by the army. Castro was fortunate that a lieutenant who arrested him placed him in a local civilian prison instead of before a firing squad. At his trial, Castro made a speech about the injustices toward the poor. Sentenced to fifteen years in prison, he was released after only two years on the condition that he leave the country. Castro left Cuba for Mexico, where he once again planned for revolution.

Surrounding himself with a group of other young adventurers such as Che Guevara and Juan Almeida, Castro returned to Cuba in 1956. As they planned to set up a base in the Sierra Maestra Mountains, they were attacked by government troops and reached the mountains with only sixteen men and a few weapons. Castro later recalled that they took their inspiration from a novel written by the celebrated American author, Ernest Hemingway, *For Whom the Bell Tolls*. From the book, Castro said, he got the idea to infiltrate Batista's army with recruits of his own and to begin to steal guns. "While I was up in the Sierra," Castro wrote, "I remembered that book a lot.... It talks about the existence of a guerrilla force... in the rear of a conventional army. Later, when we came to know that life as a guerrilla firsthand, we always came back to find inspiration."[6]

Castro's growing forces raided isolated army garrisons, gathering arms and adding men to the force. Students, priests, peasants, and others who hated Batista and the government joined up, all with a revolutionary zeal that became an increasingly serious threat to the Batista regime.

By New Year's Day, 1959, this unlikeliest of revolutions had won out. Batista resigned and fled the country to the Dominican Republic. The country gasped at the symbolism.

For the Saralegui family, the signs they observed in the early days of the revolution were symbolic not of progress but of decay. As Castro's government began to confiscate property, and as many political opponents disappeared or were executed, Cristina's father lost any confidence he had in Castro's intentions. Although Bebo Saralegui had hated Batista and everything he represented, he began to see that Castro was directing the country toward Communist rule. Both he and his father wanted no part in allowing their magazine, *Bohemia*, or any of their other publications to be merely a tool of the government.

Bebo Saralegui decided to move his family from Cuba while he was still able. Cristina's grandparents soon fled to Spain. In early 1960, Cristina, led by her mother, boarded a plane in Havana with her brothers and sisters and their nanny for the small island of Trinidad, north of Venezuela. There, they would be joined by aunts and uncles and would wait for Bebo Saralegui to follow.

Soon after his family departed for Trinidad, Saralegui managed to leave Cuba on a plane bound for Miami, Florida. In Key Biscayne, he purchased a house, found appropriate schools for the children, and traveled to Trinidad to rejoin his family and take them to the United States. Along with thousands of other refugees in Florida, the Saralegui family now prepared to begin a new life.

A HOME IN THE UNITED STATES

Having abandoned the mansion in Miramar with its swimming pools and servants, the family now occupied a relatively small, three-bedroom home in southern Florida. Although the family left behind much of its wealth in escaping from Cuba, Bebo Saralegui managed to leave with enough money to launch a new magazine in the United States. He called it *Bohemia Libre* (Free Bohemia). As Castro's government began to use the Saralegui's magazine *Bohemia* as a mouthpiece for the new regime, Bebo printed thousands of copies of his new publication and sent planes to drop them over Cuba. From his exile, he continued to try to make an impact in his former land.

As the months turned into years, the Saralegui family realized that life in Cuba was now only in their pasts. They had to put down roots in their new country and make new lives for themselves. Cristina was twelve years old.

Always a determined business leader, Bebo Saralegui soon revived another of his magazines, *Vanidades*, and established its headquarters in the Lincoln Building in New York City. In June 1961 the first issue of the new *Vanidades* in exile featured on the cover the Italian movie star Gina Lollobrigida.

Cristina's father spent the weekdays in New York working on the magazine and returned to Key Biscayne for the weekends, a routine that lasted for several years. The three-bedroom house soon filled with even more Cuban exiles, including two of Cristina's grandparents and her mother's younger brother and his fiancée, who had also left Cuba.

Cristina and her sister Vicky, along with a cousin, enrolled in Miami's Assumption Academy, a private religious school similar to the one they had attended in Cuba. As a young teenager, Cristina became a Beatles fan but was generally sheltered from the sex, drugs, and rock and roll scene in the United States that touched the lives of the 1960s generation of youngsters. Cristina went to dances only with a chaperone.

Because of her father's shrewd business acumen and his ability to rebound so quickly after losing much of his fortune to the Castro revolution, the Saralegui family became increasingly wealthy. Soon, Bebo Saralegui sold the magazine and started a construction company in Key Biscayne. He was the first contractor to develop Cape Florida, a section of the city that ultimately became one of elegance.

The family moved into a larger home and purchased a small yacht and a motorboat. The children went water-skiing. The family again hired a nanny. Gradually, they regained the smells and tastes of the life they had temporarily lost. The Cuban food, the colognes, the music—all of it again came together for the family and many of their friends.

The children were somewhat wild in an overall controlled situation. Cristina's sister, Vicky, for example, who later studied biology at the University of Miami, kept snakes and baby alligators in her room. Cristina had a monkey. Her mother often walked around with the monkey perched on her shoulder.

The hardest part of being an exile, Saralegui later wrote, was facing the prejudice of whites. Although she had blond hair and light eyes, she spoke English with a thick Spanish accent. Other children constantly asked her questions in mocking tones about life in Cuba—whether they had refrigerators and air conditioning and so on. The greatest shock, she said, was first hearing the term "spic" used as an insult. "I didn't understand why I was called 'spic,'" she said, "...until someone explained that the word came from the way a Spanish speaker pronounces the word "speak," shortening the vowel." She also cringed at the terms used to describe African Americans and the treatment they received in the American South, even in the 1960s. One of her aunts whose skin was very dark had to sit at the back of buses. In Cuba, whites and blacks had sat together.[7]

Saralegui got her first job while still in high school. She was sixteen and worked part-time at an exclusive department store in Miami called Jordan Marsh. After graduating from high school she enrolled at the University of Miami, where she studied communications with a minor in creative writing. She looked forward to a career in journalism. Unquestionably, her interest in writing and communication was influenced by two generations of her family whose lives were involved in various ways in the world of publishing.

STARTING A CAREER

While at the University of Miami, she chose to do an internship at *Vanidades* magazine, not only because of her family's deep ties to the publication but also because she wanted to increase her fluency in Spanish. Since arriving in the United States at age twelve, all of her schooling had been in English. She first worked as an assistant and then as a writer. Her first article was on the Catholic Church's position on birth control; her supervisor rejected it. Characteristically, Cristina was determined to write better and did so quickly.

In 1970, Bebo Saralegui's business crumbled. Always a man to make quick decisions and often seduced by elaborate business ventures, he fell into too many financial holes and watched his fortune slip away. So devastated were the family's business affairs in 1970 that her father did not have enough money to continue to help finance Cristina's final year at the University of Miami. At the same time, however, he managed to pay for her brother Patxi's tuition at a military school. Saralegui always bitterly looked back on her father's decision as typically sexist. She remembered his words to her: "Well, your brother was going to have to take care of a wife someday, and I thought you would find someone to take care of you."[8]

Saralegui began to turn out articles on subjects as varied as beauty tips and international news. *Vanidades* was sold in twenty-three countries, so shse learned how to write in a so-called "pan-American" style of Spanish, one that can be understood throughout Latin America even though many of the words and phrases in Spanish vary from county to country. She later attributed some of her success in radio and television to the ability she developed in these early years at the magazine to be understood throughout various Spanish-speaking countries. "Our magazine had the peculiarity in that it circulates all over Latin America, not just in the United States," she wrote. "Basically, I had to learn to write and edit the other writers in a Spanish that really doesn't exist anymore. You can't find it in any dictionaries, it's colloquial, so it doesn't sound like a textbook, but everybody understands it."[9]

In 1973, young Saralegui received an important career break; she was selected to become a writer for a new Spanish version of *Cosmopolitan*, one of the giants of women's magazines. *Cosmopolitan* was established in the late 1880s and later became part of William Randolph Hearst's publishing empire. Throughout most of its history, it was primarily a family-oriented publication and, for a time, a literary magazine. By the 1960s its popularity had declined significantly, and it was in danger of succumbing to the stiff competition of several other publications.

In 1965 Helen Gurley Brown, a young writer who had published a best-selling book called *Sex and the Single Girl*, became chief editor of *Cosmopolitan*. Soon, its entire image changed. It became something of a reflection of her book, a magazine that set a style for young career women. Usually featuring the picture of a sexy woman on the cover in a low-cut dress or bikini, it explored the world of dating, fashion, sex, and other issues that seemed slightly daring. Although Brown received much criticism from long-time readers, the sales of the magazine soon soared. It now became known as *Cosmo*, and young women eagerly awaited each new issue.

The first foreign edition of the magazine was published in 1973 in Great Britain. As a result of the immediate success of the British *Cosmo*, the Hearst Company decided to begin production of a second foreign edition, this one to be written in Spanish and sold throughout Latin America.

Frank Calderon, a long-time friend of the Saralegui family, became the editor of *Cosmopolitan en Espanol*. He asked Cristina to explore new ways to reach the audience of young Latin-American women. "That's how I became the first Latin American Cosmo Girl!" Saralegui wrote. "Frank himself sent me on a cruise ship throughout the Caribbean to find out what turned on a single guy, and I was photographed riding horseback in a bikini."[10]

Many of her first articles for the magazine were frivolous; many were not. She traveled to Mexico City to interview artist Jose Luis Cuevas. She wrote about the emerging feminist movement, the drive to instill in women the understanding they were not second-class citizens to their male counterparts, that they had rights and beliefs that must be respected. She researched the laws in various Latin-American countries as they applied to women's rights.

In 1976, Saralegui again made a quick career turn. The *Miami Herald*, the newspaper with the largest circulation in southern Florida, decided to create a Spanish supplement to appeal to the increasingly large numbers of Latinos still streaming into the area. The supplement would be called *El Herald*. As editor-in-chief Frank Soler recruited a team of writers for the new publication, he naturally sought the services of the young *Cosmo* Latina. He offered her a larger salary, better benefits, and great latitude in the kind of articles she could take on, even though they were to be about the Miami area. Saralegui accepted the offer.

She was now a young, successful career woman living on her own with a glamorous job and dating several men, including some entertainers. Nevertheless, for an individual who had recently been touring a number of countries in Latin America, the job in Miami began to seem more and more confining. She tired of it quickly.

At age twenty-eight, Saralegui decided to settle down into a life of domesticity. She wanted a child. She made what she later regarded as a rather impulsive choice and married a real estate salesman and firefighter named Tony Menendez. A year later she had a daughter they named Cristina Amalia Menendez y Saralegui, whom they simply called Titi. Saralegui spoke often about how this was the very first baby that she knew of in her family who was not blond. She and others in her extended family began to call Titi "*la mulata de fuego*" (the fiery mulatto).

For the first time in the last ten years of a whirlwind life, Saralegui did not have a job. For a year, she stayed home, took on household chores, and watched as the family's financial situation became increasingly dire. With her husband's real estate sales bringing in little income, the family had so little money to spend that they used a corn plant for a Christmas tree.

Cristina decided to resume her career. Because of the rash of quick moves, her former employers were reluctant to offer her another job. Finally, she managed to convince the editors at *Vanidades* to give her a writing job at the lowest entry scale allowed. She had come full circle and was once again at the bottom looking up. Nevertheless, she had behind her now several years of experience, better writing skills, a basic knowledge of a number of Latin American countries, proven ways in which to communicate with a broad range of their people, and growing personal maturity. And so, she was back at work, this time carrying her young Titi to her office in a basket. By the time the child was one year old, Saralegui and her husband decided to dedicate a large portion of their salaries to hire a woman from Colombia to live in their house and care for the child.

Within a year of taking the job at *Vanidades*, Saralegui was again asked to take another fork in her career road. Don Armande de Armas, owner of the magazine, decided to publish an additional, small-format magazine called *Intimidades*. Its theme was to be primarily about human sexuality. Because the salary was substantially greater than the small amount she was making in the job for *Vanidades*, she accepted the job.

The new publication began to soar in popularity. Saralegui was named editor. It was the first magazine she directed. On the cover of the magazine, she announced the editorial purpose—to deal openly with "the psychological, emotional, and intimate problems every couple faces, and help them achieve a better understanding of their relationship." She put a mighty effort into the job, often working until one or two o'clock in the morning with only a few staff members to help out. She rarely had time for her daughter except on Sundays, when she was almost always exhausted. From the hard work came exceptional results. So successful was Saralegui in running the publication that it soon was outselling *Vanidades*.[11]

Her career was now on a roll of popularity and success that would never end. In 1979, when Frank Calderon, Saralegui's former boss at *Cosmopolitan en Espanol*, left his job as editor-in-chief, management turned to Saralegui.

Within a few years of returning to work after having a child, she had risen from the lowly writer on the *Vandidades* staff to the position of editor in chief of one of the most important publications in Latin America. "I was terrified," she said.[12] But Saralegui, at thirty years old, was much more seasoned in her views and experienced in the field than she appeared. She still looked as if she were in her early twenties. She saw the Latin American *Cosmopolitan* somewhat differently than her predecessor and her own boss, Helen Gurley Brown.

For Latin American women, she believed, the "New Cosmo Girl" would represent more than just sexual liberation; it would also represent a vision of what could be possible for every Latino woman reader—the ways that women could look at their lives and themselves differently than the roles that society had for so long prescribed to them. Women, she believed, needed to understand that they too could gain political and economic power, that they did not need to be forever on a subservient level to men. They could fashion their own careers, make their own marks, be creative, and contribute in various ways they never before dreamed.

Although Brown sometimes chafed at some of the new directions that Saralegui was taking the Latin American *Cosmopolitan*, she recognized the young woman's great talent and instincts and did not try to rein in her creativity. The two developed a strong friendship. Saralegui later said, "I had the opportunity to work alongside many good editors who taught me a lot. My biggest role model was Helen Gurley-Brown, *Cosmopolitan's* editor-in-chief emerita. She's a great friend and feminist. I call her my "Professional Mama," and she still is a great inspiration."[13]

Her years as editor-in-chief were productive, and her professional life arched upward, but the demands on her personal life took a toll. For her husband, Tony Menendez, this was not the life he had envisioned as a husband and father. Because of the enormous time demands of her career, the two saw very little of each other. He was also uncomfortable with the swirling atmosphere into which his wife's career had moved. Although they remained good friends, the two decided to divorce in 1983.

Personally reeling from the divorce and physically strained from the pressure of the job, Saralegui had the good fortune to turn to individuals in a singing group who had already begun to make a profound impact on her life. Later, she said that one could look at her life and divide it into two parts—before Miami Sound Machine and after Miami Sound Machine.

Emilio Estefan founded a local band in the early 1970s called "Miami." In 1974, he asked Glorita (Gloria) Fajardo and her cousin Merci Navarro to join the group, and they changed their name to Miami Sound Machine. One of the original group members was a dark, short, good-looking bass player named Marcos Avila.

When Estefan and Gloria married, they often socialized with Saralegui. Saralegui helped promote the band's work by including news and photos of their concerts in nearly every issue of *Cosmopolitan*. When Estefan told

Saralegui of his plans to feature his wife solo with the band as a backup, Saralegui featured Gloria in her first international cover spread. The group would be called Gloria Estefan and the Miami Sound Machine. Within a few years, the band was acclaimed throughout Latin America and the Spanish-speaking world. The group also gained popularity in the United States and the Anglo market.

At the same time, Saralegui and the bass player, Marcos Avila, who had also recently divorced, began a passionate relationship and they soon married. She was thirty-five years old; Avila was twenty-four. Both Saralegui and Avila had one child from a previous marriage and together they would soon have another. Their baby boy was born prematurely, and they called him Jon Marcos. Shortly after birth, Jon Marcos was close to death on a night when his father was on the road with the band. The baby was suffering from a strangulated hernia. During the night in the hospital, Saralegui said later, she became a woman. "Until that moment," she wrote, "I had thought I'd become a woman when I gained financial independence. Not true. I was an idiotic woman, totally immature, who thought that the important things in life were my job, material belongings, money, and getting ahead." That night, she said, changed her outlook on life. She had to call on her emotional and deeply personal resources to realize what was truly important. Her beloved baby boy survived.[14]

When she looked back at her marriage years later and the love and partnership that it represented, she said, "The secret is to get a partner for life. I've been with my husband for twenty-three years now. You know, there are women who will fret about what dress to wear to a party, but they won't pay half as much attention to whom they will be with for the rest of their lives. You can't pick someone because he's cute or he dances great."[15]

TELEVISION PERSONALITY

In 1988, the Hallmark Corporation bought a Spanish-language television network and changed its name to Univision. Headed by its new president Joaquín Blaya, a Chilean, the new network would grow to become a huge enterprise with local stations in markets with large Latino populations. Establishing its headquarters in New York, Univision built its major production facilities and operations in Miami. By 2002, it was the fifth largest cable television network, with its viewers outnumbering those in such markets as HBO and ESPN.

When Blaya took over as the president of Univision, he decided to create a series of programs made by Latinos in the United States primarily for Latinos in the United States. One of his first major efforts was to convince Saralegui, whom to he had known socially for several years, to step down from her editorship of *Cosmopolitan en Espanol* and join the world of television.

Always eager to take on new challenges and encouraged by her husband, she decided to make an enormous career leap.

Saralegui first joined Univision on a variety show called *Sábado Gigante* (Super Saturday), a program hosted by the well-known entertainer Mario Kreutzberger, better known as Don Francisco. She contracted for ten segments to address the kinds of issues that she had presented in *Cosmo*. So popular were the segments that she soon agreed to host a woman's magazine show.

For a time, she was editorial consultant on a program *TV Mujer* (TV Woman). Saralegui scoffed at the original pilot that had been made for the show which seemed to her as if it might have been filmed in the early 1950s in black and white—mostly images of women in kitchens wearing aprons and wrestling with their blenders and cooking utensils. Instead, she turned the show into something entirely different, something with the content that had inspired her work on various publications, something that would speak in a special way to modern women. She even used a segment called "Vida en Pareja" (Life as a Couple), in which she dispensed ideas and advice about relationships. She created another segment for a fictional gossip columnist called Tia Virtudes (Auntie Virtue). The character, whose face was concealed, was adorned with a hat, cape, and veil and looked very much like the wicked witch in *The Wizard of Oz*.

In 1988, the success of "TV Mujer" led Blaya to offer Saralegui a unique opportunity. She was asked to create her own talk show for a Spanish-speaking audience, similar in approach to such talk show productions as hosted by Oprah Winfrey and Phil Donahue. When Saralegui asked Blaya why he decided to launch such a show with someone who had little experience before a camera, he told her that he had never met anyone who could talk a person's ear off on any subject as she could. Blaya's instincts proved to be sound.

Saralegui once told an interviewer that there seemed to be no connection between her brain and her mouth and everything that she said came out unedited. It was a tremendous defect, she said, but probably her greatest virtue.

As she entered into this phase of her career, she and Marcos decided that he should become her manager. He would take over the business dealings of what would eventually be nothing less than a financial empire. They would call the business Cristina Saralegui Enterprises. Throughout the contractual dealings, Saralegui and Marcos demanded that she have editorial control. Although executives of the network were reluctant to move forward under such a condition, they relented. She became executive producer and host of the show.

At 5:00 P.M. on April 17, 1989, the one-hour *El Show de Cristina* (The Cristina Show) debuted. It was the beginning of one of the most successful enterprises in the history of television. "She explores subjects and themes that have never been discussed on television," said Univision president and chief operating officer Ray Rodriguez. "She sees her mission as much more than just entertainment, but also as an opportunity to inform and motivate her audience."[16]

El Show de Cristina was not an immediate success. Without previous television experience, Saralegui sometimes struggled on stage. She had always been shy speaking in public, and in her first months on the show some of that fear became somewhat noticeable. She had difficulty at times reading text from the teleprompters, the devices that magnified scripts so that performers onstage would appear to be working without notes.

She also had problems convincing Latino viewers that a blonde, blue-eyed, white Cuban from Miami could represent Latinos from various countries and cultures. At times, she received mail scolding her for her brashness, her looks, and even her heavy Cuban accent. She worked hard reviewing her own performances on videotape. She lost weight and invigorated her health with better attention to exercise and nutrition. If she was going to stand in front of a camera with millions of viewers watching, she was determined to present not only the best material but also the best image.

But she never attempted to change her Cuban accent. That is what she was, she said, and that was how it was going to stay. She became especially irritated that a Cuban accent, even to some Cubans themselves, appeared to some viewers to be less educated than accents from other Latin American countries. That view was, she said, not only wrong-headed but also highly prejudiced.

The show soon took off to unprecedented ratings heights. Saralegui was daring and innovative. As in her work as a print journalist, she plunged into subjects that had been previously off limits in commercial television, especially on usually conservative Latino broadcasting. She explored issues such as gay marriage, homeless children, sex addiction, spousal rape, child abuse, menopause, and even her own facelift, pictures of which she showed to impress women with some of the drawbacks and possible disasters of the procedure. On some occasions, her shows took off in rather odd directions. For example, she invited experts to delve into their investigations of alien abductions and the existence of vampires.

Boston Globe writer Alisa Valdes wrote, "Every weekday afternoon, millions world-wide watch Oprah Winfrey's talk show; thus, the moniker: 'Queen of Talk.' But—Surprise!—there is an American talk show host with as many viewers, if not more, at any given moment. ... From Chile to the South Bronx, Saralegui (sah-rah-leh-ghee), with her platinum bob and rapid-fire Miami Spanish, claims to be the most watched show host on earth."[17]

Although the show concentrated on controversial subjects, Saralegui never tolerated the kind of shouting and, in some cases, actual physical violence that often occurred on some of the other daytime talk shows, such as *The Jerry Springer Show.* Especially with the problems associated with gang violence in urban areas and domestic violence that had become increasingly an issue among viewers, she refused to allow the program to sink into a morass of rude and threatening images.

"It is irresponsible to show violence on television," she said. "Totally. Especially TV that is real, like the people and panelists on my show. We're not just doing a movie where everybody understands that it's fiction. So I never show violence on my show. If guests start fighting, we stop the taping. The guards come in and when everybody's calmed down, then we proceed. I say no to violence. Flying saucers, that's OK, because I am going after the ratings."[18]

Although she strictly avoided situations on the show that might lead to physical confrontation, a number of the subjects she raised enraged certain elements of the viewing public. In January 1996, *El Show de Cristina* aired a homosexual marriage ceremony. The marriages on television of two women and two men by a Methodist minister from Los Angeles led to an immediate attack by a number of clerics, especially an Episcopalian minister named Oscar Agüero. Angry letters flooded Univision.

The incident even affected the family directly. On the weekend after the program, as Cristina's father, Bebo, was attending mass, he heard attacks by the priest lambasting his oldest daughter from the pulpit. Cristina's son, Jon Marcos, now eleven years old, came home from Catholic school frightened by a number of nuns who verbally attacked his mother. "That week I got my whole family together," said Saralegui. "I told them that if they wanted me to stop, I would. But everyone told me to keep at it."[19]

For the most part, Saralegui's shows did not provoke anger but tremendous support. She did a program with the Surgeon General of the United States, Antonia Novello, a Puerto Rican physician. The program advocated the benefits for children who take science courses. For Saralegui, Antonia Novello represented the best role model of a woman crusading for an important cause. In another segment, she interviewed Edward James Olmos, highly respected actor and director and activist for human rights causes. Olmos suffered from dyslexia and represented to the viewers the kind of success and respect that can be achieved despite handicaps. A woman in the audience during a taping of one of the shows said, "Cristina is like a teacher. I learn so much from her, about things I never even thought about."[20]

Looking back at some of the memorable programs aired by *El Show de Cristina*, Saralegui remembered the one with the largest audience ever—a three-part sketch on the life and death of the Tejano singer Selena. The most frightening show, she said, was one on the phenomenon of multiple personalities. She and the audience watched as some of the panelists actually changed their personas during the program.

On reflection, Saralegui has said that the most entertaining program she ever produced was one titled "Old, but Not Over the Hill." A group of women over sixty years old came on the show and merrily stripped off some of their clothing to music. One of the saddest shows introduced one of Cristina's friends who had worked for the Peruvian edition of *Cosmopolitan*. Her friend had contracted AIDS from her husband and had given birth to a child with AIDS. The later death of her friend was one of the personal events that would lead Saralegui to become a staunch champion of AIDS prevention.

The pace of Saralegui's career was exhausting. In addition to the regular preparation and taping of shows, there was the travel and special events to break ground in new media markets, to allow the public to get a glimpse of the increasingly popular celebrity. In addition to jaunts to foreign countries, in one year she taped a program in New York, took part in a Puerto Rican parade in Trenton, New Jersey, was queen of a music festival in Philadelphia, and grand marshal of a Christmas parade in Santa Ana, California.

Saralegui appeared in fiestas in Latino neighborhoods around the country, and she gave out scholarships to underprivileged Latino children. At the end of one year, Univision decided to film its Christmas special at Saralegui's home. Cristina and Marcos survived the tension, the physical demands, and the frequent outbursts of frustration but realized they could not keep up the pace forever.

For an audience of daily viewers that reached in excess of one hundred million people from the Bronx and Los Angeles throughout Latin America and to other countries, Saralegui became something of a friend and adviser. She took her role seriously, and those who regularly followed her show sensed her dedication. "You just feel she could be your mother, your sister, or your friend," said a viewer from Los Angeles whose grandmother had come to the United States from Cuba. "She has that vibe about her."[21]

The *Cristina Show* became Spanish-language television's top-rated daily talk show. In 2003, the show switched from the grueling daily format to a weekly format and remained the number one Spanish-language television talk show in the United States.

"What I like most about our show is its variety," she said. "One day you may tune in and find a very funny show, and the next you may hear us tackling a very difficult subject or featuring a celebrity. I think this mix makes us unique and quite entertaining; as long as people continue to be people, ideas or topics for new shows will continue to flow."[22]

BUILDING A MEDIA EMPIRE

In 1991, Saralegui started two additional ventures—a radio program and a magazine. The new radio show was called *Cristina Opina* and was produced by Marcos on a national network called Cadena Radio Centro, broadcast in Spanish twenty-four hours a day via satellite. The program consisted of Saralegui delivering a series of messages and motivational segments, each lasting for two and half minutes. Mostly she talked about interpersonal relationships surrounding love affairs and life crises. She also talked about such national issues as that of requiring Spanish to be used in the classrooms. This was a forum in which Saralegui, one to one with the audience, could become even more the confidant and adviser to her listeners than she was in the television series, where many of the programs involved many people, sometimes in near-chaotic conditions.

In the summer of 1991 she also launched a monthly magazine called *Cristina La Revista* (Cristina the Magazine), which soon reached a circulation of more than 160,000 in the United States and Latin America. Considering the enormous demands on her time, Cristina herself was reluctant to leap once again into the magazine industry. Her husband and the company's business executives worked hard to change her mind. From the time she was a small girl, her life had been surrounded by magazines, publishers, and writers. She remained an avid magazine reader. As she said later, magazines were in her soul.

And so she gave her assent to the new publication. Cristina became the executive editor of the magazine; a young Colombian woman named Luz Maria Doria, who had begun an apprenticeship at *Cosmopolitan*, would take on the role of editor-in-chief. With this publication it would not be Saralegui who would be deeply involved with the layout and photographs as she had done for so many years in her magazine career; she would now oversee the publication. As with so many of her ventures, Saralegui's magazine became successful almost immediately. Over the course of its fifteen-year life, it would reach millions of readers.

In addition to her television and publishing ventures, Saralegui often appeared on many national and local television programs, including, for a time, the Univision soap opera *Amandote*.

In October 1998, Saralegui started a bilingual website, Cristina Online (www.cristinaonline.com), providing access to all of the subsidiaries of her corporation, Cristina Saralegui Enterprises, Inc. Replete with news, biographical information, photographs, and other aspects of her life and career, the website continued to attract heavy use.

In 1997, Saralegui licensed her name for the first time. Although she had been approached in the past to lend her name to products ranging from clothing to perfume, she finally decided to endorse eyewear. The Cristina Collection, distributed by the Miami-based Cadore Moda USA, was targeted specifically to Hispanic women.

In 2001, she became only the fourth woman in the history of American entertainment to own her own studio, joining Mary Pickford, Lucille Ball, and Oprah Winfrey. Her Blue Dolphin Studios in Miami became a state-of-the-art television facility.

By 2004, Saralegui's name was licensed to fifteen manufacturers of home-related products from couches, to mattresses, candles, bed linens, towels, dishes, glasses and rugs. Casa Cristina, a furniture line manufactured by Pulaski, reflected the culture in which Saralegui was raised. One of lines, "Costa Dorada" (Golden Coast), was influenced by the coastal region of Spain where her grandparents once called home.

"Casa Cristina," she said, "is a fusion of my exposure to our culture and tastes, from my early years in Havana to my roots back in Spain and the Basque country and my many travels as a journalist throughout Latin America. My home furnishings line brings to life these sensibilities that I hope will make our Latino consumers feel proud to be part of the whole experience and environment we have worked hard to create."[23]

Much like Oprah Winfrey and Martha Stewart, to both of whom she was often compared, Saralegui, in her late fifties, had become something of a brand name. She had swept through several industries like a brush fire—her magazines, the talk show, a Miami television studio, a furniture line, a website, a constant presence on radio, television, and a book she authored titled *Cristina: My Life as a Blonde*, published by Warner Books in 1998.

In August 2005, *Time* magazine named her one of the "25 Most Influential Hispanics in America." She became the first Spanish-language television personality to receive a star on the Hollywood Walk of Fame. She was presented a Lifetime of Achievement Award in Hispanic Television by Multichannel News and Broadcasting & Cable.

In May 2006, the American Association of Retired Persons (AARP), a nonprofit organization for people over fifty years old, announced the launch of a Hispanic/Latino marketing campaign that included the "celebrity icon Cristina Saralegui." It marked the first time that AARP had used a Hispanic celebrity as part of a marketing campaign. "Cristina Saralegui is a great voice to reach the Hispanic community, and, like AARP, she understands the importance of providing information and services that can contribute positively to Hispanic/Latino families," said the CEO of AARP, Bill Novelli. "Working together with Cristina we hope to introduce more Hispanics to AARP and to show how AARP can improve the lives of Hispanics and their families."[24]

"The community pays attention when she endorses a product or service," said Ken Cervantes, vice president and activation director at MediaVest's multicultural agency Forty-Two Degrees. "Because of this, I believe that she is very aware of what she endorses. If she doesn't believe in it, she doesn't do it."[25]

In the course of her life and career, Cristina Saralegui had never particularly seen herself as a woman with expansive sights in business. As she and Marcos began to expand the various enterprises in which she was engaged, she later recalled the influence of her father. "As a child, my role model was my dad," she said. "He was bigger than life. He was very entrepreneurial and was always creating new business ventures. I always called him my 'Pirate Love'. He had such energy."[26]

CRUSADER AGAINST AIDS

"When I started on television," Saralegui wrote, "it was April 1989. That first week, I taped a show tackling the HIV/AIDS issue, and I was surprised at my total ignorance about this very important health issue. That show motivated me to learn more about HIV/AIDS, and that's how I became more involved and finally an activist."[27]

Saralegui was among the first television personalities to discuss HIV and AIDS. Her show regularly focused on sex and relationship issues, which had been formerly considered taboo on Spanish-language television. "That, to me, is one of the biggest contributions she has made,'" said Hector Orci, cofounder of Los Angeles–based La Agencia de Orci. "Latinos are very private and generally hold onto the intimate details of their lives. In the case of Cristina, she handled it sensitively and she made it relevant. Now, we can talk about these things in relation to her program."[28]

Through various charities and efforts, Saralegui raised hundreds of thousands of dollars for AIDS research and treatment facilities in Mexico and the United States. In 1996, she and her husband founded an AIDS organization called "The Arriba la Vida/Up With Life Foundation," which is dedicated to providing information, medicine, and support to Hispanic people afflicted with AIDS. She has also served on the council for the American Foundation for AIDS Research (Am Far), founded by actress Elizabeth Taylor and Mathilde Krimm. In December 1996, in front of the General Assembly at the United Nations on World AIDS Day, Saralegui began her remarks by saying, "I am the lady that fights AIDS in Spanish."[29]

Saralegui has constantly cited the alarming statistics about the effects of the AIDS epidemic among Latino populations. One out of every four cases of AIDS among infants is a Latino child. One of every five cases of AIDS among adolescents is a Latino youth. "For these reasons," she said, "and after witnessing a lot of human misery, many lives cut short in the flower of youth, and a lot of wasted potential, I donate my life and money and all the means of communications at my disposal to warn and inform, and raise the public consciousness in regards to this epidemic. We cannot afford to let up in the fight against this disease, which is decimating our population and represents an imminent danger for our future generations. Remember: They are our future."[30]

HELPING BUILD LATINO PRIDE

Cristina Saralegui has been one of the most influential and valued voices in the Latino community. Reaching a worldwide audience of more than one hundred million viewers with her celebrated television show and millions of others through her radio programs, magazines, and website, she has helped shape views of modern Latinos in ways unprecedented in scope. Weathering criticism and her own personal doubts, she addressed issues in frank and honest ways in mediums through which they had been before little explored.

For millions of Latinos, it was as if there suddenly was a friend, an *amiga*, with easy laughs and mild reprimands, who was there on screen or on the air that you could call on for advice. There was someone who dared talk about issues that might have filled you with fear or uneasiness and that now were being brought forth for discussion. She was there with information and encouragement along with entertainment. Many structured their days around the time that they could see or hear Cristina.

The Latino culture in which modern women found themselves was generally conservative. There were things that were mostly hushed or forbidden in public settings but were of crucial interest in ways that affected their health, happiness, self-esteem, and emotional stability. Many have credited Saralegui with helping break down certain Latino norms by engaging in subjects traditionally off-limits such as machismo, domestic violence, and menopause. Her goal, she said, was clear—to "raise my people's self-esteem and knowledge quotient so they can succeed in this very competitive country, and make them feel that they are supported in their efforts."[31]

Saralegui helped millions bridge large gaps in information, equipping them with honest and open discussion of issues and controversies. If many were uncomfortable and tuned her out, others welcomed her into their homes as they had no other media personality before. According to a number of polls, Latinos chose Cristina as their most trusted television personality. In 2004, 80 percent of Hispanics twenty-five to fifty-four years old polled by the Chicago-based research firm Synovate said they trusted Saralegui, and 70 percent considered her a role model.

Part of Saralegui's success was attributable to the exploding Latino population in the United States. "Americans have to understand that we are here, and we are Americans," she told the *Boston Globe*. "In a few years we will outnumber African Americans. Americans have to wake up and realize we're not going away. We're not foreigners. This is our country."[32]

She traveled frequently, making appearances at benefits and accepting awards from charities and social service agencies across the country that she had supported. At a benefit in California hosted by Lieutenant-Governor Cruz Bustamante, she said, "I'm a Cuban from Miami, but I'm here because Cruz Bustamante, who is a Mexican American, is a friend of mine, and he asked me to come. I think we all need to help bring about positive changes in the lives of Latinos wherever we can."[33]

Gloria Estefan, her close and supportive friend for many years, has marveled over her endurance. Saralegui, she said is "a testament to what one can achieve through talent, perseverance, and determination."[34]

In 2007, Saralegui could look back over a long career and still look forward to extraordinary times ahead. "It's about being able to get in there with some information that I think is needed, but to entertain at the same time," she said. "Being able to influence public opinion as a mom and, as of three months ago, a grandmother, is important. That's why I stick around."[35]

Reflecting on her career, she said that the Cristina that was on the television show was not just Cristina Saralegui; it was the people, the audience themselves, "real people, honest people, people who live, work, suffer, have fun, dream, question, doubt, and continue to suffer. In short, people like your neighbor, your children's teacher, the gardener, the student, the secretary, the bricklayer, the retiree, you, and—last of all—me." Her goal, she said, was to help improve the lives of Latinos everywhere, "to help them raise their economic level and better their personal situations. And, of course, to help them be more productive in their communities."[36]

NOTES

1. Jeanne Dequine, "The Hispanic Oprah: Spanish-speaking TV viewers know this talk show host and magazine publisher simply as Cristina," *Time*, January 24, 2005, 10.

2. Deborah Wilker, "¿Quien Habla Success? In the world of Spanish-language talk shows, it's Cristina Saralegui," *Hollywood Reporter*, May 24, 2004, 10.

3. Cristina Saralegui!: *Cristina!: My Life as a Blonde*, New York, Warner Books, 1998, 22.

4. Ken Kerschbaumer, "Cristina Saralegui," *Broadcasting & Cable*, October 10, 2005, 30.

5. Saralegui, 35.

6. George Rush and Joanna Molloy, "Fidel tells all about his beard, books, and Bush," *New York Daily News*, December 14, 2007, 28.

7. Saralegui, 51.

8. Saralegui, 72–73.

9. "A Latina Icon with Multimedia Presence: After 18 years on the air, talk show host Cristina Saralegui is a brand all her own." *TelevisionWeek*, October 16, 2006, 26, http://find.galegroup.com/itx/start.do?prodId=GRGM.

10. Saralegui, 77.

11. Saralegui, 83.

12. Alisa Valdes, "Talk TV's Numero Uno," *Boston Globe*, February 10, 1998, http://www.cristinaonline.com/html/bostonglobee.html.

13. Ana Figueroa, "A Live Wire," *AARP Segunda Juventud*, 2004, http://www.aarpsegundajuventud.org/english/entertainment/2004-jan/cristina.htm.

14. Saralegui, 128.

15. "A Latina Icon."

16. Kevin Downey, "The Power of Cristina," *Broadcasting & Cable*, October 1, 2007, 8A, http://find.galegroup.com/itx/start.do?prodId=GRGM.

17. Valdes.

18. "A Latina Icon."

19. Valdes.

20. Valdes.

21. Downey.

22. Figueroa.

23. "What Is Cristina Saralegui Doing these Days?" *Latino Leaders*, April 2007, 52.

24. "A Latina Icon."
25. Downey.
26. Figueroa.
27. Figueroa.
28. Downey.
29. "A Latina Icon."
30. CristinaOnline, http://www.cristinaonline.com/english/album/index.asp.
31. "She Made It: Cristina Saralegui," The Paley Center for Media, http://www.shemadeit.org/meet/biography.aspx?m=50.
32. Valdes.
33. Figueroa.
34. "She Made It."
35. Downey.
36. Saralegui, 205–206.

FURTHER READING

CristinaOnline, http://www.cristinaonline.com/english/album/index.asp.

"Cristina Saralegui." *Contemporary Hispanic Biography*. Vol. 2. Gale Group, 2002. Reproduced in Biography Resource Center, Farmington Hills, MI, Thomson Gale, 2007, http://galenet.galegroup.com/servlet/BioRC.

Dequine, Jeanne. "The Hispanic Oprah: Spanish-Speaking TV Viewers Know This Talk Show Host and Magazine Publisher Simply as Cristina." *Time*, January 24, 2005, 10.

Downey, Kevin. "The Power of Cristina." *Broadcasting & Cable*, October 1, 2007, 8A, http://find.galegroup.com/itx/start.do?prodId=GRGM.

Figueroa, Ann. "A Live Wire." *AARP, Segunda Juventud*, 2004, http://www.aarpsegundajuventud.org/english/entertainment/2004-jan/cristina.htm.

Kerschbaumer, Ken. "Cristina Saralegui." *Broadcasting & Cable*, October 10, 2005, 30.

"A Latina Icon with Multimedia Presence: After 18 Years on the Air, Talk Show Host Cristina Saralegui Is a Brand All Her Own." *TelevisionWeek*, Oct 16, 2006, 26, http://find.galegroup.com/itx/start.do?prodId=GRGM.

Saralegui, Cristina. *Cristina! My Life as a Blonde*. New York: Warner Books, 1998.

Valdes, Alisa. "Talk TV's Numero Uno," *Boston Globe*, February 10, 1998, http://www.cristinaonline.com/html/bostonglobee.html.

Courtesy of Photofest

Selena

Selena Quintanilla Perez, a Mexican-American singer from Texas, achieved fame early, first as a performer of Tejana music and then as one of the first crossover artists melding Latin and American pop music.

On a night in August 1995, outside Craig's Record Factory in a shopping center parking lot on the south side of Corpus Christi, Texas, four thousand people jammed into an area designed to hold fifteen hundred. Most were teenagers. They were there to buy a record album, but this was not just any record. To the fans of Selena this was something like her last will and testament. A few months earlier, the twenty-three-year-old sensation, known as the Tejano music queen, had been gunned down in the sunrise of her career, shot to death in a bizarre twist of fate by the president of her fan club.

At 12:00 A.M., the release of Selena's album *Dreaming of You* would mark her posthumous entry into American music's pop mainstream. As they waited in the parking lot, groups of young girls dressed up in the style of the slain Tejano music queen danced and lip-synched to an earlier Selena song called "Bidi Bidi Bom Bom." The store managers at Craig's kept orderly control on the growing crowd that began to swell to mosh-pit conditions. They played Selena's music. They talked about her career. They held a lip-synch contest for contestants ranging from toddlers to some in their twenties. They even passed out free food. At every mention of Selena's name, the crowd cheered. Some wept.

Finally, at the appointed hour, the store opened its doors. A thirty-year-old housewife named Alice Doria had the honor of purchasing the first album at Craig's Record Factory that evening. She had started the line at 12:30 in the afternoon with her ten-year-old daughter, two nieces, and a neighbor. "I bought a cassette and a CD," said Doria. "I'm gonna put one away and play one till it wears out. Then I'm gonna buy another."[1]

Dreaming of You was not extraordinary artistry. It included four songs that Selena wrote and sang in English, two bilingual cuts, including one with the Talking Heads' David Byrne, two mariachi numbers from the movie *Don Juan DeMarco*, in which she made a cameo appearance, and a number of Spanish songs. But Alice Doria and the others at Craig's Record Factory were only a few who purchased the album that week. It sold 175,000 copies the first day and 331,000 copies in the first week. It shot up to *Billboard* magazine's top spot and stayed in the top ten for several weeks.

For a variety of reasons, the album made an enormous impact: the circumstances of Selena's death, the sudden emergence of Tejana music fusing with rock and roll and other musical forms, and the great popularity of the beautiful, magnetic star from Corpus Christi who was making a name for herself far outside the boundaries of Texas.

In an interview after the release of the album soon after her death, Selena's father, Abraham Quintanilla, Jr., said, "The mainstream market was her dream, a goal. This is what she would have wanted. So I don't want to deny my daughter, even though she's dead, that dream that she had."[2]

Selena made much more than a crossover to the mainstream record market. Soon after her death, the signs of how much she meant to the Latino community became increasingly dramatic. Fans from across the country, especially from Los Angeles, areas of the Southwest and even from Chicago, began to make the trek to Corpus Christi. It became something like a pilgrimage. The visitors traveled to the family residences, three homes built side by side behind a chain-link fence in the working class district of Molina. Selena's parents lived in the middle house, Selena's brother, A.B., occupied a house flanking his parents, and on the other side was where Selena's widower lived. The sidewalks surrounding the house were chalked with inscriptions soon after her death. Visitors then drove over to Q Productions, the family's recording business that Selena made famous. A converted autobody shop in a stretch of small industrial businesses, the place was soon filled with remembrances and gifts from fans. Some visitors drove to the Day's Inn where Selena was shot. Some stayed the night there. Room 158, the room where she spent her final hours, now has a new number.

At the Seaside Memorial Park, the simple gravesite was soon covered in flowers and messages. Shortly after her death, cemetery officials said, over a thousand visitors a week paid homage. There is almost a mystical quality to her story, how this young Tejano artist, through her short career and tragic death, became a revered symbol and Latina icon. It all began with the music.

CHILD OF TEJANO MUSIC

Selena was born on Easter Sunday, April 16, 1971, in Lake Jackson, Texas, a small industrial town near Houston. Her father, Abraham Quintanilla, Jr., worked as a shipping clerk at the Dow Chemical plant; he and his wife Marcella had three children: Abraham III (A.B.), Suzette, and Selena, the youngest.

Abe Quintanilla had been born and raised in southern Texas. His roots lay in Mexico, with a family that had joined thousands of migrant farm workers crossing the Rio Grande to pick vegetables, cotton, and other seasonal crops. Later, they had settled in Corpus Christi and, finally, in Lake Jackson. Selena's mother, whose maiden name was Marcella Samora, had moved from Washington state where she had spent much of her childhood. Her roots also were from migrant workers from Mexico.

Both Abe and Marcella were part of a generation whose cultural roles were a blend of Mexican and North American. They were neither Anglo, as the normal sense of the term was used, nor Mexican, as those born in Mexico were called in Texas. Some Anglos used the word "Spanish" in referring to individuals such as Abraham and Marcella. A Mexican term used to define those of Mexican heritage born in Texas was "Tejano." That word also defined the kind of music that had been at the heart of Abraham's life since he was a youngster.

Abe Quintanilla loved Tejano music. For about fourteen years he had been in a Tejano band called Los Dinos and, although his own musical career as a performer did not succeed as he wished, music remained his passion. Quintanilla had also been the band's business representative, the member responsible for making contacts with dance-hall operators, record-label executives, and those in the jukebox business. The band may have disappeared, but he still had the keen musical instincts and business acumen.

By the time A.B. was six years old, his father was teaching him to play guitar. As A.B. became increasingly skilled, Selena began to sing along with the music. Her father recognized immediately that she had a gift—a clear voice, with perfect pitch and even a sense of timing and effect that seemed innate. She had something special, her father said, and he could see it from the first day she began to sing.

Neighbors of the Quintanillas in Lake Jackson remembered Selena as something of a tomboy, playing kickball and football with the boys, roller-skating on the sidewalk, athletically talented in everything she tried. Harold Lindloff, an officer at First State Bank, recalled: "Everyone had a feeling that she was destined to be more than the average child. She was so beautiful. She was so vibrant… she always had a twinkle in her eye… you could always cut up with her. She had that aura, something magical."[3]

Selena herself remembered her early years in Lake Jackson fondly. "I remember how green it was," she said. "I loved Lake Jackson because of the green grass, the trees. I remember eating at the Sonic and the Daily Bar." One of her close friends in those years, Meredith Lynn Cappel, said, "Selena could run faster than anybody. We wanted to show everybody we were stronger. We did not like the prissy little girls."[4]

Many friends later recalled how the Quintanilla's religious beliefs affected Selena's early life. Meredith Lynn Cappel said that birthday parties were prohibited for Jehovah's Witnesses. "In our school that meant any time there was a party, she had to go the library or she went home. She missed out on all the fun and I hated that. I had a birthday party and she couldn't come." Although Selena told a friend that the restrictions of the Jehovah's Witness faith were not that confining, all of her friends agreed that they must have constantly been a source of disappointment.[5]

For Abe Quintanilla, his children now became his own life's focus. Even at early ages, he pushed hard to instill in them his own love of Tejano music. It originated from Texas natives of Mexican descent who forged elements of both cultures into a unique sound appreciated on both sides of the border. "A lot of people say that Tejano music is like country music but in Spanish," said Pete Garcia, a program director at Abilene's KJTZ-FM, an all-Tejano FM station. "This music can really touch on what's happening in your life, whether you lost someone, divorced someone, whatever. And even if it's a sad song, it has a great beat and you can dance to it. It just speaks to their lives."[6]

Fusing Mexican, pop, polka, country, and big band sounds, Tejano music combined history and pride, speaking to the hard times and struggles of working people and their hopes, fears, and loves lost. It was a complicated mixture of traditional Mexican folk music and European styles. It spoke of the despair of migrant workers in the cotton and onion fields of southern Texas. It is not surprising that Tejano bands often played new renditions of the song "Las Nubes," one of the theme songs for the United Farm Workers.

Its distinctive accordion sound derived from the Czech and German immigrants of the nineteenth century. Their polkas had fused with traditional Mexican music in a style called *conjunto*. The accordion and its distinctive "oom-pah" sound propelled the music. It took root in the cantinas and bars of Mexican workers. In the 1930s and 1940s, migrant farmworkers who played music and had heard the popular American big band sounds added some orchestra instrumentation such as the saxopohone to the cantinas of southern Texas, turning *conjunto* into Tejano.

Bandleader and vocalist Isidro "El Indio" Lopez was the first big-name Tejano star and many credit him with creating its sound when he combined the saxophone with the accordion. Tejano performers sang and played themes for those whose lives straddled the two cultures. Mostly it was music of hard work and struggle. The sound became increasingly popular in San Antonio and, especially, Corpus Christi.

Lopez inspired other Texas-Mexicans, a number of performers who became household names in the border towns. Little Joe Hernandez, for example, used heavy brass and string ensembles. Nearly all Tejano artists were born in the United States, spoke fluent English, and sang in Spanish, a gesture to their Mexican roots and their culture that, at the same time, embraced the real situations they all faced as modern American citizens on the border.

Bob Pena, a program director of a music radio station in Corpus Christi, said, "Tejanos are fiercely proud of our culture. That's why we embrace the music so much. It's ours, it was born here. Most of our audience, their parents speak English in the house, but maybe their grandparents only speak Spanish. They flip back and forth." Around 1980, he said, groups like La Mafia and Grupo Mazz revolutionized the music, using synthesizers and bits of international pop sound. "In California, people are much more influenced by Mexican culture. We embrace that culture, but we don't mind the music changing."[7]

Quintanilla himself described Tejano music as "a fusion, with all these influences of rock and roll, pop, country, jazz. We're Americans who happen to be of Mexican descent. When [the musicians] play a Mexican song, they infuse it with all the influences in their heads."[8]

Abe used whatever extra cash the family could afford to buy used musical instruments—a guitar for A.B. and a drum set for Suzette. This would be the family hobby, he said. Although his oldest daughter was not immediately taken with the idea that she should be a drummer, she eventually went along with the idea. Music for the young members of the Quintanilla family was for the most part imposed by Abraham. He transformed the family garage into a soundproof music studio so that neighbors would not complain about the noise.

None of the children relished the idea of practicing musical instruments when they could be engaging in other activities with their friends. At first, Quintanilla required only fifteen minutes a day of practice. Gradually, he increased the time and, with it, the constant bickering. Nevertheless, he pushed on and his intention was clear. He saw in his young children the beginnings of a small band.

Quintanilla soon quit his job at Dow Chemical and put all of his savings into a new business venture. In the summer of 1980, he started a Mexican restaurant called Papa Gayo's. Although the area of the town where he began the restaurant was populated by a high percentage of Latinos and there were no Mexican restaurants in the immediate vicinity, the venture struggled. The local economy was suffering, and most residents did not have the extra cash to spend at a restaurant. Quintanilla forged ahead. He planned to put in the center of the restaurant a dance floor for live entertainment and a platform for live performances. The performers he had in mind for the platform were the family's band. And he already had a name planned—"Los Dinos," the name of his own group that had disbanded a number of years earlier.

Selena did not grow up speaking Spanish. The family did not speak the language in the home, and she did not hear much Spanish spoken in Lake Jackson's Oran M. Roberts Elementary School or on the playgrounds. For her to be a credible Tejano singer, Abe Quintanilla knew, Selena would have to have a reasonable facility with the language. Johnny Herrera, an award-winning Tejano songwriter who later composed some of Selena's music, told Abe, "If you're going to make it, you'll have to record in Spanish. You can't compete with the big companies."[9]

Thus, Selena's father and brother now became her speech coaches. A.B., who also wrote many songs, spent hours together with Selena teaching her to sing the ballads and lively songs phonetically. Fortunately, she had a facile mind for understanding both language and music. Although she would not be able to speak Spanish fluently until she was in her late teens, she did learn enough pronunciation and idioms phonetically to begin to practice songs in Spanish. By the age of nine, she could belt out a number of rousing tunes to the accompaniment of her brother on guitar and her sister on the drums. The Spanish sound came to her easily, and even at an early age her songs did not betray anything of an English accent.

Selena not only played the new music written by her brother and other Tejano pieces, she also enjoyed trying out the soul music of Little Anthony and the Imperials and the rhythm and blues of Michael Jackson. Through countless jam sessions with her brother and sister, the small family band was coming together.

Los Dinos began playing regularly at Papa Gayo's. Advertisements in the local paper invited customers to enjoy the best flautas in the area and to hear the sensational nine-year-old singer. After visiting Papa Gayo's, a local disc jockey named Primo Ledesma from a Spanish-language radio show was so impressed by Selena that he asked her father if he could tape the band. When Ledesma played the recording the next day on his show, callers flooded the phones.

The family itself was becoming even more close-knit. Selena later remembered these early days of the band quite fondly. Despite the reluctance of the children to get involved in music, the effort had brought them closer together. Abe Quintanilla later said, "Every time we saw each other, even if it was ten or fifteen times a day, there would always be hugs and kisses."[10]

But Abe's venture into the restaurant business ended a year after it started. Inexperienced in the technical matters of running a restaurant and hurt by an unfavorable location for the business, he was forced to close it down and declare bankruptcy. With the close of Papa Gayo's, with little savings upon which to fall back, and with no immediate prospects for employment, he and Marcella faced a crisis. In November 1981, the family moved in with one of Abe's brothers in a trailer park about seventy-five miles west of Lake Jackson. It was there that Selena attended the fifth grade. For a time, Abe worked for a trucking business delivering gravel. The band, however, played on. He managed to find gigs for Los Dinos at weddings and other occasions.

Within a year the family moved again, this time back to Lake Jackson. While driving a dump truck during the day, Quintanilla continued to work with the band. Finally, he began to see the hard times as an opportunity. Although he had seen the professional development of the band as something further down the road, perhaps this was the time to take a gamble. He decided to use his music connections and savvy to turn his small family band into a successful business venture.

But Lake Jackson was not the base from which to launch a fledgling Tejano group. The town existed mainly for the Dow Chemical Company and its employees. It did not have any particular roots to the Tejano music scene. Soon, the family sold the Lake Jackson house and headed for Corpus Christi, one of central locations for lovers and practitioners of the music Abe Quintanilla loved so much.

ON THE TOUR BUS AND IN THE RECORDING STUDIO

The Quintanilla family arrived in the Gulf coast town where Abe had spent much of his childhood. Corpus Christi was one of the few towns in the

United States where Tejano music had created a stir. This was the ideal location, Quintanilla reasoned, where he could launch the new band. His hopes centered on the young girl singer with the strong, mellifluous voice and the natural stage presence that seemed to have come to her as a birthright. Her father decided to change the name of the band slightly. It would now be called Selena y Los Dinos.

Selena was eleven years old and she was on center stage. A.B., who had a unique gift for writing music, furiously began to write some songs for his younger sister while he played guitar and Suzette became increasingly proficient at the drums.

After settling down in Corpus Christi for a short time and playing the rural dance halls and urban nightclubs where Tejano music had already achieved a foothold, Quintanilla decided to take the band on the road. The family purchased an old, dilapidated van with one foldout bed in the back. The ancient vehicle, belching out its noxious diesel fumes, was not only an irritant to those who traveled in it. In many cases, people enveloped by its choking smoke would ask Abe to turn the thing off. He always refused, saying that it might not start again.

In the classic tradition of traveling musicians, they packed up their instruments and started down the highway. They hit small towns in southern Texas, playing everything from weddings to honkytonks, usually to very small audiences. On occasion, Abe would join the band, playing guitar and sometimes singing duets with Selena.

"That's when we began our musical career," recalled Selena. "We had no alternative.... If we got ten people in one place, that was great," she said. "We ate a lot of hamburgers and shared everything." Looking back on those hard times, she later said, "I lost a lot of my teenage period... but I got a lot out of it too. I was more mature."[11]

Selena managed to complete the seventh grade at West Oso Junior High School in Corpus Christi. Nevertheless, she increasingly missed long periods of school while on the road. School officials threatened to report her father to the Texas Child Services Department for forcing her to work and depriving her of an education.

Marilyn Greer, Selena's seventh-grade reading teacher at West Oso, had been particularly vociferous in objecting to the way in which Selena was being deprived of much of her schooling. She said later that she regarded Selena as potentially an outstanding student, perhaps of valedictorian quality. Beautiful and intelligent, Selena conducted herself, Greer said, like a "lady, which coming from the barrio was not an easy thing to do. You're talking someone who was bright, a minority, and a female. This child could have gotten a four-year scholarship with any major university in the country."[12]

Rebuffing all such ideas, Abe finally pulled Selena out of the eighth grade. Later, Selena finished a high school equivalency degree through a correspondence course program developed in Chicago. Selena herself increasingly regretted what she had missed in her early teenage years. She later told interviewers that she had missed being around kids her own age. She missed going to dances and to football games. Because of her isolation and the degree of control over her life demanded by her father, she was at the same time known by thousands but befriended by few. One thing was certain. Her achievements would not be in an academic setting. The family, and an increasingly growing number of people who saw her perform, saw her as a rising musical star. The young Tejano singer was not the first woman to make a mark in the field. Lydia Mendoza and Chelo Silver, Mexican-American singers in the 1930s, and Laura Canales, a pioneer orchestra singer in the 1970s, had paved the way for Tejano female vocalists. Lydia Mendoza had been particularly notable. Like Selena, she had begun her career at an early age with her family band. She had traveled extensively the roads of migrant workers in Mexico and recorded over twelve hundred songs.

But Selena had special qualities that seemed destined to launch her career to a new level of influence in the world of music. Even on those early tours around Texas and into Mexico, she was a growing sensation. A magnetic stage presence in her early teens, she was also an increasingly serious student of the blends of sounds and arrangements that could set the small group apart. With A.B. writing most of the music and with Selena and her father and sister all making contributions, the musical group experimented and developed its own unique sound.

Early on, her songs were cheerful with a tinny, Tijuana brass sound that brought to mind a sunny day at the fairground merry-go-round. Later, the music incorporated a range of new pop sounds. The music remained very much Spanish in influence but with a more pronounced beat and rocking sound that revved up audiences and drew the attention of record producers.

In 1984, the group recorded an album with Freddie Records called simply "Selena y Los Dinos." In the next few years, they recorded a number of records with regional Texas-based record labels and started a steady climb to the top of the Tejano music world. The band now appeared in larger venues, including ballrooms. They crossed into the national Latino and Latin American market, recording with the Puerto Rican band The Barrio Boyzz. They began to gather a following in such areas south of the border as Matamoros. Playing alongside Tejano music singer Emilio Navaira, Selena y Los Dinos appeared before an enormous crowd in Monterrey. Her stadium concerts regularly drew more than sixty thousand fans. Selena would later record duets with Navaira. Selena also began to appear on Latin American television. By the age of thirteen she had made appearances on such shows as the Johnny Canales Show, "Sábado Gigante," and "Siempre en Domingo."

In 1986, GP Records released two Selena albums. One of the songs, "Dame un Beso," became a modest hit and helped her win a Hispanic Music Award (Female Vocalist of the Year) and two Tejano Music Awards (Female Vocalist of the Year and Performer of the Year). In 1987, the fifteen-year-old

sensation was Tejano Music Awards winner for best female vocalist and performer of the year. Slowly, steadily, she and the band were becoming more
successful, sometimes playing to overflow crowds and drawing invitations
from numerous venues.

But the days and nights on the road were a constant, grueling swirl of
towns and cities, bars and nightclubs, and little time for play or quiet or, for
Selena, working on her correspondence courses. A typical run could be an
afternoon performance in San Antonio, followed by a night gig in Dallas,
and an afternoon appearance the next day in Waco. There were always bags
to be packed and unpacked, equipment to be lugged around, and the usual
irritations over money owed the group for their work.

In 1989, at the Tejano Music Awards at the San Antonio Convention Center, Selena was approached by a producer who had the power to catapult
her career beyond the still narrow field of Tejano music. He was Jose Behar
and he was president of Capitol/EMI Latin Records. By the next morning at
breakfast, Selena's father and Behar had agreed to a deal that would bring
her talents to a worldwide market. He made it clear to Selena that EMI was
looking for an artist who could bridge the cultural range of music types, a
"bi-cultural" performer that could appeal to both Latino and Anglo audiences. He saw in the radiant youngster with the commanding stage presence the
perfect prospect to fill that niche.

Selena's look was unmistakably Tejano: shiny boots, tight jeans, large belt
buckles, colorfully adorned Western shirts, and neatly brimmed cowboy
hats. In her late teens, as her career and her music developed, and as she
wove pop, country, and Caribbean dance music into the Tejano sound, her
fashion matured.

Many began to call her the "Latin Madonna." Her long black hair and
striking features, made even more alluring with rich, red lipstick, rouge,
tight leather pants, and her use of heavily-jeweled, elaborate, spangled bust-
iers that showed off her midriff, belied her Jehovah's Witness upbringing.
Although her father was not pleased with the new look, Selena would not
be deterred. Her interest in the latest fashion and in making her own mark
not only as a singer but also as a sparkling, vivacious performer surprised
many who had seen her act in the early years. "I love shiny things and I love
clothing," she said simply.[13]

"She could do more with a bra and rhinestones than anyone I ever knew,"
quipped Rosabel Lopez, a longtime friend. "I used to tell her, 'Girl, my daddy
would kill me if he saw me in something like that.'"[14] Selena became so interested in fashion that she often talked about designing her own line of clothing. Throughout her early years as a traveling singer, she read books on
fashion and created and drew thousands of designs. Often, fashion became
nearly a preoccupation. She longed to make her mark and to express her
identity in other ways than on the stage and in the recording studios. She
spoke often with many friends and relatives about a yearning to open

boutiques. As with most things that she explored, she tackled her interests with creativity and dogged determination.

If Selena's look was alluring and sexy, her private life was still controlled and, in some ways, nearly sheltered. She rarely went anywhere without a chaperone or in the company of one of the family members.

At the time Selena signed with Capitol/EMI, Abe Quintanilla decided to expand the small family music group into an eight-piece band. He hired Pete Astudillo, a musician, singer, and writer from Laredo, Texas. Astudillo and Selena recorded a number of successful duets. On two occasions, they were nominated for Vocal Duo of the Year at the Tejano Music Awards. Astudillo also helped write several of Selena's songs.

The Quintanilla family also hired a young guitarist named Chris Perez. Handsome, with slicked-back hair worn in a ponytail, Perez was an artful musician, creative and serious. From the moment Selena heard him play, she was convinced that he would make a striking addition to the band.

Keenly aware of the crossover prospects of the young sensation, EMI records soon asked Selena and the band to cut three English tracks. They included "Only Love," "Where Did the Feeling Go?," and "Is It the Beat?"

Soon, major advertisers saw the enormous potential of Selena to tap into several markets including young people, women and girls, and, especially, the growing Latino population. Coca-Cola USA signed Selena to a six-figure, five-year contract.

ALBUM GOLD

By the 1990s, most knowledgeable Tejano music lovers acknowledged that Selena was becoming the most popular Tejano artist in history. Her 1990 album "Ven Conmigo," which included a variety of ballads, cumbias, and pop, was the first Tejano album to reach Gold Record status. EMI had managed to enlist the renowned accordion player David Lee Garza for the album. The song "Baila Esta Cumbia," written by A.B., was a rousing success in both the United States and Mexico. Music critic Joey Guerra described the album as a breakthrough for Selena: "Tejano superstar Selena begins to fully embrace her unlimited potential on this slick collection, which features a standard mix of *rancheras* and pop tracks. Every song, however, is a gem, thanks to Selena's sultry delivery and brother A.B. Quintanilla III's solid production."[15]

Selena now had scores of fans, not only in Corpus Christi, but also in predominantly Latino communities across the United States and in Mexico. Teenage girls hoarded her records, danced to her music, and began to dress in outfits resembling those worn by Selena in concert. With this growing fan base, it was a logical step in the progression of a celebrity to have a formal fan club.

If an individual was interested in forming a Selena fan club, the proper first step was to approach Abe Quintinalla, her highly protective father and manager. Quintanilla, after all, looked after Selena's affairs with intense care and scrutiny. In 1991, a woman named Yolanda Saldivar asked for a meeting with Quintanilla. Her hope, indeed her mission, she said, was to head a fan club that would help bring the glorious talents of Selena to the world's attention. She told Quintanilla that from the first time she saw Selena at a concert in San Antonio in 1989 she had been her most devoted fan.

Short and heavy-set, Saldivar was a loner who lived in a modest house near San Antonio, next to her relatives. Her father had supported the family as a headwaiter at a local Mexican food restaurant. She was eleven years older than Selena. A registered nurse who had worked in two hospitals, Yolanda had never married or had children of her own but had taken custody of three of her brother's children after he had abandoned them. She was an aunt of one of Selena's childhood friends. Her obvious enthusiasm won over Quintanilla, and he gave her his permission to start the fan club, although there would be no immediate salary involved.

From the beginning, Saldivar seemed awed and devoted to Selena and spent much of her spare time organizing the fan club. "She never talked about having any boyfriends," said Esmeralda Garza, a friend who agreed to be the secretary of the Selena Fan Club. "She never had time."[16]

Soon after Saldivar launched the fan club, Selena expressed much enthusiasm and appreciation for her work. Selena had soon felt that Saldivar was something like a new family member. She called her "Buffy," the nickname her own family had given her that was short for buffalo. "She's doing exceptionally well," Selena said. "Fan clubs can ruin you if people get upset and turned off by them. But she's doing really good." Indeed, within four years, Selena's fan club boasted nine thousand members.[17]

Selena showed her gratitude to Saldivar by giving her numerous gifts. "Yolanda was crazy about spotted cows," says Garza. "So Selena bought an $800 rug with a cow on it. She bought her a cow phone in Los Angeles. They really splurged on her."[18]

One visit to her house would have convinced anyone she was Selena's biggest fan. Or it might have convinced them that Saldivar had obsessive feelings toward the singer. Yolanda had decorated the place something like a Selena shrine or museum complete with photographs and memorabilia, topped off by a life-size, cardboard figure of the singer.

As Selena's popularity grew, she remained very close to her family, not only in spirit but also in location. Although Suzette moved out of the neighborhood in Corpus Christi where the family had moved in 1981, the other members remained there in three adjoining houses. The only sign of affluence that the family allowed themselves was Selena's red Porsche Carerra that she drove around the city and parked in the driveway of her modest house. She seemed to her friends and the family the same warmhearted, sweet individual they had known throughout her life, playing softball, shopping at Wal-Mart, and picking up ice cream at a nearby store.

But Selena was now harboring a secret infatuation. For two years she had toured with Chris Perez, the young guitar player. One day Selena's brother, A.B., hinted to Perez that Selena might be more interested in Chris than just as a fellow member of the group. "I remember I was nineteen," Chris said later, "and her brother said to me 'Chris, what do you think about Selena?' I said, 'Oh, yeah, she's cool.' 'No, what do you think about Selena because she was asking me about you.'" Although traditional dating was difficult because of concert life, "little by little it all started coming together," said Perez.[19]

By 1991, the romance had become strong. "I never wanted to see anyone else, I never went out with anyone else; it was just Selena and me."[20] As the relationship intensified, Selena's father, increasingly aware of some of their stolen moments together, began to show his displeasure. So upset did he become that he fired the young guitarist. When Perez moved to San Antonio and took another job, Selena was inconsolable. With the future of the band in jeopardy, with his daughter now showing anger and bitterness against him that she had never before shown, Abe relented. He rehired Perez but continued to show his unhappiness with the relationship. Her mother, realizing the seriousness of the romance, warned her that marriage was a sacred commitment that should not be taken lightly.

But on April 2, 1992, Selena told her parents that she going out shopping. Instead, she headed to the Nueces County courthouse with Perez. Wearing a Coca-Cola jacket, the twenty-year-old singer married the twenty-two-year-old guitarist. Both wore Levis. The judge waived the normal seventy-two-hour waiting period and the couple said their vows.

"Ever since I was a little girl," Selena later remembered, "I'd dreamed of a big, wonderful wedding, with a long white gown and a bouquet of flowers. But my love was so strong I couldn't wait any longer for us to be husband and wife. I couldn't even wear my nicest dress because that would have made my father suspicious."[21]

Abe took the news with regret. He believed that Selena was too young. Nevertheless, his mind remained focused on the band. He encouraged Selena not to mention the fact that she was married in interviews. He also asked that she and Chris refrain from any flirtations on stage. There was no cataclysmic fracture of the family over the marriage. Chris and Selena moved in together in the lower-middle class family property in Corpus Christi.

Selena's album *Entre A Mi Mundo*, the first recorded after her marriage, sold more than 300,000 copies, breaking another record for a Tejano artist. It was the first Tejano CD to be certified as Double Platinum. It included not only Tejano tracks but also pop and Spanish rock. It was highlighted by a cumbia called "La Carcacha," with call-and-response chants, whistles, and searing guitar riffs from Perez accompanying Selena's scintillating vocals.

Her fame was growing. From Los Angeles to Washington, D.C., Selena appeared at various events. In Washington, D.C., Coca-Cola sponsored a celebration for the Hispanic caucus of the United States Congress. At the musical show, with radio disc jockey Johnny Canales as the host, Selena made a special impression on U.S. Representative Solomon Ortiz of Texas. The congressman told Canales that the entertainer was heading to the top.

From the early days on the road with the decrepit bus, the traveling Selena y Los Dinos troupe now had three vehicles carrying sixteen people along with several trucks hauling production gear. They were rapidly becoming a big-time show-business group.

On February 7, 1993, they pulled into the Memorial Coliseum in Corpus Christi for a free concert before three thousand fans. City officials, nervous about the possibility that an announced free concert by Selena would cause major pandemonium and an enormous traffic nightmare, asked Abe to print up free tickets—first come, first serve. The Memorial Coliseum event was recorded. In May 1993, Capitol-EMI released *Selena Live*, the fourth album produced by the company. It drew huge sales and enormous radio play.

Tejano music, with Selena's electricity and glittering acclaim, was gaining surprising popularity. After the Corpus Christ concert, she shared the stage with David Lee Garza at the Houston Livestock and Rodeo in the Astrodome. Every night for two weeks, sixty thousand fans packed the seats, cheering and clapping to the beat.

In clothing stores in the southwest, youngsters began buying black hats and black leather coats and matching black boots, a look Selena had popularized in a Coca-Cola advertisement. She and her music and her look were on fire.

In November 1993, Selena signed an international recording contract with SBK Records, a sister company of EMI. This was the beginning, Abe Quintanilla believed, of the great breakthrough for the Tejano artist. With SBK, Selena y Los Dinos would get its chance to crack the American pop music field with recordings sung in English. For Selena, this was a challenge that she accepted with much eagerness, a chance to expand in different musical directions, and an opportunity to break into an enormous new market. One of the SBK executives involved in the negotiations with the Quintanillas admitted that he had never before heard Tejano music. "But I was so impressed seeing this girl up there on stage," he said. "I think she has every element for international success. An amazing voice, a phenomenal stage presence, gorgeous looks, and a great personality."[22]

On March 1, 1994, at New York's Radio City Music Hall, *Selena Live* received a Grammy Award for best Mexican-American album. Selena, who attended the ceremonies, became the first Tejano artist ever to receive a Grammy. The album sold six hundred thousand copies in the United States alone. The fourth single from the album, "Fotos y Recuerdos," reached the top ten on *Billboard* magazine's Latino charts.

In 1994, EMI records produced "Amor Prohibido." Destined to become the signature album by Selena, the collection included a number of singles that became hits both in the United States and Mexico and established the artist as one of the superstars of the Latino music market and the most prominent of the young singers that were making a serious move into the crossover market. "No Me Queda Mas" and "Bidi Bidi Bom Bom" became instant classics, as did the unforgettable single used as the album title, "Amor Prohibido," a song written by Selena herself about the relationship between her grandparents. In Mexico, her grandmother had been a servant girl in the home of a very wealthy family and had fallen in love with one of the sons.

The album quickly rose to number one on Billboard's Latin Track Charts, easily breaking Gloria Estefan's record fifty-eight weeks for "Mi Tierra." The album also managed to make the Top 200 of Billboard's Pop Charts.

Selena was gaining confidence in her ability to run her own life outside the constraints of her father. "More and more decisions were being made by Selena," said Rudy Trevino, executive director of the Texas Talent Musicians Association, which produced the Tejano Music Awards. "There was a growing independence with commercial endorsements. She and Chris were talking about having a family."[23]

Selena also began actively to seek ways to contribute her time and efforts to help children and women. She spoke frequently at schools, encouraging students to stay in school, avoid drugs, and earn diplomas. She performed in a public service video entitled "Mi Musica," sponsored by Agree Shampoo, in which she spoke about the roots of Mexican music and the importance of education. She participated in many "Stay in School Jamborees." She became a spokesperson for D.A.R.E. (Drug Abuse Resistance Education), the highly regarded organization dedicated to giving children the skills they need to avoid involvement in drugs, gangs, and violence. She also recorded announcements for a Battered Women's Hotline. According to family members, friends, and fans, Selena, throughout her growing success, remained a caring and unassuming individual. As a show business celebrity, she seemed uniquely grounded in the roots of her family, culture, and personal perspective.

BUSINESSWOMAN

In 1994, Selena, in the midst of a meteoric rise in the music world, expanded her personal horizons. As she had dreamed for a number of years, she started a women's fashion business. She opened Selena Etc., Inc., in Corpus Christi, and she established another store in San Antonio. In addition to selling Selena's signature line of fashions and jewelry, the boutiques featured hairstyling and manicures. She also launched Selena Design House, Inc., a company that manufactured her line of clothes. She hoped to expand her operations in other United States cities as well as in Mexico. Early on, she planned to open a clothing factory in Monterrey, Mexico.

On the advice of Abe Quintanilla, Selena asked Yolanda Saldivar, the head of the fan club, to manage the boutiques. Saldivar worked hard at the job, accompanying Selena on a number of occasions to Mexico to plan for business expansion. Nevertheless, Saldivar began having difficulties with a number of the employees. She was demanding, stern, and envious of any of the professionals hired by the company who befriended Selena.

Designer Martin Gomez, who had been brought in to help the fashion line, always found Saldivar to be a source of tension. "She was mean, she was manipulative," he said. Gomez became so exasperated with the situation that he quit. "I told Selena I was scared of Yolanda," he says. "She wouldn't let me talk to Selena anymore. She was very possessive."[24] Despite the tensions, the business thrived. So did Selena's singing career. She began to record her English album with SBK Records in the fall of 1994.

On September 19, 1994, at the Jacob Javits Center in New York, Selena joined a few other bands to celebrate Mexican Independence Day. *New York Times* music critic Peter Watrous was there. "It is easy to see why," Watrous wrote, Selena "has such a large and adoring audience; she obviously loves her job, dancing with the freedom of somebody who has spent a good portion of her life onstage, and singing with a lovely and fluid voice." The crowd jammed to the front of the stage, the critic said, "and the occasional unconscious audience member was lofted over the front barrier, to be resuscitated backstage."[25]

In 1995, Selena made a brief appearance in the movies. In *Don Juan DeMarco*, she played the part of a mariachi singer and also performed music for the soundtrack. The film starred Johnny Depp as a man who believed that he was Don Juan, the greatest lover in the world. It was directed by Jeremy Leven, produced by Francis Ford Coppola, and also starred Marlon Brando and Faye Dunaway. Selena and her family left Hollywood hoping that this film would be the first of many to come.

In early 1995, Selena's "Bidi Bidi Bom Bom" won song of the year at the Tejano Music Awards. She also won five more of the fifteen awards, including best female entertainer, best female vocalist, album of the year, Tejano crossover song, and record of the year. Upon receiving the awards, she exclaimed, "Never in my dreams would I have thought I would become this big. I am still freaking out."[26]

On February 26, 1995, Selena appeared at the Houston Astrodome before a record crowd of more than sixty-one thousand people. After the opening act, Selena walked out into the stadium and stepped into an elegant horse carriage that took her to the stage. She sang for nearly an hour—Tejano hits along with newer music that would mark her crossover into the English market. After she finished, the crowd erupted with boisterous cheers and applause. She never seemed to disappoint.

BLACK FRIDAY

But all was not right with the management of Selena, Etc., Inc. and with the Selena fan club. The problem was Yolanda Saldivar. In addition to complaints by employees that she was overbearing, there was growing evidence that something was amiss with the financial side of the business. Several employees of Selena's San Antonio boutique raised concerns that Saldivar was likely embezzling money.

At the same time, Abe Quintanilla also received word from a number of Selena's fans that they were not receiving t-shirts and other Selena merchandise they had purchased from the fan club. Both Abe and Selena confronted Saldivar about the charges and asked to see books and records she had kept both as manager of the boutiques and as the head of the fan club. Saldivar emphatically rejected any notion that she had stolen money or defrauded the Quintanilla family. The books, she said, would prove her innocence.

At first, Selena rejected any notion that Yolanda was stealing from the company. After all, the two had become close. Saldivar seemed devoted to Selena and her career. Nevertheless, as the evidence mounted, Selena herself realized that perhaps the whispers and charges were true, that the head of her fan club and manager of her business dealings was secretly betraying her.

On Thursday, March 30, Saldivar phoned Selena to tell her that she was staying at the Days Inn in Corpus Christi and that she wanted Selena to come by the hotel to discuss the rumors. She claimed she had the papers that Selena and her father had requested.

Perez took Selena to the motel. As Selena went to see Yolanda, Chris stayed outside waiting at the truck. After a short time, Selena returned to the truck with the paperwork that she had demanded from Yolanda. When she returned home and began looking at the materials, she realized that much of the documentation she was looking for was not in the package.

Selena was soon back on the phone, asking Saldivar about the missing documents. They agreed to meet again the next day. Sometime after 10:00 A.M. the following Friday morning, March 31, Selena drove over to the Days Inn again, this time alone. In the motel, Selena and Saldivar argued. Yolanda then took a .38 caliber handgun that she had bought in San Antonio two weeks earlier and pulled the trigger. The bullet hit the singer in the right shoulder, severing an artery.

Selena managed to open the door and stagger out of the room. Running awkwardly past the swimming pool, screaming that she had been shot, she reached the front entrance of the motel and collapsed in the lobby. A number of motel workers rushed to her side and called the police. Though Selena remained conscious until paramedics arrived, she was rapidly losing blood. The response team rushed Selena to the hospital. Despite several blood transfusions, she died shortly thereafter.

After the shooting, Saldivar had run to her red GMC truck, jumped inside, locked the doors, turned the gun to her head, and began talking to police on her cell phone. For nine and a half hours the standoff continued between Saldivar and the police S.W.A.T. team. Finally, the police were able to coax her out of the truck. She surrendered at 9:30 P.M. and signed a confession that she later retracted.

In the hours after these tragic events, the chain-link fence in front of the Quintanilla family's house became a bereavement memorial. People draped flowers, pictures, messages, ribbons, teddy bears, and flags.

Selena Quintanilla, age twenty-three, was laid to rest on April 3, 1995. Six hundred persons attended her private Jehovah's Witness funeral. Prior to the funeral, thousands viewed her casket at the Bayfront Plaza Convention Center in Corpus Christi. In Los Angeles, four thousand people gathered at the Sports Arena Memorial to honor the slain singer. Mourners also gathered in San Antonio. The gravesite services were broadcast live by San Antonio and Corpus Christi radio stations.

In October, Yolanda Saldivar stood trial for murder. Because the defense argued successfully that the defendant could not get a fair trial in Corpus Christi, the venue was moved to Houston. After two weeks of testimony, many of the basic questions remained cloudy. Why had Yolanda bought a gun? Did she plan to kill herself or Selena? Was the shooting an accident or had Yolanda, her world with Selena crumbling about her, planned it all along? Was Yolanda simply an unstable, mentally disturbed individual who finally cracked under pressure?

The jury acted swiftly. After less than three hours of deliberation, the decision was announced: Yolanda Saldivar was guilty of murder, and was sentenced to life in prison. Whatever the nature and source of the demons that drove Yolanda Saldivar to kill Selena, there was no question about the reaction of millions of the singer's fans. March 31, 1995, became forever known as "Black Friday."

LATINA LEGEND

Soon after Selena's death, barrios not only in Texas but also in other Latino communities around the state and in Mexico featured street murals, souvenirs, homes decorated with quilts, paintings, and other remembrances. The tragic, slain singer was elevated to reverence usually reserved for saints.

Texas dance and music writer and editor Sarah Wimer said, "Selena will be an icon for all time for the sheer glory of her human spirit. Not many saints manifest themselves in these latter days, but for me, with her death, Selena became an instant saint. Her not-quite twenty-four years among us not only increased her own people's pride in themselves—especially young women—but she lived and sang and danced with all her being trying to get more respect for the living cultural legacy of her people and died trying to achieve the Great American Dream."[27]

A symbol of success as both a Latina and as a woman, Selena soon took on an identity as a pop icon, much like Elvis Presley. A visit to Corpus Christi for fans of Selena became much like a visit to Graceland by fans of Elvis. And in the Latino culture, icons often take on a quasi-religious symbolism—altars with her picture and other remembrances, for example, began to grace the homes of fans throughout the country and in Mexico.

"Pop culture icons offer insights into religion," said Gaston Espinosa, writer and teacher. "Selena also provided broader cultural appreciation for Latinos by challenging stereotypes and projecting a new image. "She destroyed the Latino stereotype of Cheech and Chong," Espinosa said. "Her power as a cultural symbol is based on her ability to represent, embody, and signify the values, attitudes, traditions, and struggles of her subculture: 'We don't want to live in the shadow lands; we are a people; we live in this country; there are 39 million of us; we do more than just eat tacos.'"[28]

Sara Wimer's own house reflected the reverence of many to Selena's life and tragic end. "I have an ofrenda (Mexican, and in my case, pantheistic altar) for Selena in my home," wrote Wimer. "A photo of her looking sultry, yet remote, is surmounted by Nuestra *Senora de Guadalupe*, surrounded by many images of people and objects I venerate, including a postcard of Stevie's statue right next to Selena, Hindu gods I worship from two years living in India, Frida Kahlo, John Cage, etc., but she is the central figure, the main icon."[29]

Betty Cortina, editorial director of *Latina* magazine, was a reporter with *People* when she went to Corpus Christi ten days after Selena's death to spend time with the singer's family. Researching Selena for over ten years, Cortina concluded that the singer's cultural legacy is much more important than her musical one to Latinos, particularly Mexicans and Mexican Americans.

Selena represented a young Hispanic girl, equal parts Mexican and American, wrote Cortina, "who was successful and unabashedly living her dream, but never abandoning her identity." Selena represented enormous pride, said Cortina, "because she was representing who we are.... She was the quintessential American success story, and to have that cut off is tragic."[30]

Selena's posthumous album, *Dreaming of You*, debuted at number one on Billboard magazine's album chart in July 1995, making it the second fastest-selling release by a female singer in the history of popular music.

In 1996, Time Warner, Inc., decided to launch a Spanish-language edition, *People En Espanol*, after a 1995 issue of the original magazine was distributed with two distinct covers. One of the covers featured the slain singer and the other featured the hit television series "Friends." The Selena cover sold out while the other did not. By 2006, *People En Espanol* was the most popular Spanish-language magazine in the United States, reaching over four million readers.

Setting a Record

In its first week, *Dreaming of You*, the crossover album by Selena, the Mexican-American pop singer who was killed in March 1995, has fulfilled many of the hopes that friends and associates say she had for it. The record sold 331,000 copies, according to Soundscan, a company in Hartsdale, New York, that tracks music retail sales, becoming the first album by a Latin artist to reach No. 1 on the pop charts. On July 18, 1995, the day it was released, *Dreaming of You* sold more than 175,000 copies, becoming the fastest-selling album ever by a woman. Jose Behar, the president of EMI Latin, said about the album's early release, "We promised Selena that she was going to a major crossover act. It was our responsibility to take the message to the people." Mr. Behar estimated that the album really sold more than 700,000 copies last week, because Soundscan's figue does not include discount stores like Wal-Mart and K-Mart and many small shops specializing in Latin music.[1]

---

[1]Neil Strauss, "The Pop Life," *New York Times*, July 27, 1995, C13.

In 1997, Esparza/Katz Productions released *Selena*, directed and written by Gregory Nava. The film starred Jennifer Lopez as Selena and Edward James Olmos as Selena's father. It also introduced Becky Lee Meza, a ten-year-old Texas native chosen from thousands of hopefuls who auditioned for the chance to portray their heroine.

All of the Quintanilla family provided insights and details to Lopez as she prepared for the role. For a time, Lopez moved in with Selena's sister Suzette. Lopez said later that she was once scolded by Selena's mother for her bad eating habits. "She told me I was just like Selena." The film introduced the life of Selena to an enormous international crossover audience that Abe Quintanilla had hoped to reach with her planned series of new albums. The horrible irony was that Selena was no longer there to enjoy the success or build on it.[31]

The city of Corpus Christi built a $600,000 monument for her in 1997, on the bay front, called "Overlook of the Flower," and they re-named the Bayfront Auditorium as "The Selena Auditorium." The Selena Foundation was established by her family to help Hispanic youth stay in school and fulfill their dreams.

Suzette Quintanilla took over Selena Etc., Inc. The "SELENA" label became internationally recognized and sold in such well-known chain stores as J.C. Penney's and Sears.

A.B. Quintanilla joined other Latino bands and eventually formed his own band. Chris Perez also formed his own band.

Ana Castillo, Chicana novelist, poet, short story writer, said, "Selena's generation comprises individuals whose parents have migrated, merged, and commingled with the enemy. They are Jewish/Protestant, Anglo-Irish, African-American Catholic, ready-for-the-White-House Puerto Rican, corn-fed, milk-bred Mexican-Polish Midwestern. They are salsa-dancing Laotians from East L.A. They are bilingual, bicultural, bisexual individuals giving the term multiculturalism kaleidoscopic dimensions. They speak the same language and rock to the same beat. What do we know of them—those of us not of that generation, of their world? Among these too—from preadolescents to young adults—were Selena's people."[32]

Ten years after Selena's death, many fans still make the pilgrimage to Corpus Christi. Standing next to a bronze statue of Selena, Marta Solis and Patricia Mora of Pasco, Washington, talked of their journey to visit the singer's landmark sites. They had driven thirty-six hours. "I still remember being in sixth grade and crying uncontrollably after hearing she had been shot," said Solis, twenty-two years old, a teacher and longtime fan. "For me she is a role model, because she got far for a Latina woman."[33]

The esteemed Latino author Ilan Stavans saw the death of Selena from the perspective of the cultural symbols and the fight for identity among Latino peoples on the border. For those in mourning for her, Stavans wrote, she was brave and courageous, never ashamed about her background. Driving her Porsche to the Wal Mart, she remained near to those with whom she shared common roots and culture. People told Stavans about seeing Selena shopping in the local mall, working at home, and how she was such a "sweetheart." "They like to recall how accessible she was," Stavans wrote. "Selena performed in Mexican variety shows and soap operas, from the long-running Siempre en Domingo to the melodrama "Dos mujeres, un camino." Small parts, no doubt, but the real sabor: corny and sentimental. Had Selena been visited by the angel of death only a few years later, a very different story would have been told. She would have been an American star, and her misfortune would not be useful today to highlight the reticence with which *la frontera* in particular, and Latino culture in general, is taken in by the rest of the country."[34]

SELECTED RECORDED MUSIC

Amor Prohibido. EMI Latin, 1994. CD.
Dreaming of You. EMI Latin, 1995. CD.
Remembered. EMI Latin, 1997. DVD.
All My Hits—Todos Mis Exitos. EMI Latin, 1999. CD.
Ones. EMI Latin, 2002. CD/DVD.
Selena: Greatest Hits. EMI Latin, 2003. CD.
Selena Live—The Last Concert. Image Entertainment, 2003. DVD.
Forever Selena. Madacy Special Markets, 2007. CD.
Selena (10th Anniversary Two-Disc Special Edition). Directed by Gregory Nava. Warner Home Video, 2007. DVD.

NOTES

1. John Morthland, "Selena Born Again," *Entertainment Weekly*, August 18, 1995, 18.

2. Morthland.

3. Joe Nick Patuski, *Selena: Como La Flor*, Boston, Little, Brown, 1996, 31.

4. Patuski, 34.

5. Patuski, 38.

6. Mario Tarradell, "A Decade after Selena's Death," *The Dallas Morning News*, April 4, 2005.

7. John Leland, "Born on the Border," *Newsweek*, October 23, 1995, 80.

8. Leland.

9. Leland.

10. Himilce Hovas and Rosemary Silva, *Remembering Selena*, New York: St. Martin's Griffin, 1995, 29.

11. "Before Her Time," *People Weekly*, April 17, 1995, 48.

12. Patoski, 58.

13. "Selena's Complete Biography," http://www.selenalareina.com/bio.html.

14. Barbara Kantrowitz, "A year after her death, family and fans are still haunted by memories of Selena," *People Weekly*, April 1, 1996, 110.

15. "Ven Conmigo," http://www.amazon.com/Ven-Conmigo-Selena/dp/B000000VKD.

16. "Selena's Complete Biography."

17. "Before Her Time."

18. "Selena's Complete Biography."

19. "As fans pay tribute to a fallen star, Chris Perez mourns the woman he loved," *People Weekly*, July 10, 1995, 40.

20. "As fans pay tribute …"

21. Patoski, 99.

22. Jill C. Wheeler, *Selena: The Queen of Tejano*, Minneapolis, MN: Abdo Consulting Group, 1996, 14.

23. Kantrowitz.

24. "Selena's Complete Biography."

25. Peter Watrous, "Mexican independence in New York," *New York Times*, September 19, 1994, C12.

26. Hispanic Heritage, "Selena," Gale Free Resources, http://www.gale.com/free_resources/chh/bio/selena.htm.

27. Sarah Wimer, "Amor Prohibido: Selena's crossover dream," *Austin Chronicle*, http://www.austinchronicle.com/issues/vol15/issue43/books.selena.html.

28. Bruce Murray, "How pop culture icons become religious-like figures: Latina singer Selena offers cultural redemption for Mexican-Americans," FACSNET, http://www.facsnet.org/issues/faith/selena.php.

29. Wimer.

30. Michael Clark, "Selena: She Left a Cultural Legacy," *Houston Chronicle*, April 6, 2005, http://www.chron.com/disp/story.mpl/special/selena/3110398.html.

31. Richard Corliss, "Viva Selena! The Queen of Tejano was murdered in 1995. Now Hollywood and her father present their version of her life." *Time*, March 24, 1997, 86.

32. Ana Castillo, "Selena Aside," *The Nation*, May 29, 1995, 764.

33. Olga Rodriguez, "Ten Years after Her Death, Selena's Legacy Still Growing," *The America's Intelligence Wire*, March 21, 2005.

34. Ilan Stavans, "Dreaming of You," *The New Republic*, November 20, 1995, 24.

FURTHER READING

Corliss, Richard. "Viva Selena! The Queen of Tejano Was Murdered in 1995. Now Hollywood and Her Father Present Their Version of Her Life." *Time*, March 24, 1997, 86.

Hispanic Heritage, Selena, Gale Free Resources, http://www.gale.com/free_resources/chh/bio/selena.htm.

Leland, John. "Born on the Border," *Newsweek*, October 23, 1995, 80.

Murray, Bruce. "How pop culture icons become religious-like figures: Latina singer Selena offers cultural redemption for Mexican-Americans, FACSNET, http://www.facsnet.org/issues/faith/selena.php.

Novas, Himilce, and Rosemary Silva. *Remembering Selena*. New York: St. Martin's Griffin, 1995.

Patuski, Joe Nick. *Selena: Como La Flor*. Boston, Little, Brown, 1996.

Richmond, Clint. *Selena! The Phenomenal Life and Tragic Death of the Tejano Music Queen*. New York: Pocket Books, 1995.

Stavans, Ilan. "Dreaming of You," *The New Republic*, November 20, 1995, 24.

Wheeler, Jill C. *Selena: The Queen of Tejano*. Edina, Minnesota, Abdo and Daughters, 1996.

AP Photo/Hans Deryk

Lee Trevino

At the Oak Hill Golf Club in Rochester, New York, in June 1968, a jovial, short, stocky Mexican American accepted the trophy for one of the most prestigious tournaments in golf—Lee Trevino had just won the United States Open.

With a shock of black hair pushing up against his golf cap and a wide, infectious grin, Trevino joked with reporters and answered questions with a disarming honesty and graciousness. He did seem somewhat out of place— this Latino at the center of a sport almost totally dominated by Anglos. But nearly everyone who saw him that day in person or on television knew very little about the real magnitude of his achievement or, for that matter, of his even being in a position to compete in such an internationally famous sporting event.

The vast majority of golfers who made it to the highest level in the sport came from country club backgrounds where their economic and social status provided them an opportunity to play on challenging courses and receive instruction from experienced professionals. Most of them first learned how to swing a golf club from their fathers or uncles or friends of friends who were talented and knew how to direct a youngster just beginning to learn the sport. Most of them, by an early age, had developed smooth golf swings, honed by hours and hours of training under the most advantageous conditions. In a sport where the cost of playing can be quite high, most of them had the best equipment.

Lee Trevino's rise to the top echelon of golf did not begin as a member of a country club or in a golf instruction camp or on the links of a manicured golf course. His family lived in a small shack on the outskirts of Dallas. The shack was near one of the holes of a golf course that had exceptionally high grass where errant shots often landed and players lost balls. Trevino's introduction to the game of golf was finding lost balls in the high grass and then selling them for small amounts of money.

Trevino's story is one of the most unique examples of a young Latino from a background of poverty rising in American society to unprecedented levels. As fans and admirers got to know him, they called him "Super Mex."

Prominent Latino Golfers

Throughout most of the history of the Professional Golfers' Association (PGA) Tour and the Ladies PGA Tour, almost all of the professional golfers have been white. In recent years the Tours have seen a growth in the number of Black, Latino, and Asian players.

The game itself remains confined largely to middle and upper class individuals. According to a 2003 World Golf Foundation study, 14.5 percent of whites play the game versus 13.7 percent of Asian Americans, 7.0 percent of African Americans, and 5.4 percent of U.S. Latinos. About 15 percent of all golfers are minorities (versus 32 percent of the total population), and they play about 11 percent of all rounds.

Lee Trevino was a pioneer Latino in the game—but he was not alone. The careers of Chi Chi Rodriguez, Nancy Lopez, and other younger players have inspired others to participate. When asked about the development of young Latino players, Mexican-born golfer Esteban Toledo predicted that in the near future there will be many Latinos joining the tour. Thanks to youth programs in various Latin American countries and in the United States, many youngsters who would otherwise have never had a chance to test their skills and participate in the game will get an opportunity. Several Latino players have already made significant contributions to the game.

Juan "Chi-Chi" Rodriguez

Born in Rio Piedras, Puerto Rico, in 1935, Rodriguez helped his father work in the sugar cane fields. He learned the game as a young caddy at a nearby course and first developed his golf swing by carving clubs out of guava tree limbs.

Gifted with superb hand–eye coordination, Rodriguez, at age twelve, shot a 67 on a course in Puerto Rico. In a career spanning four decades, he won eight regular PGA Tour events and more than twenty Senior PGA tournaments. A consummate showman, Rodriquez made a signature gesture when he pulled off great putts: He brandished an imaginary sword and then placed it back in its sheath with a flourish, as if the shot had been slain. Five foot seven inches tall and weighing about 120 pounds, Rodriguez was considered by almost all golf experts to be the longest hitter, pound for pound, in the game.

Rodriguez founded the Chi-Chi Rodriguez Youth Foundation in Clearwater, Florida, a home for troubled and abused youngsters. "I figure kids are the future. If I made it, anybody can do it," he said. "I think I can be a good role model for them because they could look at me and say, "Look, he's a small guy, he was poor and he worked hard and made it."[1]

Nancy Lopez

Born in Torrance, California, on January 6, 1957, into a Mexican-American family, Lopez was introduced to the game of golf at age eight by her father, Domingo, who tutored her development. She won the New Mexico Women's Amateur at age twelve and the U.S. Junior Girls Amateur in 1972 and 1974. Playing the U.S. Women's Open as a seventeen-year-old amateur in 1975, she finished tied for second. In 1978, her first season as a professional, she won nine titles on the Ladies PGA Tour. She won another eight times the following year.

Balancing her career in golf and the births of three daughters, Lopez remained in the top echelon of women's golf for well over two decades,

---

[1]Latino Legends in Sports: Juan "Chi-Chi" Rodriguez, http://www.latinosportslegends. com/chi-chi.htm.

(continued)

winning several Player of the Year awards. She was one of the great players in the history of women's golf and the best player from the late 1970s to the late 1980s. Personable, attractive, and generous, she was an admirable role model for later Latino and minority players.

Esteban Toledo

As a child in the early 1960s, Toledo lived with eleven brothers and sisters in Mexicali, Mexico, in a *choza*, a Spanish hut located on a golf course.

Toledo's first sports dreams were in boxing. In his late teens, Toledo developed into a good lightweight with a long reach, chalking up a 12–1 record with fights in locations such as Tijuana, Los Angeles, and Las Vegas. Toledo then discovered his natural talent for golf. Remarkably, he changed careers, becoming probably the first and last boxer ever to become a PGA professional golfer. Although he did not win a tournament after a number of years on the tour, he did finish second at the 2002 Buick Open after a head-to-head duel with Tiger Woods.

Toledo became deeply involved with the Get a Grip Foundation, established to introduce golf to children ages seven to eighteen at no cost. "I make sure these kids go on the right track and make sure they have dreams. Maybe that's why God sent me here," Toledo said. "I want to make sure these kids have goals. There are so many problems out there, and I think if someone can just share with them some thoughts about what direction to go in, they'll be better off."[2]

Lorena Ochoa

A golfing prodigy in her native Mexico, by age six Lorena Ochoa (born November 15, 1981, in Guadalajara in Jalisco, Mexico) had developed a golf swing so coordinated and natural that she seemed born to be an enormously successful golfer. She traveled to the United States to attend the University of Arizona in Tucson. There, she was arguably the greatest women's collegiate golfer in the history of the sport.

Lorena became a professional golfer in 2002 and experienced immediate success, winning three of her ten events that year. She joined the LPGA in 2003 and again won several titles. The year 2006 was a breakout season for Ochoa, who posted six victories, including a win at the Tournament of Champions by ten shots with a record-breaking score of 21 under par. In 2007, at The Old Course at St. Andrews, Scotland, Ochoa won the Women's British Open, her first major title. She won eight times in 2007, becoming the first LPGA golfer to win over $4 million. During the same year, she became the number-one-ranked women's player in the world.

---

[2]Jason Stahl, "Mexico native defies odds with PGA Tour success," http://www.worldgolf. com/features/estaban-toledo-profile.htm.

An all-around sports enthusiast, Ochoa, while maintaining a strict golf regimen, still found time to water ski, hike, and run marathons. Some see her in the early years of the twenty-first century as the Tiger Woods of women's golf. Ochoa is heavily involved in promoting youth golf, especially in Mexico, and has established a scholarship fund for young Mexican golfers.

PICKING ONIONS AND COTTON

Lee Trevino was born on December 1, 1939, in Parkland Hospital in Dallas, Texas. The birth records do not indicate the name of his father, whom Trevino never knew. The boy's mother was Juanita Trevino, whose own father, Joe, had moved to Texas from Monterrey, Mexico, as a young boy with his family.

When Lee was a youngster, his grandfather raised cotton and onions in Garland, Texas, a small farming area north of Dallas. By the time he was five years old, the boy was in the fields to help harvest the crops. His grandfather also took the boy on hunting and fishing trips in his 1929 Model A Ford. Trevino later remembered his grandfather fondly. Trevino's days in the fields picking onions and cotton ended when his grandfather left the farm and took a job as a gravedigger at the Hillcrest Cemetery in Dallas. Along with a small paycheck, the job also included the use of a four-room shack. Juanita Trevino, along with Lee and his two sisters, Anna and Josephine, joined Joe in Dallas, along with an uncle named Lupe.

The unpainted house, sheltered by some cottonwood trees, with a lake in the front and tall grass, had no plumbing or electricity. The kitchen had a dirt floor. The cemetery where Joe Trevino worked was located a mile south of the house. Adjacent to the house was the DAC Country Club, a golf course that later became known as the Glen Lakes Country Club.

The family used the lake water for washing and for baths. Joe Trevino brought drinking water home from the cemetery in five-gallon milk cans. The family had only one mattress, which was used by Joe. Uncle Lupe slept in one of the four rooms. Juanita Trevino and her children occupied another room.

It was a primitive existence, especially in the winters. On cold nights, Trevino said, they put a huge log in the stove that would burn half the night. "Then someone got up in the freezing cold to start another fire.... I used to joke that Mexicans are so dark from sleeping next to those stoves. We would warm the front side, then rotate and warm the back side. We were barbecued."[1] The family had a Holstein cow that provided milk. They soon acquired some hogs, and the lake had fish. The family budget was woefully small and living conditions were tough, but they made a life for themselves.

Nevertheless, there was constant anxiety and tension. "My grandfather was a knife fighter," Trevino later recalled. "He was small, but he was a scrapper, with a crooked nose, like a boxer. He was very short-fused. Very short-fused. He'd pull a knife out on you in a minute. He had scars all over his chest. I saw my grandfather and my uncle get into it once in our house. They were drunk."[2]

Although he later realized that neither his grandfather nor his mother provided the attention he should have received, he did admire them for their hard work. He appreciated his mother's humor and jokes in the midst of a life full of hardship. He later attributed much of his own sense of merriment to her personality. For both his mother and him, humor was obviously a shield to cover their inner fears. But Trevino was able to use his gift of gab and his jokester personality to disarm those who tried to put him down. He later used it to great effect on golf courses throughout the world to unnerve opponents.

Trevino came to look back on his family both with an appreciation of the struggles that many Latino families had to endure to keep going but also with a longing for a supportive relationship that he later realized he had missed. In the midst of a family constantly trying to survive there were, he remembered, too few hugs and too few quiet talks. "Rich people like to talk about their backgrounds, their ancestors and where they come from," he once said. "We were too poor to care. We were too busy existing."[3]

Although both his grandfather and mother had come to the United States at the same time, they insisted on speaking only English when he was a boy. Trevino did not learn very much Spanish until he moved to El Paso on the Mexican border when he was in his twenties.

By the time he was eight years old, the young boy had wandered over to the nearby golf course. Before his first venture on the course, he had never known that the game of golf existed. Soon, Trevino had talked his way into a job caddying for some of the members of the country club. He made friends with the older caddies, most of whom were black. When Trevino began caddying, there were no machines that could roll through driving ranges to pick up balls—the caddies picked them up. Late into the evening, the young boy stayed to chase balls hit by club members into the growing darkness.

He began borrowing clubs from some of the caddies and learning to swing entirely on his own. After gaining some skill, he played against the caddies for quarters. His natural competitiveness surfaced. When he lost, he practiced harder, hitting hundreds of shots a day when he had the time.

He also picked up some adult habits with the caddies. He began to smoke when he was ten years old and began uttering some rather foul language. He went from a country kid, he said, to a "cool kitty from the city." Some of the fellow caddies, he said, "were dangerous people who carried knives and guns. Hardly a day passed that I didn't watch a knife fight. We were shooting dice and playing cards and there always were arguments."[4] But among the caddies were individuals with whom he forged a strong bond. Some stayed nights in his crowded family shack. Some would take him on camping trips with baloney sandwiches and blankets by the lake. Some of their family members became friends with members of his family.

Trevino attended Vickery School, close to the country club. He was not a consistent attendee or a particularly attentive student. Because the family had no telephone, school officials and truant officers would have to make a special effort to find out where "the Trevino kid" had gone that day. It was usually to the golf course to hit more shots. His teachers saw much raw intelligence in the boy and kept encouraging him to apply himself to school studies. Nevertheless, they rarely saw him in school more than three days a week.

Although short and stocky, Trevino was coordinated and determined in all the sports he tried. He seemed to have a natural rhythm, whether in swinging a baseball bat, kicking a soccer ball, throwing a football, or, more important in his life, hitting a golf ball. He could not swim in the public pool because it was segregated—no blacks or dark-skinned Latinos could enter; light-skinned Latinos were allowed, but Trevino was too dark for admission.

Trevino quit school before he had entered the eighth grade. Giving in to her son's pleas that school was of little use to him, his mother filled out the necessary forms for the youngster to leave the public school system and to get a work permit. He was fourteen years old. In 1954, he got a job at the golf course working with the groundskeeper. That year, his first as a full-fledged worker, earned him $1,250 a year. Trevino kept the government income tax form from that year throughout his life to remind him of where he started.

Almost entirely self-taught, Trevino had nothing like the classic golf swings that millions of other aspiring students of the game were learning from their instructors or from golf magazines—the swings of the great Bobby Jones or Sam Snead or other early champions of the sport.

Trevino's swing was flat with an irregular arc that seemed to defy all of the known conventions. Yet, when the club head touched the ball, everything suddenly lined up. The usual "thwack" as club met ball almost always resulted in an accurate shot. Trevino once said, "My swing is so bad I look like a caveman killing his lunch."[5] Throughout his golf career, he had an uncanny ability to hit the ball accurately. What Trevino lacked in golf fundamentals, he more than made up in natural ability and long days of practice on the golf course.

Around the golf course, the young caddy and groundskeeper developed a well-earned reputation as a hustler. So proficient did the youngster become that he often made what seemed like outrageous bets at the time and, more often than not, came out on top. He learned to hit golf balls with coke bottles attached to a stick. He learned to play one-handed. He was like a pool hustler betting on circus shots. And when the time came for the competition, for the moment of winning and losing the bet, the concentration was intense. Not only was Trevino a natural athlete; he was also a naturally fierce competitor.

For a time, Trevino worked at a driving range built by a man named Hardy Greenwood, a World War II veteran who had been in charge of a Japanese prisoner camp. Greenwood encouraged Trevino to think of golf as a career and gave him advice about the game.

Trevino saved up enough money to buy a run-down 1949 Ford with a broken muffler. Dressed in his black leather motorcycle jacket, motorcycle boots, and a wide-collared shirt, he loudly motored around Dallas. But none of the 1950s dance crazes or other diversions kept the youngster from the golf course. If he had not hit balls for hours on end, it had not been a good day.

At the age of fifteen, encouraged by Greenwood, Trevino entered a tournament sponsored by the *Dallas Times Herald*. "Strange as it may seem," he wrote, "that was the first complete round of golf I'd ever played. I had hit nine billion balls by then and played a lot of competition golf with money on the line, but that always was as a caddie, sneaking in a few holes out of sight of the clubhouse or on that little layout behind the caddie shed...."[6] At the municipal course in the Oak Cliff section of Dallas, the fifteen-year-old qualified with a round of 77. Although he did not win the event, he had gotten a taste of competition in a real tournament—and he liked it.

The following year, Trevino went through some unsettling times. He argued with Greenwood and quit his job. He stole some hubcaps. He rebelled against his own self-imposed regimen of hitting golf balls and briefly played some baseball. Confused and upset, the teenager decided to leave Dallas. On December 1, 1956, his seventeenth birthday, he walked into the local recruiting office of the U.S. Marine Corps, passed their tests, and was inducted. Less than three weeks later he left for boot camp training in California.

JOIN THE MARINES, LEARN MORE GOLF

Trevino's trip from Texas to San Diego for boot camp was the first time he had ever been on an airplane. Nervous, he continuously laughed and uttered wisecracks throughout the whole trip. And, within the space of twenty-four hours of joining the Marines, Trevino was already in trouble. When the group lined up to march for the first time, he started laughing. He got hit in the stomach and slapped in the head so many times, he recalled later, that he lost count. Despite the rough start, Trevino enjoyed the camaraderie of the nearly one hundred men in the platoon. By the time he left boot camp, he had two tattoos. On his right bicep, he had the "Devil Dog," the symbol of the Corps; on his right forearm he had the name "Ann," his current girlfriend. By the time he returned to Texas, Ann was seeing another man. Trevino began to cover the name on his arm with a Band-Aid.

Soon, the new Marine was on a troop ship headed for Japan. Twenty-two long days of seasickness later, the ship finally reached its destination,

Yokohama. Trevino later quipped that at times he thought they were using oars to get there. At Middle Camp Fuji, Trevino became a machine gunner. He could take the weapon apart and put it back together again in the dark. As with every other skill requiring hand-eye coordination, Trevino excelled. "I loved the Marines," he said later. "I never knew anybody when I was a kid, and there I was around a bunch of guys my own age. Hell, I volunteered for everything—night patrols, you name it. It was like camping out to me."[7]

While stationed in Okinawa, the Marines practiced amphibious and helicopter landings in the Philippines. It was in Okinawa that Trevino, by his own estimation, got the luckiest break in his life. One of his commanding officers asked him one day whether he played any sports. Trevino gave him the obvious answer, and he was placed in a Special Services division that issued sports equipment, drove athletic teams to games, and engaged in other activities related to leisure activities in which the troops participated.

The base had a golf team, and Trevino joined. From Japan to the Philippines, the Marine golf team played tournaments with other service divisions. Trevino won a championship tournament in Okinawa. While at one of the tournaments, he met a U.S. Army sergeant named Orville Moody, who was known as the best golfer in the Far East. After their tours of duty, both Trevino and Moody joined the professional golf tour.

In 1968 Trevino won the U.S. Open; a year later Moody did the same thing. Trevino later saw the whole thing as one of the most amazing coincidences of his entire life. Just think of the odds, Trevino said: Two soldiers meeting in Japan and then coming back to the United States to win the most prestigious golf tournament in back-to-back years. He would have loved, he said, to have had a $5 bet on that one.

In November 1960, outside Treasure Island in San Francisco, Trevino was discharged from the Marine Corps. Many athletes, when they spend a number of years in the armed services, look back at them as lost years as far as their professional sports careers are concerned. For Trevino, who had been a teenager living day to day with little money, the years he served in the Marines, oddly enough, furthered his sports career. He was a much more seasoned golfer when he came back from his stint in the Far East than when he left. Although he was not quite ready to take on the big time tournament trail, he was now on the road.

GOLF AS A LIVELIHOOD

When Trevino returned to Dallas, he once again joined his friend Hardy Greenwood, working at his driving range. Greenwood constantly prodded him to hone his golf game. Working for Greenwood and spending most of his spare time belting balls, Trevino became increasingly encouraged about the possibility of making a living from the sport.

He joined the North Texas chapter of the Professional Golfers' Association (PGA) and played in a number of local tournaments in Texas. He worked hard on his golf game during his spare time, which limited much of his social life. Nevertheless, in the summer of 1961 the twenty-one-year-old Trevino started dating a seventeen-year-old high school senior at North Dallas High School, usually going to bowling alleys or to drive-in movies.

Within a few months the two, Lee and Linda, decided to get married, even though she was underage and the family was decidedly against their Anglo girl marrying a Mexican boy. To pull off the marriage ceremony, Trevino and the girl smudged her birth certificate so that the date of birth read 1942 rather than 1944. They drove to Durant, Oklahoma, found a justice of the peace, and became man and wife.

It was not until Christmas that they told the girl's family. Lee and Linda moved into a small house in Garland, Texas, and she finished her senior year of high school in Garland. In November 1962, she had a child they named Richard.

Trevino kept honing his golf game at a municipal course called Tenison Park, a challenging layout that tested all his skills. He would usually tee off shortly after six o'clock in the morning to get in as many holes as possible before going to work.

It was at Tenison that Trevino perfected a side game that became the stuff of legend. Trevino's hand–eye coordination was never more evident than when he perfected his game with a large Dr. Pepper bottle to the point where he could challenge players on a short, par-3 course nearby. He would use his Dr. Pepper bottle; they would use their clubs. He putted on the greens using the bottle like a croquet mallet. Trevino played numerous opponents and insisted later that he never lost a bet.

But Lee Trevino was soon becoming the stuff of legend without his Dr. Pepper bottle. With small bets on the line, he could with great regularity hit the small signs on driving ranges. But while his game became increasingly razor sharp, his marriage soon failed. He often later referred to himself during those early years as a "golf bum," caring little about anything or anyone other than the sport. In the fall of 1963, Linda Trevino took their child Ricky and moved in with her sister—the marriage was over. Trevino moved back to live with his grandfather.

Trevino said that these early years of golf in Texas gave him much of his personality on the course that he later took to the PGA tour. "There was always a lot of people goin' nowhere," he said, "so the loudest guy got listened to the most. You didn't necessarily have to know what you were talkin' about, because no one you're talkin' to knew anything anyway, so you just started ramblin' on. We played for quarter skins, dollar skins, and we were great needlers. Guys would give you extra strokes just to shut you up."[8]

Soon, Trevino was dating a woman named Claudia Fenley, who was seventeen years old, just as his former wife had been when he started dating her. She had dropped out of high school and now lived with her mother. During the summer, Trevino and Claudia decided to marry. In August, Trevino was again a married man. Shortly after the marriage, an invigorated Trevino received an invitation to play at Glen Gardens Country Club in Fort Worth, Texas, the club where two of the greats of golf, Ben Hogan and Byron Nelson, had once worked as caddies. Trevino proceeded to play what he said was probably the most flawless round of golf in his entire life. He shot a 61, a course record, eleven strokes under par.

Claudia knew very little about golf. She later remembered questioning Lee about what she had just seen as they rode back to Dallas. "That was the first time I'd ever seen anybody play golf. You know, I thought that was the way you were supposed to play." Trevino had not beaten par on every hole, but Claudia was encouraging. "Don't worry, honey," she said, "one day you'll birdie all eighteen holes."[9]

In February 1966, Trevino and Claudia, along with a new daughter named Lesley, headed for El Paso, Texas. A wealthy cotton farmer named Martin Lettunich who had seen Trevino play offered him a job and the promise of some serious golf competition. Trevino sensed that this could be his big break—the chance for someone to sponsor him as he tried to break into the PGA Tour.

Trevino and his small family moved into a trailer on a farm four miles from Horizon Hills Golf Course, about twenty miles east of El Paso. At first he worked as a kind of handyman for the course. "I was there, openin' the shop at five in the morning and closin' at nine at night," he said, "at a poor man's course with a motel connected to it in the desert outside El Paso. Cleanin' shoes and puttin' the carts up. I'm the last tour pro who sold shoes and gave lessons. My background was servin' the public at a drivin' range or pro shop. I always said I could sell ice cream in a blizzard."[10]

At Horizon Hill, a young Tour professional named Ray Floyd was brought in to duel a local player for a healthy sum of money bankrolled by the members of the club. As Floyd told the story, he drove up in a white Cadillac and was met by a young Mexican who helped him get his clubs out of the car, showed him to his locker, and shined his shoes. "Who am I playing today?" Floyd asked. "You're talking to him," the young man replied. "Me." For two days, the Tour pro and the clubhouse boy, Trevino, fought it out. It took an eagle (i.e., two shots less than par for a hole) by Floyd to save face and win by a shot. He left El Paso saying, "Adios. I've got easier games than this on the Tour."[11]

Horizon Hills soon offered Trevino a job as an assistant pro. When he began to give lessons at the club, his salary increased to a level where the family could move into the motel at the course. He kept practicing, played in local tournaments, and hustled for small change at the course. Although he frequently drank beer and got into a few fights, he began jogging to get his legs in better shape.

The course in El Paso was dusty, with hard-baked fairways and winds that occasionally reached fifty miles per hour. But the weather never deterred the ambitious Trevino. When winds reached near hurricane levels, he was still out there on the course, wearing scuba-diver masks to keep the sand out of his eyes. His touch with his irons, especially in those winds, was nothing short of spectacular. Around the course in El Paso, members and other guest players began to realize what other knowledgeable golf fans had already learned in Dallas—Trevino had enormous talent.

In 1966, the U.S. Open tournament was held at the Olympic Golf Course in San Francisco. Impressed by his talent and determination, two men from Texas encouraged Trevino to play in regional qualifying events leading up to the Open. If he were successful, they said, they would pay his plane fare and other expenses to play in the prestigious event. Trevino was successful in qualifying and traveled to the Olympic course to compete against the best players in the world. For the first time, the young golfer faced such well-known fan favorites as Arnold Palmer and Jack Nicklaus. Nationally televised, with reporters gathered from around the world, Trevino was in an entirely different setting than the wind-swept Texas courses where he learned the game.

The course itself was not to his liking. With intimidating rough, grass much higher than anything he had ever seen in Texas, the course seemed to Trevino as foreign as the event itself. Playing with an unmatched bag of clubs (he later said he probably had seven different brands), he found himself in the rough on several holes. The tournament, which was notable for the collapse of Arnold Palmer who lost in a playoff to Billy Casper, was also not a happy experience for Trevino. He finished in 54th place in the field, shooting over 300 for the 72-hole tournament. His winnings were far less than the costs of participating.

Trevino limped back to Texas discouraged but determined. He worked harder, if possible, to improve his game, especially on courses designed with the kind of heavy rough he faced at Olympic. A year later, Trevino did not feel ready to face another U.S. Open course and had not planned to submit the entrance papers in order to try to qualify. Without his knowledge, Claudia submitted the papers for him. She insisted that he try the Open again. At Odessa, Texas, Trevino put together two superb rounds of 69 and 67 to become the lowest local qualifier in the entire country. He would again play in the U.S. Open.

Trevino headed to New Jersey. Baltrusol Golf Club in Springfield, not far from New York City, hosted the 1967 U.S. Open. When Trevino got off the plane at Newark airport, he did not even have a reservation for a hotel. He hopped in a cab and asked the driver to take him to a nearby hotel that was rather inexpensive. He stayed at a place called the Union Motel. It was the first time Trevino had ever been east of the Mississippi River.

Baltrusol, a famous old course that oozed tradition, was a tough test of golf, but Trevino felt comfortable with its layout. He scored well in a practice round and gained confidence. Unlike the previous year in San Francisco, Trevino felt from the opening day that this experience would be different, especially after shooting a 70 and a 72 in the first two days. On the final day, Trevino found himself close enough to the lead that his name went up on the leader board, posted near the clubhouse. Looking back years later, Trevino said that most of the people who saw the name Trevino thought that he was an Italian.

When the day was over, he had shot a four-round total of 283, a remarkable score for someone so completely unknown to the golfing public. The winner that day was Jack Nicklaus. His score of 275 set a new U.S. Open scoring record, and it was his second U.S. Open title.

For Trevino, it was not only the attention that he soaked up that last afternoon in New Jersey; it was also some winnings. The paycheck was for $6,000, a hefty sum for a man in Trevino's precarious financial situation. Almost giddy, he called home with the news. He said later that the conversation was somewhat emotional. His path was now more clear than ever. He could play, as he said, with the big boys.

CHALLENGING THE BEST ON THE PRO GOLF TOUR

Lee Trevino was born approximately two months before Jack Nicklaus— Trevino in late 1939, Nicklaus in early 1940. The stories of each man's rise to golf stardom could not have been more different.

Raised in the North Arlington section of Columbus, Ohio, Nicklaus was the son of a very successful pharmacist and businessman who was also a dedicated golfer. In his earliest years, Nicklaus, who was talented in a number of sports, dreamed of being a major league baseball player. He also played football and basketball and, at the age of thirteen, ran the 100-yard dash in eleven seconds. He also played golf at the prestigious Scioto Country Club, where state legislators and governors frequently teed off. At the age of thirteen Nicklaus scored below 70. The thin, blond youngster could defeat most of the golfing members of the club.

His prowess on the links was soon the talk of many golf fans in the city. With his natural swing, long, towering drives, and superb putting, he was a phenomenon unlike anyone had ever seen in the sport. While attending The Ohio State University, he won the United States Amateur title in both 1959 and 1961. At the tournament in 1959, a young amateur from Tucson, Arizona, who played against Nicklaus head-to-head later remembered hitting a very good tee shot on the first hole. Nicklaus then stepped up, he said, and hit the ball fifty yards farther down the fairway. It was, said his competitor, as if Nicklaus were playing an entirely different sport.

In 1960, at the same time Trevino was working at a driving range in Texas, Nicklaus, still an amateur, played in the U.S. Open, finishing second to Arnold Palmer. Nicklaus turned professional in 1962, and within five years, by the time he was twenty-six years old, he had become one of only four players to have won all four of golf's most treasured titles—the U.S. Open, the British Open, the PGA Championship, and the Masters.

Nicklaus was now, almost everyone agreed, the king of golf. But surprisingly enough, one of the most ardent and determined challengers for the throne would be someone named Trevino, an Italian most likely. He was from somewhere in Texas.

In the summer of 1967, Trevino joined the PGA Tour. He bought a 1965 Plymouth station wagon, loaded some clothes, and, joined by Claudia and Lesley, headed for Minnesota. After a tournament in Minneapolis they headed off again, this time to Chicago for the Western Open, and then to the American Golf Classic in Akron, Ohio. Through the Midwest the family moved along with two-year-old Lesley sitting in the back seat on a rocking-chair duck. Although Trevino's first weeks on the tour were respectable, he made little money and the routine for Claudia was becoming unbearable. Finally, she and the baby boarded a plane for Texas, and Lee headed further east. The life of a touring pro, at least for one who arrived at the events in a Plymouth station wagon, was not as glamorous as they had anticipated.

But soon Trevino began to have greater success in some of the events. The checks got a little bigger; his confidence rose. He ended the golf season with earnings of over $26,000 and was named Rookie of the Year.

In June 1968, Trevino drove into Rochester, New York, site of that year's U.S. Open. As always, Trevino arrived chattering and making quips to the other players. His caddie, eighteen-year-old Kevin Quinn, said, "I knew Trevino was a good bag, but I couldn't believe how confident he was. I remember in one of the practice rounds he saw Nicklaus, and he yelled out, 'Hey, Jack: When did you get this in your swing?' and then did this funky back-swing. And Nicklaus just stared at him for what seemed like twenty seconds, sizing this guy up. And then he shook his head and smiled. I think he could sense Lee was a guy who wasn't afraid."[12]

On the first two days, Trevino ripped drive after drive down the center of the fairways on the way to scores of 69 and 67, an extraordinary beginning to a U.S. Open in which the courses are made especially challenging. Any score under 70 in a U.S. Open round is superb. On the third day, Trevino missed a number of fairways but putted brilliantly and once again scored below par with a 68. As the tournament reached its final day, Bert Yancey, a skilled but less than stellar pro, was leading by one stroke over Trevino. Big names such as Arnold Palmer and Jack Nicklaus were a few strokes behind. And so on this grand stage of golf, with millions watching on television and large galleries surrounding every hole, the still relatively unknown

Latino from Texas, only in his second year on the pro tour, readied himself on the first tee with his playing companion, Yancey.

A sportswriter named Mike Bryan saw Trevino as something of an ugly duckling on the tour, a startling if welcome change for professional golf. Trevino stood there, said Bryan, "with a red shirt and black slacks several unfashionable inches too short, exposing equally unfashionable fire-engine-red socks. If nothing else, the duckling is colorful. Trevino lunges at his first drive and the worm-burner—Texas talk—just carries the rough in front of the tee."[13] By the fifth hole, Trevino was leading the United States Open. Could the relatively inexperienced newcomer to the tour fight off the pressure and hang on?

In the end, it was Yancey who flinched, not Trevino. A final four-foot putt on the eighteenth hole netted a 69, a total score of 275 that tied the U.S. Open record held by Jack Nicklaus. Also, Trevino became the first player in U.S. Open history to score under 70 in each of the four rounds. As Bryan summed it up, "The short-panted, red-socked, Mexican-American ugly duckling has emerged a last-laughing swan."[14]

Thousands of golf fans, reporters, and television interviewers surrounded Trevino, along with policemen who escorted him into the press tent. He quipped later that he had not had so much attention from the police since his 1949 Ford backfired on the North Central Expressway in Texas when he was fifteen. It took several minutes for Trevino to get used to the swarm of attention. Then, he was able to summon up the usual jovial posture. When asked what he intended to do with the $30,000 prize money, he joked that he was going to buy the Alamo and give it back to Mexico.

With his win in the U.S. Open, Trevino's rise from obscurity now became a story that was big-time news, not only in the sports pages of newspapers across the country but in feature magazine pieces. How could a poor Mexican American living in true poverty on the fringes of American society develop into a top-flight pro in a sport almost totally dominated by athletes from privileged backgrounds?

Writers now began to look closely at his golf swing, a self-manufactured, awkward-looking thing that defied the usual mechanics. They began to examine his playing routines and behavior on the course. Unlike most of the quiet, hushed competitors who made up most of the pro tour, Trevino was loud, always trying for the best one-liner, a difficult playing partner for most of the other players who were trying to concentrate. He was unquestionably one of the most animated players. It was not uncommon to see him stick his tongue out at a putt that would not drop or to clown around with his caddy. On one occasion, when playing against Nicklaus, he emerged from the rough holding a toy snake on one of his golf clubs. He tried anything to break the concentration of his opponent.

Nicklaus loved to tell stories about the times he played with Trevino. On one occasion, Nicklaus walked off the first tee and said, "Lee, I just want to play golf today; I don't want to talk." "That's all right, Jack," Trevino responded, "you don't have to talk, you just have to listen."[15]

Nicklaus and Trevino played head to head in some of the most memorable tournaments in golf history. Trevino held his own against the fabled "Golden Bear," besting him in a number of major events. Nicklaus, who came to admire and respect Trevino, never did get used to facing him in key matches. He once joked to Trevino, "Go back to Mexico!" even though Trevino, who laughed, reminded Jack that he never lived there.

Other players were perplexed as to how Trevino could keep up his frantic chatting with the galleries and his rapid-fire quips and still hold together his golf game. But that was one of the secrets of his success. The jokes, the chatter—those were the very things that relaxed him, the things that eased the pressure and the feelings of insecurity. Frank Beard, one the tour regulars, a student of the game and a rather plodding player, once said, "Trevino is a tremendous golfer," he says, "but nobody can tell me that a player can keep up a constant conversation with the gallery and talk to himself on the backswing and still produce his best golf."[16]

Nobody could tell Beard those things, but the results did. As Trevino, chatting and quipping along, followed his U.S. Open win with more success, it was clear that professional golf had a new kind of superstar. One of Trevino's friends told a reporter, "Lee's secret is that when he has to, he can approach a difficult shot laughing, turn on the concentration, hit the ball, and then go off laughing again. It may not look like he's concentrating, but he is."[17]

Soon, Trevino became a popular figure on the tour with fans waving signs saying "Sock It to 'Em, Super Mex." One of Trevino's friends began calling his fans "Lee's Fleas," and the name stuck. If Arnold Palmer had "Arnie's Army," Trevino now had "Lee's Fleas." He also now had his own logo. Arnold Palmer's logo was an umbrella; Nicklaus' was the gold bear. Trevino decided on a sombrero and even had the particular drawing copyrighted. Later, when Trevino's own line of golf clubs and clothes hit the markets, they all carried the Trevino sombrero. Endorsement deals soon came his way. He signed contracts with Blue Bell clothing, Dodge cars and trucks, and Faultless golf equipment. He also signed, appropriately, with Dr. Pepper, a Texas-based company. The legend of Trevino and his Dr. Pepper bottle was now worth more than small-dollar side bets. On one occasion, Trevino gave an exhibition on the front lawn of the Dr. Pepper Company hitting golf balls with their latest 32-ounce bottle.

Trevino finished 1968 in sixth place on the money winners' list. He won the Hawaiian Open and gave $10,000 in prize money to the family of a fellow golfer, Ted Makalena, who had been killed in a surfing accident. Trevino's charitable giving continued throughout his career, almost all of it done privately and without fanfare. He never forgot his roots and background, never forgot his friends in Texas, and took many opportunities to share his winnings.

Trevino's star was clearly on the rise. When the pro tour made stops in cities across the country, an increasing number of spectators and print and television reporters were as anxious to see Trevino as some of the other top players such as Jack Nicklaus and Gary Player.

If 1968 had been the year he established his place among golf's better players, some events in the following years began to rock Trevino's confidence and emotional state. Although Trevino compiled a very respectable record in 1969 and 1970, there were some warning signs. During one period, he did not win a tournament for over a year. The night before the beginning of a tournament in New York, he made an appearance on NBC's "The Tonight Show" and had obviously had too much to drink. Some business dealings became troubling, and he began the 1971 season by dropping out of three tournaments.

He also refused invitations to play at the Masters Tournament in Augusta, Georgia, in 1970 and 1971 because he disliked the course. The layout, he said, was not suited to his game. Although there was some truth to his remarks about the famed Augusta course, his refusal to play had also resulted from some of his off-camera remarks that had been picked up by a sports reporter and given national attention. He also harbored ill feelings against Augusta because of its long-standing history of denying memberships or playing opportunities to blacks. One of Trevino's friends on the tour, Charlie Sifford, the best black player of the day, for example, had not been invited to play in the Masters.

He remembered the last days of 1970 and the early part of 1971 as mentally exhausting. But during an exhibition match in Palm Beach, Florida, in March 1971, Jack Nicklaus took him aside in the locker room and told him: "I hope you never find out how well you can play. If you do, it will be trouble for all of us." Trevino said later of Nicklaus, "I've always worshipped that man. I've idolized Palmer, too, but Nicklaus has been a closer friend. When he talked I listened.... I thought about that and it turned me around."[18]

Trevino later told a reporter that Nicklaus's words of encouragement saved his life. It stopped him, he said, from being the uncertain, nervous competitor that he was and made him realize that he could "reach the peak."

SPORTSMAN OF THE YEAR, 1971

In 1971, Trevino did, indeed, reach the peak. Trevino's remarkable success began in June at the famed Merion Golf Course outside Philadelphia, site of that year's U.S. Open. With his razor sharp drives and skillful iron play, Trevino was always a threat on the U.S. Open courses because they demanded, more than anything else, accuracy. The high roughs, so difficult for most players in the U.S. Open layouts, were not a problem for Trevino because he was usually on the fairways. The only time Trevino was off the fairway, said fellow pro George Archer, was when he was answering the phone.

Trevino felt confident before the tournament because his putting stroke seemed increasingly grooved in tournaments leading up to the event. By the fourth round on Sunday, he battled for the lead. His main opponent was a familiar one—Jack Nicklaus. At the final hole, Nicklaus was faced with a fourteen-foot putt to win the tournament. The ball rolled down the slope of the green and hung on the lip of the cup. The two played an eighteen-hole playoff the next day. Trevino shot a 68, three strokes better than Nicklaus. He had won his second U.S. Open.

Years later Nicklaus would say that Trevino's ball striking abilities, his control and accuracy, were nearly unparalleled, even by the greatest the game had ever seen. He was not long off the tee, and that hurt him on some courses, but his control was masterful. "He didn't do dumb things," Nicklaus said. "He was as tough a player to beat one-on-one as I have ever seen."[19]

The next week, the tour was in Montreal for the Canadian Open at the Richelieu Valley Golf and Country Club. Although starting the tournament poorly, Trevino steadied his game, and by the final day he was in a struggle with veteran Art Wall for the championship. Just as Nicklaus had done a week earlier at the U.S. Open, Wall missed a putt on the eighteenth hole to win. Instead of the full playoff round that decides U.S. Open tournaments in case of a tie, the Canadian Open was a simple sudden death playoff. The first player to win a hole wins the championship. On the first hole the two played, Trevino sank a twenty-foot putt to win. He had now won back-to-back championships.

Trevino and Claudia then boarded a plane for London. He prepared for the British Open, to be played on the old course of the Royal Birkdale Golf Club, built in 1889, a seaside layout with sand dunes and winds. With his low-trajectory shots and his experience on Texas desert courses, Trevino felt at home playing in sand and wind.

He had first set foot on a British course in 1968 and fell in love with the atmosphere. He loved the barren, rolling landscape of most of the courses, with few trees and often a mist in your face and the odd little bunkers that dot the courses. It smelled like home cooking, he said. "What a golf course for my game," Trevino later said about Birkdale. "All British courses really, with those high winds, are good for my low shots. I'm not afraid to run the ball on the green, and if it's hard and dry, you have to do that at Birkdale."[20]

The entire week at Royal Birkdale was a joy for Trevino. His shots were falling, he was having a great time with the galleries, and on the final day he was playing for the championship with Lu Liang Huan of Formosa. The two men had gotten to know each other from earlier tournaments and liked to exchange good-natured remarks. Trevino grabbed a healthy lead early in the round but was joking so much, he said, that he managed to lose his concentration. A five-shot lead soon became a one-shot lead as they headed to the final hole. Both men birdied the par-5 eighteenth hole, and Trevino won the British Open.

"I won my first British Open championship" he said, "with a game as good as Jack Nicklaus told me it could be. So in just twenty days I had beaten Jack in our U.S. Open playoff, taken the Canadian Open title, and then won in Britain, where Jack was defending champion." Because of the tradition that defending champions of a tournament are part of the ceremony presenting the trophy, Nicklaus, who had won the British Open a year before, gave remarks before a huge gathering. "I wish," he joked, speaking about the encouragement he had given Trevino, "I had kept my damn mouth shut."[21]

No other player in the history of golf had ever won the U.S. Open, Canadian Open, and British Open in the same year. During the 1971 season, Trevino won a total of $231,000 on the tour. From the boy who had fished golf balls out of a lake with a makeshift scoop, he was now, at this time, on top of the golf world.

Trevino was named the PGA Player of the Year. But his achievement was so great that it transcended the sport of golf. The Associated Press named Trevino the male Athlete of Year. And *Sports Illustrated* featured him on its cover as Sportsman of the Year, 1971. Sportswriter Curry Kirkpatrick wrote, "If golf ever needed a certain kind of man to dull the harsh scorn of its critics, he was found in 1971. Golf found Lee Trevino, a common man with an uncommon touch who has bewitched, bothered, and bewildered the custodians of the game's mores. What Lee Trevino has done is take the game out of the country club boardroom and put in the parking lot where everybody— not just doctors and lawyers but Indian chiefs, too—can get at it."[22]

SURVIVING LIGHTNING

On June 27, 1975, at the Western Open at Butler National Golf Club in Chicago, Trevino faced an obstacle against which he was no match—lightning. Playing with Jerry Heard and Bobby Nichols, Trevino was waiting out a rain break on the thirteenth hole when a shaft of lightning bounced off a nearby lake, shot through the metal club shafts in his golf bag, and struck him in the back.

He was knocked unconscious and rushed to the hospital. The other two players also felt the effects but not as seriously as Trevino. Hospitalized for two days, doctors found four burn marks on his left shoulder where the potentially lethal charge entered and exited his body. If the bolt of electricity had hit further to the center of his body, he likely would have died. Trevino later said, "My heart stopped, and the doctor told me if it wasn't in such good shape, I'd have been gone."[23]

Although Trevino survived the incident, he began to suffer much back pain. The lightning damaged his lower back vertebrae and affected his flexibility and strength. Many observers believed that his career as a competitive golfer had essentially ended on that day in Chicago. But tenacity and determination were deeply ingrained characteristics in the personality of Trevino. He underwent a series of painful operations in the next year, including one for a herniated disc. Later, he had a nerve ending deadened to lessen the pain. But he returned to the game, experimenting with his shot to compensate for the back injuries. He did as he always had done—he adjusted. Although he limited his appearances on the tour in the aftermath of the lightning incident, and, at the insistence of his doctors, he greatly reduced his practice time, Trevino was soon back on the tour chasing titles. Within two years Trevino again triumphed in the Canadian Open.

Trevino's personal life remained stormy. His second marriage, which had lasted seventeen years and produced three children—Tony, Lesley, and a youngest daughter named Troy—ended in 1982. Looking back, he felt much regret, especially in his treatment of his children, whom he had largely ignored for the sake of his career. "Those kids didn't get a fair shake," Trevino admitted. "I was a lousy dad. Half the time I didn't even know what grades they were in. Maybe I was selfish, but I never felt like I belonged. It's only now that I realize yes, I was talented, and I probably didn't need to put as much time into it as I did."[24]

In early 1983, Trevino married for a third time, this time to Claudia Bove, whom he had met at a golf tournament. They would have two children together, Olivia and Daniel.

Trevino was now forty-four years old with a bad back; it had been thirteen years since his glory year of 1971. He had already begun to work as a golf commentator for NBC. He was still a skilled player on the Tour, but few expected him ever to win another one of the four coveted Majors. His last tour victory was in 1981; he had not won a Major in the last decade. He had never won the Masters, but he had captured the U.S. Open twice (1968 and 1972), the British Open twice (1971 and 1972) and PGA once (1974).

The PGA Championship of 1984 opened outside Birmingham, Alabama, at a course called Shoal Creek. Luxurious but isolated, the relatively new course was in such a remote and bucolic setting that a can of bug spray was put in every player's locker to help ward off an invasion of yellow jackets and other insects. At one point in the tournament a rattlesnake over three feet long was discovered in a parking lot.

Before heading for Alabama, Trevino did not exhibit his usual confidence. Claudia, whom Lee often referred to as his psychiatrist, told him that his clubs did not know how old he was. That was the kind of reasoning and quick quip that Trevino himself often threw out at others—he loved it.

The Shoal Creek course actually favored Trevino's game. It had tight fairways that demanded accurate tee shots, and it also had treacherous rough. Before the tournament began, veteran Gary Player predicted no one would break par. In some ways, the course was something like a normal U.S. Open event. If Trevino could split the fairways with his tee shots and avoid the rough, he might be a contender. After all, his clubs did not know how old he was.

Claudia's optimism was not misplaced. Shortly before the event, rain hit the Alabama course, softening its fairways and greens. Even with his low-riding shots, Trevino now had excellent opportunities to hit his irons close to the holes without great concern that they would roll off the greens.

Trevino played as if in some kind of rarified zone. It was as if this was 1971 all over again, as if the thirteen years had never passed, as if the lightning had not damaged his back. Drive after drive rocketed down the center of the fairways. His putting was exquisite. Gary Player, one of his closest competitors in the event, said he had never seen anyone make as many pressure putts.

Trevino scored an amazing score of 273, fifteen strokes under par; he had played all four rounds under 70, and he won by four strokes. It was the lowest score in history of the PGA Tournament. It was his twenty-seventh tour victory, his sixth major championship, and his second PGA title. "When you're young, you say it's inevitable you'll win," he said. "When you're old, the inevitable is over with. Winnin' a major at my age is like findin' a diamond in a coal mine."[25]

Sportswriter Barry McDermott wrote, "What a journey it has been. Trevino has won titles and hearts, been hit by lightning, insulted the best, had two back operations, teetered on the brink of bankruptcy, been married three times, traveled around the world, and has hardly ever taken a favor from anyone. He goes his own way, powered by a heart that probably could run a small city, and now, at forty-four, he's done it again."[26]

ON THE SENIOR TOUR

In 1980 the PGA formed a schedule of tournaments to be held each year for players over fifty years old. The Senior Tour became instantly popular, not only for television audiences but for golf fans in courses across the country.

In the past, as well-known players became less competitive on the regular tour, their careers were essentially over as far as national attention. Now, with the Senior Tour, fans of players such as Arnold Palmer, Gary Player, Jack Nicklaus, and others could continue to see their idols compete. It was a showcase for the public, and, with its increasingly growing popularity, it was lucrative for the players. Lee Trevino once joked that he could not wait to get into the action on the Senior Tour. He would rather play against competitors with round bellies, he said, than those youngsters with flat ones.

He began a strict physical conditioning program and concentrated on getting his golf game ready for a new challenge. In 1990, after turning fifty years old, Trevino entered a Senior Tour event at the first opportunity. He traveled to Key Biscayne, Florida, for the Royal Caribbean Classic. He won. He then won again two weeks later. He stormed the Senior Tour his first year. Of the first twenty-six events in which he entered, he won seven, including the U.S. Senior Open, where he finished two strokes ahead of Jack Nicklaus. Trevino was number one on the tour's money list with $1,190,518, setting a record as the first senior to earn more than the regular PGA Tour's leading money winner.

Despite an injured thumb that required surgery, Trevino kept winning. In 1992, he won five events and his earnings again topped $1 million. Continuing to perform well into the mid-1990s, Trevino became PGA Senior champion in 1994, but a neck injury forced him to start cutting back somewhat on both his practice and the number of events he entered. At one point, he joked that sometimes when he went out to play, the competitive edge was not quite there, that he was counting actual birds he saw rather than birdies he made.

Nevertheless, in 1996, he won the Legends of Golf to claim a fourth victory in the event in six years. At his wife's urging and after reassessing his own priorities, he began to spend much more time with his family. Soon he was carrying daughter Olivia around to golf events, driving her to school, and watching school plays. No longer was he the father who put golf far ahead of any other concerns.

Although another operation required metal plates to be inserted in his back, he continued to work out the swing in the early years of the new century, always changing it to suit his physical condition. He did not have the distance or touch of years ago, but he still had a deep love of the game and could not wait to rejoin the Senior Tour.

LATINO LEGEND

In the usual group of professional golfers with textbook swings and quiet, serious demeanors, Trevino always stood out. The squat, dark-haired player who looked a little overweight, the one that kept up a constant conversation with himself and the galleries, the one with that flat, awkward-looking swing that somehow worked—that was Trevino. Except for those ringing shots down the middle of the fairways and those low approaches to the greens that seemed always to nestle close to the pins, he looked like an everyday duffer on a two-bit course down in west Texas.

For young Latinos just learning the sport of golf or others trying to master their games, Trevino was a legendary and inspiring figure. For many golf fans, especially the millions who watched his memorable battles through many tournaments, Trevino was often the first Latino they really followed and got to know, at least on the surface.

"I've got a lot of people rooting for me," Trevino once said, "because there's more poor people than rich people. You look at my galleries. You'll see tattoos. Plain dresses. I represent the guy who goes to the driving range, the municipal player, the truck driver, the union man, the guy who grinds it out. To them, I am someone who worked hard, kept at it, and made it. Sure, I go out of my way to talk to them. They're my people."[27]

Trevino never talked much about his charitable work. He and Claudia established a foundation to distribute funds to worthy causes such as the St. Jude Children's Research Hospital in Memphis, Tennessee. From the beginning of his success on the tour, he recognized that the golf profession was an ideal way to raise money. There are tournaments whose purpose is to fund various charitable causes and over the years Trevino was involved in many.

After almost every event, he donated portions of his winnings to charitable enterprises. He also served as National Christmas Seals Sports Ambassador, and he was a member of the President's Conference on Physical Fitness and Sports and the National Multiple Sclerosis Society sports committee. As one of his friends pointed out, you did not have to look very closely to find cases of his paying a caddie's medical bills or raising money for women who have suffered spousal abuse.

Although he lived for several years in Florida at the height of his career, Trevino eventually returned, almost literally, to his Texas roots. Trevino purchased a large, elegant, fifteen-room home in the suburbs of Dallas. It rested nearly on the same ground where he used to run as a boy, hunting rabbits and fishing in the creek. The home stood near the spot where the run-down shack had stood, the one with neither electricity nor plumbing. "From the way I was raised, it's a stone miracle where I am today," said Trevino. "But God gave me a few things. Talent and determination, sure. But he also gave me the ability to adapt to whatever the hell I take up and practice at it and make it work. I've always told people that I'm an uneducated engineer. I will figure things out, somehow."[28]

Sportswriter Sam Blair, a columnist for the *Dallas Morning News*, co-authored a book with Trevino in 1982 called *They Call Me Super Mex*. Blair talked about Trevino's big heart. "Cancer research, children's hospitals, orphanages, and golf scholarship programs have benefited from his generosity," wrote Blair. "He's a guy who drove fifty miles after a round at the Tournament of Champions in response to a spontaneous request that he do a benefit for disabled veterans. He's a guy who played an exhibition in Mississippi to raise money for a pro whose shop burned down."[29]

Many times the words "the American dream" are used to describe the lives of certain individuals who rise from poverty and obscurity to unimagined heights of success. Lee Trevino's story pretty much defines the term.

NOTES

1. Lee Trevino and Sam Blair. *They Call Me Super-Mex*. New York: Random House, 1982, 18–19.

2. Jaime Diaz, "Finding His Way Home," *Golf Digest*, August 2003, 122.

3. "Lee Trevino: Cantinflas of the Country Clubs," *Time*, July 19, 1971, http://www.time.com/time/magazine/article/0,9171,905380-9,00.html.

4. Trevino and Blair, 23.

5. "Lee Trevino," http://www.golfpunkonline.com/players-lounge/lee-trevino-pt3.asp.

6. Trevino and Blair, 29.

7. "Lee Trevino: Cantinflas"

8. Nick Seitz, "The Several Lives of Lee Trevino," *Golf World*, August 13, 2004, 20.

9. "Lee Trevino: Cantinflas"

10. Seitz.

11. John Garrity, "Lee Trevino," *Sports Illustrated*, April 25, 1994, 46.

12. Diaz.

13. Mike Bryan, "Remember When: Super Mex!" *Golf Magazine*, May 1983, 56.

14. Bryan.

15. Cameron Morfit, "The Short Goodbye: At the end of a career that's been defined by pure ball striking, competitive will, and a paradoxical personality, Lee Trevino's just looking for the nearest unlit exit." *Golf Magazine*, March 1, 2006, 84.

16. "Lee Trevino: Cantinflas"

17. "Lee Trevino: Cantinflas"

18. Trevino and Blair, 114–115.

19. Morfit.

20. "Beating Birkdale: three past winners share their strategies." *Golf Magazine*, July 1983, 50.

21. Trevino and Blair, 137.

22. Curry Kirkpatrick, "Sportsman of the Year: Lee Trevino," *Sports Illustrated*, December 23, 1971, http://sportsillustrated.cnn.com/features/2001/sportsman/1971.

23. "Western Open's Near Tragedy," *Chicago Tribune*, July 3, 2005, 2.

24. Morfit.

25. Seitz.

26. Barry McDermott, "It's an Old Man's Game After All," *Sports Illustrated*, August 27, 1984, 28.

27. "Lee Trevino: Cantinflas"

28. Diaz.

29. Trevino and Blair, xiii.

FURTHER READING

Diaz, Jaime. "Finding his way home." *Golf Digest*. August 2003, p. 122.

"Lee Trevino: Cantinflas of the country clubs." *Time*. July 19, 1971, http://www.time.com/time/magazine/article/0,9171,905380-9,00.html

Morfit, Cameron. "The short goodbye: At the end of a career that's been defined by pure ball striking, competitive will and a paradoxical personality, Lee Trevino's just looking for the nearest unlit exit." *Golf Magazine*. March 1, 2006, p. 84.

Seith, Nick. "The several lives of Lee Trevino." *Golf World*. August 13, 2004, p. 20.

Trevino, Lee, and Sam Blair. *They Call Me Super-Mex*. New York: Random House, 1982.

Luis Valdez

In the great reform movements of American history—civil rights, women's suffrage, and the labor movement—music, poetry, and other entertainment have helped infuse the causes with hope and a sense of enthusiasm and camaraderie. In the farm workers' movement of the 1960s, a young playwright gave spirit to the marchers and strikers through a unique brand of expression—the theater. His name was Luis Valdez, and his creation was El Teatro Campesino (The Farmworkers' Theater). Combining Mexican folk theater, comedy, and mime, the theater company served up a stirring comic fare on the foibles and offenses of bosses and their thugs, on outrageous abuses of a system that drove poor workers into even greater poverty and despair, and on the ways workers could combat their oppressions.

Valdez, along with the stage workers he enlisted in the cause of the farm worker, made the striking fields less ominous, inspired the workers to continue the fight, and added to their sense of belonging. "I was a social activist, a child of the '60s, so in that sense I wanted to change the world," Valdez wrote. "We were fighting for our civil rights, for our humanity, and it seemed to me that using the arts, using humor, using masks, using theatre, was the way to do it."[1]

A CAMPESINO LIFE

In Delano, California, in the heart of farm labor country, Luis Valdez was born on June 26, 1940, the second of ten children of campesinos Francisco and Armeda Valdez. Both of his parents were from Arizona. Relatives on both sides of his family had roots in the Yaqui Indian culture of Mexico.

Francisco spent his youngest years around Tucson while his own parents eked out a living doing odd jobs. Eventually the family made its way north to Mesa, Arizona, southeast of Phoenix. It is there that Luis Valdez's grandfather is buried. Eventually, much of the extended Valdez family followed one of Luis' uncles to California. There, they attempted to make a life as itinerant laborers.

The family had thus joined a growing workforce in the fields—critically important to American agriculture during the harvest seasons and yet jarring to the American social fabric—thousands of men, women, and children willing to work for meager wages and yet largely unaccounted for in the organized systems of American culture, from its schools and courts to its social programs and constitutional freedoms.

Largely illiterate, extremely poor, and divided culturally from mainstream America, itinerant farm laborers usually did not remain very long in one locale, moving with the job opportunities that opened up in the fields. Isolated at their work sites, the workers lived mostly in crude shacks constructed by the farms, and they purchased most of their living supplies from makeshift stores owned by the farmers. This was the underside of the American

Dream, where unscrupulous labor contractors skimmed off portions of the workers' wages, where contractors made fake payroll deductions for Social Security and then pocketed the money. This was the time of the short-handled hoe in the lettuce fields where workers filed along the lines of crops stooped over in painful contortion, hours on end—painstaking labor that led to many physical ailments and afflictions.

Nevertheless, the Valdez family, like so many others, persevered through the humiliations and indignities, moving from valley to valley, from harvest to harvest, trying to keep afloat. Increasingly, the work left them physically debilitated, relatively powerless to do anything to end their stifling transience. But they kept going, striving to keep their spirits high and to look forward to better days.

By the age of six, Luis joined his nine brothers and sisters in the picking fields with his parents around California's San Joaquin Valley. Cotton, cherries, apricots, grapes, peaches, plums—they moved from harvest field to harvest field. For a time the family lived on the Chagrin Ranch in San Jose. The boy was shuttled in and out of schools and was able to attend only sporadically.

Valdez later remembered that he became interested in the theater at the early age. At one of the cotton camps, the Valdez family was temporarily stalled because of the breakdown of the family Ford truck. During his stay in the camp, the boy watched as a teacher turned an ordinary paper bag into a papier mâché face of a monkey. "I was amazed, shocked in an exhilarating way, that she could do this with paper and paste," Valdez remembered. The teacher was preparing other costumes for a Christmas play and asked the boy if he would try out for a part. He passed the audition. "I was measured for a costume that was better than the clothes I was wearing at the time, certainly more colorful. The next few weeks were some of the most exciting in my short life. After seeing the stage transformed into a jungle and after all the excitement of the preparations—I doubt that it was as elaborate as my mind remembers it now—my dad got the truck fixed, and a week before the show was to go on, we moved away. So I never got to be in the Christmas play."[2]

He missed the play, but he was hooked on acting. He could see himself on stage—he could see himself creating and acting out those characters. Those moments, he increasingly believed, could take him far away from the grinding poverty of the field into a completely separate dimension.

The legendary Lalo Guerrero, the "Father of Chicano Music," was an early inspiration for Valdez. Guerrero was close to the Valdez family when Luis was a boy. Although the musician traveled constantly throughout the Southwest singing in towns and barrios and appearing nationally on tours and in recording studios, he visited the San Joaquin Valley often. Guerrero was an inspiration, said Valdez, "because it was somebody who was in show business and somebody I knew who used to come over to the house whenever he was in town. I have memories of chasing his car as a kid in the barrio.... He was very influential in the life of my family, because he was like a star way back when. In the late '30s he was already making a living as a musician, which was pretty unusual, because everybody else was still working in the fields. So to have Lalo out there, and then on the radio and making records."[3]

For twelve years, Valdez worked the fields with his parents. Although his schooling was always wildly transient and uneven, the precocious boy consistently impressed his teachers, not only with his natural intelligence but also with a refreshing curiosity and eagerness to learn. He became skillful with puppetry and gained such competence as a ventriloquist that he appeared regularly on a local television show. Not surprisingly, given his later career, he wrote his own material.

Valdez graduated from James Lick High School in the east side of San Jose and earned a scholarship to attend San Jose State College. He soon turned most of his drive and energy to studying the theater. While in college he won a writing contest for his play, *The Theft*. Later, the college's drama department produced *The Shrunken Head of Pancho Villa*, his play about the problems facing a Mexican couple in America.

Valdez developed a special interest in the work of Bertolt Brecht (1898–1956), the German dramatist, stage director, and poet, who had developed a theory of theater that encouraged audiences to identify directly and emotionally with the events on stage and to try to make the production so inspiring that audiences would go out into the world to correct its ills. In many ways, Brecht's plays were like political meetings in which actors directly engaged the audience in conversation. A Brecht play would often include odd stage lighting, exaggerated characters, music, and even placards to explain events and roles.

"Brecht looms huge in my orientation," Valdez wrote. "I discovered Brecht in college, from an intellectual perspective.... I was working in the library, so I had first dibs on all the new books. Brecht to me had been only a name. But this book opened up Brecht and I started reading all his plays and his theories, which I subscribed to immediately. I continue to use his alienation effect to this day."[4]

After graduating from San Jose State in 1964, Valdez joined the San Francisco Mime Troupe. He began to learn the techniques of agitprop (agitation and propaganda) theater, plays designed to infuse the spirit and drive into the heart of political and social change movements. He soon found a perfect vehicle.

STRIKERS IN THE FIELD

In 1965, a fledgling movement in support of farm workers fired the imagination and commitment of the young playwright. It was the National Farm

Workers Association, led by Cesar Chavez. Thirteen years older than Luis, Chavez's own youth mirrored that of Valdez. Both were born in Arizona to farm worker parents; both moved to California. As a young man, Chavez had briefly left the fields for a stint in the Navy but found it oppressive in its treatment of Latinos; he returned to California determined to take on the system of repression and prejudice that had ground down so many of his fellow field workers.

After working for a social service agency, Chavez met a priest who encouraged him to read about the non-violent tactics of reform advanced by Mahatma Gandhi in India. At the same time, Chavez learned from the dynamic work of Martin Luther King and other civil rights leaders taking on the entrenched policies of racial segregation. Through the examples of these leaders and through his own indefatigable belief in organizing and fighting for the rights of migrant laborers, Chavez formed the National Farm Workers Association, which would later join with the Agricultural Workers Organizing Committee to become the union known as the United Farm Workers.

On September 16, 1965, Chavez prepared to take on the power of the big farm companies. The membership of the farm workers' union gathered at Our Lady of Guadalupe Church in Delano. It was Mexican Independence Day, honoring the time Mexicans achieved the end of Spanish colonial rule. Chavez prepared to call for a strike.

Into the pews and balconies wedged over five hundred excited workers and their families. Chavez had sent out word through local disc jockeys on Spanish radio and in the Union's paper that something big was in the works. Dressed in an old sport shirt and work pants, Chavez stepped up to speak to the large gathering, many of whom had never before seen or met him, although his name was fast becoming known throughout the migrant communities of central California. Short in stature, his voice halting and somewhat shaky, Chavez, nevertheless, rallied the men and women to *La Causa* (The Cause).

The group voted unanimously to go forward with the strike that night at the church. The cry was now "*Viva la huelga!*" (Long live the strike!). Personally, Chavez remained cautious—the union had only $100 in its bank account, but Chavez, by his decision to move forward, had not only put himself and his union in the forefront of an unprecedented effort to improve the lives of agricultural field workers but had also staked his own ground in the struggle for civil rights.

Two months after the Delano strike began, Valdez joined Chavez in his efforts to organize the farm workers. He had returned home. The decision was a crossroads in his life. As Valdez was nearing the completion of his college work, he had received an offer from one of his former professors to go to Brandeis University in Massachusetts to enroll in a Master of Arts program. His masters' thesis would be his play on which he had already worked. In addition, an off-Broadway producer named Cyril St. Cyr was already interested in producing Valdez's work. In the end, Valdez chose to remain on the west coast and work with Cesar Chavez. Looking back later, he wrote:

> So I knew that there was a possibility, a road, going in one direction. The other road that showed up in the summer of 1965 was that there was a grape strike in the town where I was born called Delano. And as it turns out it was being led by this old pachuco that I had known back when I was six years old. He used to be the running partner of my pachuco cousin.[5]

Chavez greeted his old acquaintance from Delano with welcoming arms. Valdez, Chavez knew, could bring another, vital dimension to the farm-workers' movement. It would be a theater company of actor-laborers whose goal would be to raise funds and to publicize the farm-worker strike. The talents and imagination of Valdez would soon turn the effort into something much greater—a grass-roots theatrical movement.

On Friday evenings Chavez began to hold two-hour meetings. Meant to bolster the spirit of the strikers, the weekly gatherings included songs, testimonials from families and friends of the strikers, and presentations by guests from religious, social, and labor organizations. They also included the first performances of El Teatro Campesino, which combined Mexican folk theater, comedy, and mime to offer comic reflections on laborers, bosses, and others in the world of the farm worker. The actors themselves were campesinos. The company created short skits that they performed not only at the Friday night gatherings but also on flatbed trucks at the strike sites. They later toured towns and cities to raise money for the union. They saw themselves as fighting a battle whose outcome was uncertain, Valdez said later. They had a roving picket line. Starting at dawn, the group would drive from location to location, pull up at the sides of roads, and start performing.

The Teatro's brief ten- to fifteen-minute performances aimed a stream of attacks and ridicule against the growers and their hired strikebreakers. They used few props—an old pair of pans or maybe a wine bottle—to make certain points, but mostly they showed symbols of the strikers, such as armbands. Sometimes they would hang signs around their necks indicating the portrayed characters.

The Teatro had a willing, if relatively uneducated audience, that soon fell under its spellbinding effects. The message and humor were direct, coarse, and physical, and gave to the workers something akin to morality plays fought out in the work sites. If Chavez was the spiritual and political leader of the farm workers, Valdez became their cultural leader, bringing an artistry perfectly suited to its time and place.

Several times a week "Huelga Priests" held masses for the workers. People began to talk about Mexican history and the relationship of this strike to other battles of the poor and dispossessed. Slogans appeared on the sides of buildings and fences. Strikers waved banners of the Virgin of Guadalupe, the patron saint of Mexico, and carried both the Mexican and United States flags.

Teatro de Campesino Acto

Las Dos Cras del Patroncito (The Two Faces of the Dear Boss)

In the earliest days of Luis Valdez's career, as he worked with Cesar Chavez on behalf of migrant farmworkers, he introduced a new theatrical concept he called the *acto*. The form, often humorous and irreverent, made use of various representational methods including masks and signs hung around the necks of the actors showing their occupations. Often, the characters reversed roles. The language was that of the working class. Valdez and his small company of actors often performed this early *acto*, "Los Dos Cras del Patroncito," on flatbed trucks to audiences of workers in the fields.

The plot of this *acto* involves a simple role reversal. A powerful landowner, wishing to live the life of a worker, free of responsibility, orders one of the strikebreakers he has fired to trade identities. They change masks and thus change social roles. The landowner, now facing the injustices and demeaning demands of the field worker, realizes that he has harbored distorted ideas of the lives of the workers and their supposed freedoms and has not understood their suffering. He thus becomes a supporter of their cause.

Cast:
Castersonae Esquirol, a scab farmworker
Patroncito, the dear boss
Charlie, armed guard, rent-a-fuzz

Acto:
Greeting the audience, the farmworker tells of being brought from Mexico to work as a scab in the grape orchards. The boss, wearing a yellow pig mask and chomping on a cigar, arrives in a limousine and demands that the worker increase his production. Charlie, the hired thug, begins to attack the farmworker but the boss sends him ahead to look for union organizers.

The farmworker meekly agrees that he is not working hard enough and that he and his fellow workers deserve the rough treatment usually meted out. The boss sees his position and power as a burden and wishes he could have the freedom to wander the land, to enjoy nature, and to have little responsibility. A changing of roles, he suggests, would confirm his assumptions. Quickly, the farmworker assumes the dominant position but is rudely dragged away for a whipping by the hired thug who is unaware that the other two have changed social positions.

The boss soon realizes his errors and recants. The farmworker finally agrees to give back the house, the land, and other possessions. It was never his intention or the wish of the strikers that they seize property; they merely wished their rightful pay and fair treatment. The farmworker, however, decides to keep a cigar.

All of this helped establish a strong sense of solidarity and cultural identity among the group and discouraged other workers who heard the plays and the other Friday evening activities from staying with the growers. For many of the workers it was all exhilarating, if dangerous, and something quite out of the ordinary in the lives of farm laborers, like a drink of fine wine after years of tainted water.

After absorbing the first round of volleys from the growers, Chavez decided to raise the level of the protest. In early December 1965, he decided to call a boycott of Schenley Industries. Recruiting additional volunteers from churches, community organizations, labor organizations, and universities, the union set up boycott centers in the cities. Signs appeared urging the public to "Help Farmworkers—Do Not Buy Grapes." The protest had thus moved from the fields to the urban areas. It also attracted additional national attention. It quickly became clear that Chavez was no ordinary leader and this was no ordinary strike. This was more than a typical fight for wages and working conditions; Chavez had focused the movement on the ethnic identity of Mexican Americans and a quest for justice rooted in Catholic social teaching.

Appropriately, Valdez helped the union create a cultural center for farm workers and their families in Delano, where, through art, music, dance, and the theater, they could learn about Mexican heritage.

MARCHING TO SACRAMENTO

Through the winter months of 1965 into 1966, Chavez gathered supporters to explore ways to maintain the fervor and commitment of the strikers. In February, at a meeting near Santa Barbara, California, the union leader and his advisers, after discussing a number of strategic possibilities, decided to adopt another tactic that had been successful in the civil rights movement—a long march. It would cover a route from Delano to the California state capitol of Sacramento, through such towns as Madera, Fresno, Modesto, and Stockton.

In an attempt to connect even further the union movement with the history and culture of Mexico, Valdez suggested that they write a "Plan de Delano" to be read in each town through which they marched. The statement would follow in the tradition of a leader of the Mexican Revolution, Emiliano Zapata, who fought for the rights of native peoples against powerful landowners in Mexico. In 1911, Zapata put forward his "Plan de Alaya," a rallying statement for the underclasses.

Chavez asked Valdez to compose such a document for the farm workers. It became yet another symbol around which the strikers rallied. It talked of a pilgrimage to seek an end to the suffering of farm workers, of their determination to be heard, and of their resolve to follow their God. It promised unity with people of all faiths and races, inclusion of all races and workers across the land, and a revolution for "bread and justice."

On the morning of March 17, 1966, Chavez, along with Valdez and about one hundred individuals, gathered in Delano to begin the march. Somewhat disorganized but enthusiastic, they set off through the town and onto Highway 99, followed by members of the press, several agents from the Federal Bureau of Investigation, and other onlookers. Soon, they began to pass some of the vineyards in which they had worked and against which they had organized pickets six months earlier. They carried banners, portraits of the Virgin of Guadalupe, and union flags. Some carried large crosses. Some wore Veterans of Foreign Wars hats.

Valdez carried "The Plan of Delano" to be read at each stop and then signed by local workers. At each stop he read aloud: "WE SHALL OVERCOME. Across the San Joaquin Valley, across California, across the entire Southwest of the United States, wherever there are Mexican people, wherever there are farm workers, our movement is spreading like flames across a dry plain. Our PILGRIMAGE is the MATCH that will light our cause for all farm workers to see what is happening here, so that they may do as we have done. The time has come for the liberation of the poor farm worker. History is on our side. MAY THE STRIKE GO ON! *VIVA LA CAUSA!*"[6]

On April 3, a week before the marchers were due to reach Sacramento, Chavez received a call from a representative of Schenley Industries. Already damaged by the publicity garnered by Chavez and hurt economically by the strike and boycott, the company had decided to cut its losses. They decided to enter into negotiations with Chavez for a union contract. The company agreed to recognize formally the National Farm Workers Union. This was the first time in United States history that a grass-roots farm labor union had achieved recognition by a corporation. Schenley agreed to a substantial increase of wages and to an improvement of working conditions.

Many Chicanos in cities and towns across the country closely identified with the struggle of the farm workers. They followed the marches, strikes, and boycotts intensely, and many became politically motivated themselves. They joined the pickets in front of grocery stores in their own neighborhoods during the grape boycott and began to sing and chant the slogans of Chavez's campesino movement. And Valdez's Teatro Campesino, founded in the fields of the Chavez protests, would later become a familiar rallying group to a growing, nationwide Chicano movement.

BEYOND THE FIELDS TO A NEW CHICANO THEATER

By 1967, it was clear the United Farm Workers was well established. Valdez decided to take the teatro to a wider audience. He left the unionizing efforts in the vineyards and lettuce fields to relocate to Del Rey, California. Here,

Valdez created Centro Campesino Cultural, a cultural center, where he would work to expand Teatro Campesino's reach and address themes surrounding the Chicano experience. He took the plays on the road and was sometimes overwhelmed by the response from workers.

The first time they traveled to Texas, Valdez recalled, they got lost and spent over thirty hours on the road. When they finally arrived at Rio Grande City for the scheduled performance, they were over an hour late. "This little town had no light," he remembered. "It was economically depressed. We said, 'We must have made a mistake; there's nobody here.'" But we turned the corner and went down the street—all these campesinos were standing in front of the movie house waiting. And they saw us and they began to applaud, right? And they opened up our trunk and pulled it out and took it into the movie house, sat down, and then wanted a show. And we gave them the show. After thirty-six hours we gave a live show, and it was one of the best shows that we've ever had."[7]

He soon introduced *Los Vendidos* (*The Sellouts*), a play that explored various stereotypical attitudes about Chicanos in the setting of "Honest Sancho's Used Mexican Lot and Mexican Curio Shop." Aired nationally by the Public Broadcasting System, the play won several awards, including an Emmy. Its success fueled a national tour by El Teatro Campesino.

First performed by the company at Elysian Park in Los Angeles before a gathering of the Brown Berets, a group of Chicano activists, *Los Vendidos* tapped into the conflicts of social identity and urban pressures faced by young Latinos. To the young Latinos in the audiences that saw the play, the characters were simple, humorous, and, most of all, identifiable. Honest Sancho, a former labor contractor, is obviously dishonest, and the used cars and cheap Mexican arts and crafts he peddles, not of the highest quality.

At Sancho's establishment arrives a Miss Jimenez. She is in the employ of Ronald Reagan, Governor of California, and is there to purchase a type of Mexican to serve in the administration. Honest Sancho suggests several types—a farmworker, a revolutionary, a pachuco (a young, Mexican-American urban type), and a middle-class Mexican American. Miss Jimenez rejects the farmworker as crude and unsophisticated; she rejects the revolutionary as incapable of speaking the English language; and she rejects the pachuco as a dangerous delinquent. She decides on the middle-class Mexican American, whose language skills and progressing assimilation seem suitable for state government. After purchasing the Mexican-American model, however, Miss Jimenez is in for a rude awakening. Suddenly the model displays dysfunctional qualities, even rebelliousness. As the other models cheer on the newfound self-awareness of the Mexican American, Miss Jimenez scurries out of the store, humiliated and disillusioned.

Latinos recognized Sancho, the first of the sellouts, as a figure capitalizing on and manipulating ethnic stereotypes for money; they saw Miss Jimenez as a Latino so thoroughly assimilated as to be ignorant of her roots and culture. In the new atmosphere of Latino cultural affirmation, both of these figures were comic and pathetic, and they were rejected.

The next year, Valdez presented *The Shrunken Head of Pancho Villa*, a play on which he had been working for several years. Surreal and bizarre, the play included among its characters a bodyless head and a headless body. The play dealt closely with an issue that the playwright knew intimately—a family on welfare. At first, Valdez said, he was slightly embarrassed about revealing to the world that his own family had been forced into such poverty; nevertheless, he soon realized that most of his audience had similar experiences and to them the emotional deprivation was familiar territory. The play garnered an off-Broadway Obie Award. In 1968, Valdez performed at an international festival in Nancy, in northern France. From flatbed trucks to international venues, El Teatro Campesino was on a meteoric climb. Valdez was establishing nothing less than a revolutionary Chicano theater.

Although several Mexican folk-theatre groups in the southwest had performed before the arrival of Valdez, El Teatro Campesino dramatically altered the landscape, forging a new, contemporary mode of expression. Across America, Chicano theatrical groups sprang up to stage Valdez's one-act plays, exploring such contemporary issues as the farmworkers' struggles, the Vietnam War, and the problems of drug addiction and crime. The groups stressed ethnic pride and the preservation of cultural traditions. The movement celebrated the grassroots Chicano.

At the center of the performances of El Teatro Campesino was a form that Valdez simply called the *acto*. Valdez said that even in naming the form, he did not reach for some classical Spanish term; this theatrical form was for the La Raza, the people, and the simple word *acto*, he said, made perfect sense.

In appealing to the audience of farmworkers, he also adapted motifs that conformed to aspects of Mexican folk culture and contemporary linguistics. For example, the plays used the language of the modern-day Chicano culture, with its characteristic of switching from Spanish to English and back again.

The purpose of the *acto*, he explained, was to present a social problem, satirize the opposition, propose a solution, and inspire the audience to action. As short dramatic skits, the *actos* were designed to communicate directly with the working-class Chicano in their own language. With messages usually infused with humor, the *actos* were often improvised by the theatre company players, and many of the plays featured performers directly addressing the audience and suggesting alternative endings. Players often worked without scenery, props, or costumes, sometimes simply wearing signs around their necks with the names of the stock characters such as "Patroncito" (the boss) and "Huelgista" (the striker). The dialogue fluctuated between broken English and Spanish.

In 1969 Valdez moved the cultural center to Fresno, California, where it remained for two years. While in Fresno, Valdez taught at Fresno State College. He also helped found Tenaz, a national organization of theater groups.

In 1969, Valdez married Lupe Trujillo, an aspiring Chicana writer. She and their three sons, Anahuac, Kinan, and Lakin, worked closely with Luis and Teatro Campesino over the next three decades.

In the early 1970s, Valdez purchased land and moved the troupe into two houses in San Juan Bautista, California, a small town between San Jose and Salinas, best known for its eighteenth century Catholic mission. In this rural area, far removed from the usual entertainment venues, he built a theater out of a fruit-packing shed. Now a fully professional production company, Valdez was acutely aware that he was establishing a canon for a new Chicano theater.

In 1970 Valdez introduced two performances that dramatized the sociopolitical issues directly affecting young urban audiences. In *Vietnam Campesino* he depicted the political role of powerful agricultural interests who supported the military establishment and the war in Vietnam as they profited from increasing farm subsidies. At the bottom rung of the ladder of exploited, Valdez pointed out, were the field workers.

Huelguistas was a vignette depicting various farmworkers confronting a ranchowner (*Patroncito*) and his hired *contratista* (Coyote). The simple plot came directly from the literary arsenal he had used in the early days of the Teatro Campesino on the road with Cesar Chavez—the battle between the powerful interests and the underclasses. However, in *Huelguistas* Valdez experimented with a format more likely to draw interest from a wider community. Music now infused his work. The subtleties of the relationships between the farmworker and his bosses were now undergirded with a style less dependent on detailed understanding of Chicano life. He now began to open his work to wider audiences in the United States and, indeed, abroad.

When he published a number of *actos* in 1971, he outlined his vision. The purpose, he said, must be to create a national theater based on the identification of the Chicano population's geographic, religious, cultural, and racial heritage. It must maintain an independent organization and must never stray from the grassroots—La Raza. If La Raza did not come to the theater, Valdez declared, the theater must go the La Raza.

Valdez examined the impact of the Vietnam War and its toll on Chicano families in *Soldado Razo*. As he so often did, Valdez used the figure of Death as a kind of master of ceremonies attired in the robes of a Franciscan friar. Filled with surprising humor, given the inevitability of the death of a soldier named Johnny, the play is a tender and compassionate piece of political theater.

In *No saco nada de la escuela*, a satirical analysis of how the school systems force minorities to give up their culture, Valdez called not only for bilingual education but for instruction that included Chicano and African-American history and culture, issues that state educational systems across the country were beginning to face, especially in California.

On college campuses and in communities across the country, Chicano theater groups appeared, all appealing to ethnic pride and cultural traditions, all remaining close to the people, to the grassroots, to La Raza.

ZOOT SUIT

In addition to his introduction of the *acto* as an artistic expression of Chicano theater, Valdez also explored the theme of myth. In several of his plays, he introduced *mito*, a theatrical form inspired by Mexican dance. As a theatrical genre, the *mito* would not, as the *acto*, be adopted by other Chicano playwrights into the politically explosive issues surrounding the cultural movements of the 1970s. Indeed, after several of the new Chicano theater leaders deplored his exploration of mystical themes, Valdez publicly broke with the ranks of the Chicano theater movement that he had inspired. Its focus had, he believed, become too narrow.

In 1978, Valdez wrote, directed, and produced a play that marked his breakthrough into mainstream theater. The play was called *Zoot Suit*. Based on events in Los Angeles three decades earlier, the project drove Valdez to research extensively and seriously consider his own ethnic heritage and that of his fellow Latinos in a larger historical context. Opening at the Mark Taper Forum in Los Angeles, *Zoot Suit* ran successfully for two years and, because of record sold-out performances, it was moved to the larger Aquarius Theater. The play eventually won the Los Angeles Critics Circle Award for "Distinguished Productions" and eight Drama-Logue Awards for "Outstanding Achievement in Theater." Valdez then took the play to the Winter Garden in New York in 1979. It was the first play written and produced by a Mexican American ever to reach Broadway. Although the play did not receive critical praise from the New York critics, the film, which Valdez directed, was nominated for a Golden Globe Award.

In approaching his work on *Zoot Suit*, Valdez was inspired by the very real events that had rocked the Chicano community in Los Angeles years earlier and whose echoes had reverberated in racial relations ever since.

In Los Angeles, in the summer of 1943, with United States sailors, soldiers, and marines heading to and from the front lines of the war in the Pacific, another kind of war broke out in the streets. Mexican-American youths in large numbers were now wearing their own kind of uniform—the zoot suit—and they were carrying on their own kind of rebellion, one rooted in a cultural clash nourished through generations.

These youths were known as pachucos—Mexican-American adolescents who belonged to juvenile gangs from a time during the Great Depression to the 1950s. Over the years historians and other scholars have traced the roots of the pachuco phenomenon to Spanish gypsies, to lower class settlers of the Borderlands during the late eighteenth and nineteenth centuries, and even to the common soldiers who made up the army of Pancho Villa during the Mexican Revolution of 1910. Other scholars have simply pointed to the pressures of urbanization, ethnic prejudice, and the wracking poverty of the time as the logical, bitter reasons for development of the pachuco culture.

Although it had earlier been something of a black youth fashion identified with the jazz culture, the zoot suit had been co-opted by a generation of Mexican-American teenagers. Along with the oversize coat, with its padded shoulders as wide as the frame of a door, and gaucho-like pants, most pachucos sported the signature "ducktail" hairstyle, long, especially on the sides, and swept back in waves on both sides of the head. A pachuco also wore a broad-brimmed hat and carried a very long key chain that dangled between the clip and the pocket. For the pachuco, this look was both a statement of defiance and an assertion of identity. For the general public, however, the zoot suit represented the decline of the city and the culture.

The violence and tensions in Los Angeles between the pachuco gangs and the city of Los Angeles had escalated since the summer of 1942 when the death of a man named Jose Diaz sparked a round-up of zoot-suit pachucos as possible suspects. A young Mexican national, Diaz was found dead near a reservoir nicknamed Sleepy Lagoon. The police and local media, especially the *Los Angeles Times*, immediately laid the blame for Diaz's death on the pachuco gangs. Los Angeles police herded over six hundred Latinos through police stations on the nights of August 10 and 11. Twenty-four members of the 38th Street Gang, so called by a local tabloid, were charged with the murder of Diaz.

For several weeks before the trial and during it, the co-defendants were not allowed to change their clothes, their zoot suits. The judge reasoned that the jury must be allowed to see the pachucos in their authentic attire—the long, dark, menacing coats and oversized pants. To the jury, the judge correctly assumed, the character type of the pachucos would be obvious to all.

Throughout the proceedings witnesses blithely talked about the blood lust of the gang, the ruthlessness that defined their cultural identity. For five months, the trial mesmerized readers of the Los Angeles tabloids, and with each new revelation about the ferocity of the gangs, the fears and racial tensions in the city escalated ominously. The alien menace was no longer the Japanese, who had by order of the federal government already been moved to internment camps during the war, but the Mexicans. Across Los Angeles, citizens feared that if strong measures were not put in place, a crime wave would eviscerate the city.

On January 12, 1943, the jury convicted three of the defendants of first-degree murder and sentenced them to life in prison; nine were convicted of second-degree murder and sentenced to five years to life, and five were convicted of assault and released for time served. The twelve convicted of first- or second-degree murder began serving their sentences in January 1943 at San Quentin Prison.

Throughout the spring, racial tensions in Los Angeles rose to a combustible level. On the night of June 3, 1943, eleven sailors on leave claimed they had been attacked by a group of pachucos. The response from fellow military servicemen was particularly sudden and violent. A group of more than two hundred uniformed sailors chartered twenty cabs and charged into the heart of the Mexican-American community in East Los Angeles.

For several nights, hundreds of servicemen moved through East Los Angeles. Marching abreast, they broke into stores, bars, and theaters, assaulting any individual sporting a zoot suit or anything close to it. Not only did the police stand by and watch the grisly sport, the local newspapers portrayed the invading soldiers as heroes fighting off the Latino crime wave.

So outrageous was the spectacle that First Lady Eleanor Roosevelt, writing in her newspaper column, lamented that the racial hatred against the Mexicans was at the root of the military riots in the Latino sections of Los Angeles; wearing the zoot suits, she observed, was only an excuse and pretext for the violence. The largest newspaper in the city, the *Los Angeles Times*, along with the other papers and tabloids that had cheered on the rioting servicemen, responded to Mrs. Roosevelt's remarks with a gratuitous charge that she had been accused of communist leanings.

The impact of the Sleepy Hollow Lagoon murder case and the subsequent Zoot Suit Riots was a glaring testament to the climate of racial tension and misunderstanding that pervaded Los Angeles. For two years after the bizarre trial, a group of volunteers led by an activist named Alice Greenfield worked to overturn the convictions on the basis of insufficient evidence. Finally, the Second District Court of Appeals released the defendants.

For Valdez, the historical and cultural clashes of decades earlier were logical and bountiful themes for exploration, and he set out to capture the continuing tensions. In this instance, he was determined that the historical facts not be lost in the drama. He studied books and articles, traveled to New York to interview historian Cary McWilliams, who had written the definitive account of the period, talked to aging individuals who had been involved, and visited libraries and archives to examine documents.

The product was vivid, a dramatic and musical interpretation that breathed the heat of the racial conflict that still seethed in his own time and in his own feelings. It told the story of Henry Reyna and his friends who were unfairly sent to prison largely through the hysteria of events and the culture of racism pervading law enforcement and the justice system.

"The Sleepy Hollow case established the national image of the pachuco as street punk, an image reflected on television and in films," Valdez said. "I wanted to study the case and the stereotype and to unravel something. The pachucos were mythic characters, an American phenomenon."[8]

Valdez also stressed that the emphasis on racial prejudice was in no way exaggerated in the play, as it was in the early 1940s. "There were signs in downtown Los Angeles that read, 'No Mexicans or dogs allowed.' As ugly and exaggerated as it may seem to some people, I can only say that it's true."[9]

Valdez told a reporter that he wanted the play to reach much further than the barrio. "I wrote 'Zoot Suit' for an American audience," he said. "The Anglos have to face reality, but I didn't want to offend the Anglo community. I want the pachuco life to be part of the American experience, not just the Chicano experience."[10]

El Pachuco, the play's main character, interacts with the audience as he narrates the scenes on stage by snapping his fingers. But he is not an unaffected or dispassionate observer. Representing the Chicano spirit of pride and individualism, he is deeply offended by the unfolding events playing out before him. He is Henry Reyna's alter ego, encouraging him, pressuring him to take various actions, coaching him in the name of his own heritage. El Pachuco cheers on Henry's bold defiance and encourages Henry and the others to embrace the pachuco style.

The play features exact courtroom transcriptions of testimonies and quotes from the press in covering the historical events. Along with his adherence to the historical record, Valdez also incorporates music of the time.

In one of the scenes, the servicemen turn on El Pachuco, strips off his zoot suit, and takes his switchblade knife. At that moment, El Pachuco rises, now dressed in Aztec form. Valdez has turned a historical play, albeit an allegory, into the mythical realm. El Pachuco represents a connection between Tezcatlipoca, the Aztec god of sorcery and prophecy, and the Chicano clashes in the streets of Los Angeles. The climax of the play centers on a ritual sacrifice of the pachuco, suggesting certain parallels between the sacrifices made in the Chicano gang fights and Aztec mythology.

Valdez later attributed the success of *Zoot Suit* to the mythic power and ancestry of the Pachuco figure. The reason a half million people came to see *Zoot Suit*, Valdez claimed, was because he had given back to a disenfranchised people a sense of their roots, religion, and culture. He never could have written *Zoot Suit* without the experiences and development of El Teatro Campesino, Valdez said.

> I know that our work reaches into the streets. We attract young people, people who are confronted with rather stark realities. They have to hope for something, man. If they don't have the arts telling them about the essence and meaning of life, offering some kind of exploration of the positive and negative aspects of life, then there is no hope. I was a very angry young man not too many years ago, and I was able to channel that anger into the arts.[11]

El Pachuco, Valdez explained, represented self-image or the superego, the power within every individual that can overcome any human barrier. When El Pachuco cries out that it will take more than the United States Navy to beat him down, referring to the attack by the servicemen in the

1940s, he was talking about self-salvation. "With *Zoot Suit*, I was finally able to transcend social conditions, and the way I did it on stage was to give the Pachuco absolute power, as the master of ceremonies. He could snap his fingers and stop the action. It was a Brechtian device that allowed the plot to move forward, but psychically and symbolically, in the right way."[12]

Although some Chicano critics charged that Valdez had gone too far in tying mythical origins to the pachuco movement, the play had a profound effect in the Latino communities, especially in California. Indeed, it even inspired something of a renaissance of the zoot suit look.

And even though Valdez had been shaken by the criticism of the play in New York, he responded in a biting critique of "the white man's sense of arrogance," that history and culture lie in Western Europe and that only from the perspective of those origins are political, religious, scientific, and artistic values to be considered valid. "Naturally," Valdez said, "the entire non-white world from Africa to Asia has been victimized and colonized by this incredibly arrogant attitude, but it is in America that this ignorance has come to roost. Here, a transplanted European culture is masquerading as American culture, and the way of life of the real natives has been distorted, stolen, ignored, or forgotten."[13]

ATTACKING THE LATINO STEREOTYPES

In 1981, Valdez celebrated the opening of a new playhouse in San Juan Bautista with a historical play called *Bandido*, based on the exploits of a California horse thief and stagecoach robber named Tiburcio Vasquez. A musical play within a play, *Bandido* captures the post–Gold Rush cultural clashes between native Mexicans and new American settlers and the real-life, if legendary, bandit and self-proclaimed liberator of California. Much like the legendary bandits Jesse James and Billy the Kid, Vasquez attained heroic stature within communities that understood and shared his roots, in his case the native community who saw their country and culture threatened by the American expansion westward. Unlike *Zoot Suit*, Valdez played loose with the historical accuracy of the story, opting instead to downplay the actual criminal and violent deeds of the historical figure.

The next year, Valdez explored the fascinating world of Mexican folk ballads, once again paying homage to Chicano history and culture. The production was called *Corridos: Tales of Passion and Revolution*. Valdez strongly felt that the *corridos* were the soul of the La Raza, representing voices of the work sites, the cantinas, and dance halls. A choreographed pageant of Mexican songs, some of them over one hundred years old, *Corridos* featured inventive theatrical productions by Valdez and his troupe. With colorful costumes, creative use of props, and careful musical arrangements, the show was a celebration of cultural identity.

After the 1982 production at San Juan Bautista, *Corridos* went on to become a hit at the San Francisco Marines Memorial Theater and later reopened at the Old Globe Theater in San Diego. It was awarded eleven Bay Area Critics Awards, including Best Musical. In 1987, radio station KQED/San Francisco, in association with El Teatro Campesino, adapted *Corridos* for national television through the Corporation of Public Broadcasting; the adaptation won the prestigious George Peabody Award for Excellence.

Valdez was determined to break down the Latino stereotypes so familiar in commercial theater, radio, and television. In 1986, he introduced his play *I Don't Have to Show You No Stinking Badges*. The play gets its name from the 1947 movie *The Treasure of the Sierra Madre*. Starring Humphrey Bogart and directed by John Huston, the film was one of the first Hollywood movies to be shot outside of the United States. The location was Tampico, Mexico, and the story involved three gringos who banded together to search for gold in the Sierra Madre mountains. After striking it rich, the group is assaulted by Mexican bandits pretending to be Federales (Mexican army). It was in this scene that the famous line about "no stinking badges" was uttered by the character Gold Hat, played by Alfonso Bedoya. So engrained in the public concsiousness is this iconic quote that there now exists on the Internet a website devoted entirely to listing times in which the phrase has been used or paraphrased or bowdlerized over the years.[14]

Although the film is consistently ranked in the American Film Institute's top one hundred movies of all time, it is replete with images of the Mexican that had rankled Valdez all his life. In his own play, he set out to show the context in which some of the Hollywood images were created. The setting for the play is Monterey Park, California; the principal characters are Buddy Villa, a fifty-seven-year-old Hollywood bit-part actor who has achieved his comfortable middle-class suburban life by playing Mexican stereotypes in films, from ignorant gardeners to comical, if ruthless, banditos, and his wife, Connie, who has also played stereotypical bit-parts, especially maids. The protagonist is their son, Sonny, who resents his parents' work and drops out of college to pursue a career in show business without resorting to what he saw as his parents' sell-out of their culture.

Valdez was consciously trying to provoke contrasting images from those engrained in the public consciousness for so long, images that stood in the way of racial accord. When asked about his work and the cultural divide he attempted to bridge, Valdez said, "My work comes from the border. It is neither Mexican nor American. It's part of America, like Cajun music."[15]

LA BAMBA (1987)

Early in his career, Valdez had attacked most commercial theatre and Hollywood as superficial, destructive of creativity. Nevertheless, the siren's call of a national audience had worked its seduction on Valdez, especially after the disappointingly short run of *Zoot Suit* in New York. For a time, he tried television productions but somehow the passion and political steam were not there—and neither was commercial success.

In 1987, Valdez directed *La Bamba*, the screen biography of Ritchie Valens, the 1950s Mexican-American rock-and-roll singer. Because of Valens' fame and tragic death in an airplane crash, which also took the lives of singers Buddy Holly and The Big Bopper, Valdez knew that this was an opportunity to draw large audiences, to portray elements of the Mexican-American community to theatergoers across America. As Valdez hoped, the movie became an overwhelming box office success, despite mostly bland reviews from critics. Spanish-language versions of the film were also shown in selected American cities with large Latino populations.

In Lou Diamond Phillips, the star of the film, Valdez found an actor whose features and bearing were perfectly carved for the part. And he also found a rock group in Los Lobos that contributed inspired performances and rocketed the sales of the soundtrack.

Valens, whose real name was Ricardo Valenzuela, was a third-generation American who couldn't speak a word of Spanish. Some of his early years, like those of Valdez, were largely spent in the migrant fruit farms of California. Indeed, Valdez opens the film with a scene of Ritchie working as a migrant in an apricot grove in 1957. The story of the singer's meteoric rise to fame as a rock legend is inspiring, if tragic. His career lasted less than a year, during which time he had three hit records. In the hands of Valdez, Valens' life took on a mythic quality, with foreshadowing of a violent end mixed with the startling success of a migrant worker Latino rising to a Latino at the heights of a profession.

For Valdez the film had distinctly personal meaning. During the filming of some of the early scenes, Valdez recalled later, he was intrigued by the possibility that he and Ritchie Valens had actually worked together in the orchards near San Jose. It was possible. When the labor camp set had been constructed, Valdez took his parents to see it. "It was so real," he said, "it was like stepping back into the past."[16]

Reviewing the film for the *Washington Post*, Hal Hinson said of the film, "Valdez presents it all unapologetically, with brio, and the mood of the film is so vibrant and the energy so uninhibited that you're carried over the familiarity of the terrain. The outlines of the film are the same as those of '30s and '40s movies in which talented young kids from the Lower East Side (or wherever) rise to the top, but Valdez seems to have some primal, native resonance in his story; he's seen something immutable, classical and true in it. And darned if he doesn't believe in it so deeply that he almost convinces you it's true, too."[17]

In the 1980s several other films directed by Latinos appeared, including Edward James Olmos' *Stand and Deliver*, Cheech Marin's *Born in East*

L.A., and Moctesuma Esparza's *The Milagro Beanfield War*. All were successful in the American marketplace. But *La Bamba* has remained the highest-grossing Latino feature film of the twentieth century.

CULTURAL IDENTITY AND *MUMMIFIED DEER*

After the death of both of his parents in the 1990s, Valdez became even more introspective about his religious and cultural roots. Because his family had no written record that he could find easily, he went looking for it. Because the Yaquis usually did not register the names of their children at birth, and because family members often changed their names to protect themselves, the trail of Valdez's research into his past was rocky. Nevertheless, he persisted.

"So I went back to the state of Sonora with my wife Lupe to do some research for a new play commissioned by the San Diego Repertory Theater," he said, "and went back to my ancestral towns in the northern state and discovered quite a bit about why I'm in the theatre, why I love masks, why I love improvisation, why I'm an American."[18]

Valdez was reaching back to America before Columbus to feel the rhythms within him from that heritage. "I'm not just a Mexican farmworker. I'm an American with roots in Mayan culture. I can resonate and unlock some of the mysteries of this land which reside in all of us. I've just been in the neighborhood a little bit longer. I'm a great believer in dreams. I've had some fantastic dreams. I dream when I'm standing up. I try to make my dreams come true."[19]

Into the play *Mummified Deer* Valdez put his own personal revelations and understanding about his ancestry, about the little-known history of Yaqui wars in Mexico that nearly wiped out his people, and about the myths and mysticism surrounding his culture. To Valdez this was a spiritual journey, one that gave him new insights and appreciation of his roots, and he poured out his personal discoveries in a deeply mysterious and penetrating work of the history and spirituality of Yaquis and their descendants.

The play is set is 1969, when a Chicana university student, Armida, travels to a hospital in San Diego to join her uncle, aunt, and cousin at the bedside of her eighty-four-year-old grandmother, Mama Chu. Armida's grandmother suffers from a rare medical condition caused by an encysted dead fetus that she failed to deliver six decades earlier. Valdez's idea for this central premise in the play came from a newspaper account of an actual case about which he had read years earlier. The play sets up as something of a murder, mystery tale, with Armida playing the role of the detective as she investigates the secrets of what Mama Chu herself imagines to be a mummified deer in her womb.

As Mama Chu experiences flashbacks of her life among the persecuted Indians and dreams of a Yaqui ceremonial deer dancer, the stage fills with performers in exotic costumes wandering through exotic sets—magical, mystical, hypnotic. Valdez even manages to incorporate circus acts into the play. Viewers are often transfixed on where Valdez might lead next. Armida begins to pierce the maze of myths and half-truths that have made up Mama Chu's story and the family's history. She discovers secrets about paternity and incest. But the central family pathology is rooted in the near-genocide of the Yaquis at the hands of Mexican President Porfirio Diaz and the Federales, which capped four centuries of little-known Yaqui resistance to European colonization.

Also at the center of the family pathology is the specter of war, a frequent theme in other Valdez plays. In addition to the Yaqui struggle, other wars—World War I, the Mexican Revolution, World War II, the Korean War, the Vietnam War—all profoundly shaped the family. Exploitation and the impulse to survive made all of the family members, in their own way, psychological and cultural refugees. The play was about survival and people transforming themselves, reinventing their outlook and fixed prejudices. With the feel of a Greek tragedy, the play sought to preserve something vital from generation to generation. If the play is shocking at times, even quite morbid with its descriptions and references to genocide, its colors and sounds and haunting mysticisms capture the imagination.

When *Mummified Deer* opened at the San Diego Repertory Theatre in October 2000, the cast included Valdez's son, Lakin, playing the magical Deer Dancer and an original musical score written by Valdez's brother, Daniel. Valdez told reporters how deeply personal and familial the play had been for him. "I've done years of research," he said, "traveling twice to Sonora to witness the Yaqui Easter ceremonies that are a unique mix of Catholic and Indian mythology. The result of this research is a humorous and surprising California story which coordinates one hundred years of history and reveals the heroic, untold story of the Yaqui nation."[20] In later discussing the importance of his ancestral culture to his own work and his immersion into the subject, Valdez said

> The Mayans and Native Americans are the root of American culture," he said. "They are the Greeks of the New World. They had communication routes set up that were amazing. They believed the sun was the center of the universe at a time when Europeans thought the Earth was the center. They could predict earthquakes and the weather and even had rudimentary mathematics. They had astonishing ideas for their time. Yet what they were has not been shared with the world.[21]

After attending a performance of *Mummified Deer*, Chicano poet Victor Payan, moved by the eerie, mesmerizing setting, wrote: "The stage is stark. It is barren. Truncated branches that could be limbs, that could be antlers, jut out from dry sloping walls that are adorned with cave paintings. There is the sense of raw nerves exposed. Behind a hospital bed on which an old woman lies is another network of nerves, translucent and winding toward the sky. They beat. Blood red. Like a drum. We are in a womb. And a silent deer dancer struts and prances, leaps and lunges, bouncing off the walls. He is waiting to be born."[22]

CONTINUING ARTISTIC QUESTS

Throughout Valdez's career, there have been setbacks, controversies, and challenges. In 1992, when Valdez attempted to cast Laura San Giacomo, a well-known actress of Italian ancestry, in a film on the life of Mexican painter Frida Kahlo, many fellow Latinos strongly criticized the decision. Although Valdez argued that compromise was sometimes necessary to get Hollywood to do movies with Hispanic protagonists at all and that the movie would offer a nonstereotypical picture of Latino life, the chorus of critics grew louder, especially Latina actresses, claiming that Valdez was doing something against which he had so long stood—selling out. Because of the controversy and resulting complications, Valdez cancelled the project, a particularly painful decision because the author of the screenplay was Lupe Valdez. It would have been her first major screenplay, and she likened its demise to a stillborn child.

Later, El Teatro Campesino faced its roughest financial crisis since its beginning and Valdez had to cut the number of staff, a wrenching experience that not only hurt the company but also dealt a severe blow to those whose acting careers were closely tied to the organization. But life at El Teatro Campesino continued into the new century. The group created an Internet site; it continued to tour and to produce films. And Valdez's towering legacy continued to grow. He had inaugurated a grass-roots Chicano movement, created new theater forms, mined and brought to life the history, music, and folklore of his cultural past, and set the stage for the further development of Chicano theater.

Valdez's movement inspired scores of other playwrights who readily pointed to his genius and energy as great influences in their careers. Actor-comedian Paul Rodriguez acknowledged his debt in an interview with the *New York Times* in 1991. His parents had been migrant farmworkers, he said, and he grew up picking strawberries, lettuce, and celery by their sides. The first time he ever saw El Teatro Campesino, he said, was as a "*chavalito* hanging on to my mama's hand, with my daddy saying, 'This is important; you've got to watch this.' As a matter of fact, I'll credit the Teatro Campesino with first allowing myself to even dream of being in this business."[23]

Latino playwright Octavio Solis said, "Luis Valdez was a trailblazer under unusual conditions. His influence is deep, profound, and far-reaching. His work has been a root source for all of us."[24]

And along his journey Valdez has held out the hope and promise of a closing of divides, a coming together. We cannot begin to approach a real solution to the social ills of integration and assimilation, he said, without dealing with the underlying attitudes and issues central to our backgrounds and heritage. In his exploration of the Mayan culture and its customs and superstitions, in the symbolism and myths that go far back into the subconsciousness of the various tribes and societies that formed what is now the Southwest, Valdez has made a powerful effort toward reconciliation and understanding.

In 1994, Valdez was awarded Mexico's prestigious Aguila Azteca Award. He was a founding member of the California Arts Council and has served on the National Endowment for the Arts. He was awarded honorary doctorates from San Jose State University, the University of Santa Clara, Columbia College of Chicago, and the California Institute of the Arts.

His odyssey from harvest fields to Broadway and Hollywood was as unlikely as it was spectacular. From campesino to college graduate to political protester, Valdez kept moving, contributing, reaching further and further into a reservoir of talent and drive. In the course of this journey he launched a new Chicano theater, vigorously explored historical themes and cultural roots long forgotten, inspired a younger generation of Chicano playwrights and directors, created a popular art form (the *acto*) and made the lives of Latinos more accessible and understandable to a larger public. He was the first Chicano writer to open a play on Broadway and the first Chicano to direct his own movie.

And his family has been with him all the way. Lupe has worked on many of the productions and in many parts of the business. His sons, as Valdez says, "were born into the business. They love it. What's great is they run the gamut; they're filmmakers, videographers, actors, writers, and directors, and so are their cousins and their friends. We've anchored it in family because it is through family that you get a sense of continuity. We have to better things for ourselves, for those who come with us and behind us. I carry my parents and grandparents in me and hope my children someday carry me. Through all the lumps and all the praises, it's not me that matters finally—it's the continuity. This younger generation cannot drop the flag."[25]

SELECTED MOVIES

Zoot Suit. Directed by Luis Valdez. Universal Pictures, 1981.
Chicanos Story. Directed by Luis Valdez. Indepdendent film, 1982.
La Bamba. Directed by Luis Valdez. Columbia Pictures, 1987.
Corridos: Tales of Passion & Revolution. Directed by Luis Valdez. El Teatro Campesino, 1987.
La Pastorela. Directed by Luis Valdez. El Teatro Campesino, 1991.
The Cisco Kid. Directed by Luis Valdez. Turner Pictures, 1994.

NOTES

1. Luis Valdez, Keynote, Texas Touring Arts Conference, 2002, http://www.arts.state.tx.us/ttac/valdez.asp.

2. David Savran, *An Interview with Luis Valdez*, In Their Own Words: Contemporary American Playwrights, Theatre Communications Group, 1988, 257–271, http://www.bookrags.com/criticism/luis-valdez-1940_2.

3. Victor Payan, "Papa's Dream: The San Diego roots of Chicano music legend Lalo Guerrero, *San Diego City Beat*, April 20, 2005, http://www.flyingserpent.net/justwords/laloguerrero.html.

4. Savran.

5. Valdez, Keynote.

6. "The Plan of Delano," http://www.sfsu.edu/~cecipp/cesar_chavez/delanoeng.htm.

7. Valdez, Keynote.

8. Mel Gussow, "Pachucos in musical 'Zoot Suit,'" *New York Times*, February 15, 1979, 14.

9. Gussow.

10. "Breaking down the barrios," *Newsweek*, September 4, 1978, 85.

11. Carl Heyward, "El Teatro Campesino: An Interview with Luis Valdez, 1985," http://www.communityarts.net/readingroom/archivefiles/2002/09/el_teatro_campe.php.

12. Savran.

13. Nicolás Kanellos, "Luis (Miguel) Valdez," *Dictionary of Literary Biography*, University of Houston, Thomson Gale, a part of the Thomson Corporation. 2005–2006.

14. Stinking Badges Homepage, http://www.darryl.com/badges/allindex.shtml.

15. "Putting the border onstage," *Newsweek*, May 4, 1987, 79.

16. "Putting the border onstage."

17. Hal Hinson, "La Bamba," *The Washington Post*, July 24, 1987, B7.

18. Valdez, Keynote.

19. Savran.

20. "*Mummified Deer* World Premier at the Rep," *La Prenza: San Diego*, October 20, 2000, http://www.laprenzasandieg.org/archive/october20/deer.htm.

21. Patricia Buckley, North County Times, April 14, 2004, http://www.nctimes.com/articles/2004/04/17/entertainment/theater/4_14_0412_42_31.txt.

22. Victor Payan, "Valdez's *Mummified Deer* is a powerful and profound new work," Just Words: Selected Writings of Victor Payan, 10/31/00, http://www.flyingserpent.net/justwords1/mummified.html.

23. Larry Rohten, "To Bethlehem by way of Mexico," *New York Times*, July 28, 1991, II, 25.

24. "A hero returns to the stage," *New York Times*, July 16, 2000, 12.

25. Sylvia Mendoza, "Luis Valdez: A trailblazer," *Hispanic*, October 2000, 84.

FURTHER READING

Broyles-Gonzales, Yolanda. *El Teatro Campesino: Theater in the Chicano Movement*. Austin: University of Texas Press, 1994.

Heyward, Carl. "El Teatro Campesino: An interview with Luis Valdez, 1985." http://www.communityarts.net/readingroom/archivefiles/2002/09/el_teatro_campe.php.

Kanellos, Nicolás. "Luis (Miguel) Valdez." *Dictionary of Literary Biography*, Thomson Gale, http://www.bookrags.com/biography/luis-miguel-valdez-dlb.

Reynolds, Julie. "Generations: Thirty Years at El Teatro Campesino," http://www.elandar.com/back/www-sep95/andar/cover/teatro.htm#thank.

Savran, David. "An Interview with Luis Valdez," In Their Own Words: Contemporary American Playwrights, Theatre Communications Group, 1988, 257–271, http://www.bookrags.com/criticism/luis-valdez-1940_2.

Valdez, Luis. Keynote, Texas Touring Arts Conference, 2002, http://www.arts.state.tx.us/ttac/valdez.asp.

Courtesy of Photofest

Ritchie Valens

Ritchie Valens' place in rock and roll history is grounded on a remarkably lean body of work. His first recording, "Come On, Let's Go," although a promising beginning, never reached the top ten on any weekly chart. His second 45-rpm record, however, produced two hits, "Donna" and "La Bamba," and his popularity soared. In the months after the release of that album, Valens was on the road playing concerts, in New York for television appearances, and then back on the road. And, then, it was over—a meteoric beginning snuffed out in a tragic plane crash in Iowa. But Valens' music, his ethnic heritage, and the circumstances of his death all combined to make him the first Latino rock and roll star, an almost mythic figure, a symbol of the American dream realized and then, so suddenly, snatched away.

CHILDHOOD IN THE VALLEY

Richard Steven Valenzuela was born in San Fernando, California, on May 13, 1941, the son of Joseph "Steve" Valenzuela, who worked at times as a tree surgeon, miner, and horse trainer, and Concepcion "Connie" Valenzuela. At the time of Richard's birth, both Steve and Connie were working in a wartime munitions plant in Saugus just north of the San Fernando Valley. The Valenzuelas had one other son, Robert, now age four, from Connie's previous marriage.

Throughout the 1940s and 1950s, the San Fernando Valley would emerge as a fast-growing industrial suburb to Los Angeles and nearby Burbank. While racial segregation barred blacks from most of the Valley, the area was an increasingly a diverse home to whites, Latinos, and Asian families.

When Richard was three years old, his parents separated and he began spending most of the time with his father at his house on Filmore Street in nearby Pacoima. Realizing early on that Richard was interested in musical instruments and singing, his father bought him a guitar and encouraged him to play and sing at every opportunity. Steve loved flamenco music and the blues, and his boy heard much of both in his early years.

David Chaubet, a childhood friend who lived next door to Ritchie and his father, said that Ritchie's father was strict yet caring and had intense feelings about wanting Ritchie to break out of their relative poverty. "Ritchie sang since he was a child," recalled Chaubet. "As he got older, his voice got better.... Steve used to throw some good-sized parties and a lot of times Ritchie would be embarrassed (to sing) and didn't want to do it." His father would always insist, Chaubet said, and Ritchie would reluctantly perform.[1]

In 1951, when Valenzuela was ten, his father died suddenly of complications related to diabetes. After Steve's death Connie moved into the house in Pacoima with her oldest son, Robert, and two young daughters, Connie and Irma, who had been born after her separation from Steve.

The Lasting Impact of "Donna" and "La Bamba"

The career of Ritchie Valens was tragically cut short, depriving the public of many other songs that the gifted rock and roll artist likely would have written. Nevertheless, his two principal hits, "Donna" and "La Bamba," have been performed and recorded again and again by various artists through the years.

In 1959 Marty Wilde, a significant early British rocker, recorded a version of "Donna." Many teen stars, including Johnny Crawford and Donny Osmond, have performed the song. The song even influenced a number of other songs, including "Donna, the Prima Donna," a 1963 hit for Dion, and the song about Donna the Virgin in the musical *Hair*.

A wide variety of performers have recorded "La Bamba" over the years, including rock and roll versions by Ronnie Hawkins, Neil Diamond, and Trini Lopez. Freddy Fender issued a Tex-Mex version. "La Bamba" even made its way into the folk music field and was recorded by Joan Baez, Harry Belafonte, and the Kingston Trio.

In 1961 two young British rockers, Mick Jagger and Keith Richards, recorded the song in a jam session in the living room of a friend. The friend later sold the tape at a Christie's auction in the 1980s for $81,000.

For a time, Ritchie stayed mostly with relatives in Norwalk and Santa Monica, California, but then joined his mother and the other children at the Pacoima residence. The clean, two-room house had only one bathroom, a very small kitchen, few furnishings, and only one bedroom. Ritchie, along with others, slept in a sleeping bag in a crawl space under the house.

With such spartan living conditions, Ritchie continued to spend much time away from Filmore Street, predominantly at the Pacoima home of his aunt and uncle, Ernestine and Lelo Reyes. Ernestine Reyes later remembered, "He came often and stayed with us. In the first place, Connie had no money.... That kid, poor thing, didn't even have a shirt to take a picture in... had to borrow all of Lelo's clothing. Connie just couldn't afford to give him the stuff to get him started."[2] Ritchie's early years, therefore, were filled with many beginnings and turns, much uncertainty and confusion. For the young boy, music seemed to fill a need for control and gave him a sense of purpose.

At the age of thirteen Ritchie entered Pacoima Junior High School. Large-boned, with long, jet-black hair, he was quiet, well liked, and somewhat reserved. He carried his guitar to school and around the neighborhood, as if it were part of his regular attire. During lunchtimes at the school he would head to the bleachers at the athletic field and play. Often, groups of students would follow and shout encouragement. Although he did not have a particularly mellifluous singing voice, he became increasingly proficient with the guitar.

From his family members, he learned many songs with Latino roots, especially Mexican folk songs. Some of his uncles and cousins who had some musical background helped him with the guitar. One of his cousins gave him something of a tutorial on the trumpet. He practiced the guitar for hours on end in a quiet room in the family house.

He heard the singing cowboy songs at the Saturday matinee movies and began to listen to various country music stars on the radio. He also began to hear the new sounds and beats of rock and roll, the blend of rhythm and blues, boogie-woogie, and gospel music that began to grip teenage audiences in the mid-1950s.

He heard Chuck Berry, Elvis Presley, Jerry Lee Lewis, and, especially, Little Richard. He became fascinated with their rhythms and driving piano and guitar sounds and the unrelenting, hard beat of the music, mesmerized by the pulsating sounds. Day after day, the boy listened and practiced, incorporating the various sounds, trying out new techniques.

Ernie Brandt, one of the boy's teachers at Pacoima Junior High, recounted the first time he saw him: "I remember him coming into the room with a big cut across either his left or right arm. He looked like a knife fighter or something and I thought, 'Oh boy! That's probably a rough kid!' But he was quiet and orderly. He seemed to do his work well and later on I discovered he had a beautiful sense of humor."[3]

Richard was an average student, recalled teachers and those in his classes. Industrial arts was a favorite class because he could bring his guitars to school and work on them in the woodshop, restoring and refinishing them over and over again.

On January 31, 1957, the town of Pacoima and Pacoima Junior High were thrust suddenly and tragically into national headlines. As over two hundred students played on the grounds of the school, a four-engine Douglas DC-7B airliner and a U.S. Air Force Northrup F-89J Scorpion jet fighter collided in the skies above nearby Sundland, California. Wreckage hurtled randomly and ferociously through the grounds of the school, killing three young boys and injuring about seventy-five others. Ritchie was not at school that day, as he was attending the funeral of his grandfather. One of the three children who perished was one of Ritchie's close friends. Years later, family members, fans, and others who appreciated his career looked back in hindsight at that tragic day in Pacoima as a foreshadowing. From that day forward, he developed a strong fear of flying, especially after one of his uncles warned him after the crash never to board an airplane.

By the time he entered San Fernando High School, Ritchie was playing the guitar at school assemblies and after school parties. He was becoming an accomplished singer and guitarist who was able to make up new lyrics and add riffs to popular songs. As a growing number of teenagers from outside his school began to watch him perform, word spread in the Latino communities about a new rock and roll singing sensation. Although his stage demeanor was somewhat reserved, he began to earn the nickname, "The Little Richard of the Valley."

In his junior year of high school, Ritchie was invited to join a local band named The Silhouettes. A racially mixed group including whites, blacks, Japanese Americans and Latinos, the band played high-school dances, church gatherings, and other local gigs in the Los Angeles area. Originally a quintet, the Silhouettes featured a piano, drums, vibes, saxophone, and Ritchie on guitar. The band grew to include trumpets and a clarinet.

Twenty-one-year old vibes player Gil Rocha led the group. Ritchie began to share vocal leads with Emma Franco and Phyllis Romano. Their repertoire consisted mainly of Little Richard songs and other popular hits of the late 1950s, as well as some traditional Mexican folk ballads, often using contemporary themes. Dave Toretta played with Richard as a member of the Silhouettes. Remembering Valens as humble and shy but talented, he said that, at the time, he never expected Ritchie's meteoric rise in popularity. "Basically, we were all amateurs," he said. "We thought nothing of it, really. We were just a bunch of kids." Nevertheless, looking back, Toretta said, "I thought he was very good. He had a melancholy voice. When he started to play there was electricity in the air."[4]

It was at San Fernando High that Ritchie met Donna Ludwig at a party at which the Silhouettes played. Before the night was over, he had asked for her phone number. "We would walk in the corridors in school all the time," she later recalled, "and he would meet me outside. The school would have noon-time dances and I would dance with him. He was always so sweet and treated me so nice." Unfortunately for the Latino teenager, Donna's father did not allow her to date him. "But I'd meet him at roller skating rinks and parties on the side. We became quite close." She remembered his appearances at school assemblies, remembered the students cheering and rocking to such songs as Little Richard's "The Girl Can't Help It" and others, and the times when the students would become so boisterous and enthused that the school principal would have difficulty calling the assembly to an end.[5]

In May 1958, a talent scout who had seen a performance of the Silhouettes suggested to a record producer that he take a look at a young Latino musician and singer that crowds were comparing to Little Richard. A few days later, the producer drove out to a Pacoima movie house to hear a performance at a Saturday morning matinee for children. On the stage, amidst a crowd of youngsters screaming and clapping, was a sixteen-year-old performer with an old guitar and a cheap amplifier. The producer was impressed by his energy and the intensity of the crowd. After the last song, he walked to the stage and introduced himself. His name was Bob Keane, and he would change the life of the young singer.

DEL-FI RECORDS

For all of his life, Bob Keane had been chasing a dream. As a child, he had heard the Benny Goodman Orchestra live and had expended considerable energy and drive in a quest to be like Goodman. He became so proficient with the clarinet that he formed his own band and later performed with numerous accomplished musicians. At one point in his budding career he was asked to lead the Artie Shaw Band.

But Keane's emergence as a clarinet player and big band leader had been ill timed. The era of the Big Bands was waning. Rhythm and blues, country music, blues, and other music forms began to capture the imagination of the American public. Disappointed with the national trends but blessed with an entrepreneurial eye and spirit, Keane changed with the times. Rushing through a number of jobs, Keane finally decided to form his own record company. Allied with a business partner, he joined a company that was instrumental in launching the career of Sam Cooke. When his own relationship with the company soured, Keane formed his own, which he called Del-Fi Records, a take-off on the Greek name "Oracle of Delphi," the messenger and interpreter of Apollo, the god of prophecy.

Keane was about twenty years older than the Latino performer he had heard at the community gathering in Pacoima. If he had learned anything in his youthful odyssey through the music and record business, it was a sense of what sounds and trends might be on the horizon. As a youngster he had lived for a short time with his parents in Mexico City and had grown to appreciate some of the folk and mariachi music. And now, with his new, if nearly broke, record label, he had already produced a record by a group called The Shadows, led by a young Latino singer named Jimmy Carlos. Some of the disc jockeys in the Los Angeles area had begun to give their work some airplay. Perhaps, Keane thought, a Latino influence could be fused to the new beats of rock and roll. And now, the sight of this kid in Pacoima stirred something deep in Keane. With the right handling and coaching, Keane's instincts told him, the kid could be a star.

"I'll never forget the first time I saw Ritchie," Keane said. "He had a small, somewhat beat-up guitar amp worth about fifty bucks. He stood up there on stage, with complete command of his audience," Keane said. Broad-shouldered, with his hazel green eyes and perfectly created waterfall hairstyle, he was, Keane thought, a teen idol in the making. "He was this bull-like kid with an opera tenor's torso. I knew he had a lot of potential. It should go without saying that what I heard impressed me, but I had no idea what to do with the raw talent I saw up there on the stage."[6]

Inviting the young singer to cut a demo in his basement studio, Keane watched as the boy pulled out a small, turquoise, electric guitar from Sears that he had purchased from a pawn shop. Although Ritchie had not written any complete songs and only knew bits and pieces of material, Keane could see right away that, although completely raw, he had considerable dexterity with the guitar. Keane began to work with the youngster not only in technique but also in creating some individual songs that they could introduce. From the beginning Keane thought that perhaps they could take some of the Latin influences engrained in the boy's chords and rhythms and work toward a "Latin rock and roll" sound.

The two worked together with much enthusiasm and mutual respect. Keane was taken by the boy's honesty and humble demeanor and his obvious dedication to the music. At one of the early meetings, the boy began to refer to Keane as "Bobbo." Keane said later, "We had almost a father–son relationship. He trusted my musical guidance, as well as many things I was able to advise him about in his personal life."[7]

Keane soon offered Ritchie a recording contract. Along with the basic financial and business arrangements, he suggested that Valenzuela take on a stage name. Looking for the widest possible audience and aware of the racial and cultural divides at work in the country, aware that most disc jockeys seeing the name Valenzuela attached to a song would likely throw it aside, Keane proposed that he change Valenzuela to Valens. He also suggested adding a "t" to the name of Richie. There were many Richies in the singing business, Keane reasoned, but no Ritchies. On that day in late May 1958, the career of Ritchie Valens began.

On July 8th, 1958, Keane brought Valens to the Gold Star Studios on Santa Monica Boulevard in Hollywood. Gold Star had already become one of the most popular recording studios in Los Angeles; over the years it became one of the most influential commercial studios in the world. When the studio had been designed in the early 1950s, the organizers installed special recording echo chambers approximately 20 feet square, with thick walls that produced pure sounds. To enter the chambers one would walk through a series of 2 foot square doors, and an opening that was only about 20 inches wide and high. Later, artists such as the Beach Boys and Phil Spector would produce many of their most renowned works at Gold Star. On this day, a young Latino walked through those doors.

Keane carefully selected the best musicians he could summon to work with the young Valens in his first recording session. Lead guitarist Rene Hall had played lead on Sam Cooke's famous recording of "You Send Me." Drummer Earl Palmer had recently moved to the Los Angeles area from New Orleans and was himself something of a legend, especially playing with the likes of Little Richard. Buddy Clark on bass, Irving Ashby on piano, and Carol Kaye, one of the few women session musicians at the time, made up the veteran team. In the session, the group used a Danelectro electric bass—a six-string instrument tuned an octave lower than a guitar—creating a unique, guttural, "twangy" sound. Valens' first recording was "Come On, Let's Go."

It took more than twenty takes for Keane to put together the final version. When the group heard the unedited master played back, the musicians erupted in cheers. When he took the tapes to the Capitol Records studios to complete the final editing, a number of onlookers also showed great enthusiasm. Keane knew then that his instincts about Valens were right on. This first record, he was confident, was destined to give his new Latino singer much visibility.

Later, drummer Earl Palmer remembered that first session vividly. "Ritchie was kind of shy," Palmer said. "He realized that he was a newly found talent and had no ego whatsoever. He had a lot of humility. He was always asking questions about whether his performance was okay, because many of the people we recorded with had been his idols."[8]

Shortly after cutting the record, Keane made the rounds of the local disc jockeys to pitch for airtime. He also took advantage of the fact that the Los Angeles County Fair was underway and one of largest stations was broadcasting live from the site. For a week, Keane drove Valens to the Fair and he would appear live on station with the various disc jockeys as hosts. The hot new talent immediately drew large crowds.

Keane watched, overwhelmed by the scene. "Now for the first time," he said, "I was made aware of the magnitude, even then, of the Latin population in Los Angeles. Possibly over half of the people at the fair were Latinos, and when they saw Ritchie and heard him sing, they went wild. Here was the first Latino artist who had made the mainstream in Los Angeles radio. Ritchie felt their acceptance and really got turned on, giving a performance I didn't know he had in him."[9] Soon, "Come On, Let's Go" was no longer a sensation just in Los Angeles. When *Billboard* magazine named the song as its "Pick of the Week" in September 1958, it climbed to Number 46 on the pop charts. Valens had, indeed, become the first Latino to crash the mainstream rock and roll market.

After the success of "Come On, Let's Go," Ritchie decided to skip his last year at San Fernando High to concentrate on his music career. In the following weeks, Keane and Ritchie set up live shows in the Los Angeles area and then toured up and down the coast to Washington and Oregon in Keane's Thunderbird convertible. Valens appeared on Jumpin' George Oxford's radio show on KSAN in San Francisco.

Keane knew that a successful follow-up to the first hit recording would be an important part of Valens' budding career. They looked for a different sound so that Valens would not be seen as a one-hit wonder, a talent with no versatility. Valens told Keane that he had been working on a simple song and melody dedicated to Donna Ludwig, the girl for whom he had strong feelings at San Fernando High.

When Keane heard the melody and the first line—"I've got a girl, Donna is her name"—he figured this would be a perfect sequel to the first hit. He would follow a rocking tune with a slow dance number that reminded Keane of Sam Cooke's "You Send Me." After considerable work with the instrumentals and some experimentation with a technique of creating reverberation,

Del-Fi released Valens' second major record. This ballad, with simple lyrics and guitar-chord changes, would inspire a generation of songs named after girls, from Neil Sedaka's "Oh, Carol!" to Randy and the Rainbows' "Denise."

When rock critic Lester Bangs first heard "Donna," he concluded that the appeal of Valens was from an uncomplicated sincerity that seemed to differentiate his voice from other rock and roll artists in those early years. Listening to the song, Bangs said, was hearing what it must have been like living as a teenager in the fifties.

If "Donna" was the right vehicle to light a second electrical charge to Valens' career, the flip side of that record was just as critical, although neither Keane nor Valens anticipated the reaction. The song was called "La Bamba."

A traditional Mexican folk song originating in Veracruz and dating back over three hundred years, "La Bamba" derived from both Spanish flamenco music as well as an African beat, and it was usually sung in falsetto. A *huapango*, a song of celebration, it was often played during weddings in Veracruz in which the newly married couple performed an accompanying dance. The word *arriba* (up) in the song prompts a faster and faster tempo.

On one of their road trips, Keane heard Valens play versions of the song and suggested that they work it up as a flip side to "Donna." At first Valens was reluctant, sensitive to the roots of the music and its culture, wary of turning such a song into a rock and roll piece. Although Valens did not speak Spanish, he knew much of the language and was able to speak fluently those words and phrases with which he was familiar. After talking to several of his family members about the possibility of doing the song on the record, he felt better about Keane's suggestion and agreed. Under Keane's direction as well as the help of Valens' Aunt Ernestine, who knew most of the lyrics, Valens recorded "La Bamba," infusing the traditional folk music with a rock beat, combining a flamenco-influenced lead guitar riff to a more visceral garage-band rhythm.

In late December 1958, "Donna" exploded onto the pop charts, becoming a Number 2 hit and lingering fourteen weeks on Billboard's charts. In Great Britain it reached Number 20. Although "La Bamba" never received the playing time or the ratings during its early release, disc jockeys around the country all began to realize that this record was a two-hit wonder. It did not matter that few Americans had no idea of what the song was about or knew any of the Spanish words, the song was an unforgettable blend of driving guitar sounds and an accelerated beat. It would become, on many music history lists, one of the most influential rock and roll songs in history. Its title would, in many ways, be the signature effort in Valens' repertoire, the song most closely associated with his name—Ritchie and "La Bamba."

From across the country, promoters began feverishly to call Del-Fi. When could Keane have this new Valens kid on the road? In early 1959, planning for the first United States tour of Ritchie Valens came together. In September and October, the tour would visit eleven midwestern and northeastern cities in twelve days—Chicago, Cleveland, Philadelphia, Buffalo, Detroit, and then north into Canada with a stop in Toronto. This was all heady stuff for a high schooler who had never flown on an airplane, had never been away from the west coast, and was only months removed from his days of playing for fellow classmates at lunchtime on the school playground.

AMERICAN BANDSTAND AND THE BIG TIME

On October 6, 1958, Valens appeared on Dick Clark's American Bandstand. Bandstand had begun as a local program in Philadelphia. In 1956, a good-looking, clean-cut host named Dick Clark took over; soon, ABC picked up the show on national television, and the first episode aired in August 1957. Dancing was a major feature of the show, featuring local teenagers from Philadelphia who knew all the steps to the latest dance crazes, from the Hand Jive to the Bop. Filmed in a cramped studio at 46th and Market Streets, the show became a barometer of pop music. An invitation from Clark to appear on the show was a sure sign that a performer's star was in the ascendancy. In the space of a few months, Valens appeared twice.

On his first promotional trip, Valens not only met Dick Clark but also Alan Freed, arguably the most popular disc jockey in the United States. At a radio station in Cleveland, Ohio, Freed, calling himself "Moondog," began to attract large audiences in the early 1950s by playing rhythm and blues for mixed-race audiences. At a concert billed as the "Moondog Coronation Ball" at the Cleveland Arena in March 1952, twenty thousand fans mobbed the venue that held seats for only half that number. Some have called the event the first "rock concert." Later, Freed moved to the largest market for radio, New York, and his popularity soared even further. Both Freed and rock and roll were taking over the airwaves. In the fall of 1958, Ritchie Valens played on Freed's television teen dance show in New York. Before his return to California, Valens had made the rounds of radio and television shows in several major markets, including The Buddy Deane Show in Baltimore, Maryland, and the Milt Grant Show in Washington, D.C.

In November 1958, Valens made his first album. Backed by many of the same band members who had performed on his earlier releases, Valens sang such songs as "That's My Little Suzie," "In a Turkish Town," and "Dooby Dooby Wah," all written by Ritchie himself. Two of the other cuts on the album were instrumentals, with Ritchie blazing on his guitar. Ritchie also wrote and sang a blues number called "Big Baby Blues," later remembered by many as "Ritchie's Blues," and a song called "Fast Freight," which featured a drumbeat simulated as the sound of the wheels clicking on the rails. Keane said later, "It was really ahead of its time. Some music historians have called this track the first jazz-rock instrumental in rock and roll's then short history."[10]

A week after the recording session, Valens was off to Hawaii, this time unaccompanied by Keane. At the Honolulu Civic Auditorium Valens performed alongside a young group called Buddy Holly and the Crickets, Paul Anka, and others. In a few months Valens would join Buddy Holly on a winter tour in the Midwest. Teddy Randozzo, former lead singer of the Chuckles, later recalled taking Valens to a steakhouse in Hawaii. The kid, said Randozzo, was not used to fancy restaurants and devoured the steak with unusual gusto.

When Ritchie returned to California, he agreed to perform at Pacoima Junior High at the behest of the principal who thought his return would be an inspiration to the younger students. Accompanied only by a drummer, Ritchie played a memorable string of songs to the tumultuous reception by the students, all of them only a few years younger than he.

In the audience that day was a friend of Ritchie named Gail Smith, who had formed a Valens fan club. Armed with a portable Motorola tape recorder backstage, she preserved that stage appearance. Years later, Del-Fi released an album titled "Ritchie Valens Live at Pacoima Junior High." Rock critic Lester Bangs wrote later: "It would be hard to find a recorded rock concert in which the performer displays more honest, humble warmth than Valens does here."[11]

With both "Donna" and "La Bamba" climbing in the national *Billboard* charts, Keane was able to book Valens as part of Alan Freed's Christmas Rock & Roll Spectacular concert series in New York at the Loew's State Theatre. The young star was now playing alongside many of the performers he had listened to on the radio just a couple years earlier, including Chuck Berry, Eddie Cochran, Bo Diddley, and Jackie Wilson.

No longer did Valens appear on stage in undistinguished clothing. Although Keane had earlier encouraged the singer essentially to hide the fact that he was a Latino by changing his name to Valens, the singer's ethnic roots by this time were fairly well known. Now, instead of concealing his Latino background, Keane took Valens to Nudie's, a famous clothing outfitter to the stars in Hollywood, to purchase a light-blue satin shirt with puffy sleeves, a black, studded vest and black pants. This was now something of a mariachi look. Valens' success, Keane concluded, had not suffered because of his Latino roots; it had made him a singular figure, revered by the Latino community itself, and of musical interest to others because of his infusion of a Latino influence into rock and roll.

What spectators and fellow musicians saw in New York that Christmas was a unique figure. Bo Diddly himself, who spent time with the young Valens during the Rock & Roll Spectacular, said later that the new talent had something different, something special. With all of musicians and performers staying at the Plaza Hotel, Ritchie had a chance to befriend a number of big-time stars, including Eddie Cochran. One of their mutual friends said that Cochran came to regard Ritchie as something like a younger brother. It was also on this trip that Ritchie met at one of the parties a woman named Diane Olsen, to whom he became attached. One of his friends later claimed that Ritchie had even talked about the possibility of offering her an engagement ring.

Valens also appeared at the famous Apollo Theater in New York. Since 1934, the Harlem venue had been host to some of the most influential performers in American music history, from Ella Fitzgerald and Billie Holiday to James Brown and Luther Vandross. A year earlier, Buddy Holly and the Crickets, whose rock and roll sounds owed much to the influence of black rhythm and blues roots, had also played the Apollo.

In January 1959, the connection that Valens had forged with Alan Freed resulted in another first-time opportunity for the new rock and roll sensation. He would make an appearance in a movie. *Go, Johnny, Go!* was the second film produced by Alan Freed in a genre best known among critics as "jukebox movies." The films gave current rock and roll talents a place in the movie industry to show off their skills. Usually built around a thin plot, the films paraded stars acting mostly as themselves set in the context of the action. In this film, a rock and roll singer named Johnny Melody, played by Jimmy Clanton, a popular singer from New Orleans, rises from life in an orphanage to his discovery by Freed (played by himself). The talents in the film included Chuck Berry, Jackie Wilson, Eddie Cochran, the Cadillacs, and Ritchie Valens.

For Valens, the experience seemed otherworldly. Here, on a Hollywood set, the seventeen-year-old was sitting in front of movie cameras in a scene with Freed and Chuck Berry, whose records he had listened to over and over again. In the film Berry says, "We always have Valens to soothe your gentle nerves!" Wearing a tweed coat, Ritchie pretends to stroke a guitar and lip-syncs a song called "Ooh, My Head," inspired by Little Richard's "Ooh, My Soul." Three girls at the table scream and throw their arms in the air as Freed says, "He's swingin'!"[12]

After production of the film, Keane arranged a contract for Valens with General Artists Corporation, an agency that put together packages for tours of musicians and other performers. Within a few days, they had booked Ritchie for an event called "The Winter Dance Party." Such package shows were popular during the 1950s and 1960s and typically featured two shows every evening that allowed each act fifteen to thirty minutes to perform their hits. The Dance Party was scheduled to begin in February and play a number of venues in the upper Midwest. The headliner for the tour was Buddy Holly and the Crickets.

FATEFUL TOUR WITH BUDDY HOLLY

With some of the earnings from his successful records, Valens was able to help his family purchase a new house in Pacoima. It was there that family and friends gathered in late January for both a housewarming and going-away party for the singer before his winter tour in the Midwest. There were tacos and beer and fresh fruit and hugs all around. When Bob Keane walked out to his car with Ritchie and wished him success on the tour, he told him that this was another major step in his becoming a rock and roll star. Before leaving, Ritchie and his mother prayed at the Guardian Angel Church on Laurel Canyon Boulevard for a safe trip. The next day, Ritchie flew to Chicago to meet up with Buddy Holly and the other members of the tour, including J.D. Richardson, known as "The Big Bopper," Dion and the Belmonts, and others. Bob Keane, who knew something of the conditions of the upper Midwest in the winter, loaned Valens a black camel hair winter overcoat.

Buddy Holly was five years older than Valens. Born in Lubbock, Texas, he was a singer and guitarist who had been inspired by seeing Elvis Presley at a local concert in Texas. His name was really Holley but when he signed a music contract the "e" was inadvertently dropped and he did not change it. Like Valens, his father had influenced him at an early age to take up music, and the boy had learned to play not only the guitar but also the violin and piano.

Early on, Holly had been interested in bluegrass music. He and a fellow student in junior high teamed up as a duo called "Buddy and Bob" and sang duets at local clubs and high school shows. When he heard Elvis, his musical interests turned to rock and roll, and he became a local sensation at it. At a local rock show, a music scout signed him to a contract with Decca Records. Holly formed his own band, The Crickets, and began recording at studios in Clovis, New Mexico. His first hit recording, "That'll Be the Day," was released in 1957.

Much of his music involved complex harmonies and the innovative use of instruments not usually heard in early rock and roll. The hard, sustained, rolling drumbeat of "Peggy Sue" was a novel sound, as was the use of the celesta in "Everyday." By the end of 1959 Holly was at the peak of his career with a number of hits that had been in the lists of top ten rock and roll songs in the United States and Great Britain.

For all of their success, Buddy Holly and the Crickets, as with many rock and roll bands through the years, could not keep private quarrels and sparring from affecting their musical relationship. When Holly began to experiment with new sounds, most of the members of the Crickets rebelled. Also, financial irregularities created mistrust and division. In addition, Holly had married an aspiring singer named Maria Santiago who was now pregnant. All of this weighed heavily on the young star. Holly decided to go on his own and left the Crickets and Lubbock for New York. He moved to Greenwich Village. With the split with the group tying up his money in legal battles, Holly found himself in a situation where he needed a winter tour to pay the bills. He put together a backup group including Tommy Allsup, Charlie Bunch, and Waylon Jennings, a friend from Lubbock, and headed off to "The Winter Dance Tour Party" in the Midwest.

Also headed to the Midwest was the"Big Bopper." A well-known disc jockey from Beaumont, Texas, Richardson had set a world record, as far as anyone knew, for continuous broadcasting—six days without stop, spinning nearly two thousand records. He was also a songwriter, best known for "Running Bear," recorded by Johnny Preston. And he had recently become something of a singer, his low speaking voice and simple rhythms best known in a rather lascivious song called "Chantilly Lace," which had already sold over one million copies. He had just recorded a take-off on the first record called "Big Bobber's Wedding." He and his wife had a young daughter and were expecting a second child when he arrived for the tour.

The tour began poorly and got progressively worse. "The Winter Dance Party" was set to cover twenty-four Midwestern cities in three weeks, from January 23 to February 15. The first stop began in a city far larger than most they would be encountering during the tour—Milwaukee, Wisconsin. At George Devine's Million-Dollar Ballroom in Milwaukee, the performers first stepped in front of the microphones on the trip; outside it was twenty-five degrees below zero.

From the beginning, a number of the performers realized that the entire concept of this particular tour was misguided. Especially for someone from Southern California, such as Valens, or others from Texas, such as Buddy Holly and Waylon Jennings, traveling through the upper Midwest in the middle of winter quickly seemed like an exercise in survival.

The central problem was that the venues, most of them in small towns scattered throughout the journey, were not booked appropriately according to location. In the frigid temperatures that hovered around zero degrees, with a schedule that shuttled the performers fairly long distances between each stop, and with mechanically impaired buses ill-prepared to withstand the demands of the weather, the musicians soon became exhausted; a number became ill.

After one of the drummers in the group was hospitalized because of frostbite, it became increasingly clear that the whole enterprise was likely doomed. Although local residents at each of the stops gave the traveling troupe enthusiastic welcomes, expressing appreciation that such national talent would brave the elements and appear in their relatively isolated locations, the performances, Holly and others feared, were suffering. Certainly the individuals themselves were.

Everything was cold—the performers, the buildings, the buses, whose heaters gave up early on the tour, even the musical instruments. Because of the bus problems, they were constantly delayed, so much so that most of the performers did not even have time to wash clothes. From the Kato

Ballroom in Mankato, Minnesota, to Fournier's Ballroom in Eau Claire, Wisconsin, to the Fiesta Ballroom in Montevideo, Minnesota, they forged ahead, sometimes through dangerous snow storms, determined to fulfill the obligations of their contracts.

By January 28, the group literally staggered into the Prom Ballroom in St. Paul, Minnesota, all of them weary and demoralized. Still, they continued. On the 29th, they played the Capitol Theater in Davenport, Iowa, and then at the Laramar Ballroom in Fort Dodge, Iowa, and at the National Guard Armory in Duluth, Minnesota.

Shortly before Valens left Duluth, he talked with Bob Keane by phone. Despite the conditions on the road, Valens was excited by the reception he had received the night before. "Man, it was unbelievable," he told Keane. "They wouldn't let me leave the stage.... The promoter told me to get back out there." Nevertheless, he told Keane, he had a bad cold and was thinking about quitting the tour. "Well, I'll try to stick it out," he said, "because I feel sorry for all those kids who've bought tickets. They'll be waiting out there in the snow to see us."[13] That night, Valens' bus again froze up, and the passengers huddled under newspapers waiting for the tow truck to rescue them. Valens decided to bail out as soon as he possibly could.

On February 2, 1959, more than a week after the ordeal had begun, the Winter Dance Party arrived in Clear Lake, Iowa, to play a dance at the Surf Ball Room. The small town was a summer resort, where Clark Gable used to spend some warm days and where bandleader Guy Lombardo brought his racing boat in the summer to speed around the beautiful lake. The lake at the time of the Winter Dance Tour was frozen. The Surf Ball Room was designed to look and feel like a tropical beach club, with low booths around the walls and a striped ceiling stretching over the place like an awning. The dance floor, where summer tourists had tried out their steps to Guy Lombardo's band, was wide, with blond wood, meant to simulate the look of a fresh beach. On each side of the small stage, faux palm trees flanked the performers. To the Winter Dance Tour musicians, it all seemed like a bad joke.

Worn out by the conditions, Holly decided to charter a small plane for himself and two of his band members, Tommy Allsop and Waylon Jennings, to travel to the next venue, Moorhead, North Dakota, approximately four hundred miles away. The destination of the flight would be Hector Airport in nearby Fargo, North Dakota, because Moorhead did not have an airport. They planned to take a car to Moorhead Armory for the performance.

Flight arrangements were made with Roger Peterson, a young local pilot who worked for Dwyer Flying Service in Mason City, Iowa. A fee of $36 per person was charged for the single-engine Beechcraft Bonanza, which could seat three passengers in addition to the pilot. Holly looked forward to a night in a hotel instead of the bus. The plane was scheduled to depart shortly after midnight.

After the concert at the Surf Ball Room, two critical conversations were underway. The Big Bopper had been stricken with the flu and wanted desperately to see a doctor. He approached Waylon Jennings about the possibility of changing the seating plans. Would Jennings be willing to continue on the buses so that Richardson could take the plane? Jennings reluctantly agreed.

In addition, Valens, despite his fear of flying and despite the fact that he had never ridden in a small plane, had also reached a point of exhaustion. He approached Tommy Allsop with the same question that the Big Bopper asked of Jennings. Would Allsop be willing to let Valens take his seat on the plane? Allsop was very hesitant, saying he had to pick up a registered letter in Fargo. Nevertheless, Valens persisted. Allsop finally decided to settle the question with a coin toss. Valens readily agreed. The coin toss occurred at the ballroom shortly before departure to the airport by one of the disc jockeys working the show that night. It was heads; Valens won.

Around 1:00 A.M., in a foggy snowstorm, the Beechcraft Bonanza, piloted by Roger Peterson and carrying Buddy Holly, Ritchie Valens, and the Big Bopper, lifted off the ground from an airport in Mason City, Iowa, close to Clear Lake. Minutes later, it crashed in a cornfield. The bodies were not found in the snow until midday on February 3. In Valens' coat pocket was a note from his mother saying how much she missed him already.

Investigators concluded that the plane was at a slight downward angle and banked to the right when it struck the ground at around 170 miles per hour. The plane tumbled and skidded another 570 feet across the frozen field before crumpling against a wire fence at the edge of farmer Albert Juhl's cornfield. The bodies of the three entertainers were thrown from the wreckage and lay nearby, while Peterson remained trapped inside. All four had died instantly, the coroner concluded.

Investigators also discovered that the pilot was inexperienced and had not even passed his instrument exam. He was unqualified to fly at night. He was especially unqualified to fly in the kind of weather that faced him. Indeed, he had not received from the airport an advisory as to just how the serious the storm and the lack of visibility were about to become. The pilot was also expected to file his flight plan once the plane was airborne, but Peterson never called the tower.

Waylon Jennings remembered later that, shortly before the buses left for North Dakota, he had encountered Buddy Holly backstage at the Surf Ballroom. "Well, he's leaning against the wall in a chair, and he'd just sent me to get some hot dogs, and I brought him one and me one. I'm sittin' there leaning against the wall in another chair, and he looks at me and says 'So you're not gonna go on the plane tonight? You let Big Bopper have your seat?' I said 'Yeah'" and he says, 'Well, I hope that old bus freezes up on ya again.' It had frozen up a night or two before. I said 'Well, hell, I hope your ol' plane crashes, then.' Jennings shouldered an immense amount of guilt, not only immediately after hearing the news about the crash but for years afterward. "I didn't know how to deal with it," he said. "I was alive, and Buddy and those boys were dead, and I didn't know how, but somehow I'd caused it.[14]

As for Bob Keane, the wrenching news reached him in his car as he listened to a local radio station. "The next morning I'm driving to work, and the DJ says, 'Now the great, late Ritchie Valens.' It was like somebody hit me in the gut with a baseball bat. I couldn't believe it. I was in front of the Palladium and my offices were around the corner, and I got up there and everybody was crying and the phones were off the hook and the reporters were there. It was a bummer. It was a real bummer."[15]

Donna Ludwig, by then at James Monroe High School, heard the news from a girlfriend. "Donna"—her song—was the Number 3 pop record in America.

Waylon Jennings and Dion and The Belmonts, who had continued on in the buses, heard the news when they reached their next stop in Moorhead. Stunned and deeply saddened, their first reaction was to stop the tour. Nevertheless, they concluded to honor the three singers by completing the journey. In order to finish up the tour they quickly hired a fifteen-year-old singer from the local area who knew all of Buddy Holly's songs. His name was Bobby Vee. In these tragic circumstances, Vee's career was thus launched.

On Saturday, February 7, 1959, a thousand mourners squeezed into St. Ferdinand's church in San Fernando for the requiem Mass. Others stood silently outside in a mist as church bells rang for Richard Valenzuela, Ritchie Valens. He was buried at San Fernando Mission Cemetery while hundreds stood with heads bowed. On his headstone are a bar of notes and the words "Come On, Let's Go." The original members of the Silhouettes served as pallbearers. One of them, the vibes player, Gil Rocha, said later that he went home after the funeral and continuously sobbed.

ROCK LEGEND

Hank Zevallos was a young boy who lived in Pacoima at the time Ritchie Valens was first breaking into the music scene around San Fernando Valley. Hank had a paper route. One morning after delivering his papers, he was riding his bike to Mary Immaculate School and reached the corner of Van Nuys and Laurel Canyon Boulevard. He remembered: "Hanging down from those elevated motorcycle handlebars on my English racer were my L.A. Examiner newspaper bags, with the customary extra copies all folded and rubber-banded inside." Suddenly, he said he was surrounded by teenagers all wanting to buy his remaining copies. "Many of them had tears flowing from their eyes. Speechless at first, I finally asked 'What's going on?' A girl with wet eyes haunted me as she looked directly into me and asked, 'Isn't there anything about Ritchie in the newspaper?' 'I don't know,' I replied, clearly confused. 'What's happening?' She burst into fresh tears and softly cried out in a quivering voice, 'We just heard on the radio he's dead.'"

During the 1990s, Zevallos said, on the land once adjoining the Laurel Drive-In Theater and the field where he and his friends created a baseball diamond, a park grew. It was named the Ritchie Valens Recreation Center by the City of Los Angeles. The facility makes guitar lessons available to young children, and the swimming pool, where Zevallos and his friends once learned how to swim, also now bears Ritchie Valens' name. "And that's just part of the story," Zevallos said, "of how much esteem this fallen teenage hero is still held in."[16]

Valens was not only a hometown hero. He was the first Latino rock and roll star. He was among the first rock and rollers to blend traditional Latino music with the new rock and roll beat. His music, limited in time and scope by the circumstances of his death at a tragically early age, was influential, inspiring other singers and musicians for generations.

In February 1959, shortly after his death, Valens' first album, titled "Ritchie Valens," was released. Demand for more of his recordings intensified and led, in October 1959, to the release of another album called "Ritchie." In December 1960, "Ritchie Valens in Concert at Pacoima Junior High," the appearance recorded by a simple tape recorder in his old school, was made available.

Suddenly, Valens was no longer a three-record wonder. In these recordings, some done in studio, others in public performances, the listeners for the first time heard songs such as "Bluebird Over the Mountain" and "Paddiwack," a variation of "Children's Marching Song" his mother used to sing to him. Later, a number of recordings made by Valens in the recording studio in Bob Keane's basement were also made available.

Over the years, musicians by the score have mentioned Valens' influence on their own music, and nearly every generation since has found a new way to pay tribute to the teen idol. John Lennon said many times that you could hear "La Bamba's" influence on the Beatles' early recordings such as their version of "Twist and Shout." Lennon called Valens an inspiration. This is the highest praise for a teenager who made records for just eight months.

Valens influenced musicians of widely differing style and fame who have praised his music and said that it both inspired and influenced their own: Freddy Fender, The Midnighters, Trini Lopez, Sunny and the Sunglows, The Rascals, Bob Dylan, R.E.M, Chris Montez, and Carlos Santana.

A wide variety of performers over the years have covered Valens' "Donna," many creating their own take on the song, which has influenced a number of other songs, including "Donna, the Prima Donna," a 1963 hit for Dion. "La Bamba" has also been performed by a host of artists including Ronnie Hawkins, Neil Diamond, and Joan Baez.

Led Zeppelin guitar legend Jimmy Page once told fellow British musician/author Ian Whitcomb during an interview that Valens was his first hero. Page said that he must have played the string combinations in "La Bamba" a thousand times. Indeed, Led Zeppelin came so dangerously close to plagiarizing Ritchie's "Ooh! My Head" for their own "Boogie With Stu" that the band was later sued by Kemo Music for copyright infringement. In 1978, Led Zeppelin and their record company, Swan Song Records, settled amicably out of court for a reported $130,000 plus future royalties with the stipulation that the settlement's incriminating terms be kept confidential. Though she was not involved in the lawsuit, Valens' mother is said to have received half the money.

Critics have even pointed out Valens' influence in the music of the punk bands. Critic Lester Bangs compared Valens' three-chord mariachi square-up in his version of "La Bamba" with such compositions as "Louie, Louie" by the Kingsmen, "You Really Got Me" by the Kinks, and "Blitzkrieg Bop" by the Ramones. The Ramones later performed Ritchie's "Come On, Let's Go" on the soundtrack to the motion picture, *Rock and Roll High School*. Around the same time, a band called The Plugz released their debut album, "Electrify Me," featuring a frantic version of "La Bamba."

In 1987, new interest in Ritchie Valens was sparked by the release of the Columbia Pictures bio-pic on his life titled *La Bamba*. Written and directed by Chicano Luis Valdez and produced by his brother Danny Valdez, who viewed Valens' life as an inspirational story for all youth, the film introduced Lou Diamond Phillips as Ritchie Valens. Much of the story in the film was fictional. For instance, Valdez, who had worked with Cesar Chavez in the farmworker' movement and who had himself labored in the fields as a young man, established the character of Valens in the film as a child of farm workers. Nevertheless, the basic framework of the story remained essentially true.

Latino artists Los Lobos and Carlos Santana made cameo appearances in *La Bamba*, and some of Valens' relatives, including a sister, were cast in the film. The release of the film's soundtrack, with Los Lobos' version of the title song, rose to number one on the pop music charts. A new generation thus began hearing Valens' music for the first time in multiplex theaters across the country. The film and the sales of the soundtrack once again made Valens an international figure.

In discussing the commercial success that the film achieved, filmmaker Valdez said that it points the way toward more stories of Hispanic assimilation and acculturation. It is the classic American drama, Valdez said, being played out not only by Chicanos but Puerto Ricans and other Latinos. Although conventional wisdom said that American audiences were by and large uninterested in social drama, "La Bamba" seemed to dispel that notion. "The fact that 'La Bamba' has been accepted by audiences who don't even know any Hispanics shows that it's really about American values," Valdez said.[17]

Numerous honors and awards have paid tribute to Valens over the years. In October 1997, he was inducted into Hollywood's Rock Walk during a special ceremony attended by hundreds of fans, family members, and members of the press. Hollywood's Rock Walk is the only sidewalk gallery dedicated to honoring those musicians who have made a significant contribution to the evolution of rock and roll as a universal art form. Valens was also one of only a few rock and roll artists to have been honored with a United States postage stamp. In 2001, he was inducted into the Rock and Roll Hall of Fame.

The young singer was the first to blend Latin rhythms with rock and roll. He set the stage for the explosion of Latino sounds in mainstream American music. Through that powerful contribution, he fostered a greater appreciation of his own roots and of the cultural contributions made by his fellow Latinos. Writing in *Rolling Stone*, Lester Bangs called Valens "a quiet, underrated yet enormously influential member of that handful of folk visionaries who almost single-handedly created rock and roll in the '50s."[18]

Looking back over his relationship with Ritchie Valens and his legacy, Bob Keane reflected on the fact that music historians generally agree that the singer and songwriter was the guiding force behind the Latino music explosion that occurred over the last half century. "The fact that a Chicano teenager in 1958 could leap into the same league as Elvis with two songs, one sung in Spanish, was something no one in the world could have imagined," Keane said. "It did happen though, and since the release of the motion picture *La Bamba*, he has become an icon of hope for all young entertainers in the United States, and throughout the world...."[19]

Waylon Jennings later said of Valens: "He was the real deal. Yes. He was great at what he did. Let me tell ya, he loved music. He was a shy kid. He was young, and I think he was homesick, you know? But we got to be pretty good friends, and we talked a lot. He was a good showman, and he had some wonderful ideas. He was only starting, but in the time he spent in the business, he made a big impact. I don't know if anybody could have made a bigger one. Part of it was dying. We give up our heroes slow.... His career and life were cut short, but what he did in that short time I'd put up against anybody. I was there. I know."[20]

SELECTED RECORDED MUSIC

Valens, Ritchie. *Ritchie Valens: The Lost Tapes.* Del-Fi Records, 1995. CD.
Valens, Ritchie. *Rockin' All Night: The Very Best of Ritchie Valens.* Del-Fi Records, 1995. CD.

Valens, Ritchie. *Come On, Let's Go*. Del-Fi Records, 1998. CD.

Valens, Ritchie. *Ritchie Valens: Greatest Hits*. Morada Music, 2003. CD.

Valens, Ritchie. *La Bamba and Other Hits*. Rhino Flashback, 2004. CD.

Valens, Ritchie. *The Ritchie Valens Story*. Rhino/Wea, 1993, 2004. CD.

Valens, Ritchie. *In Concert at Pacoima Jr. High*. Wounded Bird Records, 1960, 2006. CD.

Valens, Ritchie. *Ritchie Valens*. Wounded Bird Records, 1959, 2006. CD.

NOTES

1. Beverly Mendheim, *Ritchie Valens: The First Latino Rocker*, Tempe, Arizona: Bilingual Press, 1987, 18.

2. Mendheim, 38–39.

3. Mendheim, 20–21.

4. Mendheim, 37–38.

5. Rob Golub, "Former Ritchie Valens bandmate remembers days before stardom: 'We were just a bunch of kids,' *Racine Journal Times*, http://www.journaltimes.com/articles/2004/08/12/local/iq_3037885.txt.

6. "The Real Story of Ritchie Valens," http://www.rockabillyhall.com/RitchieValens1.html.

7. "The Real Story..."

8. Bob Keane, *The Oracle of Del-Fi*, Los Angeles: Del-Fi International Books, 2006, 68.

9. Keane, 71.

10. Keane, 88.

11. Kevin Roderick, "Ritchie Valens' Star Burned Brightly for Pacoima," March 25, 2001, http://www.kevinroderick.com/valens.html.

12. Keane, 93.

13. Keane, 96.

14. Waylon's Words of Wisdom: An interview with Waylon Jennings by D.J. Johnson, 1998, http://www.cosmik.com/aa-march02/waylon.html.

15. Colin Devenish, "Del-Fi's Keane Opens Door," http://www.rollingstone.com/artists/ritchievalens/articles/story/6525866/delfis.

16. Hank Zevallos, "Ritchie Valens: Homeboy Hero," http://www.hankstermania.com/MeasuredMovements/MeasuredMovements3.htm.

17. John Podhoretz, "'La Bamba' Is No Bomb," *U.S. News & World Report*, August 10, 1987, 48.

18. Roderick.

19. Keane, 104.

20. Waylon's Words of Wisdom.

FURTHER READING

"The day the music died," February 3, 1959, http://www.fifiesweb.com/crash.htm.

Johnson, D.J. "Bob Keane brings Del-Fi Records back for round two," 1999, http://www.cosmik.com/aa-august99/bob_keane2.html.

Keane, Bob. *The Oracle of Del-Fi*. Los Angeles: Del-Fi International Books, 2006.

Mendheim, Beverly. *Ritchie Valens: The First Latino Rocker*. Tempe, Arizona: Bilingual Press, 1987.

"Ritchie Valens," http:www/ritchievalens.net/bio/rvbio.html.

"Ritchie Valens Tribute," http:///www.ritchievalens.net/bio/bio.html.

"A Rockabilly Hall of Fame Presentation: Ritchie Valens," http://www.rockabillyhall.com/RitchieValens1.html.

Courtesy of Library of Congress

Zorro

He wore black—a wide-brimmed hat, gloves, and a mask to conceal his identity. He was a dashing figure with a whip and a cloak and a sword. He rode a black horse called Tornado. He did his deeds at night, and when he was finished he pulled out his sword and swiftly sliced a distinctive "Z" into the clothes or skin of his enemies. Clever, elusive, and bold, this was not an enemy of the people. This was an avenger for good. By day, he was Don Diego, a respected member of the upper classes, dressed in the clothes of a nobleman. But at night, he was the fearsome swordsman El Zorro, the Fox.

First as the hero of magazine serials and later of silent movies, talking films, comic books, and television, Zorro's adventures thrilled readers and audiences around the world for nearly a century. One journalist wrote, "Zorro was the Americas' first cross-cultural hero. A charismatic legend on both sides of the border, Zorro is the champion of the underdog, the Robin Hood of the New World, the hero of Latinos and Anglos alike. Riding into the night atop Tornado, his ebony steed, the black-clad masked adventurer rights the wrongs in an unjust, often rapacious world. Zorro is an icon, an archetype, and defender of the common man."[1]

Writer Jonathan Jerald who produced more than a dozen documentaries for the History Channel, wrote, "Zorro is, of course, a cultural icon of immense proportions."[2]

THE CURSE OF CAPISTRANO

The character of Zorro was introduced to the world in 1919 in the pages of an inexpensive fiction journal called *All Star Weekly*. The story opens with the grumblings of Sergeant Pedro Gonzales, proud lawman of the Spanish government of California before it became part of the United States. Sergeant Gonzales is complaining to a tavern owner and three of his fellow soldiers about the growing fame of a mysterious swordsman in black getting involved in various skirmishes in California. He talks about the mystery man's legendary prowess with the blade and about his cunning attacks at night.

Although Sergeant Gonzales has never seen the infamous warrior, he would like to teach him a lesson in swordsmanship, bring down the bandit figure, reveal his hidden identity, and claim reward money that has been offered for his capture. Gonzales admits his own sins of the past but longs for one encounter with the highwayman. Just give him one chance, he says, and it will be his own star that will shine, not that of this upstart rogue they call "the fox" or El Zorro.

Soon, Gonzales gets his wish. Into the tavern like a storm bursts a black figure. If Gonzales's fondest wish is to bring down the fabled nemesis, this is his chance. As the shrouded figure approaches Gonzales, the Sergeant can barely see the man's flashing eyes through the slits of his mask. The two men slowly approach each other. The man in black says, "Senor Zorro, at your service."

Zorro is at the tavern to punish Gonzales for beating a man four days earlier who did not deserve such treatment. With a pistol in one hand to hold off the three soldiers and the landlord, Zorro whips out his sword to face Gonzales. "The tip of his blade seemed to be a serpent's head with a thousand tongues. Zorro had Gonzales backed into a corner.... Zorro's blade took on a new life. It darted in and out with a speed that was bewildering. It caught a thousand beams of light from the flickering candles and hurled them back. And suddenly it darted in and hooked itself properly and Sergeant Gonzales felt his sword torn from his grasp and saw it go flying into the air." Zorro does not kill Gonzales. This encounter is merely to teach him a lesson. The legend of the masked man grows.[3]

The story was the creation of Johnston McCulley. Born in 1883 in Ottowa, Illinois, McCulley for a time worked as a police reporter for *The Police Gazette* and then as an Army Public Affairs Officer during World War I. A lover of history stories, McCulley began writing articles for so-called pulp magazines, publications that sold in neighborhood grocery and drug stores, newsstands, and other commerical outlets. Printed on low-quality wood pulp paper and featuring colorful, often lurid covers, the cheap publications covered a wide variety of westerns, crime stories, romances, and horror stories.

McCulley went on to write a number of novels and screenplays, everything from crime thrillers to stories about action heroes in the early west. He became especially interested in the early years of California and the growth of Spanish missions. He moved from New York in 1908 to a house near the San Bernardino mission in California and continued writing prose. He studied much of the local lore of the area and became a well-known public speaker.

The story of Zorro that McCulley first published in 1919 was called "The Curse of Capistrano." McCulley wrote a series of vignettes about the heroic figure that would appear mainly in such magazines as *All Story Weekly*, *Argosy*, and *West*. From 1918 to the 1950s McCulley produced more than sixty stories with such titles as "The Sign of Zorro," "Zorro Frees Some Slaves," "Zorro Prevents a War," "Zorro Fights for Peace," "Zorro Aids an Invalid," and "Zorro Fights with Fire."

McCulley's creation of Zorro was likely influenced heavily by at least two sources. One was the novel *The Scarlet Pimpernel*, written in 1905 by Baroness Emmuska Orczy, a Hungarian-British novelist and artist. The main character in the book is an English nobleman who dons a disguise to fight off evildoers, those who would send to the guillotine innocent French aristocrats. His persona became "The Scarlet Pimpernel" (named after a common English flower). He was a fighter for the downtrodden, a champion of those plagued by rigid class distinctions and the corruption of the government.

The second influence was likely that of the real-life bandit named Joaquin Murieta. After his Mexican family became a victim of mob violence, a young Murieta revolted to become one of the most notorious bandits of nineteenth-century American history. Joined by a band of fellow outlaws, Murieta, riding on his black stallion, avenged the killing of his family and engaged in a relentless campaign of robberies, mostly of gold. It was said by many residents of California that, for all of Murieta's ruthlessness, he gave much of his stolen gold to poor Mexicans who would protect and shelter him from lawmen on his trail.

Joaquin Murieta: A Real-Life Zorro?

When Johnston McCulley first introduced the character of Zorro in 1918, he was likely influenced by a number of literary sources. But, also, he undoubtedly knew the story of a real-life bandit of California named Joaquin Murieta, who had already, in the hands of the press and local authors, become a legend.

The legend of Joaquin Murieta was in many ways embellished and transformed in ways very similar to that of outlaw Jesse James. The story in its general outline, after the newspapers and various authors had finished their work, is as follows: Joaquin Murieta was born in Sonora, Mexico, around 1830 and moved north to California during the Gold Rush with his wife and her three brothers. He worked for a time as a ranch hand and as a miner, enduring discrimination and possibly beatings at the hands of Anglo thugs.

After five miners falsely accused his half-brother of stealing a burro and then lynched him and attacked his sister, the young man set out on a path of revenge.

He soon became the leader of a notorious gang called "The Five Joaquins." They raided mining towns, saloons, and stores, and, at one point, killed a sheriff. They held up stagecoaches, rustled cattle, stole horses, and robbed travelers, killing, it is said, up to nineteen people in the process. His victims included Mexicans as well as Anglos and a number of Chinese miners.

In 1853, Murieta and one of his notorious sidekicks, the so-called Three-Fingered Jack, were hunted down and killed by Captain Harry Love. The Chinese community in San Francisco, the story continued, who felt victimized by Murieta's killing sprees, raised an additional $1,000 reward for Captain Love, who promptly severed Jack's hand and cut off Murieta's head, which he preserved in a jar of brandy that was displayed to the public—for a charge, of course.

After the death of Murieta, poet and author John Rollin Ridge, a man of Cherokee parentage, took up his pen. As with any story, the facts needed embellishment. Ridge's ninety-page production published in 1854 was called *The Life and Adventures of Joaquin Murieta, the Celebrated California Bandit.*

As the word "celebrated" in the title implied, Ridge turned the Murieta story into something more than the usual takedown of a notorious outlaw. Under Ridge's imagination, Murieta became something of a Robin Hood figure—a misunderstood and mistreated loner who took up a life of crime for good reason and dealt powerful blows to a wretched and unjust government. Novelists would do the same kind of service to the life of Jesse James two decades later.

A few years after Ridge published his book, the story was repeatedly plagiarized and altered. First, it appeared in the pages of the *California Police Gazette*. A French publisher then picked it up and made some changes, and the story appeared in Spanish translation in Chile and other Latin American countries. With a few additional publications and changes, Murieta had become a freedom fighter and champion of the underdog.

The Murieta legend gained additional life on the silver screen. In 1936 *The Robin Hood of El Dorado* marked its first appearance in film. In 1965 Warner Brothers would follow with another film.

How much of the real life of Joaquin Murieta has been verified as fact? There is evidence of his birth and his participation in a ruthless gang during a period of extensive crime in California. Beyond that, there exists very little confirmed evidence. The rest is myth.

Whatever particular insights McCulley gained from these and other sources, the basic outlines of the character of Zorro were set in that first story and varied little over the course of nearly a century as novelists, filmmakers, animators, television producers, stage directors, and even comedy groups used the story of Zorro, the noble, masked avenger of wrongs.

The alter ego of Zorro is Don Diego Vega, son of a wealthy Spanish landowner in the pueblo or town of Los Angeles in the early part of the nineteenth century before California was a part of the United States. Born in Madrid, he immigrates to America with his parents. He returns to Spain to study art and science and to learn fencing from an English knight. His family controls vast acres of land in California as well as cattle and horses, and Don Diego lives in a large hacienda in the countryside and has a house in the town as well.

He is unlike the other young, wealthy members of the aristocracy, interested only in wasteful and reckless pursuits; he is cultured, fond of music and literature, and scornful of the idle talk and boastings of his peers. His conscience aches about the poor treatment of the underclasses and the injustices of an economic system that punishes the vast majority of peasants and native Indians for the luxury of the elite.

The ruthless governor of California uses his position of influence to exploit and rob the poor. His troops also routinely rough up Catholic priests. Upon his return to California, Don Diego is aghast at the government's oppression. He especially resents the mistreatment of Catholic priests. And so when he sees incidents of injustice or violence that he feels need revenge, he changes his clothes in the caves underneath his father's hacienda and takes on the persona of Zorro. On a black steed known as Tornado he rides forth as the highwayman Zorro.

A close friend named Felipe aids Zorro in his quests to fight oppression. Felipe pretends to be a deaf mute named Bernardo and is able to spy on government officials. Early stories introduce not only Sergeant Gonzales, whom

Zorro will outwit time and again, but also Zorro's love interest, Lolita Pulido. Her family has lost much of its fortune because of political missteps and is seeking to regain its footing in society. The Pulido family is now living in a run-down home. Lolita's father, Don Carlos, hopes that his daughter will marry the influential Don Diego in order to advance the Pulido family's standing.

Although Don Diego is mightily interested in the vivacious Lolita, she is not impressed with him. He is rather dull and witless, she thinks. She is, however, entranced with the exciting Zorro whom she has seen briefly. Charming, courageous, and handsome, he is the heroic warrior of whom she dreams. She, of course, has no idea that Zorro, the mysterious man of gallantry whose romantic interest she craves, is actually Don Diego. Not only does Don Diego fail to win over Lolita, he also disappoints his own father, Don Alejandro, who wants his son to get married. Frustrated, his father compares Don Diego with Zorro:

> Get life into you! I would you had half the courage and spirit this Señor Zorro, this highwayman, has! He has principles and he fights for them. He aids the helpless and avenges the oppressed. I salute him! I would rather have you, my son, in his place, running the risk of death or imprisonment, than to have you a lifeless dreamer of dreams that amount to nought![4]

Like Lolita, Don Alejandro does not realize that Don Diego and Zorro are the same man.

Thus, the stories of swashbuckling adventure and unfulfilled love marched on with new plots and new character development in a host of mediums, from movies to comic books. Since the creation of Zorro, numerous other heroic creations have been woven into the same basic theme: A quiet, law-abiding citizen who faces injustice and wrong takes up a mask and a secret identity to protect those who have been wronged.

In 1939, for example, a cartoonist named Bob Kane was asked by a comic book company to come up with a new character that would capture the imagination of children. Kane later recalled that he had gone to see a movie about a bandit hero named Zorro. The movie, Kane recalled, "had left a lasting impression on me." As an artist, he said, "you're influenced at one point by another character." And so, Kane went to work. The result of his efforts was the beginning of Batman, another superhero who would never die in the American imagination.[5]

The movie Kane had seen was *The Mark of Zorro*, and it starred the great silent film actor, Douglas Fairbanks, Sr., the first of many Zorros of the screen.

DOUGLAS FAIRBANKS AND *THE MARK OF ZORRO*

One year after the masked hero made his first appearance in McCulley's "The Curse of Capistrano," Fairbanks, the already legendary silent film actor, was given a copy of the work. He loved it. The character, he sensed, was perfect for a new direction in his screen career.

Fairbanks was now over forty years old but was still a physical marvel. Since his early childhood, he had been a remarkable athlete, especially good in gymnastics, and he was constantly fit as a result of rigorous training and exercise. He often trained with professional coaches and athletes. According to one French fencing master, Fairbanks was good enough to be considered in the world championship class. While training for a film, Fairbanks approached the world record for the standing high jump and broad jump. In only one instance in his entire film career did Fairbanks ever feel the need to use a stunt man.

The wealthy, internationally acclaimed actor had just formed United Artists Studios with his friends, the film legend Charlie Chaplin and director D. W. Griffith. Fairbanks had recently married his second wife, the film star Mary Pickford, and built a magnificent home in Beverly Hills.

Since 1915, he had made twenty-nine films, most of them light comedies. In all of those films, however, much of Fairbanks' appeal was centered on his acrobatic mannerisms. At the height of his career he would jog extensively and then engage in a strenuous exercise routine in a gymnasium he built on his film lot.

With this new Zorro picture, Fairbanks decided, the film public would see his athleticism in a new form. America had recently emerged from the horrors of World War I and had put down tyranny. Americans wanted, Fairbanks and his managers sensed, a hero who would stand up for simple values and face down injustice.

Fairbanks' screenplay closely followed the basic plot line and dialog in McCulley's "Curse of Capistrano." But now, on screen, Fairbanks could bring to the character a new visual dimension that readers of the adventure could only imagine. As the filming of the picture proceeded, the advance publicity built up enormous expectations. What was Fairbanks up to? What new screen invention would be forthcoming?

In 1920, at New York's Capital Theater, the largest motion picture venue in the world, *The Mark of Zorro* played over and over again to constant overflow crowds. The theater's box office later reported that nearly 20,000 patrons saw the film that first day and many hundreds of others had to be turned away. It was the largest single-day gross receipts in movie history up to that time.

Fairbanks did not disappoint either the movie fans or the critics. The film made Fairbanks the number one box office star of the year and launched his career in a new direction—that of a romantic adventure hero. From the genial, humorous characters that had marked his former roles, here now was Fairbanks flashing across the screen in Old California as the dashing, valiant *caballero*, fighting for the rights of Mexican peasants and Indians against the corrupt tyranny of hardened government officials and lawmen.

It was as if Fairbanks himself, just as Don Diego, had shed his own clothes and persona to become Zorro.

The opening text of the silent film set the stage: "Oppression—by its very nature—creates the power that crushes it. In California nearly one hundred years ago, with its warmth, its romance, its peaceful beauties, this dread disease, oppression, had crept in.... Then out of the mystery of the unknown appeared a masked rider who rode up and drown the great highway, punishing and protecting and leaving upon the vicious oppressor: The Mark of Zorro."[6]

As in McCulley's stories, Zorro protects the poor; he protects the religious. "Pick on a priest or a native," one character exclaims, "and—presto! Zorro!" At one point in the film, a priest helps Zorro elude pursuing soldiers and even provides him with a robe to enable him to pass for a monk.[7] In one sequence, a dignified old Franciscan friar, falsely accused of fraud, is flogged for "treasonous remarks." When Zorro hears of the flogging, he is incensed and retaliates.

Zorro also champions the virtue and honor of women. When a brutal captain tries to force himself on the beautiful Lolita, Zorro soundly defeats him—and then forces him to kneel and apologize to the young woman.

Near the end of the film, Zorro implores other *caballeros* to join him in his crusade for justice. "The heaven-kissed hills of California," he says, "swarm with the sentinels of oppression. Are your pulses dead? Thank God, mine is not—and I pledge you my blood's as noble as the best. No force that tyranny could bring would dare oppose us—once united. Our country's out of joint. It is for us, *caballeros*, and us alone, to set it right."[8]

Douglas Fairbanks, Jr., later wrote of his father's performance: "It turned out to be by far the most successful movie he had ever made.... Indeed, it became a more than minor classic of its kind, widely imitated and remade (without distinction) several times since. It was called *The Mark of Zorro* and it was to be his trademark for years to come."[9]

Looking back to this early silent film, movie critic Steven Greydanus, who studied subsequent Zorro films in the twenty-first century, wrote, "You haven't seen Zorro until you've seen Douglas Fairbanks, Sr. as Zorro in the 1920 silent swashbuckling classic *The Mark of Zorro....* Fairbanks's stunts have lost none of their impact; no subsequent cinematic superhero has ever been half so convincing as his Zorro leaping from rooftop to rooftop, over the heads of his enemies, tumbling in and out windows, soaring over any obstacle in his way, tables, donkeys, pigpens. It's amazing how far we haven't come."[10]

Many film historians and critics credit the film with launching a new adventure-hero genre that has continued in its popularity generation after generation. Viewers could imagine, at least up there on that screen, a world where injustice could be avenged, not through corrupt systems but surely and swiftly. It let them imagine that chivalry was still alive and that there could be the ultimate romantic gentleman and lover. It allowed them to imagine a hero of near-supernatural ability that could defy all odds, no matter how powerful the enemy or formidable the challenge.

For Johnston McCulley, the release of the film kept alive his fictional character. If it had not been for Fairbanks' performance, Zorro might have quietly died with the last of the stories McCulley had completed for pulp magazine readers. Now, the public yearned for more of the master hero. Publishers Grosset and Dunlap negotiated a deal with McCulley in 1924 for the release of his stories in a book called *The Mark of Zorro* to tie it commercially to the film.

Soon, McCulley was back at his desk writing more Zorro stories. *Argosy Magazine* was quickly in the Zorro business, publishing new McCulley creations called "The Further Adventures of Zorro." Other film producers were becoming intrigued with the character. And Fairbanks, himself, prepared to star in another film as the heroic avenger: In 1925 he starred in *Don Q, Son of Zorro.*

FROM SILENT FILM TO SOUND—ZORRO LIVES ON

Until the late 1920s, motion pictures were silent except for the musical accompaniment provided by theatre owners in the form of live musicians or orchestras. The story line and dialog appeared on the screen in written form between the film sequences.

In 1926, Warner Brothers introduced a new sound system using wax recordings that were synchronized with the film projectors. Although the film *Don Juan* was the first motion picture with sound to be introduced to the public, it was the premiere in October 1927 of *The Jazz Singer*, starring Al Jolson, that transformed the history of motion pictures. Here was a film with a recognized star that worked magic and convinced audiences and motion picture executives that the "talkies" had arrived.

For the legend of Zorro, the talkies arrived in 1936, eleven years after Douglas Fairbanks, Sr., had made *Don Q, Son of Zorro*. Released by Republic Pictures, the film was called *The Bold Caballero* and was written by Wells Root from a story idea by Johnston McCulley. The film starred Robert Livingston, a veteran actor who had played in other films about the West including *The Three Mesquiteers*. Even though it was the first sound version of the Zorro story, the film was hardly the most memorable. The film did have one fascinating plot device. At the beginning of the story, Zorro languishes in prison for killing the governor. He is able to prove his innocence, nevertheless, to the governor's daughter by pointing out that the letter Z carved into the governor was a backward Z. The mark, Zorro pointed out, would not have been made by the real Zorro, an educated and cultured man, but by an imposter of less education and refinement. It was the truth, and she believed him.

Republic Picture's success with Zorro in this major film led the studio to create a number of short Zorro films known as "serials," films that led from one to another in a series. The main production was called *Zorro's Fighting Legion*, and it featured such chapter titles as "The Flaming Z" and "Unmasked."

In 1940, popular Hollywood actor Tyrone Power stepped into the cape and mask. His Twentieth-Century Fox film, like the first of the two efforts by Douglas Fairbanks, Sr., was called *The Mark of Zorro*. Directed by Rouben Mamoulian and co-starring Basil Rathbone as Captain Pasquale, archenemy of Zorro, the film, according to some critics, rivaled any Zorro production ever filmed. The stylish Power was already Fox's leading actor but had never been cast in a role that demanded such physical action. He could not bring to the screen the sheer athletic skill that Fairbanks had displayed. Nevertheless, he prepared for the film with extensive training in sword fighting, and his handsome face and lithe physique cut a dashing Zorro on screen. Indeed, by the end of the film, Rathbone, who had played in other films requiring fencing scenes, remarked that Power had actually become a skilled fencer.

The most memorable scene of the film, and indeed one of the most memorable scenes in Hollywood productions from that period, is the climactic sword fight. Oddly, the fight takes place not between Zorro and his enemies but between Diego and Captain Pasquale. The arrogant Pasquale licks his sword and extinguishes the flame of a candle with a swish; Diego does the same thing. The flame does not go out. Pasquale roars with laughter. But Diego, with a glance and smile, lifts the top half of the candle with the flame still burning and tips it over. His flashing sword burst had been so swift and clean that it had severed the candle and left it standing.

The 1940 Zorro production was also notable for what it said or did not say about the issues of power and control in early California and the Latino labor that underpinned its existence. Unlike plots in earlier films, this story included significant twists of character and intent. In this rendition, Diego's father is actually the governor who has been overthrown. For Diego, then, the motive is primarily to avenge his father and to restore California to what it had been during his father's rule. He says to his fellow *caballeros* that California was a place of "gentle missions, happy peons, sleeping *caballeros*, and everlasting boredom" where "a man can only marry, raise fat children, and watch his vineyards grow."[11]

In the 1940 version, Zorro's commitment is not generally to right the wrongs in the land and to restore justice but to restore his father's benevolent rule. That rule, as the film does not emphasize, relies on those so-called happy peons, the Latino labor. The Zorro of 1940 was less a true Latino hero for the common man than either his predecessors or those who would follow.

THE TELEVISION ZORRO

By the mid-1950s Walt Disney and the entertainment empire he was in the process of creating were internationally famous. It had been a long and nearly miraculous business journey for Disney. In his late teens Disney had begun to develop his love of drawing. When he returned from France after serving during World War I as an ambulance driver, he sought a career in commercial art. As he saw the growth and potential of the motion picture industry, he began producing short animated films for local businesses in Kansas City, Missouri. And thus began the development of such characters as Mickey Mouse and such films as *Snow White and the Seven Dwarfs*, the first full-length animated musical feature.

By the 1940s, the Disney studio in Burbank, California, employed more than one thousand artists, animators, writers, and technicians. The production of the Disney studio was not limited to animation. It began to produce feature films and award-winning True-Life Adventure series such as *The Living Desert*, *The Vanishing Prairie*, *The African Lion*, and *White Wilderness*. By 1955, one of Disney's fondest dreams became a reality. A fabulous amusement park, built at a cost of $17 million, opened in Anaheim, California. It was called Disneyland.

And now, two years later, Walt Disney and his studio would try their hands at the legend of Zorro. By the latter part of the 1950s, a number of television series featuring western cowboy heroes had already made their mark. Such dashing figures as Hopalong Cassidy, the Lone Ranger, Gene Autry, Wild Bill Hickok, Kit Carson, and Roy Rogers had already charged around western scenery bringing down bad guys, almost all of whom wore black.

Even a Latino figure, The Cisco Kid, played by Duncan Reynoldo, had joined the gallery of cowboy heroes. The character of the Cisco Kid was inspired by a series of popular western dime novels of the nineteenth century written by William Sydney Porter, who used the pen name of "O. Henry." The folk hero, Cisco, and his portly sidekick, Pancho, were on television from 1950 to 1956.

And now, the most enduring of the Latino folk heroes was about to make his debut in a national television series. Befitting a Disney-produced series, *Zorro* became the highest-budgeted western on television.

Disney selected an actor named Guy Williams for the title role. Born Armand Catalano in New York to Italian immigrant parents, Williams had been a struggling actor and former model who had landed supporting roles in movies ranging from *Bonzo Goes to College* and *Mississippi Gambler* to *I Was a Teenage Werewolf* and *Seven Angry Men*.

Even though Williams was six feet, three inches tall, darkly handsome with a flashing smile and athletic build, his career had been stalled at the time he arranged for a screen test at Disney Studios. Looking back on those early roles, he said they were mostly "anonymous men leaning in doorways and cigarettes dangling from their lips.... There were times when I seriously doubted if I were cut out for this business."[12]

After one of his western roles, Williams took up fencing under the direction of a master teacher named Aldo Nadi. He hoped that the skill would help him land more attractive parts in either movies or television at a time when western action films were very popular. When he learned about the Zorro role, he eagerly signed up. Nearly twenty-five other actors had auditioned for the part of the television Zorro by the time Williams auditioned. He performed a screen test with a heavy Spanish accent that seemed too affected. Disney, who saw the audition, agreed that the accent would have to be toned down, but he was quite impressed with the screen test overall, delighting in Williams' energy and enthusiasm and his fencing skills. Williams, he thought, would be a worthy television successor to Tyrone Power.

On Thursday night October 10, 1957, at 7:30 on ABC, viewers first heard the stirring music: "Out of the night, when the full moon is bright, comes a horseman known as Zorro." There was the caped swordsman on his jet black steed framed against a lightning sky. For millions of viewers across the country gathered before their black and white television sets every Thursday night, Zorro was not quite like any of the other action heroes that had captured their imaginations. Sure, a few wore masks, such as the Lone Ranger. And all of them righted wrongs and rode beautiful horses and befuddled their enemies. But Zorro, with his black cape and mysterious origins and slight accent, was different.

The basic plot elements and characters remained in the Disney series very close to the original creations of Johnston McCulley. However, in the television series the character of Bernardo, Diego's mute servant, took on a new and more sophisticated role. In the earlier films, Bernardo was faithful and loyal to Diego but mostly dim-witted. In this version, the character Bernardo is more of a friend and ally to Diego than simply a servant. In this way, Bernardo is similar to the sidekicks of such other western heroes of television such as Roy Rogers and the Cisco Kid.

The mute Bernardo helped Diego by pretending to be deaf as well as mute. He secretly listened to conversations of the enemy and reported back to Diego. Bernardo also helped Zorro on a number of occasions by dressing in the clothes of Zorro, thus allowing Diego to be seen in the same place as Zorro. No one would expect, then, that Diego could possibly be the bandit hero.

The series was an immediate sensation, especially with children. Soon, youngsters began to play Zorro. One of those was a boy named Steve Rubenstein who later became a journalist and wrote:

> This was a great man, this Zorro. He righted wrongs in the early days of California. He wore a cape and mask, a cross between Batman and the Lone

Ranger. He had a secret identity; like Superman's, it was known only to tens of millions of grubby kids. But Zorro did it his way, scampering over rooftops, swinging on chandeliers, making safe the quaint pueblo known as greater Los Angeles. He swashbuckled. He kissed girls, too, but we forgave him that.[13]

Steve and his brother and many of their friends all became Zorro at one time or another. All of the kids on the block sent away for the cape and the hat and the plastic sword. He later said that they would have sent away for the horse, too, but that would have been too big for their back yards.

They took turns being Zorro and his enemies. The sword came equipped with a piece of chalk at its tip and the kids could strike the signature Z all around the neighborhood, mostly on places that their parents did not appreciate, such as on the sides of cars or on the backsides of their friends. Parents began to follow Zorro players around with wet rags. News stories circulated that Guy Williams himself had become a victim of youthful Zorro banditry— his own car had been marked a number of times with a Z.

They rode their bikes with their Zorro costumes and pretended the bikes were horses. They even tried to roll their "Rs" like they knew how to speak Spanish. And they did notice the cultural heritage that the characters in the series represented. Rubenstein wrote: "We did find it curious that Zorro, in the part of Mr. Williams, was white, that the Mexican soldiers were white, that the Indians in the plaza were white and that even the mantilla-swathed senorita whom Zorro kissed each week was white as a flour tortilla."[14]

But not all the characters on the Disney Zorro were white. The series also introduced a Hispanic actor as a regular member of the cast. George L. Lewis, son of a Welsh father and Spanish mother, was originally from Guadalajara, Mexico. In the Disney series, he played Diego's father, Don Alejandro. It would, however, take another quarter of a century before the character of Zorro, the heroic Latino character, would actually be played by a Latino actor.

The series theme song, written by Norman Foster and George Bruns, became one of the best known television themes of all time. Indeed, a popular rendition of the song sung by The Chordettes climbed into pop music's top twenty and more than one million copies of the song were sold during the two-year series run.

Zorro had two sponsors, the 7-Up soft drink company and the AC Spark Plug Division of General Motors. Both companies used animated characters in their commercials. The most successful was 7-Up's Fresh-up Freddie, a rooster in a Zorro costume. Guy Williams promoted the show in appearances around the country. One of the most popular locations was rodeos, where he received $2,500 to ride around the arena dressed as Zorro.

Zorro reached an estimated thirty-five million viewers each week. Every series that went up against *Zorro* was canceled the next year. Disney took portions of the first thirteen *Zorro* television episodes and edited them into a feature film called *The Sign of Zorro*. The film did especially well in foreign markets where viewers had not seen the television series.

Because of a bitter legal dispute between Disney and ABC, the Zorro series did not return for a third year. Zorro later returned to the air in syndication, beginning with the 1965–1966 season. Disney promoted the series by creating a new character for the Mickey Mouse comic strip: "Little Zorro."

For Guy Williams, the Zorro character was the height of his career. He made a great deal of money and gained international fame. After appearing in a few nondescript roles after the series was completed, he decided to retire from the film business. He had made guest appearances in a number of Latin American countries to promote the show, and in a number of cases was seen as almost a heroic figure, especially in Argentina. Williams fell in love with the country and its people and retired to Buenos Aires, returning to the United States only infrequently to visit. Although press reports in 1975 and in 1982 indicated that he was considering an offer to don the mask and the cape once again, the project never materialized. He died in Argentina in 1989.

But *Zorro* did not die with Guy Williams. The television series gained a new generation of viewers when Disney colorized the black and white series and introduced it to a new generation of viewers. For decades to come, in VHS and DVD formats, the series continued to sell to markets across the world.

There were new Hollywood renditions of the character and the story. In 1974, Frank Langella played the lead role in *The Mark of Zorro*. A year later, the accomplished French actor Alain Delon took on the role in *Zorro*. In 1981, George Hamilton played a comedic spin-off of the Zorro character in a film called *Zorro, The Gay Blade*. And in 1990, a new Zorro series began on the Family Channel on cable television. The series starred Duncan Regehr, a Shakespearean actor who had once been on Canada's Olympic boxing team. Unlike the other Zorro films and television productions, this one was filmed in Spain. Regehr added a new dimension to the Zorro character. "I've played him more like a Renaissance man," said Regehr, "interested in art, science and music, more bookish."[15]

FINALLY, A LATINO ACTOR AS ZORRO

Since the beginnings of the Zorro legend, numerous actors have played the great Latino character. None of them had been Latino. In 1998, that all changed. Into the cape and mask slipped Antonio Banderas.

The blockbuster film from Tristar Pictures and Amblin Entertainment was called *The Mask of Zorro*. Directed by Martin Campbell and produced by Steven Spielberg, the film starred not only Banderas but also the acclaimed actor Anthony Hopkins, who played an aging Don Diego, and Catherine Zeta-Jones, who played the beautiful love interest of Zorro.

Banderas was born in 1960 in Malaga, Spain. His father was a police-man; his mother was a teacher. When he was fifteen years old he saw a stage production of "Hair" and, at the show's intermission, said he wanted to be an actor. He dropped out of high school and studied at the School of Dramatic Art in Malaga. For a time, he was a struggling stage actor in Madrid, until he began to appear in Spanish movies in the early 1980s. His first Hollywood production was with Tom Hanks in the film *Philadelphia* in 1993, and he followed up with roles in such films as *House of the Spirits* and *Interview with the Vampire*.

When Banderas first earned the starring role as Zorro and after filming had begun in Mexico, he indicated to reporters how seriously, as a man of Spanish descent, he took this particular role. As a child he had grown up reading the adventures of Zorro and watching the Disney television version. He said that to him Zorro was a classic hero, a figure of discipline and respect. "Zorro is the only Hispanic hero ever created in Hollywood," said Banderas. "He fought for justice. He fought against poverty. This is an espe-cially important model for kids, especially today...."[16]

The Mask of Zorro veers sharply away from the original plot line estab-lished by Johnston McCulley nearly eighty years earlier in *The Curse of Capistrano*. In this film, Don Diego's identity as Zorro is discovered by gov-ernment authorities who lay a trap to catch him. In a swordfight in Diego's mansion, his wife, Esperanza, is accidentally killed; Diego is captured and imprisoned, and his home is burned to the ground. His infant daughter, Elena, is taken away to be brought up as Rafael Montero's daughter in Spain.

The film then jumps to a period twenty years later. Montero returns to California to take power. In addition, Diego escapes from prison in Califor-nia, not only to take revenge on Montero but also to tell Elena, his daugh-ter, her true origins—that he is her father. Diego trains a young bandit, Alejandro Murieta, to be the new Zorro. Under his tutelage, the undisci-plined wretch becomes a *caballero* and selfless champion of the underdog; he changes from a young criminal bent on self-destruction to a man who fights for a cause greater than himself and the love of a woman.

In the final fight, both Montero and Diego die. The new Zorro and Elena marry. With the support of his wife and son, Joaquin, Zorro continues the fight against injustice beyond the time California becomes the thirty-first state of the United States.

The film was the first to link the lives of the real-life Murieta to that of the fictional character Zorro. It was the first to take the story to the end of the life of Don Diego de la Vega. It introduced a number of new characters. It was the first to feature two separate Zorros. It was also the first to under-take extensive research into the history and culture of Mexican life in the early nineteenth century. Headed by production designer Celia Montiel, the staff researched libraries, archives, and museums to locate paintings and other architectural materials to create the look and feel of each stage set at the Churbusco Studios in Mexico City.

Producer David Foster said, "It was important that the locations reflected the era in which our story is set. We needed great expanses of land as it existed in Southern California, circa 1820, and we needed several classical haciendas of the period."[17]

The central Mexico City location afforded a wealth of nearby haciendas, prisons, town squares, gold mines, and shorelines that fit all of the needs of the production staff to make this Zorro the most authentic-looking film ever. Over seven thousand Mexican extras were employed on the film. More than any other production, it represented a determined commitment to create the kind of Latino atmosphere that existed in California at the time in which the story was set. From the architecture to the costumes, this production made the time of Zorro come alive. A reviewer wrote:

> A solid tale of honor, betrayal, oppression, love and family spanning a generation, *The Mask of Zorro* integrates the genre's traditional moral themes—protection of the poor and defenseless, resistance of oppression, the supporting role of religious leaders—into a cleverly structured, action-packed spectacle that makes room for such elements as a passionate, sword-wielding heroine, and an explosive finale...."[18]

ISABEL ALLENDE'S ZORRO

In 2005, the story of Zorro was in the hands of an internationally acclaimed author. Isabel Allende was born in Peru and raised in Chile. The niece of the deceased Chilean president Salvador Allende, whose government was overthrown in 1973, she forged a successful career first as a journalist and then as a novelist whose stories, lyrical and often mystical, made literary news almost from the beginning. Her first novel, *The House of Spirits* (*La casa de los espíritus*), a family saga spanning four generations, took the publishing world by storm in 1982. She proved to be a versatile and complex author and followed her first literary success with books such as *Of Love and Shadows* (*De amor y de sombras*), *Eva Luna*, *The Infinite Plan* (*El plan infinit*), and *Paula*, among others.

In the summer of 2003, executives from Zorro Productions, a company incorporated in 1986 that controlled the worldwide trademarks and copyrights of the Zorro name and promoted films, television, stage productions, and publishing projects, approached Allende. They asked her to write a novel about Zorro. Fascinated by the historical period and challenge of writing an original story about the character, she agreed.

In 2005, HarperCollins released Allende's *Zorro: A Novel*. She indeed created a compelling story, adding to the rich legend. She took readers to the beginning years of Diego, examining how the young *mestizo* boy turned into the adult character of Diego and Zorro and how, in that transformation, he gained insight into his culture and the various paths of his ancestors.

Born in Alto, California, at the end of the eighteenth century, Don Diego de la Vega, in Allende's telling of the story, is the son of a Spanish aristocrat and military man and the daughter of a Shoshone native. Diego learns from his maternal grandmother, White Owl, the ways and legends of her tribe. From his father, he learns the art of fencing and cattle branding. Diego is raised alongside Bernardo, the son of an Indian servant, and the two become inseparable throughout their lives. In California, they see European settlers continually engaging in acts of violence against the Native American population. They learn from the Shoshone about legends and lore and how to seek a vision as they go through their rites of manhood.

When Diego is bitten by a rattlesnake, the vision of a fox leads Bernardo to find help. With the fox's guidance, Diego's life is saved, and the small animal becomes his emblem. White Owl tells Diego that the fox is his spiritual guide. "You must cultivate its skill, its cleverness, its intelligence. Your mother is the moon, and your home, the cave. Like the fox, you will discover what cannot be seen in the dark, you will disguise yourself, and you will hide by day and act by night."[19]

Confused, Diego questions White Owl about how he is supposed to act, about what deeds he is to perform. She replies simply that he must prepare to be ready for the day that will come.

Diego is sent to Barcelona at the age of sixteen for a European education. As he had seen in California as a child, he sees in Spain the corruption of the government under the control of the Emperor Napoleon, so he joins a secret society dedicated to helping the poor and powerless. When he returns to California, the scene is set for his growth as the legendary Zorro.

The story sings with history, magic, and legend. It weaves together Spanish and Californian history, mystical folk tales, pirate adventures, and Native American legends. And it gives a riveting image of the "Z" the character carved in legend and on his victims:

> Alcazar kept backing up toward his desk, and when he lost his sword for the second time, he pulled a loaded pistol from a drawer. Before he had time to aim, Zorro kicked his weapon from his hand, then marked his cheek with three dizzying slashes, forming the letter Z. Alcazar screamed, fell to his knees, and clutched his cheek."[20]

It is not a mortal wound, Zorro told his enemy. It is merely the mark that ensures that he will never forget him. It was the mark that the character of Zorro had left for generations.

Allende said the character was all about justice. "The idea of justice, the idea of fighting for the underdog," she said, "is always current and always needed. What is extraordinary about Zorro is that he's funny, and that he does all of this because he loves danger and he loves justice. He wants to help, and he's willing to risk his life for that—but always in a lighthearted way. He's not violent; he doesn't want to kill his enemy, but humiliate him. So whenever possible, he does not kill."[21]

Publishers Weekly raved about the book: "Allende's lively retelling of the Zorro legend reads as effortlessly as the hero himself might slice his trademark "Z" on the wall with a flash of his sword."[22]

A review in *The Baltimore Sun*, stated, "This is not your tired matinee idol Zorro, nor the sexy cartoon Zorro of the comics. This is Diego de la Vega (the man who, with the flash of a sword, becomes Zorro), a swashbuckler of the first order: complex, compassionate, romantic, and sometimes ruthless. Allende is in rare and absolutely peak form in her just-plain-super dissertation on this folk hero of Spanish-American lore, the eighteenth-century California version of Robin Hood."[23]

As the plot unfolds in two continents and in several countries, Allende creates a journey for the reader, recreating a kind of melodramatic novel similar to those written in the nineteenth century, when the action takes place. She plays with language and expands on the characters from the earlier Zorro stories. She especially transforms the character of Bernardo. "I wanted to redeem the character of Bernardo," she said, "which TV series have traditionally treated as some sort of clown, a silly servant to Diego de la Vega. I wanted to confer him dignity, pride, an important role in the life of Zorro, but I had to keep to his non-speaking attribute. Instead of making him dumb, I decided that he wouldn't speak because he was traumatized. Telepathic communication with his brother-friend, Diego de la Vega, was a way around the issue."[24]

As she researched the Zorro legend, she found a special meaning for herself in the story. "Perhaps because inside each one of us sleeps the child," she said, "the teenager, the young person we once were. I haven't forgotten the stories I used to make up during my childhood, in which I was always the protagonist: brave, proud, adventurous."[25]

She remembered the story from her own childhood and loved the character "because he is brave and smart, he is not particularly violent, he is playful, histrionic, and eternally young. He risks his life to help the underdog but he does it with a lighthearted and ironic attitude. There is nothing tragic about him. He is fun![26]

ZORRO IN 2005

Zorro proved to be one of the most enduring heroic characters in American literature. From the earliest writings of Johnston McCulley, the image had spawned numerous imitations and take-offs. And in the year 2005, Zorro continued his remarkable run. The year was marked not only by Allende's fabulous novel. In addition, a new Zorro comic book series by the writer-artist team of Don McGregor and Sidney Lima appeared in print. A number of comic book series had been issued over the years, including a version published by Dell in the 1950s and a series issued by Marvel comics in the 1990s.

The year 2005 also saw the release of the film sequel to the 1998 *Mask of Zorro* starring Antonio Banderas, Anthony Hopkins, and Catherine Zeta-Jones. The film was titled *The Legend of Zorro*. The first Banderas Zorro film had generated an astonishing $251 million, much of it coming from foreign viewers. Seven years later, even without the presence of Anthony Hopkins, the cast was essentially the same.

In this retelling of the story, the year is 1850, and the people of California are preparing for a special election to become the thirty-first state of the union. Zorro's ten-year marriage to Elena is riding on rough waves, and his dual life is also affecting his relationship with his young son, Joaquin, who does not know the true identity of his father. For a time the couple live separately, and Elena is pursued by a suave European count named Armand. The count is actually behind a plot to block statehood. He leads a campaign of terror to influence the public to vote against the measure. Thus, Zorro is not only riding to the rescue to save California for the United States; he is riding to save his own marriage.

Banderas later talked about the physical demands of playing the role. "For one thing, I'm seven years older, and you have to confront that," he said. After finishing the film, Banderas said, "The last month was almost traumatic" as he recounted the bruises and back pain incurred by the forty-five-year-old actor who was not used to jumping on and off horses all days. And then he mentioned the heat, the limited visibility of the mask, and the unwieldiness of the cape as he fended off the swords of fellow actors. "Of course," he laughed, "if there's a good result, and people like the film, you quickly forget about all that."[27]

Directed again by Martin Campbell, the film once again came through with hard riding, exquisite sword fighting, and stirring romance. And once again the Banderas Zorro conquered United States box offices as well as those abroad.

ZORRO ON STAGE

The Latino/Chicano comedy and theater group Culture Clash, created in San Francisco in 1984, first gained the national spotlight in a play called *The Mission*. Blending social and political satire, the troupe played such major venues as New York's Lincoln Center and Los Angeles's Mark Taper Forum.

The Culture Clash had been known in California for their innovative works that focused on racial issues in the culture wars of Los Angeles. One of their plays examined the differences between the barrio and the greater Los Angeles community during the creation of the Los Angeles Dodgers baseball park at Chevez Ravine, a construction that displaced a thriving Latino community. In 2006 the three performers—Ric Salinas, Richard Montoya, and Herbert Siguenza—were asked to take on a new project. Could they create a show based on the great Latino icon, Zorro? They agreed to take on the project.

The play was called *Zorro in Hell*, and, directed by Berkeley Repertory Artistic Director Tony Taccone, it opened at the Ricardo Montalban Theater in Hollywood. Culture Clash created the character of a Chicano writer hired to develop a new work about Zorro. Holed up in an old hotel, he discovers that the place is run by a two-hundred-year-old woman, played by Sharon Lockwood of the San Francisco Mime Troupe. She supplies him with the material he needs to become the next Zorro.

Montoya was surprised by how much the work on Zorro affected him. When the troupe began the project and began to do research, they all thought of the cultural history that was behind the Zorro legend. Every time he picked up one of the history books of the era, he said, he saw white kids with the mask and cape trying to make a "Z" on suburban sidewalks. "And that warms an old cynical heart," he said, "because Zorro, even manufactured, was a phenomenon. So much of the first act is about unmasking this thing, and then by the second act it's about—I never thought I'd hear myself say this as a lefty Chicano—earning the privilege to don the mask."[28]

The theater critic of the *San Francisco Chronicle* wrote: "Jokes fly thick and fast for most of the show's two hours—political gibes, quick quips, pop culture, and literary references ranging from common to arcane, and sight gags of every description, including hilarious film spoofs, acted onstage and projected in clever combinations of movie clips and animation." But beneath it all, he said, there was in the play a serious and cutting edge to Zorro's blade.[29]

Or, as Richard Montoya said, "We steal the masked hero's white horse to take on the governator and overall laziness. Rise up L.A.! Rise up and take to the streets! Pick up some litter or take that doggie on a walk or better yet the next time there is a march for immigrants' rights, walk alongside the fifty-five-year-old mother from Oaxaca who is waving a small American flag...."[30]

THE LEGEND LIVES ON

Throughout the history of the Zorro legend and its production from silent films to television and blockbuster movies, few Latino characters had played the starring roles. Except for Antonio Banderas' appearances in two films as Zorro, the other lead roles in the major films had been played by Anglos or, in one case, a French actor.

In February 2007, the series *Zorro: la Espada y la Rosa* premiered on Telemundo affiliates across the United States. Now, for the first time, the cast of a major Zorro production included a host of actors with surnames such as Favela, Peniche, Rios, and Elías. The series opened with Peruvian actor Christian Meier in the lead role.

Filmed in Colombia, the series was developed by Telemundo, RTI Colombia and Sony Pictures Television. It was written by Venezuelan screenwriter Humberto Olivieri, who had long been a fan of the original Disney television series in the 1950s. The series melded characters from the Disney series and those developed by Isabel Allende in her novel. It featured a Los Angeles filled with everything from gypsies, slaves, and cannibals, to Amazon warriors, along with the usual population of Spanish settlers, soldiers, and native peasants.

In this rendition, Zorro falls in love with a young widow named Esmeralda Sanchez de Moncada. The theme song, called "Amor Gitana," was performed by Beyonce and Alejandro Fernandez. The production ran for 122 one-hour episodes. They were developed, written, and shot entirely in Spanish.

The Zorro legend marched on. In late 2007, BKN International, a German-based company that produced animated children's television programs licensed in nearly one hundred countries, introduced the series *Zorro—Generation Z, Zorro—Return to the Future.*

Available in DVD, the series is set in a mythical city much like Los Angeles called Pueblo Grande, about ten years in the future. Here is a modern-day Zorro, not astride his dashing black stallion Tornado but astride his Tornado Z motorcycle. His female lead character is "The Scarlet Whip."

Thus, from the earliest days of Johnston McCulley's first serial publication of the legend, the Zorro story has developed, overlapped, conflicted, and spread over time. Nevertheless, the basic form of the central character never changed. He was and has remained a masked crusader for justice.

At the end of Isabel Allende's story of Zorro, two men and a woman gather to carry on Zorro's work. They put on the disguises and form a circle. They each make a cut on their left hand with a knife. They exclaim, "For justice!"

"At that moment," Allende writes, "when the mixed blood of the three friends dripped onto the center of the circle, they thought they saw a brilliant light surge from the depths of the earth and dance in the air...."[31] The legend and the cause endure.

SELECTED MOVIES AND TELEVISION

The Mark of Zorro. Directed by Fred Niblo. Douglas Fairbanks Pictures, 1920. Film.

Don Q, Son of Zorro. Directed by Donald Crisp. Elton, 1925. Film.

The Bold Caballero. Directed by Wells Root. Republic Pictures, 1936. Film.
Zorro Rides Again. Directed by John English and William Witney. Republic Pictures, 1937. Film.
Zorro's Fighting Legion. Directed by John English and William Witney. Republic Pictures, 1939. Film.
The Mark of Zorro. Directed by Rouben Mamoulian. Twentieth-Century Fox, 1940. Film.
Zorro's Black Whip. Directed by Spencer Gordon Bennet and Wallace Grissell. Republic Pictures, 1944. Film.
Son of Zorro. Directed by Spencer Gordon Bennet and Fred C. Bannon, 1947. Film.
Ghost of Zorro. Directed by Fred C. Bannon. Republic Pictures, 1949. Film.
"Zorro." Walt Disney Productions. 1957–1959. TV.
The Sign of Zorro. Directed by Lewis Foster and Norman Foster. Walt Disney Productions, 1958. Film.
Zorro, the Avenger. Directed by Charles Barton. Walt Disney, 1959. Film.
The Mark of Zorro. Directed by Don MacDougall. Twentieth-Century Fox, 1974. Film.
Zorro. Directed by Shibu Mitra. Mondo TV, 1975. Film.
"The New Adventures of Zorro." Filmation Associates, 1981. TV (animation).
Zorro, The Gay Blade. Directed by Peter Meldak. Melvin Simon Productions, 1981. Film.
"Zorro," or "The New Zorro." Directed by Donald Paonessa. Ellipse Programme, 1990–1993. TV.
"The Legend of Zorro." Directed by Mino Guti. Mondo TV, 1992. TV (animation).
"The New Adventures of Zorro." Fred Wolf Films, 1997. TV (animation).
The Mask of Zorro. Directed by Martin Campbell. Amblin Entertainment, 1998. Film.
The Legend of Zorro. Directed by Martin Campbell. Columbia Pictures, 2005. Film.
"Zorro: Generation Z." BKN New Media, 2006. TV (animation).
"Zorro: The Sword and the Rose." Sony Pictures Television International, 2007. TV.

NOTES

1. Marc Alexander, "Zorro behind the mask: Was he a thief, scoundrel, murderer, or savior of his people? New critical interpretations explore the many identities of one of the New World's most swashbuckling icons." *Americas*, January/February 2007, 44.

2. Jonathan Jerald, "Interview: Culture Clash Donning the Mask: Zorro in Hell," http://www.citizenla.com/index.php?option=com_content&task=view&id=255.

3. Sandra Curtis, *Zorro Unmasked: The Official History*. New York, Hyperion, 1998, 8.

4. Johnston McCulley, "The Curse of Capistrano," http://www.zorrolegend.com/origin/curse.html#Synopsis.

5. "The Evolution of 'Batman,'" AMCTV, June 21, 2007, http://blogs.amctv.com/future_of_classic/2007/06/the-evolution-o.html.

6. "The Mark of Zorro (1920)," http://video.google.com/videoplay?docid=-5440302924781357611.

7. "The Mark of Zorro (1920)."

8. "The Mark of Zorro" (1920).

9. Curtis, 30.

10. Steven Greydanus, "The Mark of Zorro (1920)," http://decentfilms.com/sections/reviews/1831.

11. "Projections: What Latin America tells us at the movies: The Mark of Zorro (1940)," http://screened.blogspot.com/2005/09/mark-of-zorro-1940.html.

12. Curtis, 124.

13. Steve Rubenstein, "Farewell, Zorro, you old fox," *San Francisco Chronicle*, May 10, 1989, E8.

14. Rubenstein.

15. Jay Sharbutt, "Masked Zorro returns Friday to make his mark on cable TV," *Los Angeles Times*, January 4, 1990, 8.

16. Mark Fineman, "Movies: Baja Hollywood: With tax breaks, cheap labor and fresh scenery, Mexico is vying to be a major film location." *Los Angeles Times*, May 25, 1997, 5.

17. Curtis, 224.

18. Stephen Greydanus," The Mask of Zorro," http://www.decentfilms.com/sections/reviews/maskofzorro.html.

19. Isabel Allende, *Zorro: A Novel*, New York: HarperCollins Publishers, 2005, 80.

20. Allende, 357.

21. Jeff Troiano, "A Conversation with Isabel Allende," *San Francisco Reader*, http://www.sanfranciscoreader.com/interviews/allende%20interview.html.

22. "Zorro: Editor Reviews—from Publishers Weekly," http://www.amazon.com/Zorro-Novel-Isabel-Allende/dp/0060778970/ref=sr_1_1?ie=UTF8&s=books&qid=1200374111&sr=8-1.

23. Victoria Brownworth, "Viva Zorro," *The Baltimore Sun*, http://www.isabelallende.com/zorro_reviews.htm.

24. Ascen Arriazu, "Memories, fight and fantasy at the hand of the great superhero of the Spanish narrative: Isabel Allende in interview," http://www.threemonkeysonline.com/article_isabel_allende_interview.htm.

25. Arriazu.

26. "A Conversation with Isabel Allende," http://www.bookbrowse.com/author_interviews/full/index.cfm?author_number=321.

27. Michael O'Sullivan, "Antonio Banderas dons the mask once more," *The Washington Post*, October 28, 2005, T41.

28. Jerald.

29. Robert Hurwitt, "Culture Clash's funny 'Zorro' slashes to the heart of the matter," *San Francisco Chronicle*, March 24, 2006, E6.

30. Jerald.

31. Allende, 384.

FURTHER READING

Alexander, Marc. "Zorro behind the mask: Was he a thief, scoundrel, murderer, or savior of his people? New critical interpretations explore the many identities of one of the New World's most swashbuckling icons." *Americas*, January/February 2007, 44.

Allende, Isabel. *Zorro: A Novel*. New York: HarperCollins Publishers, 2005.

Arriazu, Ascen. "Memories, fight and fantasy at the hand of the great superhero of the Spanish narrative: Isabel Allende in interview," http://www.threemonkeysonline.com/article_isabel_allende_interview.htm.

Cotter, Bill. "Zorro: A history of the series," http://www.billcotter.com/zorro/history-of-series.htm.

Curtis, Sandra R. *Zorro Unmasked: The Official History*. New York: Hyperion, 1998.

McCulley, Johnston. *The Mark of Zorro*. New York, American Reprint Co., 1924, 1976.

Toth, Alex. *Zorro: The Complete Classic Adventures*. Forestville, California: Eclipse Books, 1988.

"Zorro," Zorro Productions, Inc., http://www.zorro.com.

"Zorro: The Legend Through the Years," http://www.zorrolegend.com.

Selected Bibliography

Allende, Isabel. *Zorro: A Novel*. New York: HarperCollins Publishers, 2005.

Arnaz, Desi. *A Book*. Cutchogue, New York: Buccaneer Books, 1994.

Beltran, Mary Caudle. *Bronze Seduction: The Shaping of Latina Stardom in Hollywood Film and Star Publicity*. Dissertation for the Degree of Doctor of Philosophy, University of Texas at Austin, August 2002. http://dspace.lib.utexas.edu/handle/2152/1154.

Berg, Charles Ramírez. *Latino Images in Film: Stereotypes, Subversion, and Resistance*. Austin, Texas: University of Texas Press, 2002.

Cabeza de Baca, Fabiola. *We Fed Them Cactus*. Albuquerque: University of New Mexico Press, 1994.

Cisneros, Sandra. *Caramelo*. New York: Alfred A. Knopf, 2002.

Cruz, Celia. *Celia: My Life*. New York: Rayo/HarperCollins Publishers, 2004.

Curtis, Sandra R. *Zorro Unmasked: The Official History*. New York: Hyperion, 1998.

Domingo, Placido. *My First Forty Years*. New York: Penguin, 1984.

"Free Resources: Hispanic Heritage." http://gale.cengage.com/free_resources/chh.

Garcia, Mario. *Ruben Salazar: Border Correspondent*. Berkeley: University of California Press, 1998.

Griswold del Castillo, Richard, and Richard A. Garcia. *Cesar Chavez: A Triumph of Spirit*. Norman Oklahoma: University of Oklahoma Press, 1995.

Harvey, Robert, and Gus Arriola. *Accidental Ambassador Gordo: The Comic Strip Art of Gus Arriola*. Jackson, Mississippi: University Press of Mississippi, 2000.

Loza, Steven Joseph. *Tito Puente and the Making of Latin Music*. Urbana, University of Illinois Press, 1999.

Maraniss, David. *Clemente: The Passion and Grace of Baseball's Last Hero*. New York: Simon & Schuster, 2006.

Mathews, Jay. *Escalante: The Best Teacher in America*. New York: Henry Holt & Company, 1988.

Meier, Matt. *Notable Latino Americans: A Biographical Directory*. Westport, Connecticut: Greenwood Press, 1997.

Novas, Himilce. *Everything You Need to Know about Latino History*. New York: Plume, 1998.

Patuski, Joe Nick. *Selena: Como La Flor*. Boston: Little, Brown, 1996.

Regalado, Samuel O. *Viva Baseball!: Latin Major Leaguers and Their Special Hunger*. Chicago: University of Illinois Press, 1998

Santana, Deborah. *Space Between the Stars: My Journey to an Open Heart*. New York: One World-Ballantine Books, 2006.

Saralegui, Cristina. *Cristina!: My Life as a Blonde*. New York: Warner Books, 1998.

Shorris, Earl. *Latinos: A Biography of the People*. New York: W. W. Norton & Company, 2001.

Stavans, Ilan and Lalo Alcaraz. *Latino USA: A Cartoon History*. New York: Basic Books, 2000.

Walsh, Robb. *The Tex-Mex Cookbook*. New York: Broadway Books, 2004.

Index

About the Author

ROGER BRUNS is a prolific author of such works as *Preacher: Billy Sunday and Big-Time American Evangelism* (2002) and biographies of Cesar Chavez, Martin Luther King, Jr., Jesse Jackson, and Billy Graham for Greenwood Press.